# ENCYCLOPEDIA OF DEPRESSION

# ENCYCLOPEDIA OF DEPRESSION

## Volume 1
### [A–L]

Linda Wasmer Andrews

GREENWOOD

AN IMPRINT OF ABC-CLIO, LLC
Santa Barbara, California • Denver, Colorado • Oxford, England

Copyright 2010 by ABC-CLIO, LLC

All rights reserved. No part of this publication may be reproduced, stored in a retrieval system, or transmitted, in any form or by any means, electronic, mechanical, photocopying, recording, or otherwise, except for the inclusion of brief quotations in a review, without prior permission in writing from the publisher.

**Library of Congress Cataloging-in-Publication Data**

Andrews, Linda Wasmer.
  Encyclopedia of depression / Linda Wasmer Andrews.
    p. cm.
  Includes bibliographical references and index.
  ISBN 978-0-313-35378-9 (vol. 1 : alk. paper) — ISBN 978-0-313-35379-6 (vol. 1 ebook) — ISBN 978-0-313-35380-2 (vol. 2 : alk. paper) — ISBN 978-0-313-35381-9 (vol. 2 ebook) — ISBN 978-0-313-35366-6 (set : alk. paper) — ISBN 978-0-313-35367-3 (set, ebook)
  1. Depression, Mental—Encyclopedias. I. Title.
  RC537.A567 2010
  616.85'27003—dc22          2010001363

ISBN: 978-0-313-35366-6
EISBN: 978-0-313-35367-3

14  13  12  11  10    1  2  3  4  5

This book is also available on the World Wide Web as an eBook.
Visit www.abc-clio.com for details.

Greenwood
An Imprint of ABC-CLIO, LLC

ABC-CLIO, LLC
130 Cremona Drive, P.O. Box 1911
Santa Barbara, California 93116-1911

This book is printed on acid-free paper ∞

Manufactured in the United States of America

For Victor,
My personal antidepressant

# Contents

## Volume 1

## Volume 2

# LIST OF ENTRIES

# QUICK REFERENCE

Use this outline as a quick study guide to depression. Items in **bold font** are titles of entries in this encyclopedia. Items not in bold font are addressed in the higher-level entries under which they fall.

DEPRESSION

1. **Mood Disorders**
   a. **Major Depression**
      i. **Atypical Depression**
      ii. **Catatonic Depression**
      iii. **Chronic Depression**
      iv. **Melancholic Depression**
      v. **Postpartum Depression**
      vi. **Psychotic Depression**
      vii. **Recurrent Depression**
      viii. **Seasonal Affective Disorder**
   b. **Dysthymia**
   c. **Depressive Disorder Not Otherwise Specified**
   d. **Bipolar Disorder**
      i. Bipolar Episodes
         1. **Mania**
         2. Hypomania
         3. Depression
         4. **Mixed Episode**
      ii. **Bipolar I**
         1. **Rapid Cycling** Bipolar Disorder
      iii. **Bipolar II**
   e. **Cyclothymia**
   f. **Bipolar Disorder Not Otherwise Specified**
   g. **Mood Disorder Due to a General Medical Condition**
   h. **Substance-Induced Mood Disorder**
2. Symptoms of **Major Depression**
   a. **Depressed Mood**

# Topical Guide

Use this guide as a starting point for exploring a dozen lesser-known but wholly fascinating aspects of depression.

**What Are Some Controversial Social Issues Related to Depression?**

Environmental toxins—*See:* **Pollution**
Ethnic disparities—*See:* **Ethnicity**
Insurance coverage—*See:* **Insurance Parity**
Managed care—*See:* **Managed Care**
Pharmaceutical advertising—*See:* **Serotonin Norepinephrine Reuptake Inhibitors**
Psychologist prescribing—*See:* **Clinical Psychologist**
Residential treatment centers—*See:* **Continuum of Care**
Stigma of mental illness—*See:* **Stigma**

**What Are Some Key Laws and Legal Cases Related to Mental Illness?**

Americans with Disabilities Act—*See:* **Americans with Disabilities Act**
Andrea Yates case—*See:* **Postpartum Depression**
Individuals with Disabilities Education Act—*See:* **Individuals with Disabilities Education Act**

Kenneth Donaldson case—*See:* **Hospitalization**
Section 504 of the Rehabilitation Act—*See:* **Individuals with Disabilities Education Act**
Wellstone-Domenici Mental Health Parity and Addiction Equity Act—*See:* **Insurance Parity**

**Who Are Some Eminent Poets and Authors Who Suffered from Depression?**

Emily Dickinson—*See:* **Seasonal Affective Disorder**
Herman Melville—*See:* **Bipolar Disorder**
John Keats—*See:* **Melancholia**
William Styron—*See:* **Styron, William**
Numerous authors—*See:* **Mood Disorders**
Numerous poets—*See:* **Creativity**

**Who Are Some Other Famous Depression Sufferers?**

Abraham Lincoln—*See:* **Mental Health**
Brooke Shields—*See:* **Postpartum Depression**
Marie Osmond—*See:* **Postpartum Depression**

# PREFACE

Depression touches virtually every aspect of a sufferer's life—mental, emotional, physical, and social. Its impact on society is equally wide-ranging, leaving a mark on fields as diverse as medicine, psychology, history, and literature. Capturing such a multifaceted condition in all its gloomy glory is a daunting challenge. This encyclopedia aims to meet the challenge by providing a far-reaching survey of the people, events, theories, and therapies that have shaped our view of depression.

In these two volumes, you will find more than 300 entries arranged alphabetically. You can start your research at any point; each entry is designed to stand alone as an introduction to its topic. Of necessity, that requires some repetition of basic information from one entry to another. But every entry also provides unique information and fresh insights about the nature of depression.

## Easy-to-Use Features

Exploring a topic as large as depression can easily lead to information overload. This encyclopedia includes several user-friendly features designed to help you sift through information to find exactly what you need quickly and efficiently. In many cases, you have the option of drilling down farther for more detail if you want it. But you will never feel overwhelmed by more detail than you need.

### Cross-References

Within each entry, you will find terms in **bold font**, which are titles of other related entries in this encyclopedia. In addition, at the end of many entries, there is a *see also* list of other related titles. Use these cross-references as pointers to additional topics of interest.

### Further Information

After many entries, you will find a further information list, which steers you toward organizations and Web sites related to that topic. Some of these resources provide a wealth of information to the public on the Web. Others are membership groups for patients, families, students, or professionals. In the Organizations appendix at the end of Volume Two, there is also a handy master list of 79 resources for support, information, treatment, and suicide prevention.

## *Bibliography*

After every entry, you will see a brief bibliography with citations to print and online publications. These citations are good starting points for digging deeper on a topic. In the "Further Reading" section at the end of Volume Two, you will also find a list of 69 recommended books, including general reading, first-person memoirs, and professional texts.

## **Quick-Reference Tools**

Whether you are a student writing a term paper or a depression sufferer educating yourself about your condition, this encyclopedia includes tools to organize and focus your search for information.

Near the front of each volume of the encyclopedia, you will find a quick reference guide, which is an outline of major topics related to depression. The outline format lets you see at a glance the relationship among various subtopics. Bolded terms in the outline direct you to pertinent entries for more information.

You will also find a topical guide, which serves as an entry point for exploring a dozen timely topics and interesting sidelights. If you are a student looking for a standout topic for a term paper—or simply a reader with a curious mind—you will find some tantalizing leads here. The guide offers pointers to controversial social issues, key laws and legal cases, cutting-edge treatments, and more.

Preceding the entries in Volume One, you will see a depression timeline, which highlights the emergence of important theories, key discoveries, and relevant cultural events. The timeline includes dates for 57 significant moments in the history of depression, stretching from the fifth century BC to 2008. A quick look at the timeline is an easy way to orient yourself temporally as you read through the various entries.

## **Multidisciplinary Approach**

Depression is equal parts mental disorder and cultural phenomenon. Most self-help books and professional texts focus on the former, but many personal memoirs of depression sufferers emphasize the latter. This encyclopedia melds the two perspectives, using a wide-angle approach to provide a panoramic view of the landscape of depression.

There are entries drawn from the latest scientific research and clinical practice on psychotherapies (e.g., Mindfulness-Based Cognitive Therapy), antidepressants (e.g., Serotonin-Norepinephrine Reuptake Inhibitors), biochemistry (e.g., Brain-Derived Neurotrophic Factor), and genetics (e.g., Tryptophan Hydroxylase Gene). But there are also entries rooted in other experiences (e.g., Grief), other diseases (e.g., Heart Disease), other times (e.g., Melancholia), other places (e.g., Traditional Chinese Medicine), other cultures (e.g., Susto), and other disciplines (e.g., Creativity, with its discussion of the arts). In addition, there are entries packed with practical information about real-world aspects of living with depression, addressing topics such as diet, exercise, insurance parity, workplace issues, social support, and stigma. Throughout the encyclopedia, connections are drawn among the many and varied facets of this fascinating disorder.

Many entries also include sidebars and charts, which complement the main text in meaningful and often unexpected ways. You would probably never think of an encyclopedia—much less the *Encyclopedia of Depression*—as light reading. But if you do nothing else, skim through the sidebars on these pages. You might be intrigued by some of the facts you find there, including lists of famous people with mood disorders, movie references to electroconvulsive therapy, quotes from celebrity-moms on postpartum depression, and tips for coping with the holiday blues.

## Getting Started

A truly exhaustive study of depression throughout history and across many contexts would take libraries, not volumes. Nevertheless, the sheer size of this two-volume encyclopedia allows for a much more comprehensive treatment of the subject than is found in other books for nonspecialists in the field. You may want to begin by reading the introduction following this preface, which will give you a quick grounding in the subject.

Then let your personal interests dictate where you go from there. You might be surprised by where your journey takes you.

# INTRODUCTION

Depression, the mental disorder, is one of the greatest challenges facing public health experts today. When number-crunching researchers compare the impact of different diseases, they look at things such as years of life lost to premature death and years of productivity lost to disability. Based on such calculations, depression is the third-leading contributor to the global burden of disease, according to the World Health Organization. And in wealthier countries, such as the United States, it tops the list.

Depression, the human experience, is much harder to quantify. It is a phenomenon so fundamental and universal that it cuts across all lines of space and time. Some form of depression has been identified in every country and culture where it has been studied, and written references to depressive states date back 3,000 years. Given the ubiquitous nature of the malady today, however, there is good reason to believe it might be much older than that—perhaps as old as humanity itself.

Ask a researcher how many adults will be depressed in the United States this year. The answer will probably be about 7 percent to 8 percent, depending on which survey the researcher consults, with about twice that many Americans experiencing a bout of depression at some point in their lives. But ask any group of 10 adults if they have ever felt depressed, and there is an excellent chance that 100 percent will say yes. It is a discrepancy that spotlights the critical difference between the disease state and the everyday feeling. This two-volume encyclopedia, unlike smaller books, is big enough to encompass both.

## Major Depression

Depression is a mental disorder, a state of mood, a cultural phenomenon. A good portion of the entries that follow take the mental disorder tack and present the latest medical/psychological viewpoint on the prevalence, causes, diagnosis, treatment, and prevention of depression. This viewpoint is informed by research, and research relies on standardized, objective criteria to determine who is depressed and who is not.

Based on standard diagnostic criteria, depression is a persistent, pervasive disorder that causes a low, sad, or hopeless mood and/or an inability to take interest or find pleasure in almost anything. Other mental, emotional, physical, and behavioral symptoms occur as well, and the net effect of all these symptoms is serious distress or significant problems in daily life.

Several depressive disorders have been defined, but the most familiar one is major depression. Far more than just a short-term case of the blues, it is a debilitating illness that saps people's energy, drains the joy from their lives, and makes simply getting out of bed in the morning a daunting chore. Left unrecognized and untreated, it can cause great suffering, destroy relationships, and contribute to substance abuse, anxiety disorders, and a host of other ailments. In the worst case, it can culminate in the most permanent of all symptoms: suicide.

When the term "depression" is used in the context of clinical care or scientific research, it typically refers to major depression unless otherwise specified. Many of the entries herein are really about major depression, then, including the symptoms that define it, the risk factors that predispose toward it, the protective factors that protect against it, the medications and psychotherapies that relieve it, and the lifestyle steps and complementary therapies that help keep it under control.

## Charting the Course

There is nothing minor-league about major depression. It is a miserable illness that can touch every facet of a person's life at home, at work, and in relationships. In addition to a low mood and general apathy, other possible symptoms include feelings of worthlessness, thoughts of death, and changes in appetite, sleep, thinking ability, energy, and activity level. By definition, symptoms must last for at least two weeks. But the harsh truth is that they are likely to hang on for months without treatment.

Although major depression can strike at any age, it most often starts during the teens or early twenties. Those with close relatives who have suffered depression or died by suicide have an increased risk of becoming depressed themselves. And for reasons that are still not entirely clear, women are twice as likely as men to be affected—a ratio that holds up regardless of ethnicity or socioeconomic status.

The fact that depression tends to run in families implies a genetic component, but other factors play a role as well. It is a person's unique mix of genetic, biological, environmental, and psychological factors that set up a vulnerability to the disorder. But even then, depression is not inevitable. Often, a stressful life event is the first domino that makes the others fall.

After an initial bout of depression, some people get better and stay that way. For many others, though, keeping the disorder at bay is a lifelong struggle. About 60 percent of people who have recovered from one episode of depression go on to have another, and the risk of a recurrence just gets higher with each subsequent bout.

## Changing Your Mind

The good news is that appropriate diagnosis and treatment can help relieve the distress and reduce the disruption caused by depression, and it may also interrupt the downward spiral into frequent recurrences. Drug therapy and psychotherapy, either alone or in combination, remain the cornerstones of treatment, as they have been for half a century. But the number of different medications and therapies is expanding rapidly, and so is the evidence to support their effectiveness.

In the realm of drug therapy, there are currently 27 different antidepressants from seven different classes available in the United States. Now scientists are racing to discover the next Prozac that will forever change the face of depression treatment. Some drugs in development have radically different modes of action from any medication on the market today. Compared to existing antidepressants, they may hit targets closer to the beginning of a long chain of chemical reactions that ultimately control mood, which may speed up the beneficial effects.

In the realm of psychotherapy, cognitive-behavioral therapy has been the gold standard in depression treatment since the 1960s. But interpersonal therapy, cognitive behavioral analysis system of psychotherapy, and problem-solving treatment now have a solid base of research support as well. Meanwhile, fresh options—including acceptance and commitment therapy, dialectical behavior therapy, and mindfulness-based cognitive therapy—may represent the next wave in psychological treatment.

Medications and therapy are by far the most common treatments, but they are not the only game in town. For people with particularly severe, urgent, or persistent symptoms, electroconvulsive therapy (ECT)—in which a carefully controlled electric current is used to stimulate a brief brain seizure—is still unsurpassed in speed and effectiveness. For people with depression that comes on in fall or winter and subsides in spring, light therapy—in which a special light box is used to provide daily exposure to a very bright light—is another proven option. But these are just the start.

The next frontier may be brain stimulation, which uses electrical current or magnetic fields to induce changes in brain function. ECT is the old standby in this category, but several newer approaches—including transcranial magnetic stimulation, vagus nerve stimulation, deep brain stimulation, and magnetic seizure therapy—have been recently approved or are currently being tested. On the low-tech end of the spectrum, wake therapy or controlled sleep deprivation shows promise as a means of jumpstarting depression relief.

## Widening the Lens

In research settings, focusing on people who have depression alone, with no other health concerns, helps keep unintended influences from muddying the results. In theoretical models, it helps keep the discussion sharply focused. But in real life, more often than not, this is a fiction. The majority of people with depression also have another mental or physical disorder, and often these conditions interact in ways that worsen symptoms or complicate diagnosis and treatment.

More than half of people with depression have a coexisting anxiety disorder. Compared to those with depression alone, these individuals tend to have worse depressive symptoms, greater problems in daily life, a poorer response to treatment, and a higher risk of suicide. Other mental and behavioral disorders that may exist side by side with depression include substance abuse, eating disorders, attention-deficit hyperactivity disorder, and borderline personality disorder.

Depression is also common in people with heart disease, stroke, cancer, diabetes, Parkinson's disease, and numerous other medical ailments. People who have both depression and a physical illness tend to have worse symptoms of both and higher medical bills.

The good news is that suffering is reduced and outcomes are improved when both depression and the coexisting condition are treated appropriately. In clinical practice, the trend today is toward a more integrated view of total health. And in research, studies such as the groundbreaking STAR*D (Sequenced Treatment Alternatives to Relieve Depression) trial are starting to include a broader range of patients in an effort to more closely mimic real-life situations.

## *Exploring the Brain*

In less enlightened times, depression was sometimes regarded as a shameful secret or character flaw. But the more researchers learn, the more apparent it becomes that depression is an illness like any other. It is a disease of the brain, just as arthritis is a disease of the joints or asthma is a disease of the lungs—and there is no more need to apologize for having depression than there is for having these other conditions.

Some of the most exciting research on depression today is aimed at discovering the brain pathways and chemicals that underlie it. Neurotransmitters—naturally occurring chemicals that relay messages between brain cells—seem to play a crucial role. Since the 1950s, scientists have suspected that a group of neurotransmitters called monoamines might be particularly important. This group, which includes serotonin, norepinephrine, and dopamine, is targeted by all antidepressants on the market today.

Yet it turns out that monoamines are just one piece of the puzzle—and perhaps not even a corner piece. Another neurotransmitter called glutamate may be more fundamental. And looking beyond neurotransmitters, other kinds of substances—such as neurotrophic factors, which promote nerve cell growth and survival—may be key players as well.

Such discoveries are only possible thanks to recent advances in neuroscience, a young discipline that is a hybrid of biology, chemistry, physics, anatomy, physiology, and psychology. This multidisciplinary approach is brought to bear on studying the nervous system in action. Tools ranging from sophisticated computers to special dyes are used to examine molecules, nerve cells, neural networks, and brain regions. In research labs around the country, neuroscientists are the adventurers of modern science, exploring that most daunting of frontiers: the human brain.

## *Changing the World*

Although science is rooted in precise, rigorous evaluation, life keeps happening in its wonderfully messy, imprecise way. So far, science is the best method humans have devised to study the occurrence of depression in groups of people, explore underlying changes in brain structure and function, develop promising drugs to target those changes, and investigate possible treatments for safety and effectiveness. But when it comes to elucidating the individual experience of depression, science has definite limitations.

To truly understand depression in all its magnificent darkness means shining a light not only on medicine, psychology, and neuroscience, but also on pop culture, social trends, and the nightly news. Most of all, it requires listening to the individual voices of people who share their personal experiences by writing books, creating art, or simply talking about their lives.

The politics of depression is an important topic that is all too often glossed over. The best treatments in the world are useless if people are unwilling to seek help due to stigma and discrimination or are unable to access care due to lack of insurance. Certainly, for anyone interested in studying depression, it is vital to become fluent in neurotransmitter reuptake, selective serotonin reuptake inhibitors, and cognitive distortions. But for anyone living with depression, it may be equally crucial to become conversant in the Americans with Disabilities Act, Individuals with Disabilities Education Act, and Wellstone-Domenici Mental Health Parity and Addiction Equity Act. Without the underpinnings of strong societal support, scientific progress is rendered moot.

A convincing argument can be made that personal activism is as important to an individual's long-term recovery as taking the right pill or seeing a good therapist. Mental health advocacy groups—such as the Depression and Bipolar Support Alliance, National Alliance on Mental Illness, and Mental Health America—give people with depression a chance to take a stand on issues of vital importance to society at large and their personal well-being in particular.

## Subjective Depression

We rely on depression sufferers to speak out, because there is no other way to know what they are going through. Depression is a private experience, and even when skilled professionals get involved, it is only partially amenable to objective assessment. People who might be depressed cannot simply get a blood test or brain scan to confirm the diagnosis. Instead, they must communicate what they are feeling through what they say and how they behave.

If someone says he or she is depressed, does that automatically mean it is so? Perhaps not, from a treatment standpoint, because the symptoms that person calls depression might not be the same ones a drug or therapy is designed to treat. But that does not make the person's experience any less authentic or painful. So to get a full picture of all that a particular person is going through, it is necessary to consider not only depression, the mental disorder, but also depression, the subjective experience.

The arts offer one window into this highly personal world. Our understanding of depression is enriched immensely by noticing how it is represented in a Herman Melville novel, Sylvia Plath poem, Edvard Munch painting, or Ingmar Bergman film—and it comes as no surprise to learn that all four of these individuals knew their subject intimately. Music is another medium that expresses mood eloquently—what would the blues be without the blues?

Other cultures are another source of insight into the nature of depression. In Western culture, where the mind and body are generally viewed as separate entities, the primary symptoms of depression are thought to be a low mood and lack of interest. Physical symptoms—such as changes in sleep or appetite, lack of energy, and unexplained aches and pains—are acknowledged, but they are relegated to secondary status. However, in non-Western cultures where the mind/body is viewed as a single unit, physical symptoms may be a much bigger part of the total picture.

History offers yet another lens for viewing this timeless condition. More than two millennia ago, Greek physicians such as Hippocrates, Aretaeus, and Galen attributed depression to physiological causes. "Black bile" and "animal spirits" are no longer found in medical textbooks, but after a long spell where depression was regarded as strictly psychological in origin, the tide has turned. Today's scientists realize that the ancients were onto something when they looked for physiological explanations.

## 2,500 Years of Depression

The systematic study of depression has been around since at least the time of Hippocrates in the fifth century BC. Theories about the cause of depression have continued to evolve since that day, and the speed of change has only picked up pace in the late twentieth and early twenty-first centuries. Below is a brief overview of 2,500 years of theory.

### Humoral Theory

The ancient Greeks—building on even older traditions from Egypt, India, and China—believed that the natural world was composed of four basic elements: earth, air, fire, and water. Hippocrates applied this notion to the human body, which he thought to be filled with four basic fluids, called humors. The humors, in turn, were thought to correspond to specific temperaments. A humor called "black bile" was associated with a melancholic temperament, and excessive black bile could lead to despondency, sleeplessness, irritability, restlessness, and lack of appetite, among other symptoms. The humoral theory spread from the Greeks into Roman, Islamic, and European medicine, where it proved to be remarkably enduring, holding sway until the eighteenth century.

## Animal Spirits

In the second century AD, Greek physician Galen further elaborated the humoral theory. He described three forms of melancholia, one of which involved a buildup of black bile below the rib cage, leading to psychological symptoms as well as abdominal pain, gas, and belching. Galen also believed that the functioning of nerves was mediated by something called "animal spirits," which were formed in the brain and passed through the nerves to the body's feeling and moving parts. A strikingly similar notion turned up centuries later when modern scientists discovered neurotransmitters.

## Acedia

In the fifth century, Scythian ascetic writer John Cassian outlined eight principal vices encountered by monks. One of these vices was acedia, a state of spiritual malaise that involved despondency, discouragement, and disinterest. Cassian's acedia was different from depression; it was a spiritual problem, not a medical disease. Yet the symptoms were similar enough that it is easy to see how the two could have become confused over the centuries, contributing to the notion of depression as a character flaw.

## Lovesickness

Starting in the late thirteenth century and continuing into the fourteenth, love was a core concept in Islamic medicine. In one scenario, pining over the object of unrequited love could lead to lovesickness. People in the grips of lovesickness, their judgment impaired by obsession, believed that the object of their desire was the only one in the world who could satisfy their need. Failing to attain the love object was therefore a severe blow to their well-being, leading to a profoundly melancholic mood. If the love object became available, lovesickness was instantly cured, and the person's mood immediately lifted. But if their love remained unrequited, lovesickness could be lasting and dangerous—even fatal. Through the centuries, the central importance of interpersonal loss has remained a core theme in theories of depression.

## Delirium without Fever

The notion of melancholic illness was still going strong in the late sixteenth century. In 1597, French physician André du Laurens published a treatise on melancholia, which became well known throughout Europe and was frequently cited in the seventeenth and eighteenth centuries. Du Laurens considered melancholia a form of delirium—in his words, "a kind of dotage without any fever." In this state, people were subject to delusions, and du Laurens provided several memorable examples, such as one man who feared he had become a rooster and another who thought himself made of glass.

## Circulatory Model

In 1628, William Harvey announced his discovery of the principles of blood circulation. Over the next century, various theories arose attributing melancholic states to circulatory mechanisms. Many stressed thickening of the blood, which was thought to cause sluggish circulation in the brain. That, in turn, was believed to affect the flow of animal spirits. Two noteworthy examples of such physiologically oriented theories were advanced by Scottish physician Archibald Pitcairne and German physician Friedrich Hoffmann.

## Delusional Disorder

By the late eighteenth century, theories of depression based mainly on physiological factors fell out of favor, and those that based largely on psychological factors began to dominate the field. French physician Philippe Pinel, considered one of the founders of modern psychiatry, linked melancholia to delusional thinking. He attributed a wide range of symptoms to the disorder, including not only sadness, gloominess, and inactivity, but also extremes of anger, fear, passionate love, and even convulsive gaiety. In fact, Pinel's definition of melancholia was so broad that it encompassed virtually any chronic psychosis, including not only psychotic depression, but also schizophrenia.

## Monomania

Pinel's student, Jean-Etienne Esquirol, subdivided melancholia into narrower disorders, called monomanias. In these disorders, the mind focused on a single subject. Esquirol coined the term *lypémanie,* from the Greek for "sad-madness," to signify the monomania focused on a sad mood. He considered lypémanie to be primarily an emotional disturbance.

## Psychoanalytic Theory

Starting in 1895, Austrian neurologist and psychiatrist Sigmund Freud elaborated psychoanalytic theory, which had a profound impact on both science and society at large. Psychoanalytic theory stressed the influence of unconscious drives and wishes on behavior. It also emphasized the central role of childhood events in shaping later experiences. Freud viewed depression as hostility turned inward, a reaction to the loss of someone for whom the depressed person had intensely ambivalent feelings. To reduce the sense of loss, the depressed person took on some characteristics of the lost individual. But because the lost individual was viewed with mixed feelings, hostility that would once have been directed outward toward that individual was now directed inward. This led to harsh self-criticism and set the stage for depression.

## Depressive Temperament

Temperament is the inherited component of personality, which emerges at an early age and has lifelong repercussions. In 1921, German psychiatrist Emil Kraepelin, who pioneered the modern classification system of mental disorders, described what he called a depressive temperament. People with this temperament tended to be gloomy, serious, guilt-ridden, and self-reproaching, laying the groundwork for becoming depressed.

### Monoamine Hypothesis

The monoamine hypothesis stated that depression was caused by an imbalance in monoamine neurotransmitters, a group of brain chemicals including serotonin, norepinephrine, and dopamine. The hypothesis dates back to work done in the 1950s by scientists such as U.S. pharmacologist Julius Axelrod. It signaled the return of biological models of depression, and it stimulated research leading to all of the antidepressants currently on the market. However, efforts to find direct support for the hypothesis yielded conflicting results. It soon became apparent that monoamines were not the whole story.

### Cognitive Theory

In the 1960s, U.S. psychiatrist Aaron T. Beck introduced his cognitive theory of depression, which continues to be influential today. According to Beck, people with depression tended to have unrealistically negative thoughts, even in the face of objective evidence to the contrary. This tendency was due to relatively stable, underlying thought patterns, called schemas. A particular schema could remain latent for some time until it was triggered by a specific relevant event, unleashing a stream of spontaneous negative thoughts. These thoughts—which involved viewing the self, the world, and the future in an unduly negative light—helped cause and perpetuate depression.

### Learned Helplessness

The theory of learned helplessness, first advanced by U.S. psychologist Martin E.P. Seligman in the 1960s, linked depression to a giving-up reaction that stemmed from exposure to unpleasant events beyond the individual's control. The theory was used to explain why some people became depressed after a traumatic or stressful event, but others did not. According to this view, individuals who believed they were powerless to escape their situation were more likely to give up and become depressed. Seligman later reformulated the theory to include explanatory style—the way people habitually explained negative events to themselves. Depressed individuals were apt to have a pessimistic explanatory style, which meant they saw negative events as long-lasting, wide-ranging, and due to their own flaws.

### Attachment Theory

Attachment theory, first proposed by British psychiatrist John Bowlby, stated that infants had an innate need for close emotional bonds with caregivers, and the way this need was met in infancy shaped later relationships and emotional stability. Lack of secure attachment was thought to cause enduring relationship problems as well as a tendency toward depression. By the 1970s, this theory was a major force in developmental psychology.

### Pleasant Activities Model

Also in the 1970s, U.S. psychologist Peter M. Lewinsohn proposed a theory based on learning principles. Lewinsohn noted that depressed individuals found fewer activities pleasant than their nondepressed counterparts, and they also took part in pleasant activities less often. Due to their lower participation, people with depression had less opportunity to receive positive reinforcement, and this led to other depressive symptoms.

## Five-Factor Model

The five-factor model, introduced in the 1990s, was the brainchild of U.S. psychologists Robert R. McCrae and Paul T. Costa Jr. This theory stated that personality had five major factors: Openness to Experience, Conscientiousness, Extraversion, Agreeableness, and Neuroticism (OCEAN). Individuals varied along a continuum on each of these factors, with most people falling between the two extremes. People high in Neuroticism—a propensity for emotional instability and psychological distress—were at increased risk for depression.

## Diathesis-Stress Model

A diathesis is an inherited predisposition to a particular disease. The diathesis-stress model tied together several previous ones. Depression was thought to develop when a genetic predisposition was coupled with a stressful situation, triggering or worsening symptoms. This view, now widely accepted, lies at the heart of much current theory and practice.

## Depression in the Twenty-First Century

Depression can be explored in one way or another through a wide array of academic disciplines—history, anthropology, literature, art history, philosophy, religious studies, nursing, and social work, to name just a few. However, the fields most closely associated with the study of depression today are psychiatry, psychology, neuroscience, and pharmacology.

Knowledge about the field is growing at an explosive pace. A search of PubMed, the National Library of Medicine's vast database of biomedical literature, turns up more than 13,000 studies on "major depressive disorder" alone published in the 15-year period between 1994 and 2009. The Pharmaceutical Research and Manufacturers of America lists 39 drug compounds in current U.S. clinical trials being tested as potential depression treatments.

In everyday life, depression has assumed the familiarity of arthritis or diabetes. With an estimated 16.5 million U.S. adults having an episode of major depression this year, there is a good chance you will know someone suffering from the disorder. And given the unprecedented level of openness in society today, there is a better chance he or she will talk about it, following the lead of celebrity sufferers such as actress Brooke Shields, singer Beyonce Knowles, novelist J.K. Rowling, astronaut Buzz Aldrin, sportscaster Terry Bradshaw, journalist Mike Wallace, comedian Sarah Silverman, oil tycoon T. Boone Pickens, and a host of others.

It is an exciting time in the age-old story of depression. The next chapter is already being written.

# DEPRESSION TIMELINE

| | |
|---|---|
| **5th century BC** | Greek physician Hippocrates ascribes melancholia—a condition including despondency, sleeplessness, irritability, restlessness, and lack of appetite—to an excess of "black bile" leading to dysfunction of the brain. |
| **2nd century AD** | Greek physician Aretaeus of Cappadocia states the first coherent theory linking the mood extremes of melancholia and mania. |
| **2nd century AD** | Greek physician Galen concludes that nerve function is controlled by "animal spirits," which are formed in the brain and passed through the nerves to the body's feeling and moving parts. |
| **5th century AD** | Scythian monk John Cassian (ca. 360–435) writes about the sin of acedia (also spelled accidia), a state of spiritual malaise that involves despondency, discouragement, and disinterest. |
| **11th century AD** | Persian philosopher and physician Avicenna writes *The Canon of Medicine,* which carries forward the notion that melancholia and mania are manifestations of a single disorder. |
| **13th–14th centuries AD** | Arab physicians stress that pining over an unrequited love can lead to lovesickness, causing dejection and low spirits. |
| **1514** | *Melencolia I,* an engraving by German artist Albrecht Dürer depicting a winged personification of melancholia amid an array of symbolic objects, becomes one of the most famous artistic depictions of this state. |
| **1586** | English physician Timothy Bright publishes a treatise on melancholy that influences his contemporary, William Shakespeare. |
| **1597** | French physician André du Laurens publishes a book that focuses attention on delusional aspects of melancholy. |
| **1621** | English clergyman Robert Burton publishes *The Anatomy of Melancholy*, one of the most influential books about depression ever written, which attributes an excess of black bile to a wide range of possible causes. |
| **1695** | German physician Friedrich Hoffmann attributes melancholy to animal spirits that have turned sluggish and acidic. |

| | |
|---|---|
| **1718** | Scottish physician Archibald Pitcairne, in a book published posthumously, attributes melancholy to thick blood and sluggish circulation in the brain. |
| **1751** | English physician Richard Mead theorizes that the animal spirits underlying melancholy might be electrical in nature. |
| **1774** | German author Johann Wolfgang von Goethe publishes a novel titled *The Sorrows of Young Werther*, a seminal work in the literature of depression, which echoes themes of lovesickness. |
| **1798** | French physician Philippe Pinel stretches the medical meaning of melancholy to encompass not only marked inactivity and gloomy taciturnity, but also violent passion and outbursts of gaiety. |
| **1838** | French psychiatrist Jean-Étienne Esquirol suggests narrowing the medical definition of melancholy to focus strictly on a sad mood and giving it a new name: *lypémanie,* from the Greek for "sad-madness." |
| **1855** | German psychiatrist Wilhelm Griesinger describes a seasonal mood disorder characterized by melancholy in fall or winter and mania in spring. |
| **1856** | French psychiatrist Louis Delasiauve begins using the term "depression" in place of the word melancholy. |
| **1899** | German psychiatrist Emil Kraepelin identifies "manic-depressive psychosis"—a term encompassing all mood disorders—as one of the main types of severe mental illness. |
| **1917** | Austrian neurologist and psychiatrist Sigmund Freud publishes an essay titled "Mourning and Melancholia," which conceptualizes depression as anger turned inward. |
| **1921** | Kraepelin describes "depressive temperament" as an inherited disposition characterized by traits such as gloominess and self-reproach that lays the foundation for depression. |
| **1924** | German psychoanalyst Karl Abraham puts forth the idea that depression results from a present loss that reactivates a past blow to self-esteem. |
| **1938** | Italian neurologist and psychiatrist Ugo Cerletti introduces electro-convulsive therapy (ECT) as a treatment for mental illness. |
| **1946** | Hungarian psychiatrist and psychoanalyst René Spitz proposes the concept of anaclitic depression, an extreme reaction seen in some infants who are abruptly separated from their mothers. |
| **1949** | Australian psychiatrist John F. Cade publishes a journal article on the calming effect of lithium, the first mood stabilizing medication. |
| **1952** | The first edition of the *Diagnostic and Statistical Manual of Mental Disorders* (*DSM*) describes a "depressive reaction" as a low mood and poor self-esteem that serve to allay anxiety triggered by a loss. |
| **1954** | Scientists report the mood-boosting effect of a tuberculosis medication called iproniazid, an observation that leads to monoamine oxidase inhibitors being the first class of antidepressant medications. |

| 1957 | U.S. pharmacologist and neuroscientist Julius Axelrod discovers reuptake, the process by which certain neurotransmitters are taken back up by the cells that originally released them. |
|------|---|
|      | U.S. psychologist Albert Ellis publishes *How to Live With a Neurotic*, the first book about his pioneering form of cognitive therapy. |
| 1958 | Swiss psychiatrist Roland Kuhn discovers the depression-lifting effect of imipramine, which becomes the first tricyclic antidepressant. |
| 1960 | The Hamilton Depression Rating Scale, the most widely used test of depression in antidepressant research, is published. |
| 1961 | Axelrod shows that imipramine acts partly by blocking the reuptake of a neurotransmitter called norepinephrine. |
|      | The Beck Depression Inventory, a widely used assessment tool, is introduced. |
| 1963 | U.S. psychiatrist Aaron T. Beck publishes a journal article about "thinking and depression"—an early formulation of his cognitive model of depression. |
| 1967 | U.S. psychologist Martin E.P. Seligman describes the phenomenon of learned helplessness—a giving-up reaction stemming from exposure to unpleasant events that cannot be controlled. |
| 1969 | British psychiatrist John Bowlby asserts that depression occurs when a loss brings up old feelings of being unlovable and abandoned, which are rooted in an insecure attachment to early caregivers. |
| 1972 | Missouri senator Thomas Eagleton steps down as Democratic candidate for vice president amid reports of previous ECT and hospitalizations for depression. |
|      | U.S. psychologist Peter M. Lewinsohn introduces pleasant activity scheduling, a mainstay of behavioral therapy for depression. |
| 1980 | The third edition of the *DSM* uses the term "major depression" and defines it by symptom clusters rather than presumed causes. |
| 1984 | The first study of light therapy for seasonal affective disorder appears in print. |
|      | U.S. psychiatrist Gerald L. Klerman publishes *Interpersonal Psychotherapy for Depression*, the first book on interpersonal therapy. |
|      | U.S. psychologist James P. McCullough Jr. introduces the cognitive behavioral analysis system of psychotherapy, designed for treating chronic depression. |
| 1985 | A National Institutes of Health Consensus Development Conference concludes that ECT is a superior treatment for the short-term management of severe depression. |
|      | Bupropion (Wellbutrin), the first of the second-generation antidepressants, is approved for marketing in the United States. |
|      | The Depression and Bipolar Support Alliance (formerly called the National Depressive and Manic Depressive Association) is founded. |
| 1987 | Fluoxetine (Prozac), the first selective serotonin reuptake inhibitor to reach the U.S. market, is approved. |

| | |
|---|---|
| **1990** | *Darkness Visible*, a memoir by U.S. author William Styron about his personal struggles with depression, opens the door for other memoirs to follow. |
| **1994** | *Prozac Nation*, a memoir by U.S. writer Elizabeth Wurtzel, helps secure Prozac's place as a pop culture icon. |
| **2000** | The American Psychiatric Association publishes practice guidelines on major depression, which state that antidepressants should be provided for moderate to severe major depression unless ECT is planned. |
| | Fluoxetine (repackaged as Sarafem) becomes the first medication approved specifically for treating premenstrual dysphoric disorder. |
| **2004** | The Treatment for Adolescents with Depression Study shows that combining an antidepressant with psychotherapy is generally the most effective treatment for adolescents with depression. |
| **2005** | Drug company Lilly launches its highly successful "depression hurts" ad campaign for duloxetine (Cymbalta). |
| | The Food and Drug Administration asks drug companies to add a black box to their labeling for antidepressants warning about an increased risk of suicidal thoughts and behavior in children and adolescents. |
| | Vagus nerve stimulation is approved as an add-on treatment for people with hard-to-treat depression. |
| **2006** | Bupropion extended-release tablets (Wellbutrin XL) becomes the first antidepressant approved specifically for preventing depression in people with a history of seasonal affective disorder. |
| | The Sequenced Treatment Alternatives to Relieve Depression study shows that even people with treatment-resistant depression can often get well after trying multiple treatment strategies. |
| **2008** | A transcranial magnetic stimulation system is cleared for the treatment of major depression. |

# A

**ABRAHAM, KARL (1877–1925).** Karl Abraham was a German psychoanalyst who became part of the inner circle of **Sigmund Freud** (1856–1939). Psychoanalysis emphasizes the importance of childhood experiences as well as the influence of unconscious drives and wishes. Abraham studied the role of infant sexuality in the development of personality and psychological disorders. He also pioneered efforts to use psychoanalytic techniques to treat manic depression, now known as **bipolar disorder**. This is a mental disorder characterized by alternating periods of depression and **mania**, an overly high mood.

Abraham believed that people who have suffered a severe blow to their self-esteem as children are susceptible to depression as adults. A loss or disappointment in adulthood can stir up intense anger toward others as well as anxiety or guilt over the anger. To defend against such unpleasant feelings, people attribute their anger to other people. However, this just makes them feel as if other people are hostile toward them, which leads them to conclude that they must be disliked because of some inadequacy. The sense of being scorned, in turn, causes their depression.

***Biographical Highlights.*** Abraham was born in Bremen, Germany. While working as a psychiatrist's assistant at a mental hospital in Zurich, Abraham met Carl Jung (1875–1961), a Swiss psychologist and psychiatrist. Jung introduced Abraham to Freud's psychoanalytic theory. Moving from Zurich to Berlin in 1907, Abraham became the first German psychoanalyst.

Abraham founded the Berlin Psychoanalytic Society and helped established the first branch of the International Psychoanalytic Institute. His most important publication was a book titled *A Short Study of the Development of the Libido, Viewed in the Light of Mental Disorders,* published in 1924. Abraham died the following year in Berlin.

## Bibliography

"Abraham, Karl." *Encyclopedia Britannica Online,* 2007, http://www.britannica.com/eb/article-9003380/Karl-Abraham.

Busch, Frederic N., Marie Rudden, and Theodore Shapiro. *Psychodynamic Treatment of Depression.* Washington, DC: American Psychiatric Publishing, 2004.

Gabbard, Glen O., and Tanya J. Bennett. "Psychoanalytic and Psychodynamic Psychotherapy for Depression and Dysthymia." In *The American Psychiatric Publishing Textbook of Mood Disorders,* by Dan J. Stein, David J. Kupfer, and Alan F. Schatzberg, eds., 389–404. Washington, DC: American Psychiatric Publishing, 2006.

**ACCEPTANCE AND COMMITMENT THERAPY.** Acceptance and commitment therapy (ACT, said as the word "act," not as the letters "a-c-t") is a form of **psychotherapy** that focuses on the past and current context in which behaviors occur. ACT melds here-and-now awareness techniques with behavior change strategies. For someone who is depressed, the ultimate goal is not to eliminate the depression. Rather, it is to increase psychological flexibility, which means fully experiencing the present moment and, based on what is happening, either changing or continuing a behavior in the service of personal values.

As its name implies, two core components of ACT are acceptance and commitment. Acceptance is closely allied with mindfulness, a practice derived from Buddhism that involves focusing attention, fully and non-judgmentally, on whatever the person is experiencing from moment to moment. ACT does not aim to deliberately change the nature or frequency of unwanted thoughts and feelings. Instead, it promotes acceptance—not passive toleration or helpless resignation, but an active choice to accept even unpleasant thoughts and feelings without trying to control them.

Commitment is closely related to **behavioral therapy**, an approach to psychotherapy that helps people identify and change maladaptive behaviors. In ACT, personal values guide the intentional pursuit of certain actions. Thus, changes in overt behavior are an important part of therapy, but only when the changes are value-driven. Change for its own sake or as a way of restructuring thoughts is not encouraged.

***Third-Generation Behavioral Therapy.*** ACT was founded by U.S. psychologist Steven C. Hayes (1948–), a professor at the University of Nevada, Reno. Hayes has argued that ACT is part of a third wave of behavioral therapy, which also includes several other treatment options that venture into areas traditionally reserved for philosophy or religion rather than science. These approaches fuse concepts such as mindfulness, values, and spirituality with proven behavioral techniques.

*First Wave.* The first wave of behavioral therapy, dating back to the 1920s, sought to change problem behaviors through the application of basic principles of classical and operant conditioning. In classical conditioning, an initially neutral stimulus (the conditioned stimulus) is paired with another stimulus (the unconditioned stimulus) that elicits a reflex response. After repeated pairings, the conditioned stimulus becomes able to elicit the response by itself. In operant condition, behavioral change occurs as a function of the consequences of a behavior.

Early behavioral therapy was largely a rebellion against the prevailing treatments of the day, which were grounded in case studies rather than controlled research. Behavioral therapy rejected the quest for insight into unconscious influences on behavior. Instead, it focused on techniques that would change behavior directly, whether or not people gained any understanding of deeper influences. In the process, it tended to downplay the role of thoughts and feelings in maintaining problems.

*Second Wave.* The second wave of behavioral therapy, dating back to the late 1950s, was a reaction against the first wave's overemphasis on outward behavior. It led to the rise of **cognitive therapy**, which aims to help people recognize and change self-defeating thought patterns. The focus was still on bringing about change directly, but now the targeted behaviors were often internal rather than external.

Older strategies for behavior change were not abandoned. Instead, they were assimilated into the new approach, creating the hybrid known as **cognitive-behavioral therapy**

(CBT). Today CBT remains the gold standard for the treatment of depression with psychotherapy.

*Third Wave.* By the 1990s, the benefits of CBT had been well established—and so had the limitations for treating certain groups, including people with **treatment-resistant depression** and those with both depression and a personality disorder. The time was ripe for another paradigm shift.

Third-generation approaches include not only ACT, but also **dialectical behavior therapy** and **mindfulness-based cognitive therapy**. In these new approaches, the emphasis is no longer exclusively on changing thoughts or behavior directly. At least some of the focus is on processes such as mindfulness, acceptance, and valuing that are seen not just as means to an end, but also as valid ends in themselves. The assumption is that changing these processes may indirectly affect thoughts or behavior, but that is not always the explicit goal.

Third-wave therapies still have a long way to go before they have an evidence base that can rival that of CBT. More research is needed to establish their effectiveness for treating depression. But taken together, such therapies may represent an important next step in the continuing evolution of therapy.

***The Process at a Glance.*** The underlying premise of ACT is that psychological suffering results when people become so entangled in their own thoughts that the thoughts overshadow everything else. In an effort to avoid pain, people try to suppress more difficult thoughts and the unpleasant feelings that go along with them. But this is a losing battle, and it distracts people from taking action based on their values. The failure to act, in turn, just perpetuates and intensifies their misery.

ACT teaches people to take a mental step back and simply focus on the process of thinking itself, noticing and uncritically accepting whatever thoughts arise without passing judgment. It also shows people that they can begin to act in accord with their values right now, without having to wait for difficult thoughts and feelings to go away.

During treatment sessions, some time is spent discussing these principles. But much of the time is spent putting them into practice through a variety of exercises; for instance, asking people not to think about something as a way of demonstrating that trying to control a thought just makes it stronger. Metaphors—for instance, comparing depression to a tug-of-war with a monster—are often employed to illustrate key points.

Questionnaires may be used to help people pinpoint their personal values. Homework may be assigned between sessions to encourage people to keep practicing newly learned skills at home.

***Benefits for Depression.*** In one study, 101 people with moderate to severe depression or anxiety were randomly assigned to receive either ACT or cognitive therapy. The groups showed equivalent improvements in depression, anxiety, daily functioning, quality of life, and satisfaction with their lives. But the results suggested that these groups may have arrived at the same destination by different paths. Those in the ACT group seemed more influenced by "acting with awareness," for example, and those in the cognitive therapy group seemed more influenced by "describing" their experience.

Although such results are promising, more studies are needed before it is possible to draw any firm conclusions about ACT's effectiveness as a depression treatment. Time will tell whether ACT and its third-wave cousins will make an indelible mark on twenty-first-century psychology, just as the two previous waves did in the twentieth century.

*See also:* Treatment of Depression

***Further Information.*** Association for Contextual Behavioral Science, www.contextualpsychology.org.

## *Bibliography*

*An Interview With Steven Hayes.* New Harbinger Publications, 2004. http://www.newharbinger .com/client/client_pages/monthinterview_HAYES.cfm.

Forman, Evan M., James D. Herbert, Ethan Moitra, Peter D. Yeomans, and Pamela A. Geller. "A Randomized Controlled Effectiveness Trial of Acceptance and Commitment Therapy and Cognitive Therapy for Anxiety and Depression." *Behavior Modification* 31 (2007): 772–799.

Hayes, Steven C. "Acceptance and Commitment Therapy, Relational Frame Theory, and the Third Wave of Behavioral and Cognitive Therapies." *Behavior Therapy* 35 (2004): 639–665.

Hayes, Steven C. *Get Out of Your Mind and Into Your Life: The New Acceptance and Commitment Therapy.* Oakland, CA: New Harbinger, 2005.

Hayes, Steven C., Kirk D. Strosahl and Kelly G. Wilson. *Acceptance and Commitment Therapy: An Experiential Approach to Behavior Change.* New York: Guilford Press, 1999.

Hayes, Steven. *Acceptance and Commitment Therapy.* Association for Contextual Behavioral Science, May 1, 2005, http://www.contextualpsychology.org/act.

Zettle, Robert D. *ACT for Depression: A Clinician's Guide to Using Acceptance and Commitment Therapy in Treating Depression.* Oakland, CA: New Harbinger, 2007.

**ACUPUNCTURE.** Acupuncture is a therapeutic technique used in **traditional Chinese medicine** (TCM). It involves the stimulation of specific points along the body by various means. In the form of acupuncture most familiar to Westerners, hair-thin, metal needles are inserted at these points. But the points also can be stimulated by tiny electrical charges (electroacupuncture), sound waves (sonopuncture) or the heat from burning herbs (moxibustion). Several small, preliminary studies suggest that acupuncture may help relieve the symptoms of depression.

In TCM, health is seen as a delicate balance between the complementary forces of yin and yang. Yin stands for the cold, slow, or passive principle; yang, for the hot, excited, or active principle. Disease is viewed as the result of an imbalance in these forces. Such an imbalance blocks the flow of vital energy, called qi, along internal energy channels, called meridians. Acupuncture sites, called acupoints, lie along these meridians, and it is thought that stimulating various combinations of points can help remove blockages and restore balance.

Western science offers an alternative explanation for how acupuncture might work. Many scientists regard acupuncture points as sites for stimulating nerves, muscles, and connective tissues. Stimulating these points seems to increase blood flow and boost the production of **endorphins**, protein-like compounds in the brain that have natural pain-relieving and mood-lifting effects.

***Historical Roots.*** Acupuncture originated in China more than 2,500 years ago. From its birthplace, the technique spread first to other parts of Asia, where it continued to evolve for millennia. The acupuncture practices used in the United States today incorporate traditions from not only China, but also Korea, Japan, and other countries.

Originally, 365 acupoints were identified, but that number has grown to more than 2,000. Traditional acupuncture needles were made of bone, stone, or metals such as gold or silver, but modern needles are made of sterile stainless steel.

Acupuncture has been familiar to Asian communities in Europe and the Americas for generations. But the technique was not widely known to the U.S. public at large until

1971, when *New York Times* reporter James Reston (1909–1995) wrote about how acupuncture helped ease his pain after surgery. By 1997, the procedure had become prominent enough in medical circles that the National Institutes of Health (NIH) issued a Consensus Development Conference Statement on acupuncture.

The NIH statement concluded that there was promising evidence for acupuncture's effectiveness at treating pain after dental surgery as well as nausea and vomiting following surgery and chemotherapy. The statement added that there were other conditions for which acupuncture might be helpful, including addiction, stroke rehabilitation, headache, menstrual cramps, tennis elbow, fibromyalgia, myofascial pain, osteoarthritis, low back pain, carpal tunnel syndrome, and asthma.

Research over the past decade has only expanded the list of acupuncture's potential uses. Depression is one of the conditions for which encouraging results have been obtained.

***The Process at a Glance.*** Acupuncture usually involves a series of weekly or biweekly treatments. Each visit to the acupuncturist may include an exam and questions about current symptoms, the stimulation of acupoints, and a discussion of self-care steps. The whole visit typically lasts about half an hour.

When acupuncture needles are inserted, people may feel a slight sensation, but there usually is no pain. The needles are left in place for several minutes. During this time, the acupuncturist may twirl the needles or apply a weak electrical current or heat to heighten the effects. Some people report feeling energized by the treatment, and others say it is relaxing.

In the hands of a skilled practitioner, acupuncture is generally a low-risk procedure. The most common side effects are soreness, bleeding, or bruising. Choosing a qualified acupuncturist is important, though, because improper needle placement can lead to pain or, in rare cases, punctured organs. To prevent possible infection, acupuncturists should always use a new set of disposable needles taken from a sealed package for each treatment. Acupuncture may not be safe for people with bleeding disorders and those on anticoagulant medications ("blood thinners" taken to prevent blood clots).

Some variations on the acupuncture theme are needle-free. Electroacupuncture uses low-level electricity with or without needles, and sonopuncture uses sound waves delivered by an ultrasound device. Other methods that are sometimes used to stimulate acupoints include heat, pressure, friction, suction, magnets, or laser beams. However, these variants have not been tested as thoroughly as needle acupuncture.

*Choosing an Acupuncturist.* Most states require a license to perform acupuncture, but requirements for education and training vary. Typically, a licensed or registered acupuncturist has a master's-level degree or diploma from a school approved by the Accreditation Commission for Acupuncture and Oriental Medicine and has been awarded the diplomate in acupuncture (DiplAc) designation after passing an exam given by the National Commission for the Certification of Acupuncture and Oriental Medicine.

**Pressure Points**

Acupressure uses pressure or touch rather than needles to stimulate acupoints. It may also involve massage and stretching, which are thought to help rebalance and restore the flow of energy in the body. A few preliminary studies have found that acupressure can help reduce depression in people with chronic medical conditions, such as chronic obstructive pulmonary disease and end-stage kidney disease.

Medical acupuncturists are physicians with an MD or DO degree who incorporate acupuncture into their practice. Psychiatry is one of the medical fields to which acupuncture may be applied, but the number of psychiatrists who are cross-trained as acupuncturists is small. It is more common for physicians to refer patients who are interested in acupuncture to an outside provider who performs the treatment.

***Benefits for Depression.*** Several small studies suggest that acupuncture may be beneficial for depression. Some found that electroacupuncture was as effective for treating moderate depression as an antidepressant. Large, well-controlled studies are needed before any firm conclusions can be drawn, however.

In rigorous research assessing the effectiveness of **antidepressants**, the medications are compared to sugar pills, which serve as a placebo treatment. One challenge for future research is determining what the best placebo for acupuncture studies might be, because it is difficult to devise a sham version of the procedure. Some researchers have tried inserting needles at places that are not acupuncture points or using needle-like devices that do not pierce the skin. But uncertainties remain, because a number of studies have found that sham acupuncture works about as well as the real thing.

Although acupuncture might help manage depression, many questions about its effectiveness are still unanswered. Until more research is done, acupuncture should not take the place of proven treatments, such as **psychotherapy** and antidepressants. People currently being treated for depression who want to try acupuncture should talk to their health care provider about how to incorporate it into their overall treatment plan.

***Further Information.*** Accreditation Commission for Acupuncture and Oriental Medicine, Maryland Trade Center #3, 7501 Greenway Center Drive, Suite 760, Greenbelt, MD 20770, (301) 313–0855, www.acaom.org.

American Academy of Medical Acupuncture, 4929 Wilshire Boulevard, Suite 428, Los Angeles, CA 90010, (323) 937–5514, www.medicalacupuncture.org.

American Association of Acupuncture and Oriental Medicine, P.O. Box 162340, Sacramento, CA 95816, (866) 455–7999, www.aaaomonline.org.

## Bibliography

*Acupressure, Shiatsu, and Other Asian Bodywork.* American Cancer Society, May 22, 2007, http://www.cancer.org/docroot/ETO/content/ETO_5_3X_Acupressure_ShShiat_and_Other_Asian_Bodywork.asp.

*Acupuncture.* American Cancer Society, May 23, 2007, http://www.cancer.org/docroot/ETO/content/ETO_5_3X_Acupuncture.asp.

"Acupuncture." *National Institutes of Health Consensus Development Conference Statement* 15 (1997): 1–34.

*Acupuncture: An Alternative and Complementary Medicine Resource Guide.* Alternative Medicine Foundation, August 15, 2007, http://www.amfoundation.org/acupuncture.htm.

*Acupuncture: Can It Help?* Mayo Clinic, December 13, 2007, http://www.mayoclinic.com/health/acupuncture/SA00086.

*An Introduction to Acupuncture.* National Center for Complementary and Alternative Medicine, May 27, 2008, http://nccam.nih.gov/health/acupuncture.

Cho, Y. C., and S. L. Tsay. "The Effect of Acupressure with Massage on Fatigue and Depression in Patients with End-Stage Renal Disease." *Journal of Nursing Research* 12 (2004): 51–59.

*Know Your Acupuncturist.* Council of Colleges of Acupuncture and Oriental Medicine, http://www.ccaom.org/downloads/KnowYourAcupuncturist.pdf.

*Moxibustion.* American Cancer Society, May 23, 2007, http://www.cancer.org/docroot/ETO/content/ETO_5_3X_Moxibustion.asp.

Smith, C. A., and P. P. J. Hay. "Acupuncture for Depression." *Cochrane Database of Systematic Reviews* 3 (2004): art. no. CD004046.

Thie, Julia. "Chinese Medical Treatments." In *Complementary and Alternative Treatments in Mental Health Care,* by James H. Lake and David Spiegel, eds., pp. 169–194. Washington, DC: American Psychiatric Publishing, 2007.

Wang, Hao, Hong Qi, Bai-song Wang, Yong-yao Cui, Liang Zhu, Zheng-xing Rong, et al. "Is Acupuncture Beneficial in Depression? A Meta-analysis of 8 Randomized Controlled Trials." *Journal of Affective Disorders* (June 10, 2008): e-publication ahead of print.

Wu, Hua-Shan, Li-Chan Lin, Shiao-Chi Wu and Jaung-Geng Lin. "The Psychologic Consequences of Chronic Dyspnea in Chronic Pulmonary Obstruction Disease: The Effects of Acupressure on Depression." *Journal of Alternative and Complementary Medicine* 13 (2007): 253–262.

**ACUTE TREATMENT.**    Treatment for depression falls into three stages: acute, continuation, and maintenance. These stages apply to treatment with **antidepressants** and **psychotherapy** alike. During the acute phase, the goal is to relieve symptoms and begin to restore normal functioning in daily life. This phase covers the time period between the start of treatment and the initial treatment response—in other words, the first signs of a 50 percent or greater reduction in symptom severity.

For people taking antidepressants, the acute phase typically lasts six to eight weeks, during which people often visit the prescribing doctor every week or two. The doctor monitors symptoms and side effects, and makes any necessary adjustments in dosage. For people in psychotherapy, the phase usually lasts six to 20 weeks, during which people often meet with the therapist weekly.

One common problem in the acute phase is quitting treatment early. In studies, dropout rates are often as high as 30 percent to 40 percent, and an even greater percentage of people fail to follow the treatment plan exactly. Some people have unrealistic expectations about how quickly they will get better, and they become discouraged when their depression does not lift overnight. Others are bothered by medication side effects or feel ambivalent about taking medicine or seeing a therapist. Still others are derailed by cost or inconvenience.

Among those who stick with it, studies show that about half of people with depression respond to the first-choice antidepressant or psychotherapy. For those who do not get better, another treatment approach can be tried. Finding the best treatment for a given individual often takes some trial and error.

When several types of medication and psychotherapy have been tried without success, other options are available. The best-known alternative is **electroconvulsive therapy** (ECT), which involves passing a carefully controlled electrical current through the person's brain to induce a brief seizure. ECT is thought to alter electrochemical processes involved in brain functioning.

*See also:* Continuation Treatment; Maintenance Treatment

*Bibliography*

Gitlin, Michael J. "Pharmacotherapy and Other Somatic Treatments for Depression." In *Handbook of Depression.* 2nd ed., by Ian H. Gotlib and Constance L. Hammen, eds., 554–585. New York: Guilford Press, 2009.

Kupfer, David J. "Acute Continuation and Maintenance Treatment of Mood Disorders." *Depression* 3 (1995): 137–138.

U.S. Department of Health and Human Services. *Mental Health: A Report of the Surgeon General.* Rockville, MD: U.S. Department of Health and Human Services, 1999.

**ADJUSTMENT DISORDER WITH DEPRESSED MOOD.** An adjustment disorder is a psychological response to a stressful situation that leads to more distress than would normally be expected or causes problems in the person's work, school, or social life. Adjustment disorders can be subdivided based on the main symptoms they cause. An "adjustment disorder with depressed mood" is characterized by symptoms such as a low mood, **crying** spells, or feelings of hopelessness.

This diagnosis is only made when a person's symptoms don't meet all the criteria for **major depression** or **dysthymia**, yet are still distressing or disruptive enough to warrant treatment. Although milder in some ways, an adjustment disorder is not trivial by any means. Left untreated, an adjustment disorder increases the risk of **substance abuse** and **suicide** attempts. It also may impede recovery from a physical illness; for example, by decreasing people's ability to stick to a treatment plan.

The good news is that people who are struggling to bounce back from a stressful situation don't have to just tough it out alone. Treatment can help them adjust to difficult changes in their lives and regain their emotional balance. It also may help keep an adjustment disorder from turning into a more severe problem, such as major depression.

*Criteria for Diagnosis.* The symptoms of an adjustment disorder with depressed mood are defined by the ***Diagnostic and Statistical Manual of Mental Disorders, Fourth Edition, Text Revision*** (*DSM-IV-TR*), a diagnostic guidebook published by the American Psychiatric Association and widely used by mental health professionals from many disciplines. According to the *DSM-IV-TR,* the symptoms arise within three months after the start of a stressful situation. They involve either (1) marked distress that is out of proportion to the situation or (2) significant problems getting along at work, school, or in social settings. Even a normal reaction to a very upsetting situation can be considered an adjustment disorder if it causes enough turmoil in daily life.

Of course, many mental disorders, including major depression and dysthymia, may be set off by **stress**. If a person's symptoms are long-lasting, wide-ranging, and serious enough to qualify as one these other disorders, that is the diagnosis made. The adjustment disorder category is only used as a last resort, when no other diagnosis is available but treatment might still be helpful in the judgment of a professional.

The symptoms of an adjustment disorder go away within six months after the stressful situation or its consequences have ended. If the source of stress is a one-time event—for instance, getting fired at work or breaking up in a romantic relationship—the symptoms usually fade away within a few months. But if the stress or its consequences are long-term—for instance, having financial problems as a result of being out of work or going through a protracted custody battle—the symptoms may last for longer, too.

When an adjustment disorder occurs along with a depressed mood, it is characterized by symptoms such as being in a down mood, crying often, feeling hopeless, and losing interest in activities that were once enjoyed. In other individuals, an adjustment disorder may occur along with anxiety symptoms (such as nervousness, worry, or the jitters), conduct disturbance symptoms (such as reckless driving, fighting, skipping school, or not paying bills), or various nonspecific symptoms (such as withdrawing socially or having problems at work or school). And in still other individuals, there may be a mixture of depression, anxiety, and/or conduct disturbance.

***Causes and Risk Factors.*** Adjustment disorders are relatively common in people of all ages. Prevalence estimates vary, though, depending on the group being studied and the assessment methods being used. Among **children**, **adolescents**, and **older adults**, for instance, the disorders are estimated to affect 2 percent to 8 percent of the general population.

Certain subgroups who are dealing with high-stress situations are at much greater risk, however. For instance, adjustment disorders occur in up to 12 percent of hospitalized patients and as many as half of those recovering from cardiac surgery.

*Stressful Events.* Stressful life events are the triggers for adjustment disorders. Common sources of stress include being diagnosed with a serious illness, getting divorced, losing a job, going away to school, being the victim of a crime, or surviving a natural disaster. Positive events that produce major life changes can lead to considerable stress—and increased risk of an adjustment disorder—as well. Examples include getting married, having a baby, starting a new job, or retiring from work.

In some cases, the source of stress is not a single event, but an ongoing set of circumstances. For instance, being impoverished or living in a crime-ridden neighborhood can cause chronic stress, which, in turn, can contribute to a long-lasting adjustment disorder.

Of course, not everyone exposed to such stressful situations goes on to experience adjustment problems. In general, people who have not developed good personal coping skills and a strong social support network may have more trouble adapting to tough situations.

Extreme stress in childhood—for example, physical or sexual abuse, loss of a parent, or frequent moves—may set the stage for an excessive reaction to stress later in life. One theory is that some children learn to feel powerless in the face of adversity. When difficulties arise at a later age, they may not feel capable of responding effectively.

---

### Bouncing Back from a Setback

Resilience is the process of adapting successfully to life-altering experiences and stressful situations. Being resilient does not mean being immune to emotional pain. After a major loss or trauma, it is normal—even healthy—to feel distressed. But although some people are overwhelmed by the pain, others are able to bounce back. The thoughts and behaviors that underlie this ability form the core of therapy for adjustment disorders, and they can be cultivated in everyday life, too. Based on scientific research and clinical experience, these steps may help:

*Nurture Your Relationships*
- Family and friends can be invaluable sources of emotional support and practical assistance when times are tough.

*Give Back to Others*
- Volunteering for a civic group, religious organization, or charitable cause not only benefits other people, but also helps the helper make new social connections and find a sense of purpose in life.

*Adopt a Healthy Lifestyle*
- Exercising regularly, eating wisely, and getting enough sleep help keep your mind and body primed for effective action.

*Boost Your Self-Esteem*
- Notice the lessons you have learned and strength you have gained by dealing with a difficult situation. Pat yourself on the back for your ability to solve problems and overcome hardship.

***Treatment of Adjustment Disorder with Depressed Mood.*** **Psychotherapy** and counseling are the mainstays of treatment for adjustment disorders. The person may meet one-on-one with a therapist or take part in **group therapy** or **family therapy**.

Short-term **cognitive-behavioral therapy**, which helps people recognize and change maladaptive thought and behavior patterns, has proven to be especially helpful. Therapy typically focuses on helping people improve their problem-solving and **stress management** skills. More specifically, people might work on understanding the role they play in their own stress, reviewing their methods of handling stress in the past, developing more effective coping strategies for the future, and learning to think about stress as an opportunity for growth rather than a threat. These skills help them not only overcome their current problems, but also weather future situations more successfully.

When symptoms don't improve with therapy or start to get worse, **antidepressants** may be prescribed. Research has shown that these medications can be effective for treating an adjustment disorder with depressed mood, just as they are for treating other forms of depression. With proper treatment, most people with an adjustment disorder start to feel better and are able to move on with their lives again.

*See also:* Reactive Depression

## Bibliography

*Adjustment Disorders.* Mayo Clinic, May 23, 2007, http://www.mayoclinic.com/health/adjustment-disorders/DS00584.

American Psychiatric Association. *Diagnostic and Statistical Manual of Mental Disorders.* 4th ed., text rev. Washington, DC: American Psychiatric Association, 2000.

Frances, Allen, Michael B. First and Harold Alan Pincus. *DSM-IV Guidebook.* Washington, DC: American Psychiatric Press, 1995.

Hameed, Usman, Thomas L. Schwartz, Kamna Malhotra, Rebecca L. West, and Francesca Bertone. "Antidepressant Treatment in the Primary Care Office: Outcomes for Adjustment Disorder Versus Major Depression." *Annals of Clinical Psychiatry* 17 (2005): 77–81.

Sampang, Jennifer A. "Adjustment Disorder With Depressed Mood: A Review of Diagnosis and Treatment." *Advance for Nurse Practitioners* 11 (2003): 51–54.

*The Adjustment Disorders.* National Cancer Institute, April 29, 2008, http://www.cancer.gov/cancertopics/pdq/supportivecare/adjustment/HealthHealthProfes/page5.

*The Road to Resilience.* Discovery Health Channel and American Psychological Association, http://apahelpcenter.org/dl/the_road_to_resilience.pdf.

**ADOLESCENTS.** At one time, depression in adolescents was regarded as nothing more than teen moodiness. Today, that has changed. Experts now recognize that adolescence is a high-risk period for the onset of depression serious enough to warrant professional help. Fortunately, more is also known about the best way to treat the disorder in this age group.

Before puberty, about 3 percent of **children** experience depression, and girls and boys are equally affected. Those prevalence and distribution figures change sharply after puberty, however. By late adolescence, the prevalence rate for full-blown **major depression** is nearing that of adults, with about 14 percent of adolescents having experienced an episode at some point in their lives. Another 10 percent or more have symptoms of depression that fall short of meeting all the diagnostic criteria for the disorder but still may be distressing.

Around ages 12 to 14, the risk for girls and boys also begins to diverge. By mid-adolescence, depression is twice as common in females as in males, a gender difference that persists through adulthood. Dramatic hormonal shifts associated with female puberty may explain at least part of this disparity.

Adolescent depression often exists side by side with other mental, emotional, and behavioral problems, including **anxiety disorders**, **conduct disorder**, and **attention-deficit hyperactivity disorder**. Teens with depression also are at increased risk for **substance abuse** and **eating disorders**. The risk of **suicide** spikes during adolescence as well. Although suicide is the eleventh-leading cause of death in the U.S. population as a whole, it is the third-leading cause among young people ages 10 through 24.

*Adolescent Risk Factors.* Why do depression rates rise so dramatically in adolescence? Physical maturation may be part of the answer. Some of the physiological processes underlying depression may not become apparent until the brain and **nervous system** have reached a certain level of development. Other physiological changes may be triggered by adolescent **hormones**. Because the gender gap in depression arises around puberty, researchers suspect that female hormones might be involved.

**Cognitive factors** also may come into play. Research has shown that certain thinking styles are associated with depression. This type of thinking may not be in full flower until young people become capable of adult-like thought—and adult-like errors in reasoning.

**Relationship issues** often assume great importance during the teen years. Any problems in this area may lead to considerable **stress**, which, in turn may trigger depression in vulnerable individuals. Compared to nondepressed peers, depressed teens tend to experience more social rejection and poorer relationships with friends and romantic partners.

*Diagnostic Issues.* In short, adolescence is a time of rapid physical, mental and social growth. The teen years are also fraught with challenges: establishing an identity apart from parents, coping with emerging sexuality, making independent decisions for the first time. It is normal for teens to experience some minor ups and downs as they negotiate these challenges. But major turbulence and severe mood swings are another matter. Mental health experts say it is a myth that the teen years are inevitably stormy. If changes in mood or behavior cause serious distress or disruption and last more than a couple of weeks, they might signal depression or another treatable condition.

Depression in adolescents is identified using the same diagnostic criteria used for adults. Only two developmental variations are noted in the ***Diagnostic and Statistical Manual of Mental Disorders, Fourth Edition, Text Revision*** (*DSM-IV-TR*). In adolescents, a **depressed mood** sometimes leads to feeling irritable rather than sad or empty. Also, the minimum duration of symptoms required for **dysthymia**—a relatively mild but very long-lasting form of depression—is one year for adolescents, compared to two years for adults.

In practical terms, some adolescents who are depressed act sullen or angry, and cause trouble at home or school rather than appearing overtly sad. As a result, parents and teachers may not immediately recognize that the problem is depression. Other depressed teens withdraw from friends and family, lose interest in hobbies, and become bored with life. They may miss school frequently, and their grades may suffer. Depressed adolescents also sometimes turn to **alcohol** or other drugs in a misguided attempt to feel better.

*Treatment Considerations.* For adolescent with depression, research has shown that a combination of **psychotherapy** and **antidepressants** seems to work the best and may help keep depression from recurring. When it comes to psychotherapy, **cognitive-behavioral therapy** (CBT), which aims to identify and change maladaptive thoughts and behaviors, is the best-studied approach. Several studies have shown that CBT can be an effective treatment for adolescent depression.

Another form of therapy that has proved beneficial in some studies is **interpersonal therapy**, which addresses the interpersonal triggers for mental, emotional, and behavioral symptoms. In most cases, psychotherapy is conducted in one-on-one sessions between the teen and a therapist. But both **group therapy** and **family therapy** have also been used successfully with depressed teens.

When it comes to medication, the types of antidepressants used to treat adult depression are also prescribed for adolescents. Such medications may help depressed teens feel better and enjoy a richer, more satisfying life at home, at school, and with their friends. Like all medications, though, antidepressants carry a risk of side effects. One risk that has received considerable attention is an increased likelihood of suicidal thoughts or actions in young people. In short-term studies involving children and teenagers with depression and other illnesses, four out of 100 young people who took antidepressants became suicidal, although none actually completed suicide. By comparison, two out of 100 who took a sugar pill became suicidal.

The decision to treat a particular adolescent with antidepressants is made on a case-by-case basis, weighing the possible risks against the expected benefits. To minimize the risks, parents should contact their child's health care provider right away if a teen on antidepressants experiences unusual changes in behavior or mood. Changes to watch for include (1) suicidal thoughts or actions, (2) worsening of depression, (3) new or worse anxiety or **irritability**, (4) agitation or restlessness, (5) panic attacks, (6) trouble sleeping, (7) aggressive or violent behavior, (8) dangerously impulsive behavior or (9) an extreme increase in activity and talking.

*See also:* Antidepressants and Suicide; Treatment for Adolescents with Depression Study

***Further Information.*** American Academy of Child and Adolescent Psychiatry, 3615 Wisconsin Avenue N.W., Washington, D.C. 20016, (202) 966-7300, www.aacap.org.

American Academy of Pediatrics, 141 Northwest Point Boulevard, Elk Grove Village, IL 60007, (847) 434-4000, www.aap.org.

Annenberg Foundation Trust at Sunnylands, www.copecaredeal.org.

Nemours Foundation, www.teenshealth.org.

Society of Clinical Child and Adolescent Psychology, clinicalchildpsychology.org.

TeenScreen, National Center for Mental Health Checkups at Columbia University, 1775 Broadway, Suite 610, New York, NY 10019, (212) 265-4453, www.teenscreen.org.

## Bibliography

American Psychiatric Association. *Diagnostic and Statistical Manual of Mental Disorders.* Washington, DC: American Psychiatric Association, 1952.

*Depression in Women: Understanding the Gender Gap.* Mayo Clinic, September 6, 2008, http://www.mayoclinic.com/health/depression/MH00035.

Emslie, Graham J., Taryn L. Mayes, Beth D. Kennard, and Jennifer L. Hughes. "Pediatric Mood Disorders." In *The American Psychiatric Publishing Textbook of Mood Disorders,* by Dan J. Stein, David J. Kupfer and Alan F. Schatzberg, eds., 573–601. Washington, DC: American Psychiatric Publishing, 2006.

Evans, Dwight L., and Linda Wasmer Andrews. *If Your Adolescent Has Depression or Bipolar Disorder: An Essential Resource for Parents.* New York: Oxford University Press, 2005.

Irwin, Cait, with Dwight L. Evans and Linda Wasmer Andrews. *Monochrome Days: A Firsthand Account of One Teenager's Experience With Depression.* New York: Oxford University Press, 2007.

Rudolph, Karen D. "Adolescent Depression." In *Handbook of Depression.* 2nd ed., by Ian H. Gotlib and Constance L. Hammen, eds., 444–466. New York: Guilford Press, 2009.

*Suicide in the U.S.: Statistics and Prevention.* National Institute of Mental Health, May 18, 2009, http://www.nimh.nih.gov/health/publications/suicide-in-the-us-statistics-and-prevention/index.shtml.

*Suicide: Facts at a Glance.* Centers for Disease Control and Prevention, Summer 2008, http://www.cdc.gov/ViolencePrevention/pdf/Suicide-DataSheet-a.pdf.

*The Depressed Child.* American Academy of Child and Adolescent Psychiatry, May 2008, http://www.aacap.org/cs/root/facts_for_families/the_depressed_child.

Treatment for Adolescents With Depression Study (TADS) Team. "Fluoxetine, Cognitive-Behavioral Therapy, and Their Combination for Adolescents With Depression: Treatment for Adolescents With Depression Study (TADS) Randomized Controlled Trial." *JAMA* 292 (2004): 807–820.

**AFRICAN AMERICANS.**   African Americans are the second-largest ethnic minority in the United States, comprising 13.5 percent of the total population. In general, rates of mental illness in African Americans are similar to those in the population as a whole. Looking specifically at depression, evidence on the relative prevalence of the disorder is mixed. Although most studies have found that African Americans have lower rates of depression than their white counterparts, some have found equivalent or even higher rates.

Such contradictory results may partly reflect differences in how depression is defined by various researchers. A large, nationally representative survey found a higher lifetime prevalence of **major depression** in white Americans than in African Americans. However, the pattern was reversed for **dysthymia**, a milder but very long-lasting depressive disorder.

Disparities in diagnosed depression also may partly reflect differences in how African Americans react to emotional distress. African Americans, like many other Americans, often dismiss depression as nothing more than "the blues." Initially, African Americans frequently seek mental health support from their family, friends, church, and community rather than health care providers.

As a result, symptoms of major depression may be relatively severe by the time a formal diagnosis is made. This helps explain why, once diagnosed, African Americans with major depression are more likely than their white counterparts to have severe and persistent symptoms.

*Treatment Issues.*   **Antidepressants**, **psychotherapy**, or a combination of both are the primary treatment options for depression. Generally speaking, these treatments are safe and effective for African Americans. Nevertheless, under-treatment remains a concern. A large, national study of U.S. adults who had experienced major depression within the past year found that just 60 percent of non-Hispanic African Americans received treatment, compared to 73 percent of non-Hispanic whites.

An even bleaker picture emerged for youth ages 12 through 17. In this age group, only 29 percent of non-Hispanic African Americans received treatment for depression, compared to 41 percent of non-Hispanic whites. Clearly, this is an area where improvements are needed.

*Antidepressant Treatment.*   Studies suggest that antidepressant treatment may be less acceptable to African Americans, on average, than to white Americans. At the same time, research shows that treatment providers may be less likely to prescribe antidepressants for African American patients. And when they do, they may be less apt to prescribe newer antidepressants, which tend to cause fewer troubling side effects than older medications. The worse the side effects, the greater the risk that people will stop taking their medication prematurely.

In addition, a greater percentage of African Americans than white Americans metabolize some antidepressants slowly and therefore might be more sensitive to their effects. This could manifest as a faster response rate, but it might also lead to more severe side effects.

Taken together, these factors help account for a lower rate of antidepressant use among African Americans with depression than among their white counterparts. Statistics show that non-Hispanic white Americans are more than twice as likely to receive antidepressants as non-Hispanic African Americans.

***Barriers to Care.*** Financial barriers to high-quality care affect African Americans disproportionately. In 2007, just 49 percent of African Americans used employer-based health insurance, compared to 66 percent of white Americans. In contrast, Africans Americans are more likely to be uninsured or to rely on public health insurance.

In addition, African Americans tend to be overrepresented in high-need groups that are particularly at risk for mental health problems. For example, African Americans make up 40 percent of the homeless population in the United States. They are also more likely to be victims of serious violent crime than white Americans.

Yet African-Americans are under-represented among those receiving outpatient services for mental health disorders. When they do receive treatment, it is more likely to come from a primary care physician rather than a mental health specialist. Compared to the general population, African Americans also are more likely to stop treatment early and less likely to receive follow-up care.

***Cultural Considerations.*** Historically, research on depression was based largely on European and white American populations. Ethnic and cultural differences in traditions, values, and beliefs were rarely addressed. As a result, less is known about **risk factors**, **protective factors**, symptoms, diagnosis, and treatment as they relate specifically to depression in African Americans.

Even studies that address ethnicity tend to lump all black Americans into a single group. Yet there is considerable cultural diversity within black communities today, with growing numbers of recent immigrants from Africa, the Caribbean, and Central America. More research is required to identify the mental health needs of these immigrant groups.

*See also:* Cultural Factors; Ethnicity

***Further Information.*** Association of Black Psychologists, P.O. Box 55999, Washington, D.C. 20040, (202) 722-0808, www.abpsi.org.

Office of Minority Health, U.S. Department of Health and Human Services, P.O. Box 37337, Washington, D.C. 20013, (800) 444-6472, www.omhrc.gov.

## *Bibliography*

*African American Profile.* U.S. Department of Health and Human Services Office of Minority Health, July 31, 2009, http://www.omhrc.gov/templates/browse.aspx?lvl=3&lvlid=23.

*African Americans.* American Psychiatric Association, http://healthyminds.org/More-Info-For/African-Americans.aspx.

*African Americans.* U.S. Department of Health and Human Services Office of the Surgeon General, http://mentalhealth.samhsa.gov/cre/fact1.asp.

Cooper, L. A., J. J. Gonzales, J. J. Gallo, K. M. Rost, L. S. Meredith, L. V. Rubenstein et al. "The Acceptability of Treatment for Depression Among African-American, Hispanic, and White

Primary Care Patients." *Medical Care* 41 (2003): 479–489.

*Mental Health and African Americans.* U.S. Department of Health and Human Services Office of Minority Health, July 27, 2009, http://www.omhrc.gov/templates/content.aspx?lvl= 3&lvlID=9&ID=6474.

Riolo, Stephanie A., Tuan Anh Nguyen, John F. Greden, & Cheryl A. King. "Prevalence of Depression by Race/Ethnicity: Findings From the National Health and Nutrition Examination Survey III." *American Journal of Public Health* 95 (2005): 998–1000.

*2008 National Healthcare Quality and Disparities Reports.* Agency for Healthcare Research and Quality, http://www.ahrq.gov/qual/qrdr08/index.html.

U.S. Department of Health and Human Services. *Culture, Race, and Ethnicity: A Supplement to Mental Health: A Report of the Surgeon General.* Rockville, MD: U.S. Department of Health and Human Services, 2001.

Williams, David R., Hector M. González, Harold Neighbors, Randolph Nesse, Jamie M. Abelson, Julie Sweetman et al. "Prevalence and Distribution of Major Depressive Disorder in African Americans, Caribbean Blacks, and Non-Hispanic Whites: Results from the National Survey of American Life." *Archives of General Psychiatry* 64 (2007): 305–315.

**AGOMELATINE.**    Agomelatine is an antidepressant that has a different mode of action from other medications currently on the market. It is still considered an experimental drug in the United States, where it is not expected to be cleared for sale until at least 2012. However, it already received marketing authorization as a treatment for **major depression** by the European Commission in 2009.

People with depression often show disturbances in **circadian rhythms**, including sleep-wake cycles and daily **cortisol** secretion. Agomelatine is unique among **antidepressants** in that it binds with and activates **melatonin** receptors. That action, in turn, helps reset disturbed circadian rhythms.

Agomelatine also blocks the action of certain **serotonin** receptors in the frontal cortex, part of the brain involved in mood, emotion, and thought. Normally, these **receptors** receive messages telling the cells when it is time to stop releasing two brain chemicals, **dopamine** and **norepinephrine**. But agomelatine keeps that message from going through, so cells keep pumping out dopamine and norepinephrine, which are thought to have mood-lifting effects.

***Benefits and Risks.***    In research to date, the effectiveness of agomelatine seems to compare favorably to that of other antidepressants. Among other things, it improves sleep quality, which is often disrupted in depression, without causing daytime drowsiness. This improvement may start as early as the first week of treatment.

Many antidepressants can cause unpleasant symptoms if stopped abruptly, so when patients are ready to stop the medication, they are usually advised to taper off gradually. This may not be necessary with agomelatine, however, because it does not cause symptoms when discontinued.

Based on studies so far, agomelatine does not seem to produce some of the more troubling side effects associated with other antidepressants, including sexual problems, weight gain, and cardiovascular effects. It may cause dizziness and nausea, however. In rare cases, it may also lead to liver problems, so it should not be taken by people who already have liver disease. Anyone taking agomelatine should get periodic liver function tests.

Agomelatine is currently in Phase III clinical trials in the United States. This is the phase in which randomized placebo-controlled trials are conducted in large numbers of patients to confirm that a drug is effective and to identify side effects. It is possible that the outlook for agomelatine will change as testing proceeds. For now, though, it looks to be one of the most promising and innovative antidepressants on the near horizon.

*See also:* Antidepressants; Melatonin

*Bibliography*

*Clinical Pipeline.* Novartis, July 2009, http://www.novartis.com/research/pharmaceutical-product .shtml.

Greener, Mark. "Agomelatine: A New Approach to Depression." *Progress in Neurology and Psychiatry* (June 24, 2009).

*New Medicines Database.* Pharmaceutical Research and Manufacturers of America, 2009, http://newmeds.phrma.org.

Sen, Srijan, and Gerard Sanacora. "Major Depression: Emerging Therapeutics." *Mount Sinai Journal of Medicine* 75 (2008): 204–225.

*Valdoxan (Agomelatine), A Novel Antidepressant, Received European Marketing Authorisation,* Servier, February 25, 2009, http://www.servier.co.uk/healthcare-professionals/article-details.asp ?StoryID=120.

*Valdoxan (Agomelatine): Frequently Asked Questions (FAQS).* Servier, http://www.servier.co.uk/healthcare-professionals/Valdoxan/frequently-asked-questions.asp.

**ALCOHOL.**   Alcohol abuse refers to a drinking pattern that leads to serious adverse consequences, such as traffic accidents, interpersonal conflicts, or missed days at school or work, yet the person continues drinking too much or too often. The result may be a downward spiral, in which alcohol-related problems get progressively worse over time. Eventually, alcohol abuse may escalate to alcoholism, which is characterized by physical and psychological dependence on alcohol. People with a history of alcohol problems are at increased risk for depression. In one study of former drinkers who had been abstinent from alcohol, nicotine, and other drugs for at least a year, past alcoholism increased the risk for current **major depression** by fourfold.

Alcohol acts as a central **nervous system** depressant. In some people, it may have a stimulating effect at first, but as drinking continues, it becomes sedating. Alcohol lowers inhibitions and impairs judgment, speech, and coordination. Excessive amounts can severely depress vital centers of the brain, and a very heavy drinking binge can even cause a life-threatening coma.

A repeated pattern of abusing alcohol can lead to a wide array of personal, social, occupational, academic, and legal problems. If continued long term, it can also result in alcoholism, a disease with four cardinal signs: (1) a strong craving, or urge, to drink alcohol, (2) loss of control over drinking behavior, (3) withdrawal symptoms after giving up drinking, and (4) the need to drink increasing amounts to get the same high.

Over time, excessive drinking can cause fatigue, short-term memory loss, and problems with the eye muscles. Other health problems may ensue as well, including liver disorders, digestive problems, cardiovascular disease, diabetes complications, bone loss, neurological disorders, and several types of cancer. Chronic alcohol abuse or alcoholism also can lead to erectile dysfunction in men, interruption of menstruation in women, and birth defects in the babies of women who drink during pregnancy.

Moderate drinking is usually defined as no more than one drink a day for women or two drinks for men. But even moderate or social drinking is inadvisable for some people, such as pregnant women, recovering alcoholics, anyone under age 21, and those taking certain medications. And because alcohol is involved in two-fifths of traffic deaths, getting behind the wheel after drinking is always a very bad idea.

About 40 percent of people who have **major depression** at some point in their lives will also have a problem with alcohol abuse or alcoholism, according to a survey of more than 43,000 adults across the United States. People with both depression and an alcohol problem tend to have more severe mental health symptoms and a greater risk of **suicide** compared to those with depression alone. For these individuals, getting help for both conditions is doubly important.

***Criteria for Diagnosis.*** The symptoms of alcohol abuse, dependence, intoxication, and withdrawal are defined by the ***Diagnostic and Statistical Manual of Mental Disorders, Fourth Edition, Text Revision*** (*DSM-IV-TR*), a diagnostic guidebook published by the American Psychiatric Association and widely used by mental health professionals from many disciplines. Collectively, these are sometimes referred to as alcohol use disorders. The diagnostic criteria are summarized below.

*Alcohol Abuse.* The core feature of alcohol abuse is a pattern of drinking that leads to serious adverse consequences. This pattern occurs intermittently or continuously for at least a year, and it causes significant distress or disruption in daily life. The result is one or more of the following symptoms: (1) repeated failure to live up to important obligations at home, work, or school (such as neglecting household or child care duties or showing up at work or school drunk), (2) repeated drinking in situations where it is physically dangerous (such as when driving or operating machinery), (3) repeated alcohol-related legal problems (such as arrests for disorderly conduct or driving under the influence) or (4) continued drinking despite serious social or relationship fallout (such as physical fights or divorce).

*Alcohol Dependence.* As alcohol abuse starts to cause multiple physical, mental, and behavioral symptoms, it may escalate to alcohol dependence. One common feature of dependence is tolerance, in which a person has to drink more and more alcohol to get the same effect. Another common feature is withdrawal, in which someone who has recently quit drinking experiences unpleasant symptoms as a result. When alcohol dependence includes both physiological and psychological features, it can be equated with alcoholism.

Like alcohol abuse, dependence is typified by a pattern of drinking that leads to serious distress or disruption in daily life. In addition, over the course of a year, the person has three or more of the following symptoms: (1) tolerance, (2) withdrawal, (3) drinking in larger amounts or over a longer period than intended, (4) wanting or unsuccessfully trying to cut down on drinking, (5) spending considerable time on drinking alcohol or recovering from hangovers, (6) giving up or cutting back on other important activities, or (7) continuing to drink despite recognizing that it causes problems.

*Alcohol Intoxication.* Intoxication is the medical term for getting drunk. It is characterized by maladaptive psychological or behavioral changes—for example, mood swings, aggressive behavior, impaired judgment, or workplace errors—that occur during or soon after drinking alcohol. These changes are accompanied by at least one of the following symptoms: (1) slurred speech, (2) poor coordination, (3) unsteady walking, (4) involuntary, rapid movements of the eyeballs, (5) impaired attention or memory, or (6) passing out or coma.

*Alcohol Withdrawal.* Withdrawal is characterized by unpleasant symptoms caused by giving up or cutting back on alcohol after a period of prolonged, heavy drinking. The withdrawal symptoms include two or more of the following: (1) signs of overactivity in the autonomic nervous system, such as sweating or a rapid pulse, (2) increase shakiness of the hands, (3) trouble falling or staying asleep, (4) nausea or vomiting, (5) transitory hallucinations (seeing, hearing, or feeling things that are not really there), (6) restless activity accompanied by feelings of inner tension, (7) anxiety, or (8) grand mal seizures, which lead to violent muscle contractions and loss of consciousness.

Withdrawal symptoms typically begin four to 12 hours after stopping or reducing drinking, as blood alcohol levels drop sharply. They usually peak on the second day of abstinence and improve markedly by the fourth or fifth day. But some symptoms—such as sleep problems or anxiety—may persist at a lower intensity for as long as three to six months.

Because withdrawal can be intense, people may be tempted to go back to drinking to relieve the symptoms. Treatment can help a person get through this stage safely and successfully. Detoxification (detox, for short) is the first step in the treatment process, during which alcohol is eliminated from the body and the person goes through medically supervised withdrawal. However, it is worth noting that some people with alcohol dependence never experience significant withdrawal symptoms, and only about 5 percent develop the most severe symptoms, such as hallucinations and seizures.

***The Depression Connection.***    The relationship between alcohol and depression is most likely a two-way street. A 25-year study from New Zealand found compelling evidence that alcohol abuse or addiction can lead to depression. Some scientists speculate that alcohol abuse may cause changes within the brain that trigger depression in people with a genetic tendency to develop the condition.

Other research has found equally convincing evidence that depression can lead to alcohol use disorders. For example, a study of more than 7,400 twins found that the risk for developing alcohol dependence was substantially increased by a prior episode of major depression, and this heightened risk was only partly accounted for by genetic factors. It seems that some people with depression turn to alcohol in a misguided effort to cope with their feelings. Unfortunately, such attempts at "self-medication" tend to backfire badly, compounding the original mood problem with a new drinking problem.

***Treatment Considerations.***    The bottom line: Depression may make alcohol abuse or alcoholism worse, and vice versa. That is why it is so important to get appropriate diagnosis and treatment for both conditions. When both problems are addressed, the odds of a full and lasting **recovery** are much better.

Alcohol treatment programs use counseling, education, and support to help people stop drinking. People who have been drinking every day might also need to check into a hospital or treatment center while they go through detox and recover from their dependence on alcohol. Active participation in **self-help** programs, such as Alcoholics Anonymous, can enhance recovery as well. These so-called 12-step programs offer a set of guiding principles for overcoming alcoholism and learning to live sober.

Various medications are also used to treat alcoholism. One such medication is naltrexone, which acts in the brain to reduce craving for alcohol after someone has stopped drinking. Interestingly, research shows that naltrexone may work, at least in part, by blunting the association between heavy drinking and both positive and negative moods.

*Help for Coexisting Depression.*    For people who have depression plus an alcohol problem, **psychotherapy** can be very helpful. In particular, **cognitive-behavioral therapy** (CBT) can help people change the maladaptive thoughts and self-defeating behaviors that are contributing to their depression. At the same time, CBT can help people with alcohol-use disorders identify cues that trigger their drinking—such as being in a bar or restaurant or smelling alcohol—and learn ways to handle those cues without having a relapse.

Besides psychotherapy, **antidepressants** are the other major treatment option for depression. For depressed individuals with a coexisting alcohol problem, antidepressants are often invaluable. But it is important to note that mixing antidepressants and alcohol is discouraged. Drinking alcohol could counteract some beneficial effects of the medication, and it could also worsen some unwanted side effects, such as drowsiness.

The combination of alcohol and **monoamine oxidase inhibitors** (MAOIs), an older group of antidepressants, can be particularly dangerous. This combination can lead to a spike in blood pressure, potentially causing a stroke. As a result, MAOIs generally are not recommended for people recovering from alcohol abuse or alcoholism.

*See also:* Comorbidity; Dual Diagnosis; Substance Abuse; Substance-Induced Mood Disorder

***Further Information.*** Al-Anon/Alateen, 1600 Corporate Landing Parkway, Virginia Beach, VA 23454, (757) 563–1600, www.al-anon.alateen.org.

Alcoholics Anonymous, P.O. Box 459, New York, NY 10163, (212) 870–3400, www.aa.org.

National Clearinghouse for Alcohol and Drug Information, P.O. Box 2345, Rockville, MD 20847, ncadi.samhsa.gov.

National Council on Alcoholism and Drug Dependence, 244 E. 58th Street, 4th Floor, New York, NY 10022, (212) 269–7797, www.ncadd.org.

National Institute on Alcohol Abuse and Alcoholism, 5635 Fishers Lane, MSC 9304, Bethesda, MD 20892, (301) 443–3860, www.niaaa.nih.gov.

## Bibliography

*Alcoholism.* Mayo Clinic, May 8, 2008, http://www.mayoclinic.com/health/alcoholism/DS00340.

*Alcohol-Related Traffic Deaths.* National Institutes of Health, http://www.nih.gov/about/researchresultsforthepublic/AlcoholRelatedTrafficDeaths.pdf.

American Psychiatric Association. *Diagnostic and Statistical Manual of Mental Disorders.* 4th ed., text rev. Washington, DC: American Psychiatric Association, 2000.

*Antidepressants and Alcohol: What Is the Concern?* Mayo Clinic, July 24, 2007, http://www.mayoclinic.com/health/antidepressants-and-alcohol/AN01653.

*Dual Diagnosis and Recovery.* Depression and Bipolar Support Alliance, December 22, 2006, http://www.dbsalliance.org/site/PageServer?pagename=about_publications_dualdiag.

*FAQ for the General Public.* National Institute on Alcohol Abuse and Alcoholism, February 2007, http://www.niaaa.nih.gov/FAQs/General-English.

Fergusson, David M., Joseph M. Boden, and John Horwood. "Tests of Causal Links Between Alcohol Abuse or Dependence and Major Depression." *Archives of General Psychiatry* 66 (2009): 260–266.

Fuller, Richard K., and Susanne Hiller-Sturmhöfel. "Alcoholism Treatment in the United States: An Overview." *Alcohol Research and Health* 23 (1999): 69–77.

Hasin, Deborah S., and Bridget F. Grant. "Major Depression in 6050 Former Drinkers: Association With Past Alcohol Dependence." *Archives of General Psychiatry* 59 (2002): 794–800.

Hasin, Deborah S., Renee D. Goodwin, Frederick S. Stinson, and Bridget F. Grant. "Epidemiology of Major Depressive Disorder: Results From the National Epidemiologic Survey on Alcoholism and Related Conditions." *Archives of General Psychiatry* 62 (2005): 1097–1106.

Kranzler, Henry R., Stephen Armeli, Richard Feinn, and Howard Tennen. "Targeted Naltrexone Treatment Moderates the Relations Between Mood and Drinking Behavior Among Problem Drinkers." *Journal of Consulting and Clinical Psychology* 72 (2004): 317–327.

Kuo, Po-Hsiu, Charles O. Gardner Jr., Kenneth S. Kendler, and Carol A. Prescott. "The Temporal Relationship of the Onsets of Alcohol Dependence and Major Depression: Using a Genetically Informative Study Design." *Psychological Medicine* 36 (2006): 1153–1162.

Nunes, Edward V., and Frances R. Levin. "Treatment of Depression in Patients With Alcohol or Other Drug Dependence: A Meta-analysis." *JAMA* 291 (2004): 1887–1896.

Nunes, Edward, Eric Rubin, Kenneth Carpenter, and Deborah Hasin. "Mood Disorders and Substance Use." In *The American Psychiatric Publishing Textbook of Mood Disorders,* by Dan J. Stein, David J. Kupfer and Alan F. Schatzberg, eds., 653–671. Washington, DC: American Psychiatric Publishing, 2006.

**ALZHEIMER'S DISEASE.**　　Alzheimer's disease is an irreversible, age-related brain disorder. It is the most common cause of dementia, a decline in memory and mental abilities that is severe enough to interfere with daily life. In its early stages, Alzheimer's causes mild memory loss and confusion. As the disease progresses over a period of years, people gradually develop personality and behavior changes, and up to 40 percent become seriously depressed.

Other symptoms of advancing Alzheimer's include difficulties with abstract thinking, loss of language skills, diminished decision-making ability, problems performing everyday tasks, disorientation in familiar surroundings, and trouble recognizing family and friends. As times goes on, the disease leads to a profound loss of mental function.

Alzheimer's wreaks its havoc by damaging and killing brain cells. As cell death spreads, affected regions of the brain begin to shrink. Research has found an association between depression and various Alzheimer's-related abnormalities in **brain physiology** and chemistry. There also may be genes that increase a person's susceptibility to both depression and Alzheimer's.

When people with Alzheimer's become depressed, their quality of life suffers. Depression is associated with increased physical frailty, more trouble with daily living skills, more aggression toward caregivers, and earlier placement in nursing homes. On the flip side, getting treatment for depression can help address some of these problems, making life easier and less stressful for both those with Alzheimer's and their caregivers.

*Diagnostic Challenges.*　　Diagnosing depression in someone with Alzheimer's can be difficult. The two conditions share many symptoms in common, including loss of interest in things that were once enjoyed, memory problems, poor concentration, and sleeping too much or too little. This makes it easy to either over- or underdiagnose depression, depending on how the overlapping symptoms are interpreted.

As Alzheimer's progresses, people with the disease often find it hard to explain what they are going through. They may lose both insight into their own feelings and the language skills to express themselves. At this point, health care professionals must rely heavily on nonverbal cues and secondhand reports from caregivers when making a diagnosis.

Depression in people with Alzheimer's disease tends to have distinctive features that make it slightly different from classic **major depression**. For example, symptoms tend to be less severe, and episodes of depression may not last as long or recur as often. In addition, people with Alzheimer's who become depressed may be more prone to **irritability** and social isolation, but less likely to talk about or attempt **suicide**.

*Criteria for Diagnosis.*　　The contrasts are great enough for many scientists to believe that "depression of Alzheimer's disease" should be considered a separate condition, distinct from other types of depression. In 2002, an expert panel convened by the National Institute of Mental Health published a proposed set of diagnostic criteria.

According to these criteria, people with depression of Alzheimer's disease have symptoms that last for at least two weeks and cause distress or disruption in daily life. They have one or both of two core symptoms: (1) a low mood and (2) decreased enjoyment of other people and usual activities. In addition, they experience one or more of the following, for a total of at least three symptoms: (3) social isolation or withdrawal, (4) changes in appetite, (5) sleep problems, (6) restless activity or slowed-down movements, (7) irritability, (8) constant tiredness or loss of energy, (9) feelings of worthlessness, hopelessness, or inappropriate guilt, and (10) recurring thoughts of death or suicide.

Differences from Major Depression

The proposed criteria for diagnosing depression of Alzheimer's disease differ from the criteria for major depression in several ways.

| | Depression of Alzheimer's Disease | Major Depression |
| --- | --- | --- |
| Defining Symptoms | Depressed mood<br>Decreased positive feelings or pleasure in response to social contacts and usual activities | Depressed mood<br>Loss of interest or pleasure in response to nearly all activities |
| Frequency of Defining Symptoms | Not specified | Most of the day, nearly every day |
| Associated Symptoms | Changes in appetite<br>Sleep problems<br>Restless activity or slowed-down movements<br>Fatigue or low energy<br>Feelings of worthlessness or inappropriate guilt<br>Recurring thoughts of death or suicide<br>Social isolation or withdrawal<br><br>Irritability | Changes in appetite<br>Sleep problems<br>Restless activity or slowed-down movements<br>Fatigue or low energy<br>Feelings of worthlessness or inappropriate guilt<br>Recurring thoughts of death or suicide<br>Trouble concentrating or making decisions |
| Number of Symptoms (Defining + Associated) | Minimum of three | Minimum of five |
| Excluded Symptoms | Does not include symptoms that are clearly due to a general medical condition other than Alzheimer's or are the direct result of non-mood dementia symptoms (for example, weight loss caused by physical difficulties with eating) | Does not include symptoms that are clearly due to a general medical condition |

***Treatment Considerations.*** There is currently no treatment that can stop or reverse the Alzheimer's disease process. However, for some people, various medications used to treat Alzheimer's help keep symptoms from getting worse for a limited time.

When depression is a concern, **antidepressants** are often prescribed. During the early stages of the disease, while communication skills are still intact, **psychotherapy** and **support groups** may be helpful as well.

Some people with Alzheimer's do not respond to standard depression treatments. In such cases, **electroconvulsive therapy** (ECT) often helps relieve even severe depression. ECT involves passing a carefully controlled electrical current through a person's brain to induce a brief seizure. It is thought to alter electrochemical processes that play a role in brain functioning.

*See also:* Dementia Syndrome of Depression; Mood Disorder Due to a General Medical Condition; Neurological Disorders; Physical Illness

***Further Information.*** Alzheimer's Association, 225 N. Michigan Avenue, Floor 17, Chicago, IL 60601, (800) 272–3900, www.alz.org.

Alzheimer's Disease Education and Referral Center, National Institute on Aging, P.O. Box 8250, Silver Spring, MD 20907, (800) 438–4380, www.nia.nih.gov/Alzheimers.

Alzheimer's Foundation of America, 322 8th Avenue, 7th Floor, New York, NY 10001, (866) 232-8484, www.alzfdn.org.

Fisher Center for Alzheimer's Research Foundation, 1 Intrepid Square, W. 46th Street and 12th Avenue, New York, NY 10036, (800) 259-4636, www.alzinfo.org.

National Institute of Neurological Disorders and Stroke, P.O. Box 5801, Bethesda, MD 20824, (800) 352-9424, www.ninds.nih.gov.

## Bibliography

*Alzheimer's Disease.* Mayo Clinic, January 12, 2007, http://www.mayoclinic.com/print/alzheimers-disease/DS00161.

*Alzheimer's Disease Medications Fact Sheet.* National Institute on Aging, July 24, 2004, http://www.nia.nih.gov/Alzheimers/Publications/medicationsfs.htm.

*Alzheimer's or Depression: Could It Be Both?* Mayo Clinic, January 11, 2008, http://www.mayoclinic.com/print/alzheimers/HQ00212.

Boland, Robert. "Depression in Medical Illness (Secondary Depression)." In *The American Psychiatric Publishing Textbook of Mood Disorders,* by Dan J. Stein, David J. Kupfer and Alan F. Schatzberg, eds., 639–652. Washington, DC: American Psychiatric Publishing, 2006.

*Depression and Alzheimer's.* Alzheimer's Association, http://www.alz.org/living_with_alzheimers_depression.asp.

Jankowiak, Janet. "Depression May Be Another Risk for Alzheimer's Disease: Your Doctor Can Help." *Neurology* 59 (2002): 4–5.

*NINDS Alzheimer's Disease Information Page.* National Institute of Neurological Disorders and Stroke, September 16, 2008, http://www.ninds.nih.gov/disorders/alzheimersdisease/alzheimersdisease.htm.

Olin, Jason T., Ira R. Katz, Barnett S. Meyers, Lon S. Schneider and Barry D. Lebowitz. "Provisional Diagnostic Criteria for Depression of Alzheimer Disease: Rationale and Background." *American Journal of Geriatric Psychiatry* 10 (2002): 129–141.

Olin, Jason T., Lon S. Schneider, Ira R. Katz, Barnett S. Meyers, George S. Alexopoulos, John C. Breitner et al. "Provisional Diagnostic Criteria for Depression of Alzheimer Disease." *American Journal of Geriatric Psychiatry* 10 (2002): 125–128.

**AMERICAN INDIANS AND ALASKA NATIVES.** American Indians and Alaska Natives (AI/ANs) are defined as individuals who trace their ancestry to any of the original peoples of North, Central, or South America and who maintain tribal affiliation or community attachment. Such individuals comprise 1.6 percent of the U.S. population. This relatively small minority group is quite culturally diverse, encompassing 562 federally recognized tribes as well as other tribes that are not formally recognized.

Based on the available evidence, it appears that AI/ANs are at increased risk for mental health problems. For instance, research indicates that AI/ANs are almost three times as likely as white Americans to experience depressive feelings. In addition, AI/AN **adolescents** have a **suicide** rate that is two to five times the rate for white adolescents.

It is important to keep in mind, however, that such comparisons are based on limited research. Compared to both white Americans and larger minority groups, much less is known about the prevalence, symptoms, diagnosis, and treatment of depression among AI/ANs.

***Barriers to Care.***   Historically, attempts to forcibly assimilate AI/AN individuals into mainstream U.S. society had a devastating impact on native communities. Today, the effects of these attempts still resonate. Among other lingering effects is a widespread mistrust of the mental health care system. And even when AI/AN individuals reach out to the system, they may run into cultural barriers and access issues.

*Cultural Barriers.*   Culturally specific views of mental health and mental illness mean that mainstream views of depression do not always translate effectively to AI/AN contexts. There is a great need for culturally knowledgeable and sensitive treatment providers to work with AI/AN populations. Yet there are only 101 AI/AN mental health professionals per 100,000 AI/AN individuals, compared to 173 per 100,000 white Americans.

Language differences can be an issue as well. There are over 200 native American languages, and about 280,000 AI/AN individuals speak a language other than English at home. For example, over half of Alaska Natives who are Eskimos speak either Inuit or Yup'ik.

*Access Issues.*   Lack of access is another potential barrier. The Indian Health Service is the federal agency charged with providing health care to AI/AN populations. Yet only one-fifth of the intended recipients report having access to Indian Health Service clinics. These clinics are located mainly on reservations, where just 20 percent of AI/AN individuals live today.

When it comes to paying for health care services, only about half of AI/AN individuals have employer-based health insurance, compared to 72 percent of white Americans. Another 25 percent of AI/ANs are covered by public insurance. And 24 percent have no insurance at all, compared to 16 percent of the general U.S. population.

In addition, AI/AN individuals are overrepresented in some high-need groups that are particularly at risk for mental health problems. For example, although making up less than 2 percent of the population as a whole, AI/ANs comprise 8 percent of homeless Americans. There is also a high rate of **alcohol** abuse and alcoholism in many AI/AN communities. These high-risk subgroups tend to be underserved by the mental health care system.

***The Navajo Experience.***   In many AI/AN communities, mental health is viewed within a larger spiritual, social, and environmental context. For example, the Navajo language (known to native speakers as Diné) has no direct translation for the word "depression." But many Navajo individuals believe that depressive symptoms are often caused by a spiritual imbalance or the neglect of one's responsibilities to spiritual beings. In other cases, depressive symptoms result from being shunned by others after violating the unwritten rules of Navajo society.

The gap between the Navajo view of depression and that of the majority culture can be difficult to bridge. The limited availability of culturally appropriate care is a hurdle that must be overcome. Geographical access to treatment providers is another major issue in the Navajo Nation, which covers some 27,000 square miles of often rugged, remote land in Utah, Arizona, and New Mexico.

Language is an important barrier to mental health care as well. About 150,000 Navajos speak the native tongue, making it the most-spoken American Indian language. The complexity of the language's syntax makes it extremely difficult for nonnative speakers to master. Even among Navajo individuals who also speak English, the Navajo language itself reflects a worldview that is quite different from that of the majority culture and may not be readily translated into terms that non-Navajo English speakers can understand. Consequently, there is a great need for Navajo treatment providers.

Holding onto their native language and worldview is crucial for younger Navajos who are still establishing a cultural identity. The traditional Navajo identity—which emphasizes spirituality, family, and the environment—helps guide behavioral choices, direct personal relationships, and give meaning to life. One study of 332 Navajo adolescents found that a strong Navajo cultural identity was associated with decreased depression.

*See also:* Cultural Factors; Ethnicity

**Further Information.**   Indian Health Service, Reyes Building, 801 Thompson Avenue, Suite 400, Rockville, MD 20852, www.ihs.gov.

National Center for American Indian and Alaska Native Mental Health Research, Mail Stop F800, Nighthorse Campbell Native Health Building, 13055 E. 17th Avenue, Aurora, CO 80045, (303) 724–1414, aianp.uchsc.edu.

Office of Minority Health, U.S. Department of Health and Human Services, P.O. Box 37337, Washington, D.C. 20013, (800) 444-6472, www.omhrc.gov.

## Bibliography

*American Indian/Alaska Native Profile.* U.S. Department of Health and Human Services Office of Minority Health, July 31, 2009, http://www.omhrc.gov/templates/browse.aspx?lvl=3&lvlid=26.

Gone, Joseph P., and Carmela Alcántara. "Identifying Effective Mental Health Interventions for American Indians and Alaska Natives: A Review of the Literature." *Cultural Diversity and Ethnic Minority Psychology* 13 (2007): 356–363.

*Mental Health and American Indians/Alaska Natives.* U.S. Department of Health and Human Services Office of Minority Health, July 27, 2009, http://www.omhrc.gov/templates/content.aspx?lvl=3&lvlID=9&ID=6475.

*Native American Indians.* U.S. Department of Health and Human Services Office of the Surgeon General, http://mentalhealth.samhsa.gov/cre/fact4.asp.

*Navajo Culture: Language.* PBS, October 29, 2007, http://www.pbs.org/independentlens/missnavajo/language.html.

*Navajo Nation: History.* Navajo Nation, http://www.navajo.org/history.htm.

Rieckmann, Traci R., Martha E. Wadsworth, and Donna Deyhle. "Cultural Identity, Explanatory Style, and Depression in Navajo Adolescents." *Cultural Diversity and Ethnic Minority Psychology* 10 (2004): 365–382.

U.S. Department of Health and Human Services. *Culture, Race, and Ethnicity: A Supplement to Mental Health: A Report of the Surgeon General.* Rockville, MD: U.S. Department of Health and Human Services, 2001.

**AMERICANS WITH DISABILITIES ACT.**   The Americans with Disabilities Act (ADA) is a federal civil rights law in the United States. It prohibits discrimination on the basis of disability in employment, state and local government, public accommodations, commercial facilities, transportation, and telecommunications. A disability is defined as a mental or physical impairment that substantially limits one or more major life activities.

Mental impairments consist of mental and psychological disorders, including depression. To rise to the level of a disability, the disorder must limit activities such as learning, thinking, concentrating, interacting with others, caring for oneself, speaking, performing manual tasks, or sleeping. The limitation must be substantial enough to severely affect daily functioning. It also must be long-term—continuing or recurring over a period of months or years. A person taking medication for a mental illness may still have a disability if there is evidence that the illness would cause substantial impairment without ongoing treatment.

***ADA at Work.*** In the workplace, Title 1 of the ADA requires employers with 15 or more employees to give qualified individuals with disabilities an equal shot at employment-related opportunities. Title 1 prohibits discrimination on the basis of disability in all kinds of employment practices, including recruitment, hiring, firing, promotions, pay, fringe benefits, and social activities. The law covers people who meet legitimate skill, experience, education, or other requirements for a position, and who can perform the essential functions of the job.

Employers are required to make reasonable accommodations—modifications or adjustments to job tasks or the work environment that enable a qualified applicant or employee with a disability to apply for a job or perform essential job functions. The exact accommodations are tailored to the individual's needs. For example, someone who has trouble remembering things due to depression might be provided with written checklists of job tasks or allowed to tape record meetings. Some with low stamina due to depression might be given more frequent rest breaks or allowed to work from home part of the week.

Employers are only required to accommodate disabilities that a job applicant or employee makes known to them. In addition, employers are not required to make accommodations that would pose undue hardship on the business. A determination of undue hardship is made on a case-by-case basis. In general, though, it involves balancing the nature and cost of an accommodation against the nature, size, resources, and facilities of the business operation.

*See also:* Work Issues

***Further Information.*** Job Accommodation Network, P.O. Box 6080, Morgantown, WV 26506, (800) 526-7234, www.jan.wvu.edu.

U.S. Department of Justice, Disability Rights Section, 950 Pennsylvania Avenue N.W., Washington, DC 20530, (800) 514-0301, www.ada.gov.

U.S. Department of Labor, Office of Disability Employment Policy, 200 Constitution Ave., NW Washington DC 20210, (866) 633-7365, www.dol.gov/odep.

U.S. Equal Employment Opportunity Commission, 131 M Street N.E., Washington, DC 20507, (800) 669-4000, www.eeoc.gov.

## Bibliography

*A Guide to Disability Rights Laws.* U.S. Department of Justice Civil Rights Division, September 2005, http://www.ada.gov/cguide.pdf.

*Americans with Disabilities Act Questions and Answers.* U.S. Equal Employment Opportunity Commission, November 14, 2008, http://www.ada.gov/q%26aeng02.htm.

Duckworth, Kendra M. *Accommodation and Compliance Series: Employees with Mental Health Impairments.* Job Accommodation Network, September 5, 2008, http://www.jan.wvu.edu/media/Psychiatric.html.

*EEOC Enforcement Guidance on the Americans with Disabilities Act and Psychiatric Disabilities.* Equal Employment Opportunity Commission, March 5, 2009, http://www.eeoc.gov/policy/docs/psych.html.

*Job Accommodations for People with Depression.* Job Accommodation Network, August 18, 2008, http://www.jan.wvu.edu/pubsandres/list.htm.

**AMYGDALA.** The amygdala is an almond-shaped structure inside the brain that is involved in emotional learning and the fear response. It is a key component of the limbic system—a network of interconnected brain structures that help regulate the expression of emotion and emotional memory. The amygdala tends to be unusually active in people with depression.

Research has shown that people with depression frequently have a psychological bias toward paying attention to negative things, compared to positive or neutral things. For instance, in memory studies, currently depressed individuals have better recall for negative material than for positive material. Some of these differences may be rooted in the amygdala. In **brain imaging** studies, when people are shown pictures of sad or fearful faces, those with depression tend to have a greater increase in amygdala activity than healthy individuals do.

The combination of an overactive amygdala and abnormal activity in other brain areas can disrupt patterns of sleep and physical activity. It also can cause abnormal production of **hormones** and other chemicals that affect many body systems. These effects may lead to various symptoms of depression, such as sleep problems and changes in activity level.

*See also:* Brain Anatomy

## Bibliography

Dannlowski, Udo, Patricia Ohrmann, Jochen Bauer, Harald Kugel, Volker Arolt, Walter Heindel, et al. "Amygdala Reactivity to Masked Negative Faces Is Assocaited With Automatic Judgmental Bias in Major Depression: A 3 T fMRI Study." *Journal of Psychiatry and Neuroscience* 32 (2007): 423–429.

Drevets, Wayne C., Joseph L. Price, and Maura L. Furay. "Brain Structural and Functional Abnormalities in Mood Disorders: Implications for Neurocircuitry Models of Depression." *Brain Structure and Function* 213 (2008): 93–118.

Leppanen, Jukka M. "Emotional Information Processing in Mood Disorders: A Review of Behavioral and Neuroimaging Findings." *Current Opinion in Psychiatry* 19 (2006): 34–39.

McEwen, Bruce S. *Stress, Depression and Brain Structure.* Depression and Bipolar Support Alliance, August 30, 2006, http://www.dbsalliance.org/site/PageServer?pagename=about_depression_mcewen.

Society for Neuroscience. *Brain Facts: A Primer on the Brain and Nervous System.* 6th ed. Washington, DC: Society for Neuroscience, 2008.

**ANACLITIC DEPRESSION.** Anaclitic depression is a reaction seen in some **infants** who are abruptly separated from their mothers during the second six months of life. The concept was introduced in 1946 by Hungarian psychiatrist and psychoanalyst René Spitz (1887–1974). It was one of the first attempts to describe depression in infancy.

Spitz studied a group of infants whose mothers had given birth while in jail. For the first several months of life, these babies had a very close relationship with their mothers and no substitute caregivers. At age eight to nine months, though, the babies were suddenly separated from their mothers. About half developed a depression-like reaction, characterized by social withdrawal, weight loss, and sleeplessness. Their physical, social, and intellectual development was often stunted, and they had a greater-than-average rate of physical illness.

Infants who were reunited with their mothers within six month soon returned to normal. But those who were not reunited or given adequate substitute mothering did not improve. Over time, they showed signs of continued deterioration, including mental retardation and severe agitation or lethargy. In the most extreme cases, they slowly wasted away from malnutrition.

There is still some debate about whether this heartbreaking reaction should be considered true depression or some other type of developmental disorder. Whatever term is used, however, the reaction clearly shows the importance of the emotional bond between baby and caregiver. Spitz's observations helped stimulate scientific interest in mothering as a factor in emotional development.

*See also:* Attachment Theory

## Bibliography

"Anaclitic Depression." *Gale Encyclopedia of Childhood and Adolescence.* Farmington Hills, MI: Gale Research, 1998.

Guedeney, Antoine. "Withdrawal Behavior and Depression in Infancy." *Infant Mental Health Journal* 28 (2007): 393–408.

Schwartz, Arthur and Ruth M. Schwartz. *Depression Theories and Treatments: Psychological, Biological, and Social Perspectives.* New York: Columbia University Press, 1993.

**ANHEDONIA.** Anhedonia—from the Greek for "without pleasure"—refers to an inability to take interest or find pleasure in activities that would normally be enjoyed. It is one of the cardinal signs of **major depression**, a mental disorder that involves being in a low mood nearly all the time and/or losing interest or enjoyment in almost everything.

Most people with major depression retain at least some capacity for feeling pleasure, but it is often greatly diminished. People with depression may lose interest in work, give up hobbies, stop enjoying social activities, and generally feel as if all the fun has gone out of life. If they were sexually active before, they may find that their sexual desire has plummeted as well.

Anhedonia is especially prominent in **melancholic depression**, a subtype of major depression that, at its lowest point, is marked by a near-complete absence of the ability to feel pleasure. Even when something much desired happens, the person's mood may brighten little, if at all.

## Bibliography

American Psychiatric Association. *Diagnostic and Statistical Manual of Mental Disorders.* 4th ed., text rev. Washington, DC: American Psychiatric Association, 2000.

Frances, Allen, Michael B. First, and Harold Alan Pincus. *DSM-IV Guidebook.* Washington, DC: American Psychiatric Press, 1995.

**ANTERIOR CINGULATE CORTEX.** The anterior cingulate cortex (ACC) is part of the cerebral cortex, the outer layer of the brain that is responsible for higher mental functions and conscious experience. In evolutionary terms, the ACC is very old. It lies along several nerve cell pathways that connect with structures deep inside the brain where unconscious emotional responses occur. **Brain imaging** studies have shown structural and functional abnormalities in the ACC of people with depression.

The ACC serves as an important interface between higher, more rational circuits in the cortex and lower, more instinctive parts of the brain. It helps monitor input from the senses and select which information people attend to. Based on past learning, the ACC also helps assess risk, reward, and conflict, and it works with other parts of the cortex to select a response. In addition, the ACC monitors bodily feelings, arousal, and pain, and it helps control the voluntary suppression of these sensations.

Research suggests that at least some functions may go awry in depression. For example, the ACC is responsible for the emotional evaluation of error. In one study, people were asked to solve problems, such as picking a complex abstract pattern from four similar choices. Participants were told how they did on each problem before moving on to the next. People who were not depressed did much better after making a mistake than those with depression did. It seems that the emotional response to error was abnormal in depressed individuals, leading them to keep making mistakes rather than building on the knowledge gained from an error to improve their performance.

*See also:* Brain Anatomy; Cingulotomy

## Bibliography

Alexopoulos, George S., Faith M. Gunning-Dixon, Vassilios Latoussakis, Dora Kanellopoulos, and Christopher F. Murphy. "Anterior Cingulate Dysfunction in Geriatric Depression." *International Journal of Geriatric Psychiatry* 23 (2008): 347–355.

Drevets, Wayne C., and Jonathan Savitz. "The Subgenual Anterior Cingulate Cortex in Mood Disorders." *CNS Spectrum* 13 (2008): 663–678, 680–681.

Elliott, R., B. J. Sahakian, J. J. Herrod, T. W. Robbins, and E. S. Paykel. "Abnormal Response to Negative Feedback in Unipolar Depression: Evidence for a Diagnosis Specific Impairment." *Journal of Neurology, Neurosurgery, and Psychiatry* 63 (1997): 74–82.

*Parts of the Brain That Slow Down or Speed Up in Depression.* Canadian Institute of Neurosciences, Mental Health and Addiction, http://thebrain.mcgill.ca/flash/a/a_08/a_08_cr/a_08_cr_dep/a_08_cr_dep.html.

Whitten, Lori. *Cocaine Abusers' Pretreatment Cue Responses Predict Recovery Success.* National Institute on Drug Abuse, February 2007, http://www.nida.nih.gov/NIDA_notes/NNvol21N2/cocaine.html.

**ANTICONVULSANTS.** Anticonvulsants are a group of medications that were originally developed to prevent seizures, but that also help even out unstable moods. Several anticonvulsants are now commonly used to treat **bipolar disorder**, a condition characterized by extreme shifts in mood, energy, and the ability to function. In addition, some research suggests that anticonvulsants may add to the effects of antidepressant medications in people with hard-to-treat **major depression**.

People with bipolar disorder alternate between excessively high moods (**mania**) and excessively low ones (depression). Lamotrigine has been specifically approved by the Food and Drug Administration (FDA) for the long-term treatment of bipolar disorder to lengthen the time between mood episodes. Divalproex sodium has been approved for treating mania, and carbamazepine has been approved for treating both mania and mixed episodes, which combine features of the two mood extremes.

Anticonvulsants that are FDA approved for other conditions may also be prescribed for bipolar disorder or **treatment-resistant depression** at a doctor's discretion, even though they are not specifically approved for that use. This practice, known as off-label prescribing, is both legal and very common, and it opens up a wider range of treatment options.

Anticonvulsants are believed to work by affecting **neurotransmitters**, natural substances that act as chemical messengers in the brain. In particular, anticonvulsants may increase **gamma-amino-butyric acid** (GABA), a neurotransmitter that has an inhibitory effect, making brain cells less excitable. They also may block or reduce electrical signals in brain cells. But because the exact mode of action varies from one medication to the next, individual response varies. A person who responds poorly to one anticonvulsant might react well to another.

Given this variability, it is no surprise that the evidence for effectiveness is mixed. As a treatment for bipolar disorder, carbamazepine, valproic acid (also called divalproex sodium), and lamotrigine have the strongest evidence base. From 60 percent to 70 percent of people taking carbamazepine or valproic acid/divalproex sodium experience a decrease in symptoms during bipolar manic episodes. And over half of those taking lamotrigine experience improvement during both the manic and depressive phases of bipolar disorder, although the success rate may fall off somewhat after several months of use.

*First versus Second Generation.*   Anticonvulsants can be subdivided into two main groups: older, first-generation anticonvulsants and newer, second-generation ones. The first anticonvulsant was introduced in the United States in 1946. Others, including carbamazepine and valproic acid/divalproex sodium, soon followed.

In the 1990s, a second wave of anticonvulsants arrived. Although these anticonvulsants have sometimes been touted as safer than older ones, research does not conclusively support that claim. Nevertheless, marketing of the newer anticonvulsants led to increased use of all medications in this class for conditions other than seizures, including **bipolar disorder,** and to a lesser extent depression.

Anticonvulsants Used As Mood Stabilizers

|  | **Brand Names** |
| --- | --- |
| Carbamazepine[†] | Carbatrol, Equetro, Tegretol |
| Gabapentin* | Neurontin |
| Lamotrigine*[†] | Lamictal |
| Oxcarbazepine* | Trileptal |
| Topiramate* | Topamax |
| Valproic acid/divalproex sodium[†] | Depacon, Depakene, Depakote |
| Zonisamide* | Zonegran |

*Second-generation anticonvulsant
[†]FDA approved for treating bipolar disorder

*Risks and Side Effects.*   Anticonvulsants are generally safe, but they are not risk-free. Most side effects are mild to moderate, although some can be severe. Common side effects include dizziness, sleepiness, and nausea. For some second-generation anticonvulsants, other common side effects include swelling of the hands and feet, weight gain, blurry vision, memory problems, and difficulty concentrating.

In addition, the FDA requires that anticonvulsants come with a written warning about an increased risk of suicidal thinking or behavior. Patients taking these medications should watch closely for suicidal thoughts or actions, new or worsening signs of depression, or unusual changes in mood or behavior. If such symptoms occur, patients should contact their doctor immediately.

Although valproic acid/divalproex sodium has one of the best track records for treating bipolar disorder, it also poses some special concerns. In rare cases, it may cause serious liver or pancreas damage, so people taking this medication need regular medical checkups. Valproic acid/divalproex sodium may also increase levels of the male hormone testosterone in teenage girls, potentially leading to a condition called polycystic ovarian syndrome. In addition, it may cause birth defects in pregnant women.

Lamotrigine is the only anticonvulsant that is proven to work against both depression and mania in bipolar disorder. But in rare cases, it may cause a serious skin rash that requires hospitalization. At times, this skin condition might be life threatening or lead to permanent disability.

Numerous medications may interact with anticonvulsants. To complicate matters further, one anticonvulsant is sometimes combined with another or taken with a different type of mood medication to maximize the effects. Such combinations only increase the risk of drug interactions. To reduce the risk, people should tell their doctor about any prescription medications, nonprescription medicines, **dietary supplements**, or herbal products they are taking.

*See also:* Augmentation Therapy; Mood Stabilizers; Pharmacotherapy

## Bibliography

*Medication Information Sheet.* Depression and Bipolar Support Alliance, May 4, 2006, http://www.dbsalliance.org/site/PageServer?pagename=about_treatment_medinfosheet.

*Mental Health Medications.* National Institute of Mental Health, July 28, 2009, http://www.nimh.nih.gov/health/publications/mental-health-medications/complete-index.shtml.

*Treating Bipolar Disorder, Nerve Pain, and Fibromyalgia: The Anticonvulsants—Comparing Effectiveness, Safety, and Price.* Consumer Reports, September 2007, http://www.consumerreports.org/health/best-buy-drugs/anticonvulsants.htm.

## ANTIDEPRESSANT DISCONTINUATION SYNDROME.

Antidepressant discontinuation syndrome is a condition that can occur if people stop taking their antidepressant medication abruptly or skip several doses in a row. Possible symptoms include nausea, vomiting, diarrhea, headache, dizziness, fatigue, sadness, irritability, and anxiety. Such symptoms are not dangerous, and they usually go away within a week. They can be unpleasant, though, so it makes sense to take steps to prevent them.

To ward off antidepressant discontinuation syndrome, it is important to take any antidepressant exactly as prescribed. If people accidentally miss a dose, they should resume their medication as soon as possible. If people are thinking about stopping an antidepressant on their own due to side effects or cost, they should discuss other options with their doctor. And if the antidepressant is no longer needed, they should work with their doctor to decrease the dose a little at a time rather than stopping it all at once.

Antidepressant discontinuation syndrome is a bigger problem with some **antidepressants** than with others. Research shows that paroxetine and venlafaxine are more likely than most antidepressants to cause the syndrome, and **fluoxetine** is less likely to do so.

## Bibliography

*Antidepressant Discontinuation Syndrome.* American Academy of Family Physicians, November 2007, http://familydoctor.org/online/famdocen/home/common/mentalhealth/treatment/904.html.

*Antidepressant Medicines: A Guide for Adults with Depression.* Agency for Healthcare Research and Quality, August 2007, http://effectivehealthcare.ahrq.gov/repFiles/AntidepressantsConsumer Guide.pdf.

*Selective Serotonin Reuptake Inhibitors (SSRIs).* Mayo Clinic, December 10, 2008, http://www .mayoclinic.com/health/ssris/MH00066.

**ANTIDEPRESSANTS.**  Antidepressants are medications originally developed for the treatment of depression. Many drugs in this class are also used to treat **anxiety disorders** or other conditions. All told, antidepressants are the most prescribed class of psychiatric medications in the United States, and tens of millions of Americans take antidepressants every day.

**Neurotransmitters** are chemical messengers in the brain. The messages they convey may affect mood, emotion, thought, and behavior. All current antidepressants increase the availability of one or more neurotransmitters. This enhances the transmission of messages from one brain cell to another, which may contribute to the depression-lifting effects.

Antidepressants may also act partly by protecting brain cells from being overwhelmed by **glutamate**, a brain chemical that has an excitatory effect. Excessive glutamate activity may interfere with healthy brain function, and depression has been linked to high levels of glutamate in some parts of the brain. Antidepressants may increase the effects of brain cell **receptors** that help keep sensitivity to glutamate under control.

From 1996 to 2005, the percentage of Americans age six and older who took antidepressant medication over the course of a year jumped from 6 percent to 10 percent. During the same period, people taking antidepressants became more likely to also take antipsychotic medications and less likely to receive **psychotherapy**. Taken together, these findings suggest a growing emphasis on drug therapy as opposed to psychological treatment. Several factors may have played a role in this trend, including greater public acceptance of antidepressants and updated medical guidelines that advocate certain antidepressants as first-choice treatment options.

Roughly six out of 10 people with depression improve after the first antidepressant they try. The rest need to try other treatments before they find one that works for them. Depending on the situation, the doctor may adjust the dose, switch to a different medication, or add another treatment. Eventually, most people, even those with severe depression, can be helped to feel better again.

*Types of Antidepressants.*  There are 27 different antidepressants currently sold in the United States. They can be divided into seven categories, based on chemical structure and mode of action.

**Monoamine Oxidase Inhibitors** (MAOIs)
MAOIs are the oldest type of antidepressant, dating back to the 1950s. These medications block the activity of an enzyme called **monoamine oxidase**, which breaks down a group of chemicals called monoamines. Included in the monoamine group are three neurotransmitters—**serotonin**, **norepinephrine**, and **dopamine**—which tend to be abnormal in depression. Boosting the brain's supply of these chemicals may help relieve depression.

**Noradrenergic and Specific Serotonergic Antidepressants** (NaSSAs)
NaSSAs prevent norepinephrine and epinephrine from binding with alpha-2 receptors on brain cells. Normally, one job of these receptors is to receive messages telling the cell when it is time to stop releasing serotonin and more norepinephrine. But NaSSAs keep

the message from going through, so the cell keeps releasing norepinephrine and serotonin.

### Norepinephrine-Dopamine Reuptake Inhibitors (NDRIs)

NDRIs block the **reuptake**, or reabsorption, of norepinephrine and dopamine back into the brain cells that originally released them. They may also enhance the release of these chemicals in the first place. Consequently, a larger amount of the chemicals is available for use by the brain.

### Serotonin Antagonist and Reuptake Inhibitors (SARIs)

SARIs are dual-action medications that affect key neurotransmitters, including serotonin, in two different ways. First, they block the action of certain brain cell receptors. Second, they inhibit the reuptake of specific neurotransmitters.

### Serotonin-Norepinephrine Reuptake Inhibitors (SNRIs)

SNRIs block the reuptake of serotonin and norepinephrine, enhancing the availability of both chemicals. One of the newest antidepressants on the market is an SNRI called desvenlafaxine, introduced in the United States in 2008.

### Selective Serotonin Reuptake Inhibitors (SSRIs)

SSRIs block the reuptake of serotonin. They are the most widely prescribed type of antidepressant today. In 2008, the third most popular brand-name medication of any kind in the United States was Lexapro, with more than 26 million total prescriptions. The fourteenth most popular generic was sertraline, with more than 29 million total prescriptions. Both are SSRIs.

### Tricyclic Antidepressants and Tetracyclic Antidepressants (TCAs)

TCAs are an older type of antidepressant, introduced soon after MAOIs. In general, they block the reuptake of serotonin, norepinephrine, and, to a much lesser extent, dopamine. Tricyclics have a three-ring molecular structure, and tetracyclics have a four-ring structure. Because they are similar, tricyclics and tetracyclics are frequently grouped together.

Antidepressant Medications

|  | Brand Names* | Type of Antidepressant |
|---|---|---|
| Amitriptyline[†] | Elavil | TCA |
| Amoxapine[†] | Asendin | TCA |
| Bupropion[†] | Wellbutrin | NDRI |
| Citalopram[†] | Celexa | SSRI |
| Clomipramine | Anafranil | TCA |
| Desipramine[†] | Norpramin | TCA |
| Desvenlafaxine[†] | Pristiq | SNRI |
| Doxepin[†] | Sinequan | TCA |
| Duloxetine[†] | Cymbalta | SNRI |
| Escitalopram[†] | Lexapro | SSRI |
| Fluoxetine[†] | Prozac, Sarafem | SSRI |
| Fluvoxamine | Luvox | SSRI |
| Imipramine[†] | Tofranil | TCA |
| Isocarboxazid[†] | Marplan | MAOI |
| Maprotiline[†] | Ludiomil | TCA |
| Mirtazapine[†] | Remeron | NaSSA |
| Nefazodone[†] | Serzone | SARI |
| Nortriptyline[†] | Aventyl, Pamelor | TCA |

| Paroxetine[†] | Paxil, Pexeva | SSRI |
|---|---|---|
| Phenelzine[†] | Nardil | MAOI |
| Protriptyline[†] | Vivactil | TCA |
| Selegiline[†] | Emsam | MAOI |
| Sertraline[†] | Zoloft | SSRI |
| Tranylcypromine[†] | Parnate | MAOI |
| Trazodone[†] | Desyrel | SARI |
| Trimipramine[†] | Surmontil | TCA |
| Venlafaxine[†] | Effexor | SNRI |

†FDA approved for treating depression
*Some antidepressants are no longer sold as brand-name products, but are still available in generic form

***First versus Second Generation.***    The first two types of antidepressants were MAOIs and TCAs, introduced in the 1950s. Both MAOIs and TCAs are still available, and they work about as well as their newer counterparts. But they are not as specific in their effects on the body, so they cause a wider range of side effects.

In 1985, the U.S. introduction of an NDRI called bupropion marked the start of a new generation of more targeted antidepressants. Two years later, an SSRI called **fluoxetine** followed and quickly became one of the most influential medications in history. Although these second-generation medications were no more effective than their predecessors, they caused fewer serious side effects, which opened the door to greatly expanded use of **pharmacotherapy** (drug therapy) for depression.

Before long, newer antidepressants, especially SSRIs, had become the treatment of choice for many people with depression. Yet individuals vary in their response to specific antidepressants. Some people who do not respond well to SSRIs and other newer antidepressants find that older antidepressants work better for them.

***Brand Name versus Generic.***    New drugs have both a generic name (the scientific name for the compound) and a brand name (the trademarked name under which it is sold by a particular company). When a pharmaceutical company develops a new drug, the medication is initially protected by a patent that gives that company the exclusive right to sell it. During the period of patent protection, the brand-name version of the medication is all that is available. This period of exclusivity gives the company a chance to recoup its investment in research and development.

Once the patent expires, other companies can apply to sell generic versions of the drug. By law, the generic must be identical to the brand-name drug in dosage, safety, strength, route of administration, quality, performance, and intended use. Before a generic medication can be marketed, its manufacturer must show that it is therapeutically equivalent, which means it has an equal effect and results in no difference when substituted for the brand-name product.

Most current antidepressants are now sold in both brand-name and generic versions, although desvenlafaxine (Pristiq), duloxetine (Cymbalta), and escitalopram (Lexapro) are still available only in branded form. Although generics are chemically identical and therapeutically equivalent to their brand-name counterparts, they are usually sold at a substantially lower price. The least expensive generic antidepressants cost about $20 month, on average, but the most costly brand-name antidepressants run over $400 a month.

***Use and Precautions.***    When prescribing an antidepressant, doctors often start with the lowest dose possible. Then they monitor the patient's response, watching for side effects as well as improved functioning and decreased symptoms of depression. The dosage may be increased gradually until the optimal dose for that individual is found.

Depression is not like strep throat; people cannot simply take their medicine and expect to feel better in a couple of days. Instead, it may take several weeks for the full benefits to kick in. Even after people are feeling better, most need to stay on medication for at least six to nine months, and sometimes for years, to help keep symptoms from coming back. When it is time to stop, the dose may need to be decreased a little at a time to prevent flu-like symptoms, called **antidepressant discontinuation syndrome.**

***Risks and Side Effects.*** A side effect is an unintended effect of treatment. About 90 percent of people taking antidepressants experience at least one side effect. Many such effects are mild and temporary. But up to 30 percent of antidepressant users find side effects so bothersome that they stop their medication.

In general, side effects that tend to be mild and short-lived include diarrhea, nausea, dizziness, headaches, dry mouth, sweating, and shakiness. Side effects that are often more troublesome or severe include drowsiness, confusion, panicky feelings, trouble sleeping, sexual problems, nervousness, agitation, and weight gain. The specific side effect profile varies from one antidepressant to another, however.

In rare cases, antidepressants that increase serotonin may lead to **serotonin syndrome**, a potentially life-threatening reaction to the buildup of excessive serotonin in the body. This problem is more likely when the antidepressant is paired with another drug that also boosts serotonin. In addition, a small number of **children**,

### Dangerous Duos

A drug-drug interaction refers to a change in the way a medication acts in the body when combined with another drug. Such interactions may cause adverse effects or reduce the medication's effectiveness. Possible drug interactions vary from one antidepressant to another. However, newer antidepressants should never be used along with MAOIs. In addition, some antidepressants may interact harmfully with specific **anticonvulsants** (carbamazepine, phenytoin), **antipsychotics** (haloperidol, thioridazine), **mood stabilizers** (lithium), anti-anxiety medications (alprazolam, diazepam), blood thinners (warfarin), antibiotics (ciprofloxacin, erythromycin), antifungals (ketoconazole), and migraine medications (sumatriptan, zolmitriptan). To avoid dangerous combinations, people should be sure to tell their doctor about any prescription or over-the-counter medications they are taking.

**adolescents**, and young adults may experience worsening mood symptoms or increased suicidal thoughts and behavior after taking antidepressants. People experiencing symptoms of serotonin syndrome, unusual mood changes or suicidal thoughts and behavior should contact their doctor immediately.

Antidepressants can make a huge difference in the lives of people with depression. But like all medications that are powerful enough to help, they are also potent enough to harm, so they should be treated with respect. People taking antidepressants who run into problems should discuss them with their doctor, who may be able to adjust the treatment regimen or suggest coping strategies.

*See also:* Antidepressants and Suicide; Monoamine Hypothesis; Treatment of Depression

***Further Information.*** Food and Drug Administration, 10903 New Hampshire Avenue, Silver Spring, MD 20993, (888) 463–6332, www.fda.gov.

Pharmaceutical Research and Manufacturers of America, 950 F Street N.W., Washington, DC 20004, (202) 835–3400, www.phrma.org.

## Bibliography

*Antidepressant Medicines: A Guide for Adults with Depression.* Agency for Healthcare Research and Quality, August 2007, http://effectivehealthcare.ahrq.gov/repFiles/AntidepressantsConsumerGuide.pdf.

*Antidepressants: Comparing Effectiveness, Safety, and Price.* Consumer Reports, 2009, http://www.consumerreports.org/health/resources/pdf/best-buy-drugs/Antidepressants_update.pdf.

*Drugs@FDA Glossary of Terms.* Food and Drug Administration, June 18, 2009, http://www.fda.gov/Drugs/InformationOnDrugs/ucm079436.htm.

Gitlin, Michael J. "Pharmacotherapy and Other Somatic Treatments for Depression." In *Handbook of Depression.* 2nd ed., by Ian H. Gotlib and Constance L. Hammen, eds., 554–585. New York: Guilford Press, 2009.

*Medication Information Sheet.* Depression and Bipolar Support Alliance, May 4, 2006, http://www.dbsalliance.org/site/PageServer?pagename=about_treatment_medinfosheet.

*Mental Health Medications.* National Institute of Mental Health, July 28, 2009, http://www.nimh.nih.gov/health/publications/mental-health-medications/complete-index.shtml.

Olfson, Mark, and Steven C. Marcus. "National Patterns in Antidepressant Medication Treatment." *Archives of General Psychiatry* 66 (2009): 848–856.

*Selective Serotonin Reuptake Inhibitors (SSRIs).* Mayo Clinic, December 10, 2008, http://www.mayoclinic.com/health/ssris/MH00066.

"2008 Top 200 Branded Drugs by Total Prescriptions." *Drug Topics,* 2009, http://drugtopics.modernmedicine.com/drugtopics/data/articlestandard//drugtopics/222009/599845/article.pdf.

"2008 Top 200 Generic Drugs by Total Prescriptions." *Drug Topics,* 2009, http://drugtopics.modernmedicine.com/drugtopics/data/articlestandard//drugtopics/222009/599844/article.pdf.

*What Are Generic Drugs?* Food and Drug Administration, May 12, 2009, http://www.fda.gov/Drugs/ResourcesForYou/Consumers/BuyingUsingMedicineSafely/UnderstandingGenericDrugs/ucm144456.htm.

**ANTIDEPRESSANTS AND SUICIDE.** The relationship between **antidepressants** and **suicide** is complex and controversial. On one hand, antidepressants decrease symptoms of depression, which can include a preoccupation with suicide and death. Epidemiological studies have tended to show a link between higher rates of antidepressant use and lower rates of suicide. On the other hand, clinical trials have found that a small number of **children**, **adolescents**, and young adults who take antidepressants actually experience an increase in suicidal thoughts and behavior when the medication is first started.

In 2005, the Food and Drug Administration asked drug companies to add a "black box" warning about the risk in children and adolescents to their antidepressant labeling. In 2007, the agency asked that the warning be expanded to include young adults ages 18 through 24. Initially, there was some concern that the warnings might discourage appropriate use of antidepressants. However, a study looking at the impact of the 2005 black box and some earlier warnings leading up to it found that any effects on prescribing were modest and mostly limited to the target age group.

The explanation for the paradoxical effect on suicidal thoughts and behavior is still being debated. One possibility is that the energy boost provided by antidepressants might kick in sooner than the overall mood improvement. At this early stage, antidepressants might give some depressed individuals the energy to follow through on suicidal impulses.

However, it is still unclear if taking antidepressants increases the risk of completing, rather than just contemplating or attempting, suicide. Clinical trials generally exclude those individuals at highest risk for suicide, and most trials last only a couple of months. As a result, among the tens of thousands of trial participants over the years, there have been only a handful of suicide deaths—too few for statistical analysis.

Whatever the cause, the link between antidepressants and suicide is strongly related to age. Antidepressants are only associated with an increased risk of suicidal thoughts and behavior in the young. In adults ages 25 through 65, the increased risk disappears, and in those older than 65, the risk actually declines. At any age, the possible risks of taking antidepressants must be balanced against the proven benefits of treating depression.

***What to Watch For.*** Any increase in suicidal thoughts or behavior is most likely to occur within the first month or two after starting an antidepressant or upping the dosage. Patients taking antidepressants—or parents of younger patients—should watch for these warning signs: (1) thoughts about suicide or death, (2) suicide attempts, (3) new or worsening depression, (4) new or worsening anxiety, (5) new or worsening **irritability**, (6) panic attacks, (7) extreme agitation or restlessness, (8) aggressiveness, violence, or uncontrollable anger, (9) trouble sleeping, (10) acting on dangerous impulses, (11) extreme increases in activity and talking or (12) other unusual changes in behavior or mood.

If such problems occur, people should call their doctor right away. It is important not to stop taking an antidepressant without talking to a doctor first, because this can lead to other symptoms.

## Bibliography

*FDA Proposed New Warnings About Suicidal Thinking, Behavior in Young Adults Who Take Antidepressant Medications.* Food and Drug Administration, May 2, 2007, http://www.fda.gov/News Events/Newsroom/PressAnnouncements/2007/ucm108905.htm.

Olfson, Mark, Steven C. Marcus, and Benjamin G. Druss. "Effects of Food and Drug Administration Warnings on Antidepressant Use in a National Sample." *Archives of General Psychiatry* 65 (2008): 94–101.

*Questions and Answers on Antidepressant Use in Children, Adolescents, and Adults: May, 2007.* Food and Drug Administration, http://www.fda.gov/Drugs/DrugSafety/InformationbyDrugClass/ucm096321 .htm.

*Revisions to Medication Guide: Antidepressant Medicines, Depression and Other Serious Mental Illnesses, and Suicidal Thoughts or Actions.* Food and Drug Administration, http://www.fda.gov/downloads/ Drugs/DrugSafety/InformationbyDrugClass/ucm100211.pdf.

Stone, Marc, Thomas Laughren, M. Lisa Jones, Mark Levenson, P. Chris Holland, Alice Hughes et al. "Risk of Suicidality in Clinical Trials of Antidepressants in Adults: Analysis of Proprietary Data Submitted to US Food and Drug Administration." *BMJ* 339 (2009): b2880.

**ANTIPSYCHOTICS.** Antipsychotics are a group of medications that were originally designed to prevent or relieve psychotic symptoms, such as delusions (distorted personal beliefs), hallucinations (disturbed sensory impressions), disorganized thoughts, and agitation. These medications are sometimes prescribed to help treat **psychotic depression**, a disorder in which people have not only the usual depressive symptoms, but also psychotic ones.

Some antipsychotics are also used to treat **bipolar disorder**, which is characterized by moods that alternate between overly low (depression) and overly high (**mania**). Antipsychotics may be taken along with mood stabilizer medications for treating severe mania or mixed episodes (bouts that combine features of both mania and depression). In addition, certain antipsychotics may be added to **antidepressants** for managing hard-to-treat **major depression**, even when no psychotic symptoms are present.

There are numerous antipsychotics, but the only ones with Food and Drug Administration (FDA) approval specifically for use in bipolar disorder are aripiprazole, asenapine, olanzapine, quetiapine, risperidone, and ziprasidone. Aripiprazole has also been approved as an add-on therapy for major depression. But other medications in this class may still be prescribed for either bipolar disorder or major depression at a doctor's discretion. This practice, known as off-label prescribing, is both legal and very common, and it opens up a wider range of treatment possibilities. Yet it means that doctors may sometimes prescribe medications when there is little or no research evidence to support the drugs' effectiveness for that particular condition.

Antipsychotics are thought to affect **neurotransmitters**, natural substances that act as chemical messengers within the brain. In particular, they may decrease **dopamine**, a neurotransmitter that is essential for movement and also influences motivation, the perception of reality, and the ability to experience pleasure.

Based on limited research to date, antipsychotics seem to help calm manic symptoms in 40 percent to 75 percent of people with bipolar disorder. Evidence of effectiveness at treating bipolar disorder is strongest for olanzapine, quetiapine, and risperidone. But antipsychotics have been much less extensively studied in bipolar disorder than in schizophrenia, the primary condition for which they are prescribed.

***First versus Second Generation.*** Antipsychotics can be subdivided into two main groups: older, first-generation antipsychotics and newer, second-generation ones (also called atypical antipsychotics). Several first-generation medications introduced in the 1950s and 1960s are still available today. But second-generation medications developed over the past 15 years now dominate sales.

When second-generation antipsychotics first hit the market, they were believed to be more effective and have milder side effects than their older counterparts. More recent research indicates that this may not actually be the case, however. It turns out that the older medications work about as well as the newer ones, yet cost far less. Also, older antipsychotics do not seem to cause more frequent or severe side effects than newer ones overall. However, some new-generation medications seem to be less prone to causing muscle twitches and abnormal body movements.

Antipsychotics Used as Mood Stabilizers

|  | **Brand Names** |
| --- | --- |
| Aripiprazole*†‡ | Abilify |
| Asenapine*† | Saphris |
| Clozapine* | Clozaril |
| Haloperidol | Haldol |
| Olanzapine*† | Zyprexa |
| Quetiapine*† | Seroquel |
| Risperidone*† | Risperdal |
| Thioridazine | Mellaril |
| Trifluoperazine | Stelazine |
| Ziprasidone*† | Geodon |
| Combination Product | |
| Olanzapine + fluoxetine (an antidepressant)*†‡ | Symbyax |

*Second-generation antipsychotic
†FDA approved for treating bipolar disorder
‡FDA approved for treating treatment-resistant depression

***Use and Precautions.*** When used for bipolar disorder, an antipsychotic is typically added to a mood stabilizer for treating people in the midst of a severe manic episode. Once the episode has abated, the antipsychotic is often stopped, although it may be continued if needed to control ongoing symptoms.

With all medications, the goal is to strike a balance between a high enough dose to achieve effectiveness and a low enough dose to minimize risks. With antipsychotics, finding the right balance can be particularly challenging. Individual response varies greatly. Doctors usually start with a low dose and then gradually increase the amount until the optimal dose for that person is found.

***Risks and Side Effects.*** Antipsychotics are generally prescribed for severe symptoms of mental illness, and the benefits of reducing these symptoms often far outweigh the risks of taking the drug. Nevertheless, side effects remain a significant concern. Between 80 percent and 90 percent of people who take an antipsychotic will experience at least one side effect, and from 20 percent to 30 percent will have a side effect so serious or intolerable that they stop the medication within the first few months.

Possible side effects, ranging from mild to severe, include abnormal movements, muscle twitches, tremors, menstrual problems, blurred vision, constipation, dizziness upon standing, dry mouth, excessive saliva, increased hunger, insomnia, lack of coordination, lip smacking, male infertility, muscle stiffness or weakness, rapid heartbeat, restlessness, sedation, sensitivity to sunlight, sexual problems, skin rash, and slurred speech. These side effects often get better with time or at a lower dose, and they go away when the medication is stopped.

More serious side effects occur occasionally as well. They include blood sugar abnormalities, seizures, significant weight gain, and neuroleptic malignant syndrome (a potentially life-threatening condition characterized by high fever, increased heart rate, and high blood pressure). In addition, clozapine is more likely than other antipsychotics to cause myocarditis (inflammation of the heart muscle) or agranulocytosis (a bone marrow disorder that can lead to serious infections). First-generation antipsychotics are more apt to cause tardive kinesia (uncontrollable muscle movements and twitching, which sometimes are permanent).

Although there are real risks associated with taking antipsychotics, the risk of not treating severe psychotic symptoms or **mood disorders** may be even greater. To minimize any adverse effects, people on antipsychotics should take their medication exactly as prescribed.

*See also:* Augmentation Therapy; Pharmacotherapy

## Bibliography

*Evaluating Prescription Drugs Used to Treat Schizophrenia and Bipolar Disorder: The Antipsychotics—Comparing Effectiveness, Safety, and Price.* Consumer Reports, 2009, http://www.consumerreports.org/health/best-buy-drugs/antipsychotics.htm.

McDonagh, Marian S., Kim Peterson, Susan Carson, Benjamin Chan, and Sujata Thakurta. *Drug Class Review: Atypical Antipsychotic Drugs—Final Report Update 2.* Oregon Health and Science University, 2008, http://derp.ohsu.edu/final/AAP_final_report_update_23.pdf.

*Medication Information Sheet.* Depression and Bipolar Support Alliance, May 4, 2006, http://www.dbsalliance.org/site/PageServer?pagename=about_treatment_medinfosheet.

*Mental Health Medications.* National Institute of Mental Health, July 28, 2009, http://www.nimh.nih.gov/health/publications/mental-health-medications/complete-index.shtml.

Swartz, Marvin S., T. Scott Stroup, Joseph P. McEvoy, Sonia M. Davis, Robert A. Rosenheck, Richard S. E. Keefe, et al. "What CATIE Found: Results From the Schizophrenia Trial." *Psychiatric Services* 59 (2008): 500–506.

**ANXIETY DISORDERS.**   Anxiety disorders are a group of emotional disorders characterized by excessive fear or worry that is recurrent or long-lasting. The symptoms caused by these disorders go well beyond ordinary nervousness or uncertainty, leading to serious distress or interfering with people's ability to get along at home, work, or school. Experts have long noted that anxiety and depression often go hand in hand. More than half of people with **major depression** have an anxiety disorder as well, and the reverse is also true.

Anxiety disorders are very common, affecting some 40 million U.S. adults in any given year. Unlike a short-lived attack of nerves brought on by a first date or big presentation at work, anxiety disorders last for weeks, months, or even years, and they can get worse if not treated. Job performance, schoolwork, and personal relationships all may suffer, and some people resort to **substance abuse** in a vain attempt to keep the anxiety at bay.

When depression is added to the mix, the challenges increase as well. Compared to people with depression alone, those with a coexisting anxiety disorder tend to have more severe depression, greater problems at work and in their social life, a poorer response to treatment, and a higher risk of **suicide**. One study found that people with both major depression and a type of anxiety disorder called **panic disorder** were 15 times as likely as those with no psychiatric illness to have suicidal thoughts.

Fortunately, effective help is available. Appropriate treatment with **psychotherapy**, medications, or a combination of the two can help relieve the symptoms of both anxiety and depression. When depression is severe, it may need to be addressed first so people can regain the motivation they need to confront their anxiety successfully.

*Types of Anxiety Disorders.*   Several types of anxiety disorders are described in the ***Diagnostic and Statistical Manual of Mental Disorders, Fourth Edition, Text Revision***, a diagnostic guidebook that is used by mental health professionals from many fields. Below are brief descriptions of disorders in this category.

*Generalized Anxiety Disorder.*   **Generalized anxiety disorder** (GAD) is characterized by excessive, uncontrollable worry and tension over a number of different things. This worry occurs more days than not for at least six months. Along with the worry, adults have at least three of the following symptoms, and children have at least one: (1) feeling restless, keyed up, or on edge, (2) getting tired easily, (3) finding it hard to concentrate or having one's mind go blank, (4) having trouble falling or staying asleep, or sleeping restlessly, (5) **irritability**, and (6) muscle tension.

People with GAD anticipate disaster around every corner, and they are often overly concerned about their health, finances, job, or relationships. They cannot seem to shake their worries, even though they usually realize that their anxiety is more intense than the situation warrants. Instead, they live in a state of perpetual tension, finding it nearly impossible to ever relax and unwind.

*Panic Disorder.*   The defining feature of panic disorder is the occurrence of repeated, unexpected panic attacks. These attacks are sudden waves of intense fear and apprehension that are accompanied by four or more of the following symptoms: (1) racing or pounding heart, (2) sweating, (3) trembling, (4) shortness of breath, (5) choking sensation, (6) chest pain, (7) nausea or upset stomach, (8) dizziness or faintness, (9) feelings of unreality or detachment from oneself, (10) fear of losing control or going crazy, (11) fear of dying, (12) numbness or tingling sensation, and (13) chills or hot flushes. The symptoms come on abruptly and reach their peak within a matter of minutes.

In the aftermath of panic attacks, people with panic disorder develop persistent concerns about having future attacks or nagging worries about what the attacks might mean. For instance, they may fear that they have a life-threatening medical illness, are "out of their mind," or will lose control in a public place. Some people make major changes in their lifestyle as a result of such fears. For example, they may avoid physical exertion because they are worried about having a heart attack.

*Specific Phobias.*    A specific phobia is characterized by intense fear that is focused on a particular animal, object, or situation and is out of proportion to any real threat. Examples of common specific phobias include heights, escalators, tunnels, closed places, highway driving, water, flying, dogs, spiders, and blood. Adults with phobias recognize that their fear is excessive or irrational. Nevertheless, being around the feared object or situation almost always provokes an immediate fear reaction or panic attack.

To head off such unpleasant reactions, people begin to avoid the feared object or situation whenever they can. If the object or situation is unavoidable, it is endured only with great distress. Eventually, the avoidance, distress, or anxious anticipation about running into the feared thing starts to interfere with their daily routine, disrupt their personal relationships, or hinder their performance at work or school.

*Social Phobia.*    Social phobia—also known as social anxiety disorder—is characterized by intense fear in social situations that involve being around unfamiliar people or being exposed to possible scrutiny by others. People with social phobia live in constant fear that they will humiliate or embarrass themselves. Adults realize that their fear is excessive or unreasonable. Nevertheless, the feared social situation almost always triggers a fear reaction or panic attack. In children, the anxiety may be expressed by **crying**, throwing tantrums, freezing, or shrinking from unfamiliar people.

Social phobia can be limited to a few situations, such as talking on the phone or eating and drinking in front of people. Or it may be so broad that people experience intense fear around almost everyone except immediate family members. In either case, people start to either avoid the feared situation or endure it only at great emotional cost. They may be very anxious before the encounter, extremely uncomfortable during it, and wracked with worries afterward about the impression they made on others.

*Post-traumatic Stress Disorder.*    **Post-traumatic stress disorder** (PTSD) develops after exposure to a traumatic event that evoked intense fear, horror, or helplessness. The event involved actual or threatened bodily harm. In some cases, the person with PTSD is the one who suffered or was threatened with injury or death. But in other cases, the harm may have befallen a loved one, or the person with PTSD may have witnessed a terrifying event that happened to a stranger.

Symptoms of PTSD fall into three main categories. The first category is reexperiencing the trauma; for example, having intrusive memories or disturbing nightmares or flashbacks. The second category is emotional numbness and avoidance of things associated with the trauma; for example, feeling detached from others and trying not to think about or talk about what happened. The third category is a heightened state of arousal; for example, constant alertness and trouble sleeping. People with PTSD have all three types of symptoms, and the problems persist for more than a month.

*Obsessive-Compulsive Disorder.*    The defining features of **obsessive-compulsive disorder** (OCD) are recurrent, uncontrollable obsessions and compulsions. Obsessions are intrusive, upsetting thoughts that keep coming back despite efforts to ignore or suppress them. Because the thoughts cause so much anxiety, people try to neutralize them with some physical or mental act, which is where compulsions come into play. Compulsions are ritualistic actions that people feel driven to perform in an effort to reduce the anxiety produced by an obsession.

Obsessions often involve frequent, exaggerated thoughts about being diseased, dirty, sinful, or doing abhorrent things. Examples of compulsions include repetitively washing one's hands, cleaning, checking the locks, putting objects in order, counting, or silently saying a phrase. Healthy people may perform little rituals, too. For instance, they might check the stove more than once to make sure it is turned off. But for people with OCD, the rituals start to take over their life, consuming hours out of each day or interfering with other activities.

Who Is Anxious?

Anxiety disorders strike people of all ages, both sexes, and every ethnic and economic background.

| | Number of U.S. Adults* | Distribution by Gender | Typical Age When It Begins |
|---|---|---|---|
| Generalized Anxiety Disorder | 6.8 million | More women than men | Childhood to middle age |
| Panic Disorder | 6.0 million | More women than men | Late adolescence or early adulthood |
| Specific Phobias | 19.2 million | More women than men | Childhood or adolescence |
| Social Phobia | 15.0 million | About equally divided | Childhood or early adolescence |
| Post-traumatic Stress Disorder | 7.7 million | More women than men | Any age |
| Obsessive-Compulsive Disorder | 2.2 million | About equally divided | Childhood, adolescence, or early adulthood |

*These numbers add up to more than 40 million because some people have more than one anxiety disorder.

***Relationship to Depression.*** The close connection between depression and anxiety may be due in part to shared **genetic factors**. The evidence for some genetic overlap is especially strong for major depression and GAD. In addition, certain **environmental factors**, such as extreme **stress** in childhood, may contribute to both conditions. Yet studies show that there are real differences as well as commonalities in the underlying causes for depression and anxiety disorders.

The typical age of onset for many anxiety disorders is younger than that for major depression. As a result, it has been suggested that having an anxiety disorder early in life may predispose people to becoming depressed later. However, this does not seem to be a cut-and-dried relationship. When people have both major depression and GAD, social phobia or PTSD, the anxiety disorder comes first only two-thirds or less of the time. And when people have both dysthymia and panic disorder, PTSD or OCD, dysthymia precedes the anxiety disorder more often than not.

*Tripartite Model.* One theory that aims to define the core differences between depression and anxiety was proposed in 1991 by U.S. psychologists Lee Anna Clark and David Watson. Known as the tripartite model, this theory identifies three key features of the disorders: general distress, **anhedonia** (an inability to take interest or find pleasure in activities that would normally be enjoyed) and physiological arousal. According to the theory, both depression and anxiety are characterized by a high level of distress. But only depression is characterized by anhedonia, and only anxiety is characterized by physiological arousal.

Numerous studies have borne out the validity of this model. One implication is that the line between depression and anxiety disorders might be sharpened by emphasizing symptoms of anhedonia or physiological arousal, respectively. At the same time, for purposes of distinguishing depression from anxiety, it might be helpful to deemphasize symptoms of general distress, such as trouble sleeping and difficulty concentrating.

*See also:* Comorbidity

**Further Information.** Anxiety Disorders Association of America, 8730 Georgia Avenue, Suite 600. Silver Spring, MD 20910, (240) 485–1001, www.adaa.org.

*Bibliography*

American Psychiatric Association. *Diagnostic and Statistical Manual of Mental Disorders.* 4th ed., text rev. Washington, DC: American Psychiatric Association, 2000.

*Anxiety Disorders.* National Institute of Mental Health, 2007, http://www.nimh.nih.gov/health/publications/anxiety-disorders/summary.shtml.

Clark, Lee Anna, and David Watson. "Tripartite Model of Anxiety and Depression: Psychometric Evidence and Taxonomic Implications." *Journal of Abnormal Psychology* 100 (1991): 316–336.

Foa, Edna B., and Linda Wasmer Andrews. *If Your Adolescent Has an Anxiety Disorder: An Essential Resource for Parents.* New York: Oxford University Press, 2006.

Goodwin, Renee, Mark Olfson, Adriana Feder, Milton Fuentes, Daniel J. Pilowsky, and Myrna M. Weissman. "Panic and Suicidal Ideation in Primary Care." *Depression and Anxiety* 14 (2001): 244–246.

Klein, Daniel N., Stewart A. Shankman, and Brian R. McFarland. "Classification of Mood Disorders." In *The American Psychiatric Publishing Textbook of Mood Disorders,* by Dan J. Stein, David J. Kupfer and Alan F. Schatzberg, eds., 17–32. Washington, DC: American Psychiatric Publishing, 2006.

*Let's Talk Facts About Anxiety Disorders.* American Psychiatric Association, 2005, http://healthyminds.org/factsheets/LTF-Anxiety.pdf.

Moffitt, Terrie E., HonaLee Harrington, Avshalom Caspi, Julia Kim-Cohen, David Goldberg, Alice M. Gregory, et al. "Depression and Generalized Anxiety Disorder: Cumulative and Sequential Comorbidity in a Birth Cohort Followed Prospectively to Age 32 Years." *Archives of General Psychiatry* 64 (2007): 651–660.

Simon, Naomi M., and Jerrold F. Rosenbaum. "Anxiety and Depression Comorbidity: Implications and Intervention." *Medscape Psychiatry and Mental Health* 8 (2003): http://www.medscape.com/viewarticle/451325.

**APPETITE DISTURBANCES.** Changes in appetite and weight are common symptoms of depression. Many depressed individuals lose interest in food and feel as if they have to force themselves to eat. In severe cases, adults may lose five percent or more of their body weight in a month, and children may fail to gain weight as expected. Lack of appetite and weight loss may be particularly pronounced in people with **melancholic depression**.

Less commonly, people with depression may have an increased appetite or a craving for sweet or starchy foods (carbohydrates). Not surprisingly, this type of appetite disturbance can lead to putting on unwanted pounds. An increase in appetite or weight gain occurs in almost half of people with **atypical depression**, and overeating or a craving for carbohydrates is typical of those with **seasonal affective disorder**.

***Role of Inflammation.*** Some scientists have linked loss of appetite in depression to **inflammation**, the immune system's natural reaction to infection, irritation, or injury.

Cytokines are the chemical messengers of the **immune system**. High levels of inflammation-promoting cytokines have been linked to something called "sickness behavior," a pattern of depression-like behavior that normally helps the body rest and heal when illness strikes. Decreased appetite is a hallmark of sickness behavior, and researchers have suggested that proinflammatory cytokines might underlie it.

Tumor necrosis factor-alpha (TNF-α) is one of the proinflammatory cytokines. In a study of older women, higher levels of TNF-α were associated with increased depressive feelings as well as poor appetite. One way cytokines such as TNF-α might decrease appetite is by affecting the release of leptin, a hormone produced by fat cells that helps regulate appetite and metabolism. It is an intriguing possibility that warrants further investigation.

*See also:* Hormones

*Bibliography*

American Psychiatric Association. *Diagnostic and Statistical Manual of Mental Disorders.* 4th ed., text rev. Washington, DC: American Psychiatric Association, 2000.

Andréasson, Anna, Lotta Arborelius, Charlotte Erlanson-Albertsson, and Mats Lekander. "A Putative Role for Cytokines in the Impaired Appetite in Depression." *Brain, Behavior, and Immunity* 21 (2007): 147–152.

Blazer, Dan G., and Celia F. Hybels. "Depression in Later Life: Epidemiology, Assessment, Impact, and Treatment." In *Handbook of Depression.* 2nd ed., by Ian H. Gotlib and Constance L. Hammen, eds., 492–509. New York: Guilford Press, 2009.

Rosenthal, Joshua Z., and Norman E. Rosenthal. "Seasonal Affective Disorder." In *The American Psychiatric Publishing Textbook of Mood Disorders,* by Dan J. Stein, David J. Kupfer, and Alan F. Schatzberg, eds., 527–545. Washington, DC: American Psychiatric Publishing, 2006.

Stewart, Jonathan W., Frederic M. Quitkin, and Carrie Davies. "Atypical Depression, Dysthymia, and Cyclothymia." In *The American Psychiatric Publishing Textbook of Mood Disorders,* by Dan J. Stein, David J. Kupfer, and Alan F. Schatzberg, eds., 547–559. Washington, DC: American Psychiatric Publishing, 2006.

**ASIAN AMERICANS AND PACIFIC ISLANDERS.** Asian Americans—individuals who trace their ancestry to the original peoples of the Far East, Southeast Asia, or the Indian subcontinent—make up 5 percent of the total U.S. population. Pacific Islanders—who are descended from the original peoples of Hawaii, Guam, Samoa, or other Pacific islands—comprise another 0.1 percent. As a group, Asian Americans and Pacific Islanders (AA/PIs) are the least likely of all ethnic minorities in the United States to use mental health services. Yet research suggests that the overall prevalence of mental health problems is similar to that for other Americans.

Looking specifically at depression, the Chinese American Epidemiology Study—the largest study to date of mental health disorders in this group—found that full-blown depression was about as common in Chinese Americans as in the general population. But other studies that focused on isolated symptoms rather than a full-fledged disorder have found higher levels of depressive symptoms in AA/PIs than in white Americans.

Nevertheless, utilization of mental health services is low. One reason is the **stigma** attached to mental illness in many AA/PI communities. Such stigmatization may lead individuals to express psychological distress as physical aches and pains. This tendency is seen in culturally specific syndromes, such as the Chinese syndrome called *shenjing shuairuo.* Physical symptoms such as tiredness, dizziness, headaches, and other aches and pain are prominent, but the condition may also have psychological symptoms such as mental fatigue, trouble concentrating, and memory loss.

Another reason for lower use of specialized mental health care by AA/PIs is a cultural focus on the mind/body connection. From this vantage point, the distinction between physical and mental treatments is irrelevant. In **traditional Chinese medicine**, for example, depression may be treated with **herbal remedies**, massage, or **acupuncture**.

***At-Risk Groups.*** AA/PI individuals are sometimes stereotyped as a "model minority." Unlike some other minorities, they are not over-represented among high-risk groups such as the homeless, prisoners, and substance abusers. Yet the belief that AA/PIs are immune to mental health problems may work to their disadvantage if it interferes with getting help when needed. In truth, AA/PIs face the same mental health challenges as anyone else. Some AA/PI subgroups, such as refugees and older women, may be especially vulnerable.

*Refugees.* In the 1970s, Southeast Asian refugees fleeing war-torn countries and cruel political regimes began arriving in the United States in droves. The lasting effects of **traumatic events** experienced by many refugees before and during immigration still reverberate to this day, often manifesting as **post-traumatic stress disorder** (PTSD) and depression. In one study of Cambodian adolescents who survived of Pol Pot's concentration camps, nearly half were suffering PTSD and over 40 percent were suffering depression several years after leaving their homeland.

*Older Women.* The overall **suicide** rate for Asian Americans is about half the rate for white Americans. One exception to that rule, however, is older Asian American women, who have the highest suicide rate of all U.S. women age 65 and older. Some experts blame the devastating impact of changes in cultural and social roles. These older women may come from cultures that accord far more respect to elders than mainstream American culture does. They may also define themselves by their role as family caregiver, and when key relationships are lost—for instance, by a spouse dying or grown children moving away— they may feel isolated and purposeless. The **stress** associated with such feelings may in turn trigger depression in vulnerable individuals.

***Barriers to Care.*** The AA/PI category is quite culturally diverse, encompassing over 40 different ethnic subgroups. Although the majority of Asian Americans were born outside the United States, a large number of Chinese and Japanese Americans are fourth- or fifth-generation Americans. Most Pacific Islanders, in contrast, are descended from the original inhabitants of islands now held by the United States. These subgroups have different needs and challenges. However, language and cultural barriers affect all to some degree.

*Language.* AA/PI individuals speak over 100 languages and dialects, and about a third live in households where the adults have limited proficiency in English. Over 60 percent of Vietnamese Americans and half of Chinese Americans, for example, do not speak English at home. Bilingual treatment providers and translators are in limited supply, making it difficult for some AA/PIs to get adequate assessment and treatment for mental health problems.

*Providers.* Even when language is not a barrier, AA/PI individuals may have trouble finding culturally appropriate services. An individual's culture can influence such things as how depression is expressed, how symptoms are understood, and which treatments are most acceptable. Yet AA/PIs are underrepresented in the mental health field. There are only 70 AA/PI mental health professionals per 100,000 AA/PI individuals, compared to 173 white professionals per 100,000.

*Symptom Severity.* Those AA/PIs who receive mental health treatment tend to be more severely ill than other ethnic groups. This is probably due to delays in seeking care as a result of stigma or language and cultural barriers. It underscores the need to find better ways of reaching out to this population.

*See also:* Cultural Factors; Ethnicity; Older Adults; Yoga

***Further Information.*** Asian American Psychological Association, PMB 527, 5025 N. Central Avenue, Phoenix, AZ 85012, www.aapaonline.org.

National Asian American Pacific Islander Mental Health Association, 1215 19th Street, Suite A, Denver, CO 80202, (303) 298–7910, www.naapimha.org.

Office of Minority Health, U.S. Department of Health and Human Services, P.O. Box 37337, Washington, D.C. 20013, (800) 444–6472, www.omhrc.gov.

## Bibliography

*Asian American/Pacific Islander Profile.* U.S. Department of Health and Human Services Office of Minority Health, July 31, 2009, http://www.omhrc.gov/templates/browse.aspx?lvl=3&lvlid=29.

*Asian Americans/Pacific Islanders.* American Psychiatric Association, http://healthyminds.org/More-Info-For/Asian-AmericanPacific-Islanders.aspx.

*Asian Americans/Pacific Islanders.* U.S. Department of Health and Human Services Office of the Surgeon General, http://mentalhealth.samhsa.gov/cre/fact2.asp.

Hsu, L. K. George, Yu Mui Wan, Hong Chang, Paul Summergrad, Bill Y. P. Tsang, and Hongtu Chen. "Stigma of Depression Is More Severe in Chinese Americans Than Caucasian Americans." *Psychiatry: Interpersonal and Biological Processes* 71 (2008): 210–218.

*Mental Health and Asian Americans.* U.S. Department of Health and Human Services Office of Minority Health, July 27, 2009, http://www.omhrc.gov/templates/content.aspx?lvl=3&lvlID=9&ID=6476.

*Native Hawaiians/Other Pacific Islanders Profile.* U.S. Department of Health and Human Services Office of Minority Health, July 31, 2009, http://www.omhrc.gov/templates/browse.aspx?lvl=3&lvlid=111.

Pascual, Cathy. "Why More Elderly Asian Women Kill Themselves" *Los Angeles Times* (September 14, 2000).

U.S. Department of Health and Human Services. *Culture, Race, and Ethnicity: A Supplement to Mental Health: A Report of the Surgeon General.* Rockville, MD: U.S. Department of Health and Human Services, 2001.

**ATTACHMENT THEORY.**   Attachment theory states that **infants** have an innate need for close emotional bonds with their caregivers. The way this need is met in infancy shapes later interpersonal relationships and emotional stability. Lack of a secure attachment bond is thought to cause enduring relationship problems as well as a tendency toward depression and anxiety.

Attachment theory was first proposed by British psychiatrist **John Bowlby** (1907–1990), who argued that infants' attachment to their caregivers and distress upon separation are useful adaptations from an evolutionary point of view. Attachment behaviors—such as crying, smiling, and clinging—increase the likelihood of survival by keeping infants close to those who protect and care for them. The attachment bonds formed by infants with their caregivers create the model for future relationships.

Research by Canadian-born U.S. psychologist Mary D. Salter Ainsworth (1913–1999) and others confirmed and expanded attachment theory. By the 1970s, the theory had become a major force in developmental and child clinical psychology. Since the late 1980s, attachment theory has been extended to encompass adult romantic relationships as well.

***Early Childhood Attachment Styles.*** Different researchers have conceptualized attachment in somewhat different ways. In general, though, four basic patterns of attachment in infants and young children have been described.

*Secure Attachment.* Secure attachment is characterized by the assurance that the parent will be available and responsive. Securely attached children learn that they are worthy of love and that the world is a caring place. Put in a strange situation, securely attached young children display confidence when the parent is present, act mildly distressed if the parent leaves, and reestablish contact quickly once the parent returns.

*Ambivalent Attachment.* This attachment style stems from inconsistent caregiving, in which the parent is available and attentive at some times, but not at others. Ambivalently attached children may become preoccupied with the parent, alternately seeking and rejecting close contact. Placed in a strange situation, young children with this attachment pattern show a mixture of positive and negative responses to the parent.

*Avoidant Attachment.* This attachment style results from repeated rebuffs and rejection by the parent. Young children with this attachment pattern have little confidence that they will receive help and comfort if they need it, so they become emotionally distant and hostile. Placed in a strange situation, they ignore the parent when present, seem unfazed if the parent leaves, and may actively avoid contact once the parent returns.

*Disorganized Attachment.* This attachment style typically results from maltreatment by a caregiver. The parent is at once a source of distress and the only potential source of comfort. As a result, infants and young children display conflicted behavior; for example, simultaneously reaching for and turning away from a parent. Placed in a strange situation, they show no consistent pattern of behavior when the parent leaves and returns.

***Relationship to Depression.*** Children with an ambivalent attachment style often appear anxious, clingy, passive, and helpless. Theorists dating back to Austrian psychiatrist **Sigmund Freud** (1856–1939) have noted a link between this relationship style and depression. Freud described a type of insecure relationship in which dependency and anxiety are coupled with fear of rejection by loved ones and hostility toward them. From a Freudian perspective, adults with this pattern are vulnerable to depression following a relationship loss or separation.

In contrast, children with an avoidant attachment style may strive to be self-reliant as a defense against rejection and criticism. As adults, they may be distant from others, showing little interest in or appreciation for interpersonal relationships. At the same time, they may be overinvested in activities and achievements designed to compensate for feelings of inferiority, worthlessness, and guilt. People with this pattern are vulnerable to depression when they fail to live up to their own unrealistically high standards.

Of all the attachment styles, disorganized attachment is the strongest predictor of more severe emotional and behavioral problems later in life. This association may contribute to the well-established link between childhood physical and sexual abuse and adult depression.

*See also:* Evolutionary Perspective; Personality Factors; Relationship Issues

## Bibliography

Blatt, Sidney J. *Experiences of Depression: Theoretical, Clinical, and Research Perspectives.* Washington, DC: American Psychological Association, 2004.

Bretherton, Inge. "The Origins of Attachment Theory: John Bowlby and Mary Ainsworth." *Developmental Psychology* 28 (1992): 759–775.

Hardy, Lyons T. "Attachment Theory and Reactive Attachment Disorder: Theoretical Perspectives and Treatmetn Implications." *Journal of Child and Adolescent Psychiatry Nursing* 20 (2007): 27–39.

Hazan, Cindy, and Phillip Shaver. "Romantic Love Conceptualized as an Attachment Process." *Journal of Personality and Social Psychology* 52 (1987): 511–524.

Joiner, Thomas E. Jr., and Katherine A. Timmons. "Depression in Its Interpersonal Context." In *Handbook of Depression.* 2nd ed., by Ian H. Gotlib and Constance L. Hammen, eds., 322–339. New York: Guilford Press, 2009.

**ATTENTION-DEFICIT HYPERACTIVITY DISORDER.** Attention-deficit hyper-activity disorder (ADHD) is a condition characterized by a short attention span, excessive activity, and/or impulsive behavior. The symptoms begin at a young age and continue for a long time, sometimes lasting into adulthood. Depression is one of the most common coexisting conditions. By some estimates, up to 70 percent of those with ADHD will be treated for depression at some point in their lives.

About three percent to five percent of children have ADHD. Although the first signs of the disorder may show up in early childhood, it is difficult to make a diagnosis at that age, because even healthy preschoolers have short attention spans and limited control over their behavior. Often the condition is first diagnosed when children reach school age and ADHD symptoms begin causing problems in the classroom.

All children occasionally have trouble sitting still, blurt out things they don't mean to, or find it hard to pay attention. For children with ADHD, though, such behaviors occur more often than normal for their age. The behaviors are part of a long-lasting pattern, not just a temporary response to a short-term situation. And they occur in a variety of settings, not just in one place such as the classroom or playground.

ADHD can affect children's ability to learn in the classroom, get along with others, and behave appropriately at home and school. As a result, such children often wind up labeled as behavior problems. By their late teens, young people may grow out of some symptoms, such as hyperactivity. But other symptoms, such as being easily distracted, may be longer-lasting. From 30 percent to 70 percent of those who had ADHD as children continue to experience some problems as adults.

### Treatment of ADHD

When people have both ADHD and depression simultaneously, both conditions need to be addressed. Below are some of the main treatment options for ADHD.

#### Medication
Stimulant medications help decrease hyperactivity and impulsiveness as well as increase attention. Stimulants mainly affect **dopamine**. There is also a non-stimulant ADHD medication called atomoxetine, which affects the brain chemical **norepinephrine**.

#### Behavioral Therapy
Behavioral therapy helps people with ADHD change their behavior to solve specific problems. Key elements include setting goals, rewarding desired behaviors, and monitoring progress. When children have ADHD, parents and teachers may learn to use these techniques for modifying behavior.

#### Classroom Interventions
Classroom strategies that promote positive behavioral change include keeping a consistent routine, writing down assignments, and organizing books and supplies. If needed, extra tutoring or other special educational services can help keep students from falling too far behind.

Even when symptoms of ADHD subside as children grow older, earlier problems at home, school, and play can have far-reaching repercussions. That is why it is so important to seek advice from a qualified medical or mental health professional if ADHD is suspected. If the disorder is diagnosed, several management options are available, including ADHD medication, **behavioral therapy,** and classroom interventions. When depression is also present, such approaches may be combined with **cognitive therapy** and/or **antidepressants**.

*Criteria for Diagnosis.* The symptoms of ADHD are defined by the ***Diagnostic and Statistical Manual of Mental Disorders, Fourth Edition, Text Revision***, a diagnostic guidebook published by the American Psychiatric Association and used by mental health professionals from many disciplines. By definition, ADHD starts early in life, with symptoms serious enough to cause problems appearing by age seven. The symptoms lead to significant impairment in school, work, or social functioning, and the problems occur in multiple settings.

Symptoms of ADHD fall into two main categories: inattention and hyperactivity/impulsivity. To be diagnosed with the disorder, people must have six or more symptoms from at least one of these categories. The symptoms last for a minimum of six months and are inconsistent with what would be expected for individuals of that age.

*Inattention.* People who are inattentive have trouble keeping their mind focused on any one thing. Such individuals often (1) make careless mistakes or fail to pay close attention to detail, (2) have trouble staying focused on what they are doing, (3) do not seem to listen when spoken to, (4) do not follow instructions or finish tasks, (5) have problems getting organized, (6) dislike or avoid tasks that require sustained mental effort, such as studying, (7) lose necessary items, such as schoolbooks, (8) are easily distracted, and (9) act forgetful.

*Hyperactivity/Impulsivity.* People who are hyperactive always seem to be on the go, and those who are impulsive fail to think before they act. Such individuals often (1) fidget or have trouble sitting still, (2) leave their seat in the classroom or other places where they are supposed to stay seated, (3) run about or climb around in situations where it is inappropriate, (4) have problems engaging in quiet play or leisure activities, (5) seem to be in constant motion, (6) talk too much, (7) blurt out answers before the questions are finished, (8) find it hard to wait their turn, and (9) interrupt other people's conversations or butt into their activities.

***Relationship to Depression.*** Left untreated, ADHD and depression often feed off each other. Children with ADHD may become demoralized and develop low self-esteem if they experience repeated failures at school or hear frequent criticism at home. As the negative experiences pile up, they may begin to feel helpless and hopeless. These feelings, in turn, can contribute to depression.

Conversely, depression can make it harder to cope with the challenges of ADHD. It is a vicious cycle that can have serious consequences if allowed to continue unchecked. Fortunately, treatment can help break the cycle and create the conditions for turning failure into success.

*See also:* Comorbidity

***Further Information.*** Attention Deficit Disorder Association, P.O. Box 7557, Wilmington, DE 19803, (800) 939–1019, www.add.org.

Children and Adults With Attention Deficit/Hyperactivity Disorder, 8181 Professional Place, Suite 150, Landover, MD 20785, (800) 233–4050, www.chadd.org, www.help4adhd.org.

## Bibliography

*AD/HD and Coexisting Conditions: Depression.* National Resource Center on ADHD, February 2008, http://www.help4adhd.org/en/treatment/coexisting/WWK5C.

*ADHD: What Parents Should Know.* American Academy of Family Physicians, November 2006, http://familydoctor.org/online/famdocen/home/children/parents/behavior/118.html.

American Psychiatric Association. *Diagnostic and Statistical Manual of Mental Disorders.* 4th ed., text rev. Washington, DC: American Psychiatric Association, 2000.

*Attention Deficit Hyperactivity Disorder.* National Institute of Mental Health, April 3, 2008, http://www.nimh.nih.gov/health/publications/adhd/complete-publication.shtml.

*NINDS Attention Deficit-Hyperactivity Disorder Information Page.* National Institute of Neurological Disorders and Stroke, June 6, 2008, http://www.ninds.nih.gov/disorders/adhd/adhd.htm.

*Psychosocial Treatment for Children and Adolescents With ADHD.* National Resource Center on ADHD, February 2004, http://www.help4adhd.org/treatment/behavioral/WWK7.

**ATYPICAL DEPRESSION.** Atypical depression is a subtype of **major depression** in which the person's mood is highly sensitive to good or bad news. An episode of depression often is triggered by an interpersonal loss, such as a romantic breakup. The symptoms may greatly improve or even disappear if the loss is reversed; for instance, by getting back together or starting a new relationship.

The heightened reaction to outside events is the opposite of what is seen in another depression subtype called **melancholic depression**, in which people show almost no reaction at all when good things happen. Atypical depression and melancholic depression are mirror images in other ways, too. People with atypical depression tend to oversleep and eat too much, but those with melancholic depression tend to do exactly the opposite.

Despite its name, atypical depression is not uncommon, affecting 15 percent to 40 percent of those with major depression. The term "atypical" is an artifact of early studies of depression conducted among hospitalized patients. Those patients often had the severe symptoms typical of melancholic depression. But among people who are treated as outpatients, there is nothing particularly unusual about the symptoms of atypical depression.

***Criteria for Diagnosis.*** Atypical depression is a variant of major depression. All forms of major depression involve being in a low mood nearly all the time or losing interest or enjoyment in almost everything. These feelings last for at least two weeks, are associated with several other symptoms, and lead to serious problems functioning in everyday life.

Along with meeting the diagnostic criteria for major depression, people with atypical depression show "mood reactivity" (the first symptom listed below), which means they are able to be cheered up by good news or positive events. In addition, they have two or more other symptoms from the following list.

*Mood Reactivity.* People with atypical depression get a mood boost from positive events, and they feel relatively tranquil and contented for at least a short time. The happier mood may last for an extended period if the positive circumstances continue.

*Increased Appetite.* Almost half of those with atypical depression either notice an increase in appetite or overeat to the point where they put on weight.

*Sleeping Too Much.* Some people oversleep at night, and others take overly lengthy naps during the day. The total time spent sleeping adds up at least 10 hours a day, or at least two hours more than when not depressed.

*Sensation of Heaviness.* Another common symptom of atypical depression is "leaden paralysis"—feeling as if the arms or legs are heavy, leaden, or weighted down. The heavy sensation sometimes lasts for several hours at a time.

*Hypersensitivity to Rejection.*   Most people with atypical depression have a longstanding pattern of being hypersensitive to rejection. This is a trait that starts at a young age and lasts throughout all or most of adult life. It may lessen during nondepressed periods, but it never completely goes away. Overreacting to the slightest rebuff or criticism causes problems with other people, often leading to stormy relationships or an inability to sustain long-term bonds.

***Causes and Risk Factors.***   Atypical depression is two to three times more common in women than in men. This form of depression often starts in childhood or adolescence. It frequently comes and goes over a long period, sometimes with only **partial remission** between episodes of full-blown depression. To some people with atypical depression, it seems as if they have always felt this way.

Atypical symptoms often are seen in people with **seasonal affective disorder**, a form of major depression in which the symptoms start and stop around the same time each year. Usually, the symptoms begin every fall or winter and subside every spring.

Atypical symptoms also can occur in people with **dysthymia**, a mood disorder that is major depression's less intense but long-lasting cousin. Dysthymia involves being mildly depressed most of the day, more days than not, for at least two years.

***Treatment of Atypical Depression.***   Before the advent of newer **antidepressants**, there were two major types of depression medication: tricyclic antidepressants (TCAs) and **monoamine oxidase inhibitors** (MAOIs). Researchers discovered that, unlike people with other forms of depression, those with atypical depression were more likely to respond well to MAOIs than to TCAs. This was an important discovery, because it suggested that there was something unique about the biological underpinnings of atypical depression.

Today, though, MAOIs are rarely prescribed, in part because people who take these drugs must follow a restricted diet. **Selective serotonin reuptake inhibitors** (SSRIs), a widely prescribed class of newer antidepressants, are now usually the first-choice treatment for people with atypical depression who take medication. When SSRIs don't provide enough relief, however, an MAOI may be a good alternative.

**Psychotherapy**, either alone or combined with medication, may be helpful as well. One 10-week study of 108 people with atypical depression compared cognitive therapy (a form of psychotherapy that helps people recognize and change self-defeating thought patterns) and phenelzine (the best-studied MAOI for treating this form of depression). In this study, the two treatments were equally effective.

*See also:* Partial Remission

## Bibliography

American Psychiatric Association Work Group on Major Depressive Disorder. *Practice Guideline for the Treatment of Patients with Major Depressive Disorder.* 2nd ed. Washington, DC: American Psychiatric Publishing, 2000.

American Psychiatric Association. *Diagnostic and Statistical Manual of Mental Disorders.* 4th ed., text rev. Washington, DC: American Psychiatric Association, 2000.

Frances, Allen, Michael B. First, and Harold Alan Pincus. *DSM-IV Guidebook.* Washington, DC: American Psychiatric Press, 1995.

Jarrett, Robin B., Martin Schaffer, Donald McIntire, Amy Witt-Browder, Dolores Kraft, and Richard C. Risser. "Treatment of Atypical Depression With Cognitive Therapy or Phenelzine: A Double-blind, Placebo-Controlled Trial." *Archives of General Psychiatry* 56 (1999): 431–437.

Quitkin, Fredric M. "Depression With Atypical Features: Diagnostic Validity, Prevalence, and Treatment." *Primary Care Companion to the Journal of Clinical Psychiatry* 4 (2002): 94–99.

Stewart, Jonathan W. "Treating Depression With Atypical Features." *Journal of Clinical Psychiatry* 68 (2007): 25–29.

Thase, Michael E. "Recognition and Diagnosis of Atypical Depression." *Journal of Clinical Psychiatry* 68 (2007): 11–6.

**AUGMENTATION THERAPY.**    Augmentation therapy is the addition of another medicine to boost the effectiveness of a primary medication. When it comes to depression, the primary drug treatment is generally an antidepressant. If that antidepressant alone does not clear up all the depressive symptoms, it may be augmented with a second type of antidepressant or with a completely different kind of medication.

Some researchers use the term "augmentation therapy" in a stricter sense. They reserve it for situations in which a non-antidepressant is added to an antidepressant. These researchers use the term "combination therapy" when the second medication is an antidepressant with a different mechanism of action. But practically speaking, the distinction is largely semantic, because both strategies involve combining two drugs that affect the brain in different ways.

***Non-Antidepressants for Depression.***    Several types of non-antidepressants may be used for augmentation therapy, depending on an individual's needs and response to treatment. Below are some of the most common options.

*Lithium.*    **Lithium** is a mood stabilizer. Although it is typically used to treat **bipolar disorder**, it can also help some people with hard-to-treat **major depression**. Several studies show that lithium enhances the effects of **antidepressants**, possibly by giving a boost to a key brain chemical called **serotonin**.

*Anticonvulsants.*    **Anticonvulsants** were originally developed to prevent seizures, but they also help stabilize moods in people with bipolar disorder. Some research suggests that they may add to the effects of antidepressants in people with major depression.

*Thyroid Hormone.*    Triiodothyronine is a thyroid hormone typically used to treat thyroid problems. In the large **Sequenced Treatment Alternatives to Relieve Depression** study, some people who had not responded fully to other treatments got augmentation therapy using either triiodothyronine or lithium. About 20 percent became symptom-free, and triiodothyronine caused fewer troublesome side effects than lithium.

*Antipsychotics.*    **Antipsychotics** are medications specifically designed to relieve or prevent psychotic symptoms, including hallucinations and delusions. Such medications are sometimes prescribed to treat **psychotic depression**. However, certain newer antipsychotics also may help people with hard-to-treat depression even when no psychotic symptoms are present.

*Stimulants.*    Stimulants are medications that excite activity in the central nervous system. They are typically used to treat **attention-deficit hyperactivity disorder** and narcolepsy (a sleep disorder that causes excessive daytime sleepiness and sudden attacks of sleep). The combination of a stimulant and an antidepressant may be helpful for people who have severe problems with apathy, fatigue, and slowed-down movements and speech.

*Buspirone.*    Buspirone is an anti-anxiety medication that is typically used to treat **anxiety disorders**. Some research suggests that it may help depressed individuals who initially do not respond to a widely prescribed group of antidepressants called **selective serotonin reuptake inhibitors** (SSRIs). By enhancing serotonin receptors in the brain, buspirone may help SSRIs work better.

*Alpha Blockers.*    Alpha blockers, also called alpha-adrenergic antagonists, are typically used to treat conditions such as high blood pressure and an enlarged prostate. Research shows that alpha blockers may increase the effectiveness of the antidepressant mirtazapine, possibly by boosting a brain chemical called **norepinephrine**.

*See also:* Pharmacotherapy; Treatment of Depression

*Bibliography*

*Alpha Blockers.* Mayo Clinic, December 18, 2008, http://www.mayoclinic.com/health/alpha-blockers/HI00055.

Appelberg, B. G., E. K. Syvälahti, T. E. Koskinen, O. P. Mehtonen, T. T. Muhonen, and H. H. Naukkarinen. "Patients with Severe Depression May Benefit from Buspirone Augmentation of Selective Serotonin Reuptake Inhibitors: Results from a Placebo-Controlled, Randomized, Double-Blind, Placebo Wash-In Study." *Journal of Clinical Psychiatry* 62 (2001): 448–452.

Barbosa, L., M. Berk, and M. Vorster. "A Double-Blind, Randomized, Placebo-Controlled Trial of Augmentation With Lamotrigine or Placebo in Patients Concomitantly Treated With Fluoxetine for Resistant Major Depressive Episodes." *Journal of Clinical Psychiatry* 64 (2003): 403–407.

Blier, Pierre. "Medication Combination and Augmentation Strategies in the Treatment of Major Depression." In *The American Psychiatric Publishing Textbook of Mood Disorders,* by Dan J. Stein, David J. Kupfer, and Alan F. Schatzberg, eds., 509–524. Washington, DC: American Psychiatric Publishing, 2006.

Masand, Prakash S., Vishal S. Anand, and John F. Tanquary. "Psychostimulant Augmentation of Second Generation Antidepressants: A Case Series." *Depression and Anxiety* 7 (1998): 89–91.

Moret, Chantal. "Combination/Augmentation Strategies for Improving the Treatment of Depression." *Neuropsychiatric Disease and Treatment* 1 (2005): 301–309.

Nierenberg, Andrew A., Maurizio Fava, Madhukar H. Trivedi, Stephen R. Wisniewski, Michael E. Thase, Patrick J. McGrath, et al. "A Comparison of Lithium and $T_3$ Augmentation Following Two Failed Medication Treatments for Depression: A STAR*D Report." *American Journal of Psychiatry* 163 (2006): 1519–1530.

**AXELROD, JULIUS (1912–2004).** Julius Axelrod was a U.S. pharmacologist and neuroscientist who won the 1970 Nobel Prize in Physiology or Medicine for his pioneering work on **neurotransmitters**, chemical messengers in the brain. His research on brain chemistry in the early 1960s played a seminal role in the development of modern **antidepressants**.

Axelrod studied the process by which a neurotransmitter called **norepinephrine** is stored and released by cells as needed. He also described **reuptake**, the mechanism by which a neurotransmitter is absorbed back into the cell that originally released it as a way of regulating how much of that chemical is available in the brain. His findings were instrumental in the development of several types of antidepressants that act by blocking the reuptake of one or more neurotransmitters.

***Early Career Highlights.*** A New York City native, Axelrod earned his bachelor's degree from the College of the City of New York in 1933. After graduation, he applied to several medical schools but was rejected by all of them, so he began working instead as a lab assistant and research chemist. During this period, Axelrod took night courses in chemistry, completing a master's degree at New York University in 1941.

Axelrod also began a life-altering collaboration with U.S. biochemist Bernard B. Brodie (1907–1989), then at Goldwater Memorial Hospital in New York. Brodie and Axelrod set out to study the serious side effects associated with certain headache remedies of the day. They learned that the drugs were metabolized into two substances with toxic effects, but a third, safer metabolic product called acetaminophen was probably the painkilling agent.

The men advocated using acetaminophen alone, and their discovery, never patented, led to its marketing under the brand name Tylenol. It was the first of Axelrod's many important contributions to pharmacology.

In 1950, Axelrod took a job at the newly formed National Institutes of Health (NIH). Brodie had moved there as well, and Axelrod continued working in Brodie's lab, but with growing independence. Although Axelrod had never worked with enzymes before, he soon discovered a class of drug-metabolizing enzymes, a major pharmacological advance.

All this was accomplished before Axelrod even had a doctoral degree. In 1954, he took a leave of absence to go back to school. A year later, at the age of 42, he received a Ph.D. from George Washington University. Upon returning to the NIH, he was made head of pharmacology in the clinical science lab at the National Institute of Mental Health.

**Discovery of Reuptake.**    Axelrod's attention soon turned to neurotransmitters. Once a neurotransmitter has delivered its chemical message within the brain, it still needs to be disposed of. Because the first-known neurotransmitter, called acetylcholine, is broken down and inactivated by an enzyme, scientists assumed that was the primary disposal method. But Axelrod showed that norepinephrine is removed from the tiny gap between cells by another means: The chemical is reabsorbed into the cell that originally released it, a process he dubbed "reuptake." It soon became clear that reuptake is the rule rather than the exception for most neurotransmitters.

Axelrod also realized that drugs could work by inhibiting reuptake. Trying to improve upon the first schizophrenia medication, scientists had recently developed a drug called imipramine. Although imipramine did not help schizophrenia, it did turn out to work unexpectedly well for relieving depression. Axelrod showed that imipramine blocked the reuptake of norepinephrine, increasing the brain's available supply. This discovery spawned a whole new approach to antidepressants.

For his neurotransmitter research, Axelrod shared the Nobel Prize with German-born British biophysicist Bernard Katz (1911–2003) and Swedish physiologist Ulf von Euler (1905–1983). Katz showed how neurotransmitters are stored in and released by nerve endings, and von Euler showed that norepinephrine acts as a neurotransmitter. In announcing the prize, the Nobel Foundation noted that the independent discoveries of these three scientists "contribute in solving principal questions concerning the neurotransmitters, their storage, release, and inactivation."

**Axelrod in Perspective.**    Axelrod's description of reuptake set off a flurry of research activity. This research led to the development of antidepressants specifically designed to block reuptake, starting with the popular **selective serotonin reuptake inhibitors**. These medications revolutionized the way depression is treated.

Axelrod made other significant contributions during his long career at the NIH, including the discovery that **melatonin** is the pineal gland's key hormone. Although he formally retired in 1984, Axelrod remained a frequent fixture at the lab. Even after his death at age 92 in 2004, Axelrod's work continues to inspire the next generation of pharmacologists and neuroscientists.

*Bibliography*

*Julius Axelrod (1912–2004).* National Institutes of Health, http://history.nih.gov/exhibits/bowman/BioAxel.htm.

*Julius Axelrod: Biography.* Nobel Foundation, http://nobelprize.org/nobel_prizes/medicine/laureates/1970/axelrod-bio.html.

*Nobel Laureate Axelrod, Neuroscience Pioneer.* National Institute of Mental Health, June 26, 2008, http://www.nimh.nih.gov/science-news/2004/nobel-laureate-axelrod-neuroscience-pioneer .shtml.

Snyder, Solomon H. "Obituary: Julius Axelrod (1912–2004)." *Nature* 433 (February 10, 2005).

*The Nobel Prize in Physiology or Medicine 1970.* Nobel Foundation, October 1970, http://nobel prize.org/nobel_prizes/medicine/laureates/1970/press.html.

# B

**BECK, AARON T. (1921– ).** Aaron T. Beck is a U.S. psychiatrist who played a key role in developing **cognitive therapy**. This form of **psychotherapy** helps people recognize and change self-defeating thought patterns that contribute to their emotional and behavioral problems. Beck's approach to therapy, introduced in the early 1960s, grew out of his work with and study of depressed patients. Today it stands as one of the best-validated treatments for depression.

Beck's treatment approach is based on a model of depression that views the problem as an outgrowth of systematic errors in thinking. In early research, Beck found that people with depression had a negative bias in their views of themselves, the world, and the future. Concrete feedback that disproved these views had an immediate positive effect on their feelings and behavior. In particular, it boosted their mood and increased optimism and motivation. Thus, it gave people a way to reduce their own suffering.

Beck also is an innovator in the area of assessment. Over the years, he has developed several questionnaires for quickly and easily assessing psychological symptoms. The best known of these is the **Beck Depression Inventory**, which is widely used in both research and clinical practice.

Building upon his work with depression, Beck has since applied his theories and techniques to the identification and treatment of suicide-prone individuals. According to Beck, hopelessness is one of the key psychological factors that drives people to **suicide**. He and his colleagues have shown that hopelessness, like depression, can be objectively measured and substantially reduced by cognitive interventions.

***Early Career Highlights.*** Beck was born in Providence, Rhode Island. A sickly child, he underwent several surgeries that led to a strong aversion to blood. He later recalled that he was motivated to attend medical school as a way of confronting and overcoming this fear.

Beck graduated from Yale Medical School in 1946. Although he initially intended to pursue a career in neurology, he soon became intrigued by recent advances in psychiatry. After a stint as assistant chief of neuropsychiatry at the Valley Forge Army Hospital during the Korean War, Beck joined the psychiatry department at the University of Pennsylvania in 1954. His association with the university would span more than half a century.

Beck began his career as a psychiatrist by studying and practicing psychoanalysis, a form of long-term psychotherapy originated by **Sigmund Freud** (1856–1939). Psychoanalysis stresses the influence of unconscious drives and wishes on behavior as well as the importance of childhood events in shaping later experiences. Beck set out to scientifically test the psychoanlaytic concept of depression as inwardly directed hostility, fully expecting that the concept would be validated. But when Beck's studies failed to support his hypotheses, he began to look for an alternate explanation.

***Cognitive Model of Depression.*** Beck found that people with depression often experienced what he called automatic thoughts—streams of negative thoughts that pop up spontaneously. These thoughts involved viewing themselves, the world, and the future in an unduly negative light. Beck also discovered that helping depressed patients recognize and evaluate their automatic thoughts led to the adoption of a more realistic thinking style. The shift in thinking, in turn, led to an improvement in emotional and behavioral symptoms.

Beck went on to elaborate a cognitive model of depression. He noted that people with depression tend to cling to their self-defeating thoughts, even in the face of objective evidence to the contrary. Beck attributed this tendency to relatively stable, underlying thought patterns, which he termed schemas.

According to Beck, a schema may be latent for some time until it is activated by a particular event. For example, a person who believes he is worthless unless he is successful in his career might do quite well at weathering a personal crisis, such as getting divorced. However, being laid off at work might activate the schema, pitching him into depression. The more active his schema became, the easier it would be to evoke in an ever-widening range of situations. Eventually, any hint of real or perceived failure might activate the schema, setting off a stream of depressingly negative thoughts.

Cognitive therapy interrupts this process by helping people assess their thoughts more accurately. Over time, a shift in thinking style occurs that makes people less vulnerable to depression. The same principles have since been applied to the treatment of a wide variety of mental and physical ailments, including certain **anxiety disorders**, **eating disorders**, **substance abuse**, chronic fatigue syndrome, and **chronic pain**.

***Beck in Perspective.*** Over his long career, Beck has received numerous awards and accolades, including the prestigious Albert Lasker Award for Clinical Medical Research in 2006. He has published over 500 articles, authored or coauthored 17 books, and lectured around the world. Beck is now professor emeritus of psychiatry at the University of Pennsylvania and president of the Beck Institute for Cognitive Therapy and Research.

Cognitive therapy is a dominant force in psychotherapy today. Its value for treating depression has been particularly well documented. As one of the founders of cognitive therapy, Beck has helped shape the current view of depression and its treatment.

*See also:* Personality Factors

***Further Information.*** Beck Institute for Cognitive Therapy and Research, One Belmont Avenue, Suite 700, Bala Cynwyd, PA 19004, (610) 664-3020, www.beckinstitute.org.

## Bibliography

Beck, Aaron, T., A. John Rush, Brian F. Shaw, and Gary Emery. *Cognitive Therapy of Depression.* New York: Guilford Press, 1979.

Krapp, Kristine, ed. "Aaron Temkin Beck," in *Psychologists and Their Theories for Students.* Vol. 1. Detroit, MI: Thomson Gale, 2005.

Millon, Theodore. *Masters of the Mind: Exploring the Story of Mental Illness from Ancient Times to the New Millennium.* New York: John Wiley and Sons, 2004.

Weishaar, Marjorie E. *Aaron T. Beck.* Thousand Oaks, CA: Sage Publications, 1993.

**BECK DEPRESSION INVENTORY.**    The Beck Depression Inventory (BDI) is a brief self-report questionnaire designed to assess the severity of depression symptoms in adolescents and adults. The questionnaire, developed by U.S. psychiatrist **Aaron T. Beck** (1921– ) and his colleagues, was first published in 1961. An updated version, the BDI-II, was introduced in 1996 to reflect the diagnostic criteria in the *Diagnostic and Statistical Manual of Mental Disorders, Fourth Edition.* Today the BDI-II is widely used for both clinical and research purposes.

Like its predecessor, the BDI-II is quick and easy to administer. It consists of 21 items, each of which presents four statements about a particular symptom of depression arranged in order of severity. People choose the statement that most closely matches how they have felt within the past two weeks. The test, which takes about five minutes to complete, is intended for use by individuals from 13 through 80 years old. The higher the resulting score, the more severe a person's depression symptoms are.

The primary clinical use of the BDI-II is to measure depression in people who have already been diagnosed with the disorder. Once treatment begins, the test may be repeated periodically to monitor any change in symptoms over time and see how well treatment is working. A second use of the test is to screen for depression in people who might have the illness, but who have not yet been diagnosed. Those who score in the depressed range on the test should then undergo a full diagnostic interview. The BDI-II score alone is not sufficient for making a diagnosis.

***Pros and Cons of the BDI-II.***    The BDI-II is among the most popular self-rating scales for measuring depression in clinical practice. The questionnaire and its predecessor also have been used in thousands of scientific studies. This popularity rests on a solid foundation. Assessments of the BDI-II have shown that it has very good reliability, the extent to which the results obtained are consistent and repeatable. The test also performs well when it comes to validity, the degree to which it actually measures what it purports to measure.

One yardstick of the questionnaire's validity is its ability to discriminate depression from other disorders. Research by Beck and others has shown that people with depression do indeed score higher on the BDI-II, on average, than those with anxiety or adjustment disorders. Also, as would be expected, those with more serious forms of depression tend to get higher scores than those with less serious forms.

On the downside, the structure of the questionnaire makes it quite easy for those taking it to discern which items indicate more or less severe symptoms. Therefore, the questionnaire may not be very accurate when taken by someone who wants to fake a good or bad score.

*See also:* Diagnosis of Depression; Screening Tests

*Bibliography*

Arbisi, Paul A. and Richard F. Farmer. "Beck Depression Inventory-II." *The Fourteenth Mental Measurements Yearbook,* http://www.unl.edu/buros.

*Beck Depression Inventory-II (BDI-II).* Harcourt Assessment, http://www.harcourtassessment.com.

Beck, A. T., C. H. Ward, M. Mendelson, J. Mock, and J. Erbaugh. "An Inventory for Measuring Depression." *Archives of General Psychiatry* 4 (1961): 53–63.

Cohen, Ronald Jay, and Mark E. Swerdlik. *Psychological Testing and Assessment: An Introduction to Tests and Measurement.* 5th ed. Boston: McGraw-Hill, 2002.

Richter, Paul, Joachim Werner, Andrés Heerlein, Alfred Kraus, and Heinrich Sauer. "On the Validity of the Beck Depression Inventory." *Psychopathology* 31 (1998): 160–168.

Yonkers, Kimberly A., and Jacqueline A. Samson. "Mood Disorders Measures." In *Handbook of Psychiatric Measures,* 2nd ed., by A. John Rush Jr., Michael B. First, and Deborah Blacker, eds., 499–528. Washington, DC: American Psychiatric Publishing, 2008.

**BEHAVIORAL THERAPY.** Behavioral therapy is a form of **psychotherapy** that helps people identify and change maladaptive behaviors. In practice, it often is combined with **cognitive therapy**, which focuses on helping people recognize and change self-defeating thought patterns. This combined approach, known as **cognitive-behavioral therapy** (CBT), is one of the best-validated forms of treatment for depression.

Behavioral therapy is grounded in the principles of learning. The focus is on current behaviors and the environmental events that sustain or eliminate them. Therapy is intended to help people decrease undesirable behaviors and increase desirable ones, regardless of whether or not they gain insight into the origins of their problems.

From a behavioral perspective, symptoms of depression are viewed as behaviors that have been learned—and thus, can be unlearned. Then new, more adaptive behaviors can be learned to take their place. A number of techniques have been developed to facilitate this learning. Some have become so familiar and accepted that they are now widely used not only by behavioral therapists, but also by therapists from other orientations.

***Historical Roots.*** Behavioral therapy traces its roots back to Ivan Pavlov (1849–1936), the Russian physiologist who first introduced the concept of classical conditioning, also known as Pavlovian conditioning. In this form of learning, an initially neutral stimulus (the conditioned stimulus) is paired with another stimulus (the unconditioned stimulus) that elicits a reflex response. After repeated pairings, the conditioned stimulus becomes able to elicit the response by itself. In the classic demonstration of this principle, a bell (the conditioned stimulus) is rung when food (the unconditioned stimulus) is presented to a dog, causing the dog to salivate. Over time, simply ringing the bell is enough to make the dog salivate, even when no food is present.

Pavlov opened the door to later behavioral theorists, most notably U.S. psychologist B. F. Skinner (1904–1990). Although classical conditioning was a breakthrough discovery, it applied to only a limited number of real-life situations. Skinner greatly expanded the scope of learning theory when he introduced the concept of operant conditioning, also known as instrumental conditioning. In this form of learning, behavioral change occurs as a function of the consequences of a behavior.

In the classic Skinnerian experiment, a lab rat has to press a lever to get a food pellet or a pigeon has a peck a disk to get some grain. When the food reward is presented, it strengthens the pressing or pecking behavior, a process known as reinforcement. When the food reward is withdrawn, the behavior declines, a process known as extinction.

Modern behavioral therapy uses the principles of operant and classical conditioning to understand and change maladaptive behaviors. For instance, let's say an ambitious junior executive becomes depressed after failing to advance as quickly as expected at work. A behavioral therapist might view the person's depression as a consequence of too little reinforcement in the work environment. Therapy might focus on teaching the person how to get sufficient reinforcement, perhaps by rewarding herself for reaching goals or learning social skills that attract the attention of the boss.

***The Process at a Glance.*** Behavioral therapists take an active role in guiding the treatment process. Sessions are relatively structured, and clients may be asked to monitor their behavior or practice exercises at home. A wide variety of techniques are employed in behavioral therapy. Following are some that are commonly used for treating symptoms of depression.

*Pleasant Activity Scheduling.* This technique is based on the behavioral theory of depression developed by U.S. psychologist **Peter M. Lewinsohn** (1930– ). The theory states that depression occurs when people start receiving less reinforcement for their actions. As a result, they begin to do less, which leads to even fewer rewards. To reverse this downward cycle, clients work with a therapist to schedule more pleasant, satisfying activities in their day. The goal is to provide more reinforcement for staying active and engaged.

*Self-Control Therapy.* In this form of behavioral therapy, clients set specific goals for themselves with the aid of a therapist. Then they track their own behavior with diaries and other self-monitoring tools, and they learn how to use self-reinforcement to strengthen desired behaviors. Self-control therapy also may involve a behavioral contract, a written agreement between the client and therapist in which the client agrees to carry out certain behaviors.

*Social Skills Training.* This set of behavioral techniques is geared toward teaching people the skills they need to interact successfully in specific social situations, such as on a date or in a job interview. One key technique is behavior rehearsal, in which clients practice handling difficult social situations with the therapist as a way of preparing for the real thing. Social skills training also may include assertiveness training, in which people learn how to express their opinions, feelings, and preferences in a clear, direct, and appropriate manner.

**Benefits for Depression.** The benefits of behavioral therapy for depression have been investigated in numerous studies. Overall, the results suggest that behavioral therapy is about as effective for treating depression as cognitive therapy or **antidepressants**, and more

---

### Getting into a Vicious Cycle

In *Control Your Depression* (1978), Lewinsohn and his coauthors offer a view of depression that is rooted in behavioral principles:

> Except when we are sleeping, we are continuously interacting with our environment. Whether we are watching television, typing a report, talking to a salesperson, interacting with our children or spouse, talking to someone on the telephone, or just sitting and thinking about something from the past—we are always doing something. Our interaction with our environment is continuous.
>
> In a general way we can put our interactions into three groups: those that lead to *positive* outcomes (you finish a task and someone compliments you on it); those that have *neutral* outcomes (you drive to the store); and those that have *negative* outcomes (being criticized by someone who is important to you). When too few of our interactions have positive outcomes and when too many of them have negative outcomes, we start feeling depressed . . .
>
> With depression, it's rather easy to get into a vicious cycle. Having few interactions with positive outcomes causes you to feel depressed; the more depressed you feel, the less motivated you are to engage in the kinds of activities which might have had positive outcomes; this causes you to feel even more depressed, which, in turn, causes you to become even less active. And so it goes on and on. This circle continues until you feel very depressed and are very inactive.

effective than brief **psychodynamic therapy**—a form of therapy that emphasizes the role of past events in molding current experiences as well as the importance of unconscious influences on behavior.

Specific behavioral techniques have been studied individually as well. A recent analysis of 16 studies that looked at activity scheduling as a depression treatment found that it worked about as well as cognitive therapy. In addition, the benefits lasted after formal therapy ended, indicating that clients learned skills they were able to keep using on their own.

One of the most appealing things about behavioral therapy is its direct, down-to-earth quality. Many behavioral techniques are relatively uncomplicated, quick to learn, and easy to implement. They can be used alone, but they are also readily incorporated into other treatment approaches, making them especially adaptable tools for dealing with depression.

*See also:* Acceptance and Commitment Therapy; Treatment of Depression

**Further Information.** Association for Behavioral and Cognitive Therapies, 305 7th Avenue, 16th Floor, New York, NY 10001, (212) 647-1890, www.abct.org.

## Bibliography

American Psychiatric Association Work Group on Major Depressive Disorder. *Practice Guideline for the Treatment of Patients with Major Depressive Disorder.* 2nd ed. Washington, DC: American Psychiatric Publishing, 2000.

Cuijpers, Pim, Annemieke van Straten, and Lisanne Warmerdam. "Behavioral Activation Treatments of Depression: A Meta-analysis." *Clinical Psychology Review* 27 (2007): 318–326.

Lewinsohn, Peter M. and Christopher S. Amenson. "Some Relations Between Pleasant and Unpleasant Mood-Related Events and Depression." *Journal of Abnormal Psychology* 87 (1978): 644–654.

Lewinsohn, Peter M. and Julian Libet. "Pleasant Events, Activity Schedules, and Depressions." *Journal of Abnormal Psychology* 79 (1972): 291–295.

Persons, Jacqueline B., Joan Davidson, and Michael A. Tompkins. *Essential Components of Cognitive-Behavior Therapy for Depression.* Washington, DC: American Psychological Association, 2001.

U.S. Department of Health and Human Services. *Mental Health: A Report of the Surgeon General.* Rockville, MD: U.S. Department of Health and Human Services, 1999.

**BIBLIOTHERAPY.** Bibliotherapy refers to the use of **self-help** books to manage psychological or physical problems. The first best-selling guide to psychological issues may have been *The Human Mind* (1930), by U.S. psychiatrist Karl A. Menninger (1893–1990). In the intervening decades, the self-help genre has blossomed into a highly lucrative industry and integral part of American culture. Among the popular titles are numerous books that aim to help people take control of depression.

Most self-help books are purchased by individuals who use them on their own. However, some mental health professionals also recommend that clients read books to supplement what they are learning in formal **psychotherapy**. Many books addressed to readers with depression take a cognitive-behavioral approach, offering hands-on advice about how to identify and change maladaptive patterns of thinking and behaving.

**Benefits for Depression.** A number of studies have shown that self-help books can indeed help people with depression improve their mood. In some cases, the benefits are comparable to those seen with traditional therapy. Follow-up studies show that the improvements may be long-lasting as well.

There are several advantages to this approach. It is simple, inexpensive, and available to anyone. It empowers individuals to take charge of their own treatment, which may lead to enhanced self-confidence and independence. Plus, it educates people about mental health, making them more informed consumers if they ever need professional care. When books are combined with formal therapy, they may speed up the learning process.

On the downside, there are thousands of self-help books, and they differ widely in quality and approach. A book that relies on unproven techniques or makes unrealistic promises could do more harm than good. In addition, using even the best self-help book requires concentration and motivation, which may be in short supply when people are depressed. It also requires adequate reading skills, which is a barrier for some people.

Self-help books alone may be helpful for some people with milder depressive symptoms. Those with more severe symptoms generally need the help of a mental health professional, however. In addition, even people with milder problems might want to seek professional guidance if they try self-help to no avail. The same technique may be more successful when a trained professional is there to offer suggestions and support.

***Book-Buying Guidelines.*** In a recent study of 50 top-selling self-help books about common psychological problems, expert evaluators found that only half of the books prepared readers for possible setbacks and failures. Just 42 percent offered what were judged as reasonable expectations about the potential benefits of self-help techniques.

The same study found that the best books tended to focus on a limited range of issues; for instance, focusing specifically on depression or mood problems. But because these problems often coexist with other conditions, such as **anxiety disorders** or **substance abuse**, it is helpful if the book also discusses how such conditions may impact **recovery**.

A good self-help book should offer a clear program of self-treatment with easy-to-understand exercises. Other topics that should be addressed include how to recognize the target problem, how to monitor progress, how to keep the problem from recurring once it gets better, what to do if it fails to improve, and when to seek professional help.

---

### Recommended Reading

In the study of 50 popular self-help books, psychologists rated each book on several dimensions, including practical utility, scientific accuracy, and reasonable expectations. Following are the top-rated books on depression, presented in order with the highest-ranked book first.

Burns, David B. *Feeling Good: The New Mood Therapy.* Rev. ed. New York: HarperCollins, 1999.

Ross, Julia. *The Mood Cure: The 4-Step Program to Take Charge of Your Emotions—Today.* New York: Penguin, 2003.

Yapko, Michael D. *Breaking the Patterns of Depression.* New York: Main Street Books, 1998.

Greenberger, Dennis, and Christine A. Padesky. *Mind Over Mood: Change How You Feel by Changing the Way You Think.* New York: Guilford Press, 1995.

Gilbert, Paul. *Overcoming Depression: A Step-by-Step Approach to Gaining Control over Depression.* 2nd ed. New York: Oxford University Press, 2001.

Copeland, Mary Ellen. *The Depression Workbook.* 2nd ed. Oakland, CA: New Harbinger, 2001.

---

### Bibliography

Floyd, Mark, Forrest Scogin, Nancy L. McKendree-Smith, Donna L. Floyd, and Paul D. Rokke. "Cognitive Therapy for Depression." *Behavior Modification* 28 (2004): 297–318.

Floyd, Mark, Noelle Rohen, Jodie A. M. Shackelford, Karen L. Hubbard, Marsha B. Parnell, Forrest Scogin, et al. "Two-Year Follow-Up of Bibliotherapy and Individual Cognitive Therapy for Depressed Older Adults." *Behavior Modification* 30 (2006): 281–294.

Floyd, Mark. "Bibliotherapy as an Adjunct to Psychotherapy for Depression in Older Adults." *Journal of Clinical Psychology/In Session* 50 (2003): 187–195.

Gregory, Robert J., Sally Schwer Canning, Tracy W. Lee and Joan C. Wise. "Cognitive Bibliotherapy for Depression: A Meta-analysis." *Professional Psychology: Research and Practice* 35 (2004): 275–280.

Menninger, Karl A. *The Human Mind.* New York: Alfred A. Knopf, 1930.

Morgan, Amy J., and Anthony F. Jorm. "Self-Help Interventions for Depressive Disorders and Depressive Symptoms: A Systematic Review." *Annals of General Psychiatry* 7 (2008): 13.

Redding, Richard E., James D. Herbert, Evan M. Forman, and Brandon A. Gaudiano. "Popular Self-Help Books for Anxiety, Depression, and Trauma: How Scientifically Grounded and Useful Are They?" *Psychology: Research and Practice* 39 (2008): 537–545.

**BIOPSYCHOSOCIAL MODEL.** The biopsychosocial model states that biological, psychological, and social factors are closely intertwined, and all are important for causing disease or promoting health. As a practical matter, biological and **genetic factors** are often grouped together, as are social and environmental ones. When applied to depression, the model unifies many theories of causation under a single, broad umbrella.

As a guiding principle in modern medicine, the biopsychosocial model was introduced by U.S. psychiatrist George Engel (1913–1999) in the 1970s. It was offered as an alternative to the dominant biomedical view, which focuses almost exclusively on identifying and remediating biological causes of disease.

Researchers and clinicians working within a biopsychosocial framework look for all the biological, psychological, and social factors that might be acting together to cause depression. Rather than operating independently, these factors are thought to influence each other in an interdependent way. Current concepts of depression as a multifactorial disorder owe a debt to the biopsychosocial model.

*See also:* Causes of Depression; Cognitive Factors; Environmental Factors

*Bibliography*

Dowling, A. Scott. "George Engel, M.D. (1913–1999)." *American Journal of Psychiatry* 162 (2005): 2039.

Engel, G. L. "The Need for a New Medical Model: A Challenge for Biomedicine." *Science* 196 (1977): 129–136.

Lindau, Stacy Tessler, Edward O. Laumann, Wendy Levinson, and Linda J. Waite. "Synthesis of Scientific Disciplines in Pursuit of Health: The Interactive Biopsychosocial Model." *Perspectives in Biology and Medicine* 46 (2003): S74-S86.

Schotte, Chris K. W., Bart Van Den Bossche, Dirk De Doncker, Stephan Claes, and Paul Cosyns. "A Biopsychosocial Model as a Guide for Psychoeducation and Treatment of Depression." *Depression and Anxiety* 23 (2006): 312–324.

**BIPOLAR DISORDER.** Bipolar disorder—formerly known as manic depression—is a mental disorder that causes unusual shifts in mood, energy, and ability to function. People with bipolar disorder alternate between moods that are overly low (depression) and overly high (**mania**). The shifts are more serious and disabling than the normal ups and downs that everyone experiences in day-to-day life.

Left untreated, bipolar disorder can damage relationships and wreak havoc with life at home, work, or school. People with the disorder have an increased risk of **suicide** and **substance abuse**. During manic periods, many also engage in self-destructive behaviors, such as reckless driving, unsafe sex, and spending sprees. In severe cases, some people even experience psychotic symptoms, such as delusions (distorted beliefs that are seriously out of touch with reality) and hallucinations (sensory perceptions of things that are not really there).

The dramatic mood swings of bipolar disorder can last for weeks or months, creating chaos not only for the person with the illness, but also for family and friends. Even once the person gets better, the disorder tends to recur, and without treatment, it usually gets worse with time.

Fortunately, effective help is available. In most cases, proper treatment can reduce the frequency and severity of bipolar episodes and help people lead happier, healthier lives. But like diabetes and asthma, bipolar disorder is a chronic condition that requires long-term treatment. Often, that means lifelong attention to managing the disorder.

***Having an Episode.*** The overly high and low periods seen in bipolar disorder are known as episodes. These episodes can take four different forms: mania, hypomania, **major depression** and mixed.

*Mania.* During an episode of mania, people experience an excessively high, grandiose, or irritable mood that lasts for at least a week. (This time requirement is waived if the symptoms are severe enough to necessitate hospitalization.) When the person's mood is high or grandiose, at least three of the following symptoms must be present: (1) inflated self-esteem or exaggerated ideas about oneself, (2) decreased need for sleep, (3) unusual talkativeness or a feeling of pressure to keep talking, (4) racing thoughts or abrupt changes of topic when speaking, (5) easy distractibility, (6) increased activity or restlessness, and (7) excessive involvement in pleasurable but high-risk activities, such as sexual indiscretions or risky investments. If the person's mood is only irritable, at least four of these seven symptoms must occur. The symptoms cause marked problems in daily life or personal relationships, reach psychotic proportions, or require hospitalization to prevent harm to self or others.

*Hypomania.* The symptoms of hypomania are the same as those for mania, but they only have to last a minimum of four days. Also, although the person's mood is clearly different from usual, the change is not drastic enough to seriously impair functioning, necessitate hospitalization, or lead to psychotic symptoms. In fact, the milder burst of energy associated with hypomania may feel good to the person and lead to greater productivity. Even when family and friends come to recognize the mood swings as a problem, the person may deny that anything is wrong. Without treatment, however, hypomania sometimes turns into more severe mania or switches into depression.

### The Upside of Bipolar

From ancient Greek philosophers to nineteenth-century Romantic poets, great thinkers through the ages have remarked upon the apparent link between genius and madness. In her 1993 book *Touched with Fire: Manic-Depressive Illness and the Artistic Temperament,* U.S. psychiatry professor Kay Redfield Jamison (1946– ) traces a more specific connection between artistic creativity and bipolar disorder. Jamison, who has written about her personal experience with the disorder, argues that bipolar illness may occur disproportionately in people with creative talent, such as poets, authors, composers, and artists.

More recently, several studies have provided scientific evidence to bolster such scholarly claims. For instance, a study by Stanford researchers found that children who had bipolar disorder or who were at high risk for the illness tended to score higher on a creativity test than other children did.

*Major Depression.* In an episode of **major depression**, people have one or both of two core symptoms: (1) a low mood nearly all the time and (2) loss of interest or enjoyment in almost everything. At the same time, they may experience associated problems: (3) changes in weight or appetite, (4) trouble sleeping or oversleeping, (5) restless activity or sloweddown movements, (6) constant tiredness or lack of energy, (7) feelings of worthlessness or inappropriate guilt, (8) difficulty concentrating or making decisions, and (9) recurring thoughts of death or suicide. All told, at least five of the nine symptoms must be present for a minimum of two weeks. The symptoms are serious enough to cause significant distress or problems in daily life.

*Mixed.* During a **mixed episode**, a person simultaneously experiences the symptoms of both mania and major depression nearly every day for at least one week. The person may be in a very down, hopeless mood while at the same time feeling highly energized. Common features of a mixed state include restlessness, trouble sleeping, changes in appetite, thoughts of suicide, and psychotic symptoms.

**Criteria for Diagnosis.** The symptoms of bipolar disorder are defined by the ***Diagnostic and Statistical Manual of Mental Disorders, Fourth Edition, Text Revision*** (*DSM-IV-TR*), a diagnostic guidebook published by the American Psychiatric Association and widely used by mental health professionals from many disciplines. According to the *DSM-IV-TR*, there are three types of bipolar disorder: **bipolar I**, **bipolar II**, and **bipolar disorder not otherwise specified**.

*Bipolar I.* This is the classic form of bipolar disorder, characterized by the occurrence of at least one manic or mixed episode. Often, but not always, there also has been an episode of major depression.

*Bipolar II.* In this form of bipolar disorder, the person has never had a full-fledged manic or mixed episode. Instead, there has been at least one episode of hypomania as well as at least one of major depression.

*Bipolar Disorder Not Otherwise Specified.* This catchall category includes other forms of bipolar illness that cause problems serious enough to need treatment but don't meet all the criteria for bipolar I, bipolar II, or **cyclothymia** (a disorder characterized by moods that alternate between hypomania and relatively mild depression). For example, some people have all the symptoms of mania or major depression, but they move so quickly from one mood to the other that they don't fulfill the time requirements. Others have

---

### Melville's Melancholy

"The intensest light of reason and revelation combined, can not shed such blazonings upon the deeper truths in man, as will sometimes proceed from his own profoundest gloom. Utter darkness is then his light, and cat-like he distinctly sees all objects through a medium which is mere blindness to common vision."—U.S. author Herman Melville (1819–1891) in *Pierre* (1852)

Few novelists have written more affectingly than Melville about depression, a subject with which he was intimately familiar. Melville came from a family with a history of mental illness, and he himself may have suffered from **bipolar disorder**—a condition in which the intense lows of depression alternate with extreme highs, known as **mania**. During extended downturns in mood, he could be irritable, withdrawn, listless, pessimistic, and preoccupied with thoughts of death and suicide—classic symptoms of depression.

Yet Melville—best known for his masterpiece *Moby Dick* (1851)—was also a critically acclaimed author whose haunting prose still speaks to new generations of readers. As the quote above hints, some of the enduring truths in his writing may have emanated from his own profound gloom.

repeated episodes of hypomania without alternating periods of depression. And many children and young adolescents develop a mixture of mania and depression that is disruptive, but does not quite qualify as a mixed episode.

*Course of the Illness.* Bipolar disorder can start at any age from childhood to late life. However, it typically begins in late adolescence or early adulthood. At first, it may not be recognized as an illness, and people may suffer for years before they finally get proper diagnosis and treatment.

*Bipolar I.* More than 90 percent of people who have a first episode of mania go on to have another one in the future. Most people with bipolar I disorder are free of symptoms between episodes, but 20 percent to 30 percent have some residual mood symptoms. Even those whose mood seems to return to normal often continue to have problems getting along at work, school, or in relationships.

The interval between episodes tends to shorten as time goes on. About five percent to 15 percent of people with bipolar I disorder display **rapid cycling**, which means they have four or more mood episodes in a single year. For some, it reaches the point of multiple episodes in a single week or even within the same day. Rapid cycling is more common in women than in men.

*Bipolar II.* The course of bipolar II is similar to that of bipolar I. But only about 15 percent of those with the disorder continue to have some mood symptoms and problems in daily life between episodes. Within five years, five percent to 15 percent of people with bipolar II have a manic episode, which changes their diagnosis to bipolar I.

*Causes and Risk Factors.* Almost three percent of U.S. adults have bipolar disorder in any given year, according to the National Institute of Mental Health. The occurrence rate in older adolescents seems to be similar. And the first signs of the disorder may appear even earlier, often starting out as major depression, cyclothymia, or **dysthymia** (a relatively mild but quite long-lasting form of depression).

**Genetic factors** seem to play a role. Studies of identical twins, who share the same genes, have found that if one twin has bipolar disorder, the second twin is more likely than other siblings to also develop the illness. However, even the identical twin of someone with bipolar disorder does not always become ill, indicating that genes are not the whole story.

**Environmental factors** that may contribute to bipolar disorder include significant losses and high **stress**. Some people with the disorder also may have **circadian rhythms** (daily biological rhythms) that are out of sync with the outside world. These circadian disruptions could help explain the sleep disturbances seen in mania and depression. It is also possible that abnormal circadian rhythms don't cause the illness but do make it worse once it starts.

**Brain imaging** has shown that the brains of people with bipolar disorder tend to differ from the brains of healthy individuals. For instance, bipolar disorder has been associated with a decreased number of nerve cells in part of the **hippocampus**, a brain structure that plays a role in learning, emotion, and memory. The disorder also has been linked to a decreased number and density of support cells in the **prefrontal cortex**, part of the brain involved in higher thought, problem solving, short-term memory, and emotion.

Abnormalities in certain chemicals that act as messengers within the brain may come into play as well. Two brain chemicals that seem to play key roles in depression are **serotonin** and **norepinephrine**. The biochemical changes involved in mania are less well understood.

*Treatment of Bipolar Disorder.* With proper treatment, most people with bipolar disorder—even those who are severely affected—start to feel considerably better. Treatment helps even out mood swings and relieve symptoms. A combination of medication and **psychotherapy** is usually most effective.

Medications called **mood stabilizers** are prescribed to help keep moods on a more even keel. **Lithium**, the oldest and best-known mood-stabilizing drug, is still widely prescribed. However, other medications called **anticonvulsants**, originally developed to help prevent seizures, also help regulate moods. For maximum effect, anticonvulsant medications may be combined with lithium or with each other. When these medications alone don't provide enough relief, newer **antipsychotics**, originally designed to prevent or relieve psychotic symptoms, may help slow down racing thoughts to a more manageable speed.

**Antidepressants** were once commonly used to treat the depression phase of bipolar disorder. However, their use is now controversial, due to evidence that they may sometimes trigger a sudden switch to mania. When insomnia is a problem, a sedative may be prescribed.

*Psychological Approaches.* Psychotherapy can provide emotional support and teach useful skills to people with bipolar disorder and their families. Research has shown that appropriate psychotherapy can improve mood stability, reduce hospitalizations, and enhance the ability to get along in daily life.

Two types of psychotherapy that may be particularly helpful are **cognitive-behavioral therapy** (CBT) and interpersonal and social rhythm therapy. CBT helps people with bipolar disorder learn to recognize and change dysfunctional thought and behavior patterns that are contributing to their illness. Interpersonal and social rhythm therapy helps people improve their relationships and regularize their routines. Regular daily routines and sleep schedules may help ward off future episodes of mania.

**Psychoeducation** can help people with bipolar disorder learn how to manage their illness at home and recognize signs of a relapse so any necessary changes can be made early, before symptoms become too severe. **Family therapy** can help reduce the stress and conflict in family life that often results from or contributes to bipolar symptoms.

Bipolar disorder is a challenging condition to live with. Yet proper treatment can help smooth out extreme peaks and valleys in mood and behavior. With ongoing treatment, most people with bipolar disorder can look forward to a much-improved quality of life.

*See also:* Mood Disorders

***Further Information.*** Child and Adolescent Bipolar Foundation, 1000 Skokie Boulevard, Suite 570, Wilmette, IL 60091, (847) 256-8525, www.bpkids.org.

Depression and Bipolar Support Alliance, 730 N. Franklin Street, Suite 501, Chicago, IL 60610, (800) 826-3632, www.dbsalliance.org, www.peersupport.org, www.facingus.org.

## Bibliography

American Psychiatric Association. *Diagnostic and Statistical Manual of Mental Disorders.* 4th ed., text rev. Washington, DC: American Psychiatric Association, 2000.

*Bipolar Disorder.* Mayo Clinic, January 4, 2008, http://www.mayoclinic.com/health/bipolar-disorder/DS00356.

*Bipolar Disorder.* National Institute of Mental Health, April 3, 2008, http://www.nimh.nih.gov/health/publications/bipolar-disorder/complete-publication.shtml.

Evans, Dwight L., and Linda Wasmer Andrews. *If Your Adolescent Has Depression or Bipolar Disorder: An Essential Resource for Parents.* New York: Oxford University Press, 2005.

Jamison, Kay Redfield. *Touched with Fire: Manic-Depressive Illness and the Artistic Temperament.* New York: Free Press, 1993.

*Let's Talk Facts About Bipolar Disorder.* American Psychiatric Association, 2005, http://www.healthyminds.org/multimedia/bipolardisorder.pdf.

*Medications for Depression and Bipolar Disorder.* Depression and Bipolar Support Alliance, September 11, 2006, http://www.dbsalliance.org/site/PageServer?pagename=about_depression_medications.

Mondimore, Francis Mark. *Bipolar Disorder: A Guide for Patients and Families.* Baltimore, MD: Johns Hopkins University Press, 1999.

*Rapid Cycling and Its Treatment.* Depression and Bipolar Support Alliance, May 4, 2006, http://www.dbsalliance.org/site/PageServer?pagename=about_publications_rapidcycling.

Simeonova, Diana I., Kiki D. Chang, Connie Strong, and Terence A. Ketter. "Creativity in Familial Bipolar Disorder." *Journal of Psychiatric Research* 39 (2005): 623–631.

**BIPOLAR DISORDER NOT OTHERWISE SPECIFIED.** "Bipolar disorder not otherwise specified" (BP-NOS) is a catchall term that is used when **bipolar disorder** is serious enough to need treatment but does not fulfill the criteria for any established disorder. To make a diagnosis, mental health professionals rely on the ***Diagnostic and Statistical Manual of Mental Disorders, Fourth Edition, Text Revision*** (*DSM-IV-TR*). But this manual cannot cover every possible manifestation of bipolar disorder, so the BP-NOS category is included to give professionals more latitude for making a judgment call.

Bipolar disorder involves moods that alternate between overly high (**mania** or hypomania) and overly low (**major depression**). Some people have all the requisite symptoms during periods of mania or major depression, but they cycle so rapidly from one mood to the other that they don't fulfill the time requirements. Others have repeated episodes of hypomania without alternating periods of depression. And still others develop a mixture of mania and depression that is disruptive, but does not quite qualify as a **mixed episode**, in which the person simultaneously meets all the criteria for both mania and major depression nearly every day for at least one week.

The BP-NOS designation may be especially useful for children and young adolescents. They often fall just short of meeting diagnostic criteria, which were originally based on adult experiences. For example, young people frequently have all the requisite symptoms of mania, an excessively high, grandiose, or irritable mood that is disruptive enough to cause serious problems in daily life and relationships. However, their manic episodes may not last a full week, the minimum duration required. The BP-NOS category gives treatment providers an option for diagnosing bipolar disorder in such cases.

*See also:* Rapid Cycling

*Bibliography*

American Psychiatric Association. *Diagnostic and Statistical Manual of Mental Disorders.* 4th ed., text rev. Washington, DC: American Psychiatric Association, 2000.

Axelson, David, Boris Birmaher, Michael Strober, Mary Kay Gill, Sylvia Valeri, Laurel Chiappetta, et al. "Phenomenology of Children and Adolescents with Bipolar Spectrum Disorders." *Archives of General Psychiatry* 63 (2006): 1139–1148.

**BIPOLAR I.** Bipolar I is the classic form of **bipolar disorder**, a condition in which people alternate between extreme ups and downs in mood. The defining characteristic of bipolar I is the occurrence of a bout of **mania** (an excessively high mood) or a **mixed episode** (a combination of mania and depression). Often, but not always, there also has been an episode of **major depression** (an excessively low mood).

About 10 percent to 15 percent of people with recurrent major depression go on to have a manic or mixed episode, changing their diagnosis to bipolar I. In those who have so far experienced only depression, one clue to a high risk of later developing mania is a history of bipolar disorder in close relatives.

On the flip side, up to 20 percent of people with a history of mania have never had a bout of major depression. There is still some debate about whether all or almost all of these individuals will eventually have an episode of depression, given enough time and especially if not treated. Regardless, about 90 percent of people who have had one manic episode will go on to have another bout of mania.

Bipolar I disorder occurs about equally often in males and females, and it usually begins during adolescence or young adulthood. Men often start out with an episode of mania, and women often have a bout of depression first. As time goes on, the number of manic episodes tends to equal or exceed the number of depression episodes in men, whereas depression tends to predominate in women.

## Bibliography

American Psychiatric Association. *Diagnostic and Statistical Manual of Mental Disorders.* 4th ed., text rev. Washington, DC: American Psychiatric Association, 2000.

Frances, Allen, Michael B. First, and Harold Alan Pincus. *DSM-IV Guidebook.* Washington, DC: American Psychiatric Press, 1995.

Klein, Daniel N., Stewart A. Shankman, and Brian R. McFarland. "Classification of Mood Disorders." In *The American Psychiatric Publishing Textbook of Mood Disorders,* by Dan J. Stein, David J. Kupfer, and Alan F. Schatzberg, eds., 17–32. Washington, DC: American Psychiatric Publishing, 2006.

**BIPOLAR II.** Bipolar II is a form of **bipolar disorder**, a condition in which people alternate between extreme ups and downs in mood. In bipolar II disorder, they go back and forth between **major depression** and hypomania, an unusually high mood that is part of a disruptive pattern, but is not as disabling as full-blown **mania**.

Bipolar II disorder made its first appearance as an officially sanctioned diagnosis in the *Diagnostic and Statistical Manual of Mental Disorders, Fourth Edition,* the guidebook used by mental health professionals. The diagnosis may have important treatment implications, because taking **antidepressants** to treat depression may be more likely to trigger a switch to mania in those with bipolar II. The medications most often prescribed for this disorder are **mood stabilizers**, which help keep moods on a more even keel.

***Relationship to Other Mood Disorders.*** One area of current debate is how bipolar II relates to other **mood disorders**. Should it be considered a variant of **bipolar I** (the classic form of bipolar disorder in which full-blown mania occurs), a variant of major depression, or a distinct condition in its own right? So far, the evidence seems to point toward being a separate disorder, but one with close ties to both bipolar I and major depression.

*Bipolar II as a Separate Disorder.* People with bipolar II disorder are more likely than those with bipolar I or major depression to have a close relative with bipolar II. Also, the distinctions between the different diagnoses tend to stay fairly stable over time. Within five years, only five percent to 15 percent of people with bipolar II have a manic episode, which changes their diagnosis to bipolar I.

*Connection to Bipolar I.* People with bipolar II disorder are less likely than those with bipolar I disorder to have a close relative with bipolar I, but more likely than those with major depression. Also, people with bipolar I and II generally respond to the same kinds of treatments.

*Connection to Major Depression.*   Like major depression, bipolar II disorder is more common in women than men. Also, people with bipolar II tend to have longer and more frequent periods of depression than those with bipolar I.

## Bibliography

American Psychiatric Association. *Diagnostic and Statistical Manual of Mental Disorders.* 4th ed., text rev. Washington, DC: American Psychiatric Association, 2000.

Frances, Allen, Michael B. First, and Harold Alan Pincus. *DSM-IV Guidebook.* Washington, DC: American Psychiatric Press, 1995.

Klein, Daniel N., Stewart A. Shankman, and Brian R. McFarland. "Classification of Mood Disorders." In *The American Psychiatric Publishing Textbook of Mood Disorders,* by Dan J. Stein, David J. Kupfer, and Alan F. Schatzberg, eds., 17–32. Washington, DC: American Psychiatric Publishing, 2006.

**BORDERLINE PERSONALITY DISORDER.**   Borderline personality disorder (BPD) is a condition characterized by pervasive instability in moods, relationships, self-image, and behavior. People with BPD are prone to extreme impulsivity and exaggerated fear of abandonment. Intentional **self-injury** is common as well, and about 10 percent of those with the disorder die by **suicide**. Because BPD creates tremendous upheaval in people's lives, it often occurs side by side with other mental health problems. Research has shown that about three out of five people with BPD also develop **major depression** at some point in their lives.

The term "borderline" is a relic of theories that prevailed in the 1940s and 1950s. At that time, the disorder was seen as being on the border between neurosis (less severe mental disorders marked by anxiety or other distressing emotions) and psychosis (more severe mental disorders marked by serious impairments in thought, perception, or mood). This distinction no longer reflects current thinking, and some advocacy groups have pushed for the adoption of a new name, such as emotional regulation disorder.

BPD affects about two percent of U.S. adults, with females making up three quarters of those with the disorder. In general, the most severe problems and highest risk of suicide occur during the young adult years. By their thirties and forties, most people with BPD have attained greater stability in their personal lives and relationships, but some problems may persist for decades.

At the height of symptoms, people with BPD often need extensive mental health services. The disorder accounts for about 20 percent of all psychiatric hospitalizations. Fortunately, treatment options for BPD have improved in recent years. With help, many people with BPD improve over time and go on to have rewarding lives and loving relationships.

***Criteria for Diagnosis.***   The symptoms of BPD are defined by the ***Diagnostic and Statistical Manual of Mental Disorders, Fourth Edition, Text Revision*** (*DSM-IV-TR*), a diagnostic guidebook published by the American Psychiatric Association and widely used by mental health professionals from many disciplines. Like all personality disorders, BPD is characterized by an enduring pattern of thinking, feeling, and behaving that differs markedly from societal norms. This pattern is inflexible, which helps explain why it is maladaptive, because people with personality disorders find it difficult to adapt to the changing demands of their environment. The disorder also is pervasive, affecting all or most areas of personal functioning. The dysfunctional pattern emerges by adolescence

## Treatment of BPD

When people have both BPD and depression simultaneously, both conditions need to be addressed during treatment. Below are some of the main treatment options for BPD.

### Psychotherapy

Psychotherapy is the mainstay of treatment for BPD, and DBT is the best-validated approach for this purpose. DBT is an offshoot of **cognitive-behavioral therapy**, which focuses on helping people change maladaptive thought and behavior patterns. In DBT, two more elements are added to the mix: acceptance strategies, which let people know that they are acceptable just as they are, and dialectical strategies, which help people find a comfortable balance between the need for acceptance and the need for change. Another promising approach is transference-focused psychotherapy, which helps people learn how to have more successful relationships by focusing on the emotions and problems that arise in the relationship with the therapist.

### Medication

Medication cannot resolve the fundamental personality issues underlying BPD, but it may help manage some associated problems, such as depression, anxiety, and impulsiveness. Among the types of medication that may play a useful support role when combined with psychotherapy are **selective serotonin reuptake inhibitors** (antidepressants), benzodiazepines (mild sedatives), **mood stabilizers**, and newer **antipsychotics**.

or early adulthood, and is relatively stable over time. It leads to emotional distress and/or problems getting along in daily life.

What sets BPD apart from other personality disorders is the specific constellation of symptoms and traits that typify it. People with BPD display at least five of the following: (1) frantic efforts to avoid real or imagined abandonment, (2) a pattern of intense but tumultuous relationships that shift abruptly from idealizing the other person to devaluing him or her, (3) sudden, dramatic shifts in self-image, goals, values, and career aspirations, (4) impulsive and harmful behavior such as gambling, spending sprees, unsafe sex, **substance abuse**, binge eating, and reckless driving, (5) self-harming behavior or suicide threats or attempts, (6) intense but short-lived bouts of depression, anger, or anxiety, (7) long-lasting feelings of emptiness and being easily bored, (8) inappropriate displays of anger, such as angry outbursts, physical fights, extreme sarcasm, or enduring bitterness, and (9) short-lived, stress-related episodes of paranoid thoughts (extreme suspiciousness or exaggerated beliefs about being harassed, persecuted, or unfairly treated) or dissociative symptoms (a disconnect in the usually integrated functions of consciousness, memory, identity, or perception, such as feeling detached from one's own mind and body).

*Relationship to Depression.* A severely **depressed mood** can occur in both BPD and major depression. Although the mood lasts at least two weeks in major depression, it usually lasts only a few hours in BPD. There also are qualitative differences in the mood. People with BPD report feeling more emptiness, loneliness, and boredom than those with major depression, but less guilt, loss of appetite, and lack of energy.

People with BPD may not respond as well to **antidepressants** as those with major depression alone do. But a form of **psychotherapy** called **dialectical behavior therapy** (DBT) has been shown to reduce depressive symptoms and suicide attempts in BPD, and it also has shown early promise as a therapy for major depression when other treatments fail.

*See also:* Comorbidity; Personality Factors

***Further Information.***    National Education Alliance for Borderline Personality Disorder, P.O. Box 974, Rye, New York 10580, (914) 835-9011, www.borderlinepersonalitydisorder .com.

## Bibliography

American Psychiatric Association. *Diagnostic and Statistical Manual of Mental Disorders.* 4th ed., text rev. Washington, DC: American Psychiatric Association, 2000.

*Borderline Personality Disorder.* Mayo Clinic, May 14, 2008, http://www.mayoclinic.com/health/ borderline-personality-disorder/DS00442.

*Borderline Personality Disorder.* National Institute of Mental Health, June 26, 2008, http://www.nimh.nih.gov/health/publications/borderline-personality-disorder.shtml.

*Borderline Personality Disorder: A Costly, Severe Mental Illness.* National Education Alliance for Borderline Personality Disorder, February 2008, http://www.borderlinepersonalitydisorder.com/ documents/BPDBriefingPaperDraft_607Feb08.pdf.

*Factsheet: Personality Disorders.* Mental Health America, November 8, 2006, http://www.nmha.org/ go/information/get-info/personality-disorders.

*Fact Sheet:* Borderline Personality Disorder. National Alliance for Research on Schizophrenia and Depression, http://www.narsad.org/dc/pdf/facts.bpersonalityd.pdf.

Oldham, John M. *Guideline Watch: Practice Guideline for the Treatment of Patients with Borderline Personality Disorder.* American Psychiatric Association, March 2005, http://www.psychiatryonline .com/content.aspx?aid=148718.

*Practice Guideline for the Treatment of Patients with Borderline Personality Disorder.* American Psychiatric Association, October 2001, http://www.psychiatryonline.com/pracGuide/pracGuideTopic _13.aspx.

Yen, Shirley, Meghan E. McDevitt-Murphy, and M. Tracie Shea. "Depression and Personality." In *The American Psychiatric Publishing Textbook of Mood Disorders,* by Dan J. Stein, David J. Kupfer, and Alan F. Schatzberg, eds., 673–686. Washington, DC: American Psychiatric Publishing, 2006.

**BOWLBY, JOHN (1907–1990).**    John Bowlby is a British psychiatrist known for his **attachment theory**, which states that **infants** are primed by evolution to form close emotional bonds with caregivers. The way the need for attachment is met in infancy shapes personality development, interpersonal relationships, and emotional stability later in life. Lack of a healthy attachment is thought to predispose people to depression.

According to attachment theory, infants and young **children** with caregivers who are consistently responsive and supportive develop secure attachments. They learn to regard themselves and other people in a positive light. In contrast, youngsters with caregivers who are inconsistent, unresponsive, or unsupportive develop insecure attachments, which may lead to fear of abandonment, self-criticism, and excessive dependency. As a result, they are more vulnerable to developing depression in response to a loss or **stress**.

***Early Career Highlights.***    Bowlby was born in London in 1907, the son of a surgeon. Like many children from affluent British families of the day, Bowlby was raised primarily by a nanny, then sent to boarding school at an early age. Although he did not feel that his upbringing was out of the ordinary, it is tempting to speculate that his early experiences may have influenced his later interest in the parent-child bond.

As a young man, Bowlby attended the University of Cambridge, where he had his first taste of what is now called developmental psychology—the field that studies physical, mental, and behavioral changes across the lifespan. After completing a bachelor's degree in 1928, Bowlby did a short stint working at a progressive school for maladjusted children.

His experiences there sparked an enduring interest in the effects of early parent-child relationships on personality development. Determined to embark on a career as a child psychiatrist, Bowlby began his medical training at University College Hospital in London.

Around the same time, Bowlby also began training in psychoanalysis—an in-depth, long-term approach to psychological treatment that emphasizes the influence of unconscious drives and wishes on behavior. Bowlby was exposed to the ideas of Austrian-born British psychoanalyst Melanie Klein (1882–1960) at the British Psychoanalytic Institute. Klein believed that children's emotional problems were almost wholly caused by fantasies resulting from internal conflicts, rather than by actual events in the outside world. Over the next several years, Bowlby became increasingly alienated from this viewpoint—and increasingly convinced that family experiences were in fact the primary cause of emotional disturbance.

After completing medical school, Bowlby practiced as a psychiatrist. Although World War II interrupted his clinical career, it expanded his research repertoire. His wartime assignment was to develop officer selection procedures along with distinguished colleagues at Tavistock Clinic in London. The job gave him a level of statistical sophistication that was then unusual for a psychiatrist and psychoanalyst.

When the war ended, Bowlby was invited to stay on at Tavistock as head of the Children's Department, which he promptly renamed the Department for Children and Parents. He remained in this position for the rest of his career. In 1949, Bowlby published what is often considered the first paper on **family therapy**, describing how he achieved breakthroughs by interviewing parents about their youthful experiences in front of their troubled children.

Beginning in the early 1950s, Bowlby became intrigued by ethology, the study of innate or species-specific behavior in animals, typically in their natural habitat. This interest laid the groundwork for a key theme in Bowlby's subsequent work: the belief that attachment is a useful adaptation from an evolutionary point of view. Bowlby held that attachment behaviors—such as crying, smiling, and clinging—increase the likelihood of survival by keeping infants close to those who protect and care for them.

***Fruitful Collaborations.*** Bowlby was an original thinker who had an immense impact on child psychiatry and psychology. But he did not work in a vacuum. Instead, he formed synergistic relationships with other researchers that both informed and confirmed his own ideas.

*Mary D. Salter Ainsworth.* Canadian-born U.S. psychologist Mary D. Salter Ainsworth (1913–1999) is the researcher whose name is most closely associated with Bowlby's. Prior to meeting Bowlby, she had already based a dissertation on security theory, which states that infants and young children need to develop secure dependence on their parents before exploring unfamiliar situations.

Ainsworth joined Bowlby's research team at Tavistock in 1950. Bowlby became first a mentor and later a collaborator on research into parent-child attachment. Although Ainsworth left the clinic four years later, she continued to translate Bowlby's concepts into testable hypotheses.

In the 1970s, Ainsworth devised the Strange Situation research protocol to assess attachment in infants and young children. Using this protocol, a parent and young child are first placed in an unfamiliar setting. Then the parent leaves briefly. The child's response when the parent leaves and returns is used as a gauge of attachment. The Strange Situation remains one of the most elegant methods ever devised for testing a psychological theory.

Research using this procedure highlighted the difference between infants with secure attachment and those with two types of insecure attachment: avoidant and ambivalent-resistant. Placed in a strange situation, securely attached young children display confidence when the parent is present, act mildly distressed if the parent leaves, and reestablish contact quickly once the parent returns. Those with an insecure avoidant attachment ignore the parent when present, seem unfazed if the parent leaves, and may actively avoid contact once the parent returns. Those with an insecure ambivalent attachment show a mixture of positive and negative responses to the parent.

*Harry F. Harlow.*   Another researcher influenced by Bowlby was U.S. psychologist Harry F. Harlow (1905–1981). Unlike Ainsworth, Harlow did not collaborate with Bowlby directly. However, beginning in the late 1950s, the two scientists corresponded with each other, met several times, and cited each other's work.

Harlow studied maternal-infant bonds as well, but from the viewpoint of comparative psychology. This field investigates animal behavior, usually in a lab, with the dual objective of understanding nonhuman behavior for its own sake as well as for gaining insight into human behavior. Harlow is best known for a series of experiments on attachment behavior in rhesus monkeys. The results were dramatic, although the methods generated controversy because of the extreme distress caused to the animals.

In one set of studies, baby rhesus monkeys were raised in cages without their natural mothers, but with two surrogate objects. One surrogate, from which the monkeys could feed, was made of wire. The other, to which the monkeys could cling, was wrapped in terrycloth. When a frightening mechanical spider was placed in the cage, the monkeys ran to the terrycloth surrogates, showing that contact comfort was paramount in establishing a secure bond.

Harlow also studied the harmful effects of depriving monkeys of maternal and contact comfort. In one pair of studies, he separated baby rhesus monkeys from their mothers for two to three weeks. The young monkeys first reacted to the separation violently and vocally, then sank into a depression-like state of low activity, minimal play, and occasional crying.

These reactions closely mirrored Bowlby's earlier description of maternal separation in human children, which began with a stage he called protest, followed by a stage he called despair. In Bowlby's view, these responses made adaptive sense. Protest was seen as a way of signaling distress and location to the caregiver, and despair was seen as a way of conserving resources and avoiding predators if the caregiver failed to respond.

**Insights into Depression.**   In the 1960s, Bowlby began writing his magnum opus, the *Attachment and Loss* trilogy (1969, 1973, 1980). The final volume dealt with **sadness** and depression. Bowlby described three personalities that predispose individuals to depression after a loss. Those in insecure relationships characterized by anxious ambivalence and excessive dependence are vulnerable to depression following loss of a loved one. Those in insecure relationships characterized by anxious avoidance and excessive independence are vulnerable to depression following loss of self-esteem.

A third group of depression-prone individuals are compulsive caregivers. Bowlby described these individuals as simultaneously resentful about having to stay home from an early age to care for a sick or needy parent and anxious about leaving home. As a result, they become excessively guilty and preoccupied with caring for another person in the way they themselves would like to have been cared for.

**Bowlby in Perspective.**   Bowlby's ideas were initially attacked by traditional psychoanalysts. But as more and more evidence was amassed supporting his views, the tide began to turn. His attachment theory was hailed as innovative, and it became a major force in child psychiatry and psychology.

Some critics have interpreted Bowlby's emphasis on parental behavior as blaming the parents for anything that later goes wrong in a child's life. Although it may not have been Bowlby's intention, his ideas taken alone seem to place undue responsibility on parents. The prevailing view today is that the early relationship with a parent is only one of many factors that work together to create a vulnerability to depression.

Bowlby died of a stroke in 1990 on the Isle of Skye off the coast of Scotland, where he had a vacation home. By the time of his death at age 83, his groundbreaking work on attachment had forever changed child psychiatry and developmental psychology.

*See also:* Evolutionary Perspective

## Bibliography

Ainsworth, Mary D. Salter, and John Bowlby. "An Ethological Approach to Personality Development." *American Psychologist* 46 (1991): 333–341.

Ainsworth, Mary D. Salter. "John Bowlby (1907–1990)." *American Psychologist* 47 (1992): 668.

Blatt, Sidney J. *Experiences of Depression: Theoretical, Clinical, and Research Perspectives.* Washington, DC: American Psychological Association, 2004.

Bowlby, John. "The Study and Reduction of Group Tensions in the Family." *Human Relations* 2 (1949): 123–128.

Bowlby, John. *A Secure Base: Clinical Applications of Attachment Theory.* London: Routledge, 1988.

Bowlby, John. *Attachment and Loss (Volume 1): Attachment.* London: Hogarth, 1969.

Bowlby, John. *Attachment and Loss (Volume 2): Separation.* London: Hogarth, 1973.

Bowlby, John. *Attachment and Loss (Volume 3): Loss, Sadness and Depression.* London: Hogarth, 1980.

Bretherton, Inge. "The Origins of Attachment Theory: John Bowlby and Mary Ainsworth." *Developmental Psychology* 28 (1992): 759–775.

Milite, George A. "John Bowlby." *Psychology Encyclopedia,* http://psychology.jrank.org/pages/90/John-Bowlby.html.

Seay, B., E. Hansen, and H. F. Harlow. "Mother-Infant Separation in Monkeys." *Journal of Child Psychology and Psychiatry* 3 (1962): 123–132.

Sheehy, Noel, Antony J. Chapman, and Wendy Conroy, eds. "Ainsworth, Mary Dinsmore (Salter)" and "Bowlby, Edward John Mostyn," in *Biographical Dictionary of Psychology.* New York: Routledge, 2002.

Van der Horst, Frank C. P., Helen A. LeRoy, and René van der Veer. "'When Strangers Meet': John Bowlby and Harry Harlow on Attachment Behavior." *Integrative Psychological and Behavioral Science* 42 (2008): 370–388.

Van Duken, Suzan, René van der Veer, Marinus van Uzendoorn, and Hans-Jan Kuipers. "Bowlby Before Bowlby: The Sources of an Intellectual Departure in Psychoanalysis and Psychology." *Journal of the History of the Behavioral Sciences* 34 (1998): 247–269.

**BRAIN ANATOMY.**    The brain is the most complex organ in the human body. It is the seat of thinking, memory, and emotion. It also interprets sensory input, initiates muscle movement, and controls behavior. All these functions are carried out by a spongy mass of fatty tissue that weighs only about three pounds at full size. Normally, the various parts of the brain work with remarkable efficiency. But when there are structural flaws, a wide range of problems may occur, including depression.

The brain is housed inside a bony covering, called the cranium, which helps protect it from injury. Between the cranium and brain are three membrane layers, called the meninges, which provide further protection. Cerebrospinal fluid—a clear, watery fluid that flows through channels within and around the brain—offers additional cushioning.

The brain is something like a panel of experts. It is composed of individual parts that all work together, but each of which has its own specialized tasks and skills. These parts are organized into three basic sections: forebrain, midbrain, and hindbrain.

*Forebrain.* The largest and most highly developed section is the forebrain, which is responsible for all forms of conscious experience, including thought, emotion, and perception. The forebrain also controls the pituitary gland and helps regulate sleep, appetite, and the activities of internal organs. It consists mainly of the cerebrum and inner brain.

*Cerebrum.* The cerebrum is the major, topmost portion of the brain—the part usually seen in pictures. It is the seat of all intellectual activities, such as reasoning, planning, and imagining. This structure is divided by a deep fissure into two halves, called hemispheres. The hemispheres communicate with each other through a large tract of nerve fibers at the base of the fissure, called the corpus callosum.

On the outer surface of the cerebrum is a vital layer of tissue, called the cerebral cortex. The cortex is sometimes referred to as "gray matter," because its nerves lack the insulation that makes most other parts of the brain look white. Although the cortex is only the thickness of a stack of two or three dimes, it is full of folds that give the brain a wrinkly appearance. These folds increase the surface area of the cortex, allowing more information to be processed there.

Each cerebral hemisphere is itself divided into segments, called lobes. The largest of these segments are the frontal lobes, which are involved in voluntary movement, speech, and other intellectual and behavioral functions.

From Structure to Function

The various parts of the brain are interconnected by neural pathways, routes followed by nerve impulses as they carry information from one site to another. These two-way routes enable different parts of the brain to work together. In depression, certain areas of the brain may start to malfunction, and problems in one area may just feed problems in other areas, creating a vicious cycle.

|  | **What It Is** | **How It Might Contribute to Depression** |
|---|---|---|
| **Amygdala** | An almond-shaped structure in the temporal lobes of the cerebrum. | Generates negative emotions. |
| **Anterior Cingulate Cortex** | The front part of a long strip of cerebral cortex that arches over the corpus callosum. | Keeps the person from thinking about anything other than the negative emotions. |
| **Prefrontal Cortex** | The forward-most part of the frontal lobes of the cerebrum. | Revives bad memories associated with the negative emotions. |

*Inner Brain.* Hidden deep inside the brain are structures that act as gatekeepers between the spinal cord and cerebrum. These structures affect a person's emotional state and modify perceptions and responses based on that state. They also let a person make some movements without thinking about them.

The **hypothalamus** is only about the size of a pearl, but it serves a vital role as a joint command center for the **nervous system** and **endocrine system**. The hypothalamus also helps regulate mood and emotion, and it is thought to be involved in depression. Nearby lies the thalamus, a relay station for signals passing to and from the cerebrum and spinal cord.

An arching tract of nerves leads from the hypothalamus and thalamus to the **hippocampus**, a seahorse-shaped structure that is involved in memory, learning, and emotion. The hippocampus tends to shrink in people with depression, which may help explain why memory problems are a common symptom of the disorder.

*Midbrain.*    The midbrain is the uppermost part of the brainstem, the lower extension of the brain that connects it to the spinal cord. The midbrain is the main pathway for sensory and movement impulses passing between the forebrain and hindbrain. It also coordinates visual and auditory reflexes.

*Hindbrain.*    The hindbrain helps control bodily activities such as breathing, heart rate, blood pressure, muscle tone, and coordination of muscle movement. It consists of the cerebellum, the rest of the brainstem, and the upper part of the spinal cord.

The cerebellum is a wrinkled ball of tissue located at the back of the brain. It coordinates movements and helps people perform rapid, repetitive actions, such as playing a videogame or hitting a tennis ball.

*See also:* Brain Physiology

*Bibliography*

*Anatomy of the Brain.* American Association of Neurological Surgeons, June 2006, http://www .neurosurgerytoday.org/what/patient_e/anatomy1.asp.

*Brain Basics: Know Your Brain.* National Institute of Neurological Disorders and Stroke, May 1, 2007, http://www.ninds.nih.gov/disorders/brain_basics/know_your_brain.htm.

*Brain Facts: A Primer on the Brain and Nervous System.* 6th ed. Washington, DC: Society for Neuroscience, 2008.

*Parts of the Brain That Slow Down or Speed Up in Depression.* Canadian Institute of Neurosciences, Mental Health and Addiction, http://thebrain.mcgill.ca/flash/a/a_08/a_08_cr/a_08_cr_dep/a _08_cr_ zdep.html.

**BRAIN-DERIVED NEUROTROPHIC FACTOR.**    Neurotrophic factors are small proteins in the brain needed for the growth and survival of specific groups of brain cells. Brain-derived neurotrophic factor (BDNF), in particular, is currently being studied for its possible role in depression. Research in both humans and animals has found that depression is associated with decreased **neuroplasticity**, the brain's ability to modify connections between cells to better cope with new circumstances. BDNF affects the neuroplasticity of brain cells related to chemicals involved in depression, including **serotonin** and **dopamine**.

Scientists are still sorting out the complex relationship between BDNF and depression. But the effects of BDNF seem to vary depending on which area of the brain is involved. BDNF may have a depression-fighting effect in the **hippocampus**, a brain structure involved in learning, emotion, and memory. Conversely, BDNF may have a depression-causing effect in the ventral tegmental area (VTA), part of the brain's reward center, which promotes the repetition of behaviors that help ensure survival.

BDNF also affects other parts of the brain besides the hippocampus and VTA. But research on those two areas reveals a lot about how BDNF might influence depression and its treatment.

***BDNF in the Hippocampus.*** In the hippocampus, **major depression** is associated with low levels of BDNF as well as decreased volume in that area of the brain. In contrast, treatment with **antidepressants** or **electroconvulsive therapy** is associated with greater BDNF production and activity as well as increased hippocampal volume.

One interesting line of research uses something called the forced swim test to study depression-like behavior in rats. When rats are placed in water, they are normally eager to try swimming their way out. If they fail to react this way, researchers consider their behavior the rodent equivalent of human depression. But when BDNF is injected into the hippocampus of such rats, they outperform even healthy rats on the forced swim test, implying that the surplus of BDNF in their brain has an antidepressant effect.

Such findings have led scientists to hypothesize that antidepressant treatments work by enhancing BDNF activity. The result is an improvement in the ability of critical brain circuits to adapt to environmental demands, which may be a crucial step in the **recovery** process.

***BDNF in the VTA.*** In the VTA, however, the relationship between BDNF and depression seems to be reversed. Other studies in rats have found that raising BDNF levels in the VTA makes the animals more, not less, vulnerable to **stress** and depression.

Forced swim tests have been used here, too. When BDNF was injected into the VTA of rats, they swam just as well the next day as rats that did not get the injection. But by the second day, the injected rats stopped performing as well. In other words, they had a depression-like response to the increased BDNF.

Scientists knew that the VTA sends BDNF to the nucleus accumbens, a neighboring part of the brain's reward center. So they tried injecting a compound into the nucleus accumbens that blocks BDNF. The day after the injection, these rats swam as well as others who did not get the injection. But by the second day, the injected rats were swimming even better than the others, indicating that they had become unusually resilient.

Researchers hope that such findings will one day lead to new drugs that help humans fend off depression. The challenge will be to find compounds that have exactly the right effect on BDNF at exactly the right place in the brain.

*Bibliography*

Angelucci, F., S. Brené, and A. A. Mathé. "BDNF in Schizophrenia, Depression and Corresponding Animal Models." *Molecular Psychiatry* 10 (2005): 345–352.

Arehart-Treichel, Joan. "Researchers Try to Explain Link Between Depression, Brain Chemical." *Psychiatric News* 38 (2003): 17.

Castrén, Eero, and Tomi Rantamäki. "Neurotrophins in Depression and Antidepressant Effects." *Novartis Foundation Symposium* 289 (2008): 43–52.

Castrén, Eero, Vootele Võikar, and Tomi Rantamäki. "Role of Neurotrophic Factors in Depression." *Current Opinion in Pharmacology* 7 (2007): 18–21.

Eisch, Amelia J., Carlos A. Bolaños, Joris de Wit, Ryan D. Simonak, Cindy M. Pudiak, Michel Barrot, et al. "Brain-Derived Neurotrophic Factor in the Ventral Midbrain-Nucleus Accumbens Pathway: A Role in Depression." *Biological Psychiatry* 54 (2003): 994–1005.

Shirayama, Yukihiko, Andrew C.-H. Chen, Shin Nakagawa, David S. Russell, and Ronald S. Duman. "Brain-Derived Neurotrophic Factor Produces Antidepressant Effects in Behavioral Models of Depression." *Journal of Neuroscience* 22 (2002): 3251–3261.

*Stress: Brain Yields Clues About Why Some Succumb While Others Prevail.* National Institutes of Health, October 18, 2007, http://www.nih.gov/news/pr/oct2007/nimh-18.htm.

Taylor, Stephen Michael. "Electroconvulsive Therapy, Brain-Derived Neurotrophic Factor, and Possible Neurorestorative Benefit of the Clinical Application of Electroconvulsive Therapy." *Journal of ECT* 24 (2008): 160–165.

**BRAIN IMAGING.**   Brain imaging refers to noninvasive, computerized techniques that are used to study the structure or function of the brain. In the past, scientists had to rely on indirect evidence and postmortem examination to study links between the brain and specific disorders or behaviors. But the advent of modern brain imaging changed that. Today, doctors and researchers can study the living brain directly.

Techniques such as computed tomography (CT) and magnetic resonance imaging (MRI) provide a look at **brain anatomy**. Techniques such as functional MRI (fMRI), magnetic resonance spectroscopy (MRS), positron emission tomography (PET), single photon emission computed tomography (SPECT), and magnetoencephalography (MEG) offer a window into **brain physiology**. These latter techniques allow scientists to assess a variety of physiological and biochemical variables, including regional differences in brain blood flow, oxygen level, and glucose metabolism. Using such data, they can compare the relative activity of different parts of the brain and determine which parts are more or less active under specific conditions.

Doctors are not yet able to diagnose depression with current brain imaging technology. In the future, though, it is hoped that brain imaging might be useful for identifying individuals at high-risk for depression and diagnosing those with specific depressive disorders.

Brain imaging also might one day help treatment providers choose the best treatment for a particular patient. Several studies have shown that certain pretreatment abnormalities in brain metabolism help distinguish people who will respond to **antidepressants** from those who will not. Among people who have recovered from depression, brain imaging might prove useful for identifying those at high risk for **recurrence** so preventive measures can be taken.

*The Depressed Brain.*   Brain imaging studies show that the brains of people with depression tend to look different from those of healthy individuals. Certain parts of the brain—areas responsible for regulating mood, thought, sleep, appetite, and behavior—appear to work differently. In addition, some important neurotransmitters—chemicals that carry messages between brain cells—appear to be out of balance.

From an anatomical perspective, one of the most consistent findings is shrinkage of the **hippocampus**, a seahorse-shaped structure in the brain that plays a role in memory, learning, and emotion. There is also some evidence of volume loss in the **prefrontal cortex**, an area involved in higher mental functions, such as thinking, problem solving, short-term memory, and emotion.

From a physiological perspective, functional abnormalities have often been reported in the prefrontal cortex and the **anterior cingulate cortex**, an area that serves as an interface between higher, more rational circuits of the brain and lower, more instinctive parts. Among the best-replicated findings is a link between low prefrontal activity and greater depression severity.

Once people with depression recover, some abnormalities seen on brain scans return to normal. This normalization has been observed after several forms of treatment, including various antidepressants, **psychotherapy**, **electroconvulsive therapy**, **transcranial magnetic stimulation**, and **vagus nerve stimulation**. Interestingly, though, **cognitive-behavioral therapy** (CBT) leads to changes in different areas of the brain than drug therapy does. After treatment with CBT, metabolic activity tends to decrease in prefrontal areas and increase in the hippocampus. The reverse pattern is seen with an antidepressant.

***Types of Brain Imaging.*** Below are several imaging technologies that can be used to visualize the inner structure and function of the brain.

*Computed Tomography.* CT scanning combines special X-ray equipment with a sophisticated computer to produce cross-sectional images of brain structure. Conventional X-ray exams use a stationary machine to focus a small burst of radiation on part of the body. The result is a two-dimensional image, similar to a photograph. But CT scans of the brain use an X-ray device that rotates around the head to produce multiple cross-sectional images, like slices of brain tissue. When the slices are reassembled by computer software, the result is a detailed, multidimensional view of the brain.

*Magnetic Resonance Imaging.* MRI is a technique that uses a powerful magnetic field, radio waves, and a computer to create precise images of brain structure. It is currently the most sensitive brain imaging test in routine clinical use. MRI technology is based on the fact that different atoms in the brain resonate to different frequencies of magnetic fields. MRI scanning equipment first creates a background magnetic field, which lines up all the atoms in the brain. Then a second magnetic field, oriented differently from the first, is turned on and off very rapidly. Certain atoms resonate at specific pulse rates and line up with the second field. When the second magnetic field is switched off, those atoms swing back into alignment with the background field. The process produces signals that can be picked up and converted into MRI images, which are unsurpassed in anatomical detail.

*Functional Magnetic Resonance Imaging.* This imaging technique combines standard MRI technology with a means of detecting changes in blood oxygen levels. Such changes indicate brain activity, because increased blood flow is needed by busy areas of the brain. Therefore, unlike conventional MRI, fMRI can show the brain in action. During the scan, the person may be asked to perform simple tasks, such as answering basic question or tapping the fingers. The scan shows not only which areas of the brain become active and for how long, but also whether the activity in different spots occurs simultaneously or sequentially.

*Magnetic Resonance Spectroscopy.* MRS is an offshoot of fMRI that uses the same equipment, but in a different way. Rather than assessing blood flow, it measures the concentration of specific chemicals, such as neurotransmitters, in different areas of the brain. This technique holds promise as a method for studying the natural course of depression or monitoring treatment response.

*Positron Emission Tomography.* PET is a form of nuclear medicine imaging that uses small amounts of a radioactive material, called a tracer, to reveal how tissues and organs are functioning. The tracer generally is injected into the bloodstream, which carries it to the brain. There, it is taken up by different areas of the brain in proportion to how hard the cells are working. As positrons (positively charged particles) in the material undergo radioactive decay, they emit radioactivity, which can be detected and converted into images. PET scanning can be used to study changes in the release of certain neurotransmitters, which helps researchers understand the relationship between that neurotransmitter and particular psychological processes. In research settings, PET is used to help understand the biochemical causes of depression and to evaluate the effectiveness of various treatments.

*Single Photon Emission Computed Tomography.* SPECT is similar to PET, but the tracer has a longer half-life—the time it takes for half the atoms in a radioactive substance to decay. As a result, the tracer is less complicated and expensive to produce. However, the images created by SPECT are not as detailed as PET images. SPECT scans can be used to study blood flow differences in the brain, which indicate areas of greater or lesser activity.

*Magnetoencephalography.* MEG measures magnetic signals arising from electrical activity in the brain. An array of sensors monitors the magnetic field pattern near a person's head, pinpointing the position and strength of activity in different areas. One advantage of MEG is that it can pick up very rapid changes in activity, down to the millisecond. This allows researchers to measure precisely how long activity is sustained in different parts of the brain in response to various stimuli.

**Further Information.**    Radiological Society of North America, 820 Jorie Boulevard, Oak Brook, IL 60523, (800) 381-6660, www.rsna.org, www.radiologyinfo.org.

*Bibliography*

*CT Scan.* Mayo Clinic, January 12, 2008, http://www.mayoclinic.com/health/ct-scan/MY00309.

*CT: Head.* Radiological Society of North America, 2009, http://www.radiologyinfo.org/en/info.cfm?PG=headct.

*Functional MR Imaging (fMRI): Brain.* Radiological Society of North America, 2009, http://www.radiologyinfo.org/en/info.cfm?pg=fmribrain.

Hasler, Gregor, Stephen Fromm, Paul J. Carlson, David A. Luckenbaugh, Tracy Waldeck, Marilla Geraci, et al. "Neural Response to Catecholamine Depletion in Unmedicated Subjects with Major Depressive Disorder in Remission and Healthy Subjects." *Archives of General Psychiatry* 65 (2008): 521–531.

Mayberg, Helen S. "Brain Imaging." In *The American Psychiatric Publishing Textbook of Mood Disorders,* by Dan J. Stein, David J. Kupfer and Alan F. Schatzberg, eds., 219–234. Washington, DC: American Psychiatric Publishing, 2006.

*MRI of the Head,* Radiological Society of North America, 2009, http://www.radiologyinfo.org/en/info.cfm?pg=headmr.

*Neurological Diagnostic Tests and Procedures.* National Institute of Neurological Disorders and Stroke, May 15, 2009, http://www.ninds.nih.gov/disorders/misc/diagnostic_tests.htm.

*New Diagnostic Methods.* Society for Neuroscience, http://www.sfn.org/skins/main/pdf/brainfacts/2008/new_diagnostic_methods.pdf.

*Positron Emission Tomography (PET) Scan.* Mayo Clinic, May 8, 2009, http://www.mayoclinic.com/health/pet-scan/MY00238.

*SPECT Scan.* Mayo Clinic, March 31, 2009, http://www.mayoclinic.com/health/spect-scan/ MY00233.

*What Causes Depression?* National Institute of Mental Health, March 30, 2009, http://www.nimh.nih.gov/health/publications/depression/what-causes-depression.shtml.

**BRAIN PHYSIOLOGY.**    The brain is a marvel of functional complexity. It contains billions of neural circuits—networks of nerve cells and their interconnections. To process a single bit of information, the brain may use multiple neural circuits and many brain structures. Normally, these circuits and structures all work together with awesome efficiency. But when there is a functional breakdown, a wide range of problems, including depression, may ensue.

No nerve signal ever hits a dead end in the brain. Instead, every place a signal lands is also a potential point of departure. The ongoing communication and dense interconnections make the brain an extremely dynamic organ.

It is also a highly adaptable organ that operates on two levels at once. On one hand, the brain contains precisely wired circuits that relay messages in an orderly fashion from one cell to the next. On the other hand, some brain chemicals are able to have diffuse effects that are not tied down to circuits. Despite the apparent contradictions between these two modes of operation, they actually complement each other quite well.

**The Wired Brain.**    The classical view of the brain focuses on the wiring between information-bearing nerve cells, called **neurons**. Messages are passed from one neuron to the next by a process known as neurotransmission.

To get from one neuron to the next via neurotransmission, information must cross a tiny gap, called a synapse. It is carried across the gap by chemical messengers, called

**neurotransmitters**. Axons, the sending extensions on cells that release neurotransmitters, make up the wiring that keeps information flowing around the brain, just as electrical wiring keeps electricity flowing around a house. Yet unlike the wires in a house, the wiring in the brain is constantly changing in response to new demands.

*The Unplugged Brain.* Neurons also communicate with each other outside the wired system via a process called neuromodulation. In this process, neurons release chemical messengers not into a single synapse, but into broader areas of the brain. By this means, the chemicals can affect many synapses at once. The effects of neuromodulation are slower-acting but longer-lasting than those of neurotransmission.

Neuromodulation does not change the basic nature of the connection between two neurons the way neurotransmission does. Instead, it modifies the intensity of the connection. It does this by influencing either the release of a neurotransmitter or the response of **receptors**, specialized sites on cells that receive and react to the chemical message.

The four main chemicals used in neuromodulation are **serotonin**, **norepinephrine**, **dopamine**, and acetylcholine. The same chemicals are used in neurotransmission as well, and they are usually referred to simply as neurotransmitters. Technically speaking, though, they function as both neurotransmitters and neuromodulators. Current **antidepressants** target one or more of these crucial brain chemicals.

*Beyond Neurotransmitters.* Neurotransmitters play a crucial role in the brain, but they are not the only important players. **Hormones** are the chemical messengers of the **endocrine system**. Many hormones, including **estrogen** and **cortisol**, have receptors in the brain, where they affect various mental functions and disorders, including depression.

Neurotrophic factors are small proteins needed for the growth and survival of specific groups of neurons. One neurotrophic factor in particular, called **brain-derived neurotrophic factor** (BDNF), is currently being studied for its possible role in depression. BDNF is involved in **neuroplasticity**, the brain's ability to modify connections between neurons to better cope with new circumstances. Specifically, BDNF affects the neuroplasticity of neurons related to serotonin and dopamine.

Enzymes are proteins that act as biological catalysts, which means they speed up the rate of chemical reactions in the body without becoming part of the end product. Cofactors are substances that must be present for enzymes to work properly. Among the ones being studied in relationship to brain function are **glycogen synthase kinase 3 beta**, an enzyme, and **S-adenosyl-L-methionine**, an enzyme.

*See also:* Brain Anatomy; Nervous System; Neurological Disorders

*Further Information.* Dana Foundation, 745 Fifth Avenue, Suite 900, New York, NY 10151, (212) 223-4040, www.dana.org.

Society for Neuroscience, 1121 14th Street N.W., Suite 1010, Washington, DC 20005, (202) 962-4000, www.sfn.org.

## Bibliography

*Brain Facts: A Primer on the Brain and Nervous System.* 6th ed. Washington, DC: Society for Neuroscience, 2008.

*The Wired Brain: Beginner.* Canadian Institute of Neurosciences, Mental Health and Addiction, http://thebrain.mcgill.ca/flash/d/d_01/d_01_cr/d_01_cr_fon/d_01_cr_fon.html.

*The Wired Brain: Intermediate.* Canadian Institute of Neurosciences, Mental Health and Addiction, http://thebrain.mcgill.ca/flash/i/i_01/i_01_cr/i_01_cr_fon/i_01_cr_fon.html.

**BRAIN STIMULATION.**   Brain stimulation—also known as neurostimulation or neuromodulation—is a therapeutic technique that uses electrical current or magnetic fields to bring about changes in brain function. **Electroconvulsive therapy** (ECT) has been used for decades to treat depression. Newer brain stimulation methods that have been recently approved or are currently being tested as depression treatments include **transcranial magnetic stimulation** (TMS), **vagus nerve stimulation** (VNS), **deep brain stimulation** (DBS), and **magnetic seizure therapy** (MST).

At present, such treatments are mainly reserved for cases of severe depression in which standard treatments cannot be used, do not help, or have stopped working. With the exception of ECT, research on the safety and effectiveness of these procedures is still at an early stage. But as evidence mounts, it is possible that some of the newer approaches could one day become standard therapies rather than treatments of last resort.

All brain stimulation therapies are based on the assumption that depression is related to abnormal brain signals. The goal is to reset the brain's electrical circuitry, which, in turn, affects the output and activity of key brain chemicals. The hope is that this readjustment will reduce or eliminate symptoms.

The critical question is if the current state of the science is advanced enough to precisely target the troublemaking part of the brain and control activity there. The jury is still out on that answer. This is an area of intense scientific study, however, and brain stimulation technology is improving rapidly. The promise for the future appears bright.

*Therapeutic Approaches.*   Several types of brain stimulation may be used to treat severe depression that does not improve with standard treatments.

*Electroconvulsive Therapy.*   ECT involves passing a carefully controlled electrical current through a person's brain to induce a brief seizure. First introduced over 70 years ago, ECT is the only brain stimulation technique with a long track record. Compared to **antidepressants** and **psychotherapy**, it is quite effective and fast acting. Yet several treatment sessions are required, and potential side effects, including memory loss, remain a concern. ECT is the gold standard against which newer brain stimulation treatments are measured. These other approaches aim to build on what is good about ECT while reducing side effects or enhancing effectiveness.

*Transcranial Magnetic Stimulation.*   TMS uses rapid pulses of magnetic fields to stimulate brain cells in the targeted part of the brain. The magnetic fields are produced by a special electromagnetic coil that is placed against the patient's scalp.

*Magnetic Seizure Therapy.*   MST is an intense form of TMS. This experimental treatment uses strong, rapidly alternating magnetic fields to induce a brief seizure.

*Deep Brain Stimulation.*   DBS is the most invasive form of brain stimulation currently used to treat depression. This experimental treatment involves surgically implanting electrodes in the brain. The electrodes are connected by wires to an implanted pacemaker-like device, which transmits electrical pulses to the brain through the electrodes.

*Vagus Nerve Stimulation.*   VNS uses an implanted device, similar to a pacemaker, to deliver mild electrical pulses to the vagus nerve. This nerve then transmits the pulses to the brain, reaching areas that affect mood and other symptoms of depression.

*Pros and Cons.*   Compared to antidepressant medications, brain stimulation is aimed more directly at the brain. Because antidepressants are carried throughout the whole body in the bloodstream, they may have greater potential for causing physical side effects, such as weight gain, upset stomach, sexual problems, or dry mouth.

Unlike traditional brain surgery, which deliberately removes or destroys a small section of the brain, treatment with brain stimulation is reversible. The price of impermanence is the need for follow-up care. ECT, TMS, and MST are noninvasive, but relapse may occur unless some type of treatment is continued long term. VNS and DBS involve the surgical implantation of a pacemaker-like device, so periodic doctor visits are required to ensure that the device is still working properly and has not slipped out of place.

All brain stimulation techniques have their own set of risks and side effects. They can also be quite expensive, and insurance may cover only some or none of the cost. In addition, more research is needed to learn about how the newer approaches work and who is most likely to benefit from them. Yet for people who are desperate for relief from severe, hard-to-treat depression, brain stimulation therapies offer fresh hope.

*See also:* Treatment of Depression; Treatment-Resistant Depression

**Further Information.** International Neuromodulation Society, 2000 Van Ness Avenue, Suite 402, San Francisco, CA 94109, (415) 683-3237, www.neuromodulation.com.

## *Bibliography*

Baldauf, Sarah. "Brain Stimulation: Can Magnetic or Electrical Pulses Help You?" *U.S. News and World Report* (July 15, 2009).

Block, David R. "Brain Stimulation Therapies for Treatment-Resistant Depression." *Psychiatric Times* (January 1, 2008).

Marangell, L. B., M. Martinez, R. A. Jurdi, and H. Zboyan. "Neurostimulation Therapies in Depression: A Review of New Modalities." *Acta Psychiatrica Scandinavica* 116 (2007): 174–181.

**BURTON, ROBERT (1577–1640).** English clergyman Robert Burton was librarian at Christ's Church College at Oxford University and vicar of St. Thomas in Oxford. Yet it is as an author that he is still remembered today. His massive tome, *The Anatomy of Melancholy*, is arguably the most influential book ever written about depression. An immediate popular success when first published in 1621, the book went through continuous revision and expansion until Burton's death in 1640.

Burton himself was given to melancholy, the type of dark, despondent mood that today might be considered a sign of depression. His book is equal parts medical text, philosophical treatise, and literary masterpiece. In it, he espouses an updated version of the theory of humors—a theory that, in its original form, dates back to the ancient Greeks and their predecessors. This theory attributes different dispositions and disorders to four fundamental body fluids, called humors. Melancholy is thought to result from an overabundance of "black bile."

### "Naught So Sad As Melancholy"

In a poem titled "The Author's Abstract of Melancholy," Burton catalogs the variety of melancholic experiences—some sweet, some sour, some divine, some damned. The stanza below captures the haunting **sadness** of a melancholic mood:

> While I lie waking all alone,
> Recounting what I have ill done,
> My thoughts on me then tyrannize,
> Fear and sorrow me surprise,
> Whether I tarry still or go,
> Methinks the time moves very slow.
> All my griefs to this are jolly,
> Naught so sad as melancholy.

Burton ascribed the presumed excess of black bile to any number of possible causes, including poor diet, immoderate drinking, lack of fresh air, physical and mental inactivity, disturbed sleep, and various "passions and perturbations of the mind." In this way, he anticipated current thinking about the multiple causes and **risk factors** for depression. Burton also described "causeless" melancholy, which arose without any obvious trigger.

Samuel Johnson (1709–1784), one of the great figures in eighteenth-century English life and letters, once remarked that Burton's *Anatomy* was the only book that ever got him out of bed two hours earlier than he wanted to arise. Although the popularity of Burton's work eventually waned, it enjoyed a strong resurgence of interest in the 1800s that continues unabated to this day.

*See also:* Historical Perspective; Melancholia

## Bibliography

Burton, Robert. *The Anatomy of Melancholy.* New York: New York Review of Books, 2001.

Radden, Jennifer, ed. *The Nature of Melancholy: From Aristotle to Kristeva.* New York: Oxford University Press, 2000.

Stone, Michael H. "Historical Aspects of Mood Disorders." In *The American Psychiatric Publishing Textbook of Mood Disorders,* by Dan J. Stein, David J. Kupfer, and Alan F. Schatzberg, eds., 3–15. Washington, DC: American Psychiatric Publishing, 2006.

**CAFFEINE.**    Caffeine is a substance found in coffee, tea, cola, cocoa, chocolate, and certain medications. It has a stimulating effect on the central **nervous system,** which makes people more alert and gives them an energy boost. These effects may be positive up to a point, but excessive caffeine can worsen mood swings, nervousness, and anxiety. In some people with depression, the result can be an increase in their symptoms.

For most people, 100 mg to 300 mg of caffeine a day—the amount in two to three cups of brewed coffee—is not harmful. But too much caffeine can lead to restlessness, anxiety, irritability, sleep problems, headaches, upset stomach, and abnormal heart rhythms. Even lesser amounts—as little as a single cup of coffee—may cause unwanted effects in people who are extra-sensitive to caffeine. Several factors can increase caffeine sensitivity, including small body size and psychological **stress**.

Although caffeine use does not cause depression, it might worsen symptoms in certain individuals. Some caffeine users develop a pattern of rollercoaster moods, in which the initial pick-me-up provided by a cup of coffee or can of cola is followed by a crash when the caffeine wears off. Caffeine also makes it harder to fall asleep and stay that way, and lack of sleep can exacerbate depression.

Despite the fact that caffeine may make depression worse, depressed individuals are sometimes tempted to use more of it than usual. This paradox is explained by the temporary energy boost that caffeine provides, which offers a quick lift to people whose energy reserves have been drained by depression. But the improvement is short-lived, and it can set up a vicious cycle that ultimately does more harm than good.

***Cutting Back on Caffeine.***    People with depression may want to limit or avoid caffeine and see if their mood improves. Those who are daily users should keep in mind that caffeine can be habit-forming, however. Stopping it too abruptly can lead to withdrawal symptoms, such increased depression, fatigue, drowsiness, anxiety, nausea, or vomiting.

To lessen such symptoms, it helps to taper off caffeine gradually. For example, someone who drinks four cups of coffee a day could cut down by one cup at a time. Some people also find it easier to reduce caffeine by replacing coffee, tea, or soda with their decaffeinated versions rather than giving up their favorite drinks entirely.

*Bibliography*

American Psychiatric Association. *Diagnostic and Statistical Manual of Mental Disorders.* 4th ed., text rev. Washington, DC: American Psychiatric Association, 2000.

*Caffeine and Depression: Is There a Link?* Mayo Clinic, October 17, 2007, http://www.mayoclinic .com/health/caffeine-and-depression/AN01700.

*Caffeine.* National Library of Medicine, http://www.nlm.nih.gov/medlineplus/caffeine.html.

*Caffeine: How Much Is Too Much?* Mayo Clinic, March 8, 2007, http://www.mayoclinic.com/print/ caffeine/NU00600.

Whalen, Diana J., Jennifer S. Silk, Mara Semel, Erika E. Forbes, Neal D. Ryan, David A. Axelson, et al. "Caffeine Consumption, Sleep, and Affect in the Natural Environments of Depressed Youth and Healthy Controls." *Journal of Pediatric Psychology* 33 (2008): 358–367.

**CANCER.** Cancer is a general term for a group of related diseases in which abnormal cells begin to grow out of control and are able to invade other tissues. There are more than 100 different types of cancer, which differ in their symptoms and prognosis. Often, though, untreated cancer can cause severe or even life-threatening illness. The disease itself or the treatment used for it may lead to a host of unpleasant symptoms, such as pain, nausea, and fatigue. Many people with cancer also develop mood and emotional problems, and up to a quarter suffer from full-blown **major depression.**

It is normal to experience **sadness** and **grief** after being diagnosed with a serious disease. Many people who have just been diagnosed with cancer develop sleeping problems, lack of appetite, feelings of despair, fears about the future, or a preoccupation with dark and gloomy thoughts. Within weeks, though, most begin to adjust. To the extent that their physical condition and treatment schedule allow, they get back to daily activities and resume their roles as students, workers, spouses, or parents.

For others, however, the adjustment goes less smoothly. The depressive symptoms linger and sometimes deepen. People who already were depressed or who have a personal or family history of depression are at particularly high risk. Those who abuse alcohol or other drugs, lack family support, or have other sources of ongoing **stress** in their lives also have a heightened risk of becoming depressed. In addition, there are cancer-specific risk factors. Having advanced cancer, poorly controlled pain, or increased physical disability boosts the likelihood of depression.

Given the seriousness of cancer, it is understandable that patients and doctors alike often give depression a low priority. Yet the consequences of ignoring depression may be far from trivial. Depressed cancer patients may be more troubled by their physical symptoms and distressed over their personal relationships. Preliminary data suggest that depression may even reduce cancer survival. Plus, the **suicide** rate in cancer patients is up to 10 times higher than in the general population.

Fortunately, although depression is a common problem for people with cancer, it is neither inevitable nor untreatable. Proper treatment for depression can enhance quality of life. This is a crucial benefit in an era when treatment providers increasingly realize that it is not only how long cancer patients live that counts, but also how well.

***The Depression Connection.*** The relationship between cancer and depression is complex. On a psychological level, having cancer can be a very stressful experience. Common sources of stress include fear of death, disruption of plans, changes in lifestyle, body image problems, and financial concerns. This stress, in turn, may trigger or worsen depression in vulnerable individuals.

On a physiological level, people with cancer sometimes develop vitamin B12 deficiency, abnormal levels of thyroid hormone, chronic pain, or various metabolic abnormalities. These conditions may affect how the brain works and lead to depression in certain people.

Some scientists think that cancer not only contributes to depression, but depression contributes to cancer as well. The latter contention is controversial, however. It is grounded in the idea that depression may impair immune functioning; for instance, by reducing cell activity in the **immune system** or lowering the number of white blood cells.

In addition to fending off germs, the immune system to a lesser extent helps the body defend itself against cells transformed by cancer. This explains why having an immune system weakened by depression might, in theory, increase a person's cancer risk. However, when researchers have looked for a link between being depressed and later developing or dying from cancer, they have found inconclusive results.

*Treatment Considerations.* The treatment for cancer depends on the cancer's type and location, if the disease has spread, and the person's age and overall health. Possible options include surgery, radiation therapy, chemotherapy, hormone therapy (treatment to block the body's natural hormones, helping slow or stop the growth of certain cancers), and biological therapy (treatment to boost or restore the immune system's ability to fight disease).

When people have both cancer and depression, treatment with **antidepressants**, **psychotherapy**, or both can help relieve their mood symptoms. The safety and effectiveness of these approaches for people with cancer has been demonstrated in a number of studies.

The types of antidepressants shown to help people with cancer include **selective serotonin reuptake inhibitors** (SSRIs) and **tricyclic antidepressants**. Although side effects are usually seen as a bad thing, some have a good side for cancer patients. For example, some antidepressants produce drowsiness, which can be helpful for people with cancer who have trouble getting to sleep.

### A Closer Look: Pancreatic Cancer

As far back as the 1930s, scientists noted a link between cancer of the pancreas and depression. In a 2003 study based on the health insurance claims of nearly 749,000 people over a five-year period, researchers found that the two conditions were indeed associated. But the reason for that association is still being debated. There are at least three possible explanations.

#### Hypothesis 1: Depression Leads to Pancreatic Cancer

In the 2003 study, people with psychiatric conditions, especially depression, were more likely to later develop pancreatic cancer than those without psychiatric conditions. Depression also was more likely to precede pancreatic cancer than other types of cancer, indicating that some kind of unique mechanism may have been involved. Other research suggests that depression may suppress immune functioning in general. But it is unclear why depression might lead to pancreatic cancer more than other cancers.

#### Hypothesis 2: Pancreatic Cancer Leads to Depression

Another possibility is that pancreatic tumor cells may produce substances that affect serotonin, a brain chemical that helps regulate mood. These substances may either block serotonin receptors in the brain or reduce the amount of serotonin available for use there.

#### Hypothesis 3: Smoking Is the Common Bond

Smoking is particularly common among people with psychiatric conditions, including depression. The risk of getting pancreatic cancer is two to three times higher in smokers, which may be due to cancer-causing chemicals in cigarette smoke that damage the pancreas.

**Focus on Prevention**

Antidepressants are intended for treating depression once it has already taken hold. But in one small study, patients with melanoma, the deadliest form of skin cancer, were given an SSRI as a preventive measure before they ever became depressed. These patients were scheduled to receive high-dose interferon-alpha, a biological therapy that works well for treating melanoma but often causes depressive symptoms as a side effect. In this preliminary study, taking an antidepressant preventively seemed to minimize any depression.

*Psychological Approaches.* Psychological approaches can also help people with cancer adjust to their disease, cope with problems, and find relief from depression. Such approaches can be used alone or combined with medication.

In a recent study of 200 depressed individuals with various types of cancer, half were randomly selected to take part in a depression management program. The program consisted of up to 10 sessions over a three-month period, with a focus on helping participants learn to take antidepressants properly, handle problems better, and stay active. Interestingly, the sessions were led by nurses who received training in the program and were supervised by psychiatrists, but who were not required to have a background in psychiatric nursing. Program participants had greater reductions in depression than people in a control group, and the benefits lasted for at least a year. One advantage to this program was the modest cost of $670 per participant.

As far as formal therapy goes, there is strong research evidence that **cognitive-behavioral therapy** can help relieve depression in people with cancer. This type of therapy helps people recognize and change maladaptive thoughts and behaviors. There is also good evidence for the benefits of **supportive therapy**, which offers emotional support to people in distress using methods such as reassurance and advice, and **problem-solving treatment**, which helps people identify and address life problems that are contributing to their distress.

In addition, several studies have shown that **psychoeducation**, which offers information about a disease and its management, can reduce depression and fear of the unknown in cancer patients. Other studies have found that **relaxation techniques**, which help people release mental and physical tension, can decrease feelings of stress and depression.

*See also:* Mood Disorder Due to a General Medical Condition; Physical Illness

**Further Information.** American Cancer Society, 250 Williams Street N.W., Atlanta, GA 30303, (800) 227-2345, www.cancer.org.

National Cancer Institute, 6116 Executive Boulevard, Room 3036A, Bethesda, MD 20892, (800) 422-6237, www.cancer.gov.

National Comprehensive Cancer Network, 275 Commerce Drive, Suite 300, Fort Washington, PA 19034, (215) 690-0300, www.nccn.org.

*Bibliography*

*A New Approach for Treating Depression in Cancer Patients.* American Cancer Society, August 22, 2008, http://www.cancer.org/docroot/NWS/content/NWS_1_1x_A_New_Approach_for_Treating _Depression_in_Cancer_Patients.asp.

Akechi, T., T. Okuyama, J. Onishi, T. Morita, and T. A. Furukawa. "Psychotherapy for Depression Among Incurable Cancer Patients (Review)." *Cochrane Database of Systematic Reviews* 2 (2008): art. no. CD005537.

*Cancer: Questions and Answers.* National Cancer Institute, June 6, 2005, http://www.cancer.gov/cancertopics/factsheet/Sites-Types/general.

Carney, Caroline P., Laura Jones, Robert F. Woolson, Russell Noyes Jr., and Bradley N. Doebbeling. "Relationship Between Depression and Pancreatic Cancer in the General Population." *Psychosomatic Medicine* 65 (2003): 884–888.

*Depression (PDQ): Health Professional Version.* National Cancer Institute, October 29, 2008, http://www.cancer.gov/cancertopics/pdq/supportivecare/depression/HealthProfessional.

*Depression (PDQ): Patient Version.* National Cancer Institute, October 24, 2008, http://www.cancer.gov/cancertopics/pdq/supportivecare/depression.

*Detailed Guide: Pancreatic Cancer.* American Cancer Society, http://www.cancer.org/docroot/CRI/CRI_2_3x.asp?rnav=cridg&dt=34.

Fisch, Michael. "Treatment of Depression in Cancer." *Journal of the National Cancer Institute Monographs* 32 (2004): 105–111.

Jacobsen, Paul B., and Heather S. Jim. "Psychosocial Interventions for Anxiety and Depression in Adult Cancer Patients: Achievements and Challenges." *CA: A Cancer Journal for Clinicians* 58 (2008): 214–230.

Musselman, Dominique L., David H. Lawson, Jane F. Gumnick, Amita K. Manatunga, Suzanne Penna, Rebecca S. Goodkin, et al. "Paroxetine for the Prevention of Depression Induced by High-Dose Interferon Alfa." *New England Journal of Medicine* 344 (2001): 961–966.

National Comprehensive Cancer Network. *Distress Management: NCCN Clinical Practice Guidelines in Oncology.* Version 1. Fort Washington, PA: National Comprehensive Cancer Network, 2008.

Pirl, William F. "Evidence Report on the Occurrence, Assessment, and Treatment of Depression in Cancer Patients." *Journal of the National Cancer Institute Monographs* 32 (2004): 32–39.

Strong, Vanessa, Rachel Waters, Carina Hibberd, Gordon Murray, Lucy Wall, Jane Walker, et al. "Management of Depression for People with Cancer (SMaRT Oncology 1): A Randomised Trial." *Lancet* 372 (2008): 40–48.

*What Is Cancer?* National Cancer Institute, April 8, 2008, http://www.cancer.gov/cancertopics/what-is-cancer.

**CATATONIC DEPRESSION.** Catatonic depression is a subtype of **major depression** that is characterized by extreme changes in activity level. Most people associate a catatonic state with severe reductions in movement and responsiveness, but it can also take the form of extreme overactivity, and/or bizarre behavior.

A change in activity level is a common symptom of depression. It is only when the changes are extreme that they may qualify as catatonia. For instance, someone with ordinary depression might move so slowly that it takes two hours to get dressed. But someone with catatonic depression might stand completely immobile for days at a time.

Without treatment, catatonic depression can have severe, even life-threatening, consequences. Those in a state of catatonic stupor may fail to eat, leading to malnutrition, and those in a state of catatonic overexcitement may engage in frenetic activity, leading to exhaustion. In addition, some of the more bizarre behaviors associated with catatonic depression may lead people to injure themselves or others. Careful supervision and round-the-clock care are often needed until treatment begins to take hold.

*Criteria for Diagnosis.* Catatonic depression is a variant of major depression. All forms of major depression involve being in a low mood nearly all the time or losing interest or enjoyment in almost everything. These feelings last for at least two weeks, are associated with several other symptoms, and lead to serious problems getting along in everyday life.

In addition to meeting the diagnostic criteria for major depression, people with catatonic depression have at least two symptoms from the list below. The most severe symptoms are profoundly disabling, leaving the person completely unable to function without help.

*Lack of Movement and Responsiveness.* Catatonic depression is often marked by a sustained, extreme lack of response to the outside world. Some people exhibit catalepsy, a state in which they hold the same body position for hours or even days on end. If moved into a new position, they will maintain it indefinitely—a characteristic known as "waxy flexibility," because the body can be molded like a wax figure. Others sink into a stupor, a trance-like state in which they are immobile, mute, and seemingly unaware of their surroundings.

*Extreme Overactivity.* In other cases, catatonic depression is marked by ceaseless activity. This is different from the overactivity seen in **mania**, an overly high mood that alternates with depression in bipolar disorder. Those in the grips of mania might try to accomplish six things at once. But those with catatonic depression are in a world of their own. Their excessive activity has no obvious purpose and is not affected by external events.

*Extreme Negativity.* The negativity of catatonic depression can take a variety of forms. Some people are extremely resistant to complying with even the simplest requests. Others adopt a rigid body posture that resists all attempts to be moved. And still others refuse to speak for days or weeks.

*Bizarre Behavior.* Catatonic depression sometimes leads to very odd-looking behavior. This may take the form of bizarre postures, unusual mannerisms, or pronounced grimacing. Or it may involve stereotyped movements—nonfunctional, often self-injurious behaviors that the person seems driven to repeat over and over, such as rocking, head banging, or self-biting.

*Purposeless Imitation.* Catatonic depression may lead to imitative behavior that has no apparent purpose. Some people develop echolalia—the parrot-like repetition of another person's speech. Others develop echopraxia—the seemingly involuntary mimicking of another's movements.

***Causes and Risk Factors.*** Catatonic symptoms can occur not only in people with major depression, but also in those with other severe mental disorders, such as schizophrenia. All told, from 5 percent to 9 percent of psychiatric inpatients display catatonic symptoms. Of that group, it is estimated that one-quarter to one-half have either major depression or bipolar disorder. Compared to catatonic patients with bipolar disorder or schizophrenia, those with catatonic depression have the best outlook for **recovery**.

***Treatment for Catatonic Depression.*** Due to the urgency of catatonic depression, psychiatric **hospitalization** is sometimes required until the worst symptoms begin to subside. Hospitalization allows those with severe symptoms to receive intensive, specialized care and close, round-the-clock monitoring. The hospitalization is usually short-term, similar to hospital care for other medical illnesses.

In some cases, immediate relief is obtained by administering a benzodiazepine intravenously. Benzodiazepines are anti-anxiety drugs that have a calming effect and relax the muscles. Once the initial crisis has passed, benzodiazepines may be combined with or replaced by **antidepressants**, medications specifically designed to relieve depression.

Another treatment that may be considered early on is **electroconvulsive therapy** (ECT). This treatment involves passing a carefully controlled electrical current through the person's brain, which induces a brief seizure that is thought to alter some of the electrochemical processes involved in brain functioning. Modern ECT is painless and relatively safe, and it works faster than other depression treatments.

As the catatonic symptoms start to lessen, treatment with an antidepressant is usually continued. If the antidepressant alone isn't enough, another type of medication may be added or substituted. **Antipsychotics** are medications that are specifically designed to relieve or prevent severe symptoms of mental illness. **Lithium** is a medication that helps stabilize moods. Once the catatonic features fade, **psychotherapy** also may play a role in treating depression and preventing future episodes or keeping them from becoming so severe.

## Bibliography

American Psychiatric Association Work Group on Major Depressive Disorder. *Practice Guideline for the Treatment of Patients with Major Depressive Disorder.* 2nd ed. Washington, DC: American Psychiatric Publishing, 2000.

American Psychiatric Association. *Diagnostic and Statistical Manual of Mental Disorders.* 4th ed., text rev. Washington, DC: American Psychiatric Association, 2000.

Frances, Allen, Michael B. First, and Harold Alan Pincus. *DSM-IV Guidebook.* Washington, DC: American Psychiatric Press, 1995.

Penland, Heath R., Natalie Weder, and Rajesh R. Tampi. "The Catatonic Dilemma Expanded." *Annals of General Psychiatry* 5 (2006): 14.

**CAUSES OF DEPRESSION.**   Depression does not have a single cause. Instead, it seems to be caused by a combination of genetic, biological, environmental, and psychological factors. An individual's unique mix of factors and the complex way they interact are what ultimately determine whether that person becomes depressed.

**Genetic factors** are passed down from parent to child through the genes. Scientists have found genetic variations on several chromosomes that may play a role in depression. Each variation by itself confers only a small amount of risk. Depression seems to result from the combined effect of multiple genes acting in concert with the environment—in short, both nature and nurture.

**Environmental factors** lie outside the person, but they nevertheless influence that individual's functioning and behavior. A large body of evidence shows that both everyday life **stress** and once-in-a-lifetime **traumatic events** may trigger or worsen depression in genetically vulnerable individuals.

Biological factors that underlie depression include physiological changes in brain pathways and chemistry. **Neurotransmitters** and **hormones**—chemical messengers of the nervous and endocrine systems, respectively—seem to play a central role in causing and maintaining depressive symptoms.

Psychological factors have a major impact on depression as well. An irrationally negative thinking style seems to be a core feature of the illness. Certain personality styles—such as excessive dependence or self-criticism—may also predispose people to the development of depression.

*See also:* Biopsychosocial Model; Cognitive Factors; Diathesis-Stress Model; Monoamine Hypothesis; Personality Factors

## Bibliography

*Depression (Major Depression): Causes.* Mayo Clinic, February 14, 2008, http://www.mayoclinic.com/health/depression/DS00175/DSECTION=causes.

Gotlib, Ian H., and Constance L. Hammen, eds. *Handbook of Depression.* 2nd ed. New York: Guilford Press, 2009.

Stein, Dan J., David J. Kupfer, and Alan F. Schatzberg, eds. *The American Psychiatric Publishing Textbook of Mood Disorders.* Washington, DC: American Psychiatric Publishing, 2006.

*What Causes Depression?* National Institute of Mental Health, January 30, 2009, http://www.nimh.nih.gov/health/publications/depression/what-causes-depression.shtml.

**CENTER FOR EPIDEMIOLOGIC STUDIES DEPRESSION SCALE.** The Center for Epidemiologic Studies Depression Scale (CES-D) is a short self-report questionnaire designed to measure the severity of depression symptoms in the population at large. Published in 1977, the scale was developed by Lenore Sawyer Radloff (1935– ) while she was a researcher at the National Institute of Mental Health. Originally, it was intended for use in epidemiological studies, which look at the occurrence and distribution of a disease within a population. However, it is now commonly used in clinical settings, too.

The CES-D, which takes about five minutes to complete, consists of 20 items describing various symptoms of depression. People rate how often they have experienced each of the symptoms during the past week. Scores range from 0 to 60, with higher scores indicating more severe symptoms.

As a research tool, the test is used to conduct community surveys. In clinical practice, it may be used to screen for depression in people who might have the illness, but who have not yet been diagnosed. Those who score in the depressed range on the test should then undergo a full diagnostic interview. The CES-D score alone is not sufficient for making a diagnosis.

***Pros and Cons of the CES-D.*** The CES-D has proved to be a very useful tool for detecting depression in adults of various ages and ethnic backgrounds. It has been studied in a variety of populations, including African American, Asian American, Hispanic, French, Greek, Japanese, and Yugoslavian. But it probably is not equally appropriate for everyone. For instance, one study found that the scale had limited predictive power in low-income women.

Overall, the CES-D seems to have good reliability, the extent to which the results of the test are consistent and repeatable. However, it does not perform as well when it comes to its ability to discriminate depression from other disorders. Rather than a specific measure of depression, it may be more accurate to view it as a general measure of distress.

*See also:* Diagnosis of Depression; Screening Tests

*Bibliography*

Radloff, Lenore Sawyer. "The CES-D Scale: A Self-Report Depression Scale for Research in the General Population." *Applied Psychological Measurement* 1 (1977): 385–401.

Thomas, Janet L., Glenn N. Jones, Isabel C. Scarinci, Daniel J. Mehan, and Phillip J. Brantley. "The Utility of the CES-D as a Depression Screening Measure Among Low-Income Women Attending Primary Care Clinics." *International Journal of Psychiatry in Medicine* 31 (2001): 25–40.

Yonkers, Kimberly A., and Jacqueline A. Samson. "Mood Disorders Measures." In *Handbook of Psychiatric Measures,* 2nd ed., by A. John Rush Jr., Michael B. First, and Deborah Blacker, eds., 499–528. Washington, DC: American Psychiatric Publishing, 2008.

**CERLETTI, UGO (1877–1963).** Ugo Cerletti was an Italian neurologist and psychiatrist who developed **electroconvulsive therapy** (ECT), a treatment that involves passing a small amount of electrical current through a person's brain to induce a brief seizure. The seizure, in turn, may reduce symptoms of **major depression**, **bipolar disorder**, or schizophrenia. Today, ECT is still recognized as the most effective and fastest-acting treatment for depression. It is often helpful for severe or suicidal depression even when other treatments have failed to work.

Cerletti's collaborator in the development of ECT was his assistant, Lucino Bini (1908–1964). In the 1930s, while studying epilepsy in animals, the men realized that electricity could bring on a seizure. At the time, researchers elsewhere were experimenting with the use of medications to induce seizures, which seemed to help relieve schizophrenia. Cerletti and Bini decided to try using electricity for the same purpose. After testing the technique on dogs, they administered the first ECT treatment to a human patient with schizophrenia on April 14, 1938. With one incomplete and 11 complete ECT sessions, the patient was much improved and able to return to work. The success of this initial experiment led to further trials of ECT in mentally ill patients.

When Cerletti and Bini published their work, originally in Italian and later in English, it created a stir in the psychiatric community. During World War II, ECT was included in the training for military medical personnel, and by the 1950s, it had become a standard treatment for hospitalized patients with depression. Although **antidepressants** eventually replaced ECT as a first-choice treatment, ECT remains an important option for those with hard-to-treat depression or urgent symptoms, such as suicidal impulses.

***Early Career Highlights.***    Cerletti was born in Conegliano, Italy, in 1877. As a young man, he initially studied medicine in Rome and Turin. Later, he traveled to France and Germany to work under some of the most illustrious neurologists and psychiatrists of the day, including Emil Kraepelin (1856–1926) and Alois Alzheimer (1864–1915).

In 1919, Cerletti was appointed director of the Neurobiological Institute at the psychiatric hospital in Milan. After that, he took teaching positions, first in Bari and then in Genoa. Finally, in 1935, he became chair of the department of mental and neurological diseases at the University of Rome, where he conducted his pioneering research on ECT.

***Cerletti in Perspective.***    Although it was ECT that brought Cerletti worldwide fame, he made many other contributions to neurology during the course of his long career. For example, he studied characteristic brain changes in Alzheimer's disease, the blood-brain barrier, and the structure of neuroglia (specialized cells in the nervous system that nourish and support neurons). Among many awards and honors, he received an honorary degree from the Sorbonne (University of Paris) in 1950.

Yet it is for the development of ECT that Cerletti is best remembered. Although ECT was hailed as a great advance by some, it attracted criticism as well. In the early days, before doctors learned how to properly control the procedure, it could result in serious memory loss, broken or dislocated bones, or occasionally even death. Doctors soon learned to better modulate the dose of electricity to reduce the mental side effects, and the addition of anesthesia and muscle relaxants eliminated pain and bone-jarring physical convulsions. Technical refinements made ECT a much gentler, safer procedure, but some risks, such as milder memory loss, remain a concern to this day.

Over the decades, ECT has inspired both great enthusiasm over its effectiveness and great controversy over its risks. But more than 70 years after its introduction, ECT still has an unparalleled track record when it comes to treating the most challenging cases of depression.

## Bibliography

*A Scientific Odyssey: People and Discoveries—Electroshock Therapy Introduced.* PBS, 1998, http://www.pbs.org/wgbh/aso/databank/entries/dh38el.html.

*Electroconvulsive Therapy.* Mayo Clinic, July 11, 2008, http://www.mayoclinic.com/health/electroconvulsive-therapy/MY00129.

Sabbatini, Renato M. E. "Ugo Cerletti: A Brief Biography." *Brain and Mind Magazine* (August/September 1997).

Shorter, Edward. "The History of ECT: Unsolved Mysteries." *Psychiatric Times* (February 1, 2004).

"Ugo Cerletti 1877–1963." *American Journal of Psychiatry* 156 (1999): 630.

**CHILDREN.**   Until the last few decades, depression in children was regarded as trivial or even nonexistent. Today, that has changed. Childhood depression—also called pediatric depression—is now recognized as a serious disorder that can cause great distress and disruption. Left untreated, depression can interfere with healthy social, emotional, and intellectual development. Fortunately, like teens and adults, children with depression can be helped to feel better and get their lives back on track with appropriate treatment.

Diagnosed depression is uncommon in early childhood, affecting about one percent of preschoolers ages two through five. Once children reach school age, the prevalence rate climbs to about three percent—still lower than in **adolescents** and adults, but no longer rare. In adults, women are twice as likely as men to experience **major depression**. Before puberty, however, girls and boys are about equally likely to be affected.

Childhood depression often exists side by side with other problems, including **anxiety disorders**, **attention-deficit hyperactivity disorder**, and **conduct disorder**. Depression itself also tends to recur, and a younger age of onset only increases the risk of more episodes in the future.

*Diagnostic Challenges.*   From preschool-age onward, depression is identified using the same diagnostic criteria as those used for adults. Only two developmental variations are mentioned in the ***Diagnostic and Statistical Manual of Mental Disorders, Fourth Edition, Text Revision*** (*DSM-IV-TR*). In children, a **depressed mood** sometimes leads to feeling irritable rather than sad or empty. Also, the minimum duration of symptoms required for **dysthymia**—a relatively mild but very long-lasting form of depression—is one year for children, compared to two years for adults.

In clinical practice, though, childhood depression actually may differ more from its adult counterpart than *DSM-IV-TR* criteria imply. Children who are depressed may pretend to be sick, refuse to go to school, or have a drop in grades. They also may act clingy or develop unhealthy fears and worries, such as constantly worrying that a parent will die. Youngsters who once loved to play with friends may start to spend most of their time alone and never seem to have any fun. Older children with depression may become sullen and cranky, get into trouble at school, and feel as if nobody understands them.

Because it is normal for children's behavior to change rapidly as they grow and mature, it may be tempting to pass off such symptoms as nothing more than a temporary phase. At times, that might well be the case. But if the symptoms cause serious distress or disruption and last more than a couple of weeks, they could signal depression or another treatable condition.

A professional **diagnosis of depression** involves evaluating symptoms in light of a child's age and developmental level. In addition to talking with the child, the health care provider may gather information from parents, other caregivers, and teachers. Preschoolers present a special challenge, because they may have trouble expressing themselves verbally. With this age group, information supplied by those close to the child may be particularly important. Regardless of a child's age, a skilled professional also can learn a lot by closely observing the youngster's behavior and body language.

*Treatment Considerations.*   Just like teens and adults, children with depression generally benefit from treatment with **psychotherapy**, **antidepressants**, or a combination of both. When it comes to psychotherapy, **cognitive-behavioral therapy** (CBT) is the best-studied approach. Children who are depressed often have an unrealistically negative view of themselves and their world, and CBT can help them develop a more positive outlook. In some cases, it may be helpful to involve other family members in therapy sessions, an approach known as **family therapy**.

When it comes to medication, antidepressants may be beneficial as well, helping children who have been sidelined by depression get back to the important business of learning, playing, and growing up. Like all medications, though, antidepressants carry a risk of side effects. One risk that has received considerable attention is an increased likelihood of suicidal thoughts or actions in young people. In short-term studies involving children and teenagers with depression and other illnesses, four out of 100 youngsters who took antidepressants became suicidal, although none actually completed suicide. By comparison, two out of 100 who took a sugar pill became suicidal. In 2005, the Food and Drug Administration asked drug companies to add a black box to their labeling for antidepressants warning about an increased risk of suicidal thoughts and behavior in children and adolescents.

Another concern is that children's bodies absorb and eliminate medications differently than adults' bodies do, and their brains might be affected differently, too. Some worry that the wrong drug at the wrong time could sidetrack normal development, leading to adverse effects that last long after the medication is stopped. On the other hand, the risks of not treating depression are also apt to be greatest during the formative years, when children are still developing intellectually, emotionally, and socially.

The decision to treat a particular child with antidepressants is made on a case-by-case basis, weighing the possible risks against the expected benefits. To minimize the risks, parents should contact the child's health care provider right away if a child on antidepressants experiences unusual changes in behavior or mood. Changes to watch for include (1) suicidal thoughts or actions, (2) worsening of depression, (3) new or worse anxiety or **irritability**, (4) agitation or restlessness, (5) panic attacks, (6) trouble sleeping, (7) aggressive or violent behavior, (8) dangerously impulsive behavior, or (9) an extreme increase in activity and talking.

Antidepressants have not been studied as extensively in children as in adults. Of the numerous antidepressants on the market, only **fluoxetine** has gone through the rigorous research process that is required to be approved by the Food and Drug Administration specifically for the treatment of major depression in children. Nevertheless, doctors can use their medical judgment and clinical experience to prescribe other antidepressants for children, a practice known as off-label prescribing. This practice is both perfectly legal and very common, and it opens up a wider range of treatment options.

Clearly, though, a better-case scenario is that more research be done in the future to identify the safest, most effective medications for this age group. Until such research is completed, doctors and parents must be particularly judicious when weighing the pros and cons of antidepressant treatment.

*See also:* Antidepressants and Suicide; Infants

***Further Information.*** American Academy of Child and Adolescent Psychiatry, 3615 Wisconsin Avenue N.W., Washington, D.C.20016, (202) 966-7300, www.aacap.org.

American Academy of Pediatrics, 141 Northwest Point Boulevard, Elk Grove Village, IL 60007, (847) 434-4000, www.aap.org.

Nemours Foundation, www.kidshealth.org.

Society of Clinical Child and Adolescent Psychology, clinicalchildpsychology.org.

## Bibliography

American Psychiatric Association. *Diagnostic and Statistical Manual of Mental Disorders.* Washington, DC: American Psychiatric Association, 1952.

*Antidepressants for Children: Explore the Pros and Cons.* Mayo Clinic, November 15, 2008, http://www.mayoclinic.com/health/antidepressants/MH00059.

*Depression in Children and Adolescents.* National Institute of Mental Health, June 9, 2009, http://www.nimh.nih.gov/health/topics/depression/depression-in-children-andadolescents .shtml.

*Depression Treatment for Children: What Works?* Mayo Clinic, October 9, 2008, http://www .mayoclinic.com/health/depression-treatment/AN00685.

Garber, Judy, Catherine M. Gallerani, and Sarah A. Frankel. "Depression in Children." In *Handbook of Depression.* 2nd ed., by Ian H. Gotlib and Constance L. Hammen, eds., 405–443. New York: Guilford Press, 2009.

*How Do Children and Adolescents Experience Depression?* National Institute of Mental Health, http://www.nimh.nih.gov/health/publications/depression/how-do-children-and -adolescents-experience-depression.shtml.

*Medication Guide about Using Antidepressants in Children and Teenagers.* Food and Drug Administration, January 26, 2006, http://www.fda.gov/downloads/Drugs/DrugSafety/ InformationbyDrugClass/UCM161646.pdf.

*Questions and Answers on Antidepressant Use in Children, Adolescents, and Adults: May, 2007.* Food and Drug Administration, May 22, 2009, http://www.fda.gov/Drugs/DrugSafety/ InformationbyDrugClass/ucm096321.htm.

*Should Children Take Antidepressants?* Harvard University, 2005, https://www.health.harvard.edu/ newsweek/Should_children_take_antidepressants.htm.

*Statistics on Depression.* Depression and Bipolar Support Alliance, January 30, 2009, http://www.dbsalliance.org/site/PageServer?pagename=about_statistics_depression&printer _friendly=1.

*The Depressed Child.* American Academy of Child and Adolescent Psychiatry, May 2008, http://www.aacap.org/cs/root/facts_for_families/the_depressed_child.

*Treatment of Children with Mental Disorders.* National Institute of Mental Health, January 27, 2009, http://www.nimh.nih.gov/health/publications/treatment-of-children-with-mental-disorders/ index.shtml.

**CHILDREN'S DEPRESSION INVENTORY.** The Children's Depression Inventory (CDI) is a self-report questionnaire specifically designed to assess the severity of depression symptoms in young people ages 7 through 17. It is modeled after the **Beck Depression Inventory**, one of the most widely used measures of depression in adults. Developed by U.S. psychologist Maria Kovacs (1944– ), the CDI was first published in 1977, and it remains a popular screening tool today.

The CDI consists of 27 items, each of which presents three statements about a particular symptom of depression arranged in order of increasing severity. **Children** choose the statement that most closely matches how they have felt within the past two weeks. The paper-and-pencil questionnaire, which takes about 15 minutes to complete, is easy to read and can be given individually or to a group. There is also a shortened version, as well as versions designed to be filled out by a parent or teacher.

The CDI can be used for routine screening at schools, pediatric clinics, residential treatment centers, and other places that cater to school-aged children. In addition, it can be used for research purposes and in clinical settings to assess how well treatment is working.

***Pros and Cons of the CDI.*** Research on the CDI has found that it has good reliability, the extent to which results of the test are consistent and repeatable. The available evidence also suggests that the test does an adequate job of distinguishing depressed children from both healthy children and those with other disorders. However, more research is needed in this area.

On the downside, the CDI is prone to false negatives—scores that indicate no depression in individuals who actually have the disorder. This calls into question its value for screening groups of children in an effort to identify those who need further evaluation. The high false-negative rate means that many children who actually have depression may be missed using this test.

*See also:* Adolescents; Diagnosis of Depression; Screening Tests

## Bibliography

Brotman, Laurie Miller, Dimitra Kamboukos, and Rachelle Theise. "Symptom-Specific Measures for Disorders Usually First Diagnosed in Infancy, Childhood, or Adolescence." In *Handbook of Psychiatric Measures,* 2nd ed., by A. John Rush Jr., Michael B. First, and Deborah Blacker, eds., 309–342. Washington, DC: American Psychiatric Publishing, 2008.

Carlson, Janet F. and Stephen J. Freeman. "Children's Depression Inventory (2003 Update)." *The Seventeenth Mental Measurements Yearbook,* http://www.unl.edu/buros.

*Children's Depression Inventory.* Multi-health Systems, http://www.mhs.com.

Heisel, W. J. and J. L. Matson. "The Assessment of Depression in Children: The Internal Structure of the Child Depression Inventory (CDI)." *Behavior Research and Therapy* 22 (1984): 289–298.

Hodges, K. and W. E. Craighead. "Relationship of Children's Depression Inventory Factors to Diagnosed Depression." *Psychological Assessment* 2 (1990): 489–492.

Kovacs, M. "Rating Scales to Assess Depression in School-Aged Children." *Acta Paedopsychiatrica* 46 (1981): 305–315.

**CHRONIC DEPRESSION.**    Chronic depression refers to depression in which the symptoms last for at least two years. Typically, depression is a come-and-go illness. Each episode lasts for weeks or months, but it eventually goes away, and there is a period of **recovery** before the next episode begins. For people with chronic depression, though, the depression stretches on for years. Over time, the unrelenting low mood wears away at their mental, physical, and social well-being. Feelings of hopelessness and thoughts of helplessness become ingrained.

Because chronic depression lasts for years, people with the condition may start to believe that feeling constantly sad or dispirited is "just the way they are." They may accept the continual trouble functioning in daily life and getting along in relationships as normal for them. Yet chronic depression is a disorder that can be treated, and even people who have been depressed for many years can begin to enjoy a richer, more satisfying life.

*Forms of Chronic Depression.*    Chronic depression can take two main forms. In chronic **major depression**, the person experiences a low mood nearly all the time or loses interest or enjoyment in almost everything. These feelings are associated with several other symptoms and lead to serious problems getting along at home, work, or school. To be considered chronic, the symptoms of major depression must be present continuously for two years or longer.

In **dysthymia**, the person feels mildly depressed most of the day. These feelings occur more days than not for at least two years and are associated with other symptoms. In children and adolescents, dysthymia can lead to a mood that seems irritable rather than depressed, and the symptoms only need to last for a year before a diagnosis can be made.

*Causes and Risk Factors.*    There are several theories about why depression might be so long-lasting in some people. **Genetic factors** may play a role. Both people with dysthymia and those with episodic major depression are about equally likely to have a close relative with major depression, with a risk that is higher than in people with no mental disorder. But those with dysthymia have a higher rate of that disorder among their close relatives than either those with no mental disorder or those with episodic major depression. This suggests that there may be one set of family factors that predispose certain people to depression in general, and another that confers a specific risk of chronic depression.

**Stress** also seems to be an important risk factor. Studies suggest that very stressful experiences in childhood, such as sexual and physical abuse or parental neglect and rejection, may predispose people to developing chronic depression. Once depression begins, interpersonal problems may play a role in maintaining and prolonging the symptoms. In fact, any form of severe long-term stress, such as having a serious medical illness or a loved one who is incapacitated, may trigger and maintain chronic depression in people who are vulnerable to becoming depressed.

Thinking style may contribute to chronic depression as well. U.S. psychologist Susan Nolen-Hoeksema (1959– ) has theorized that depression may be prolonged by **rumination**—repetitive, passive thinking about the dark side of life. People with this thinking style tend to brood over negative feelings and distressing symptoms ("I feel terrible all the time") and worry about their meaning ("Will I ever stop feeling so bad?"). Several studies have shown that people who ruminate when they are sad or blue are prone to higher levels of depression over time than people who don't ruminate, even when initial levels of depression are taken into account.

People with chronic depression also are more likely than those with episodic depression to have a personality disorder—a pervasive, long-lasting pattern of thinking, feeling, and behaving that deviates from cultural expectations and leads to distress or dysfunction. The reasons for this connection are difficult to untangle. On one hand, the chronic stress and interpersonal problems caused by a personality disorder could trigger and maintain depression. On the other hand, chronic depression that starts in childhood could adversely affect personality formation. It is also possible that chronic depression and personality disorders share a common genetic or environmental cause. Further research is needed to sort out the nature of this relationship.

***Treatment of Chronic Depression.*** Treatment for chronic depression typically involves **antidepressants**, **psychotherapy**, or a combination of both. In general, though, psychotherapy alone may be somewhat less effective than it is for episodic major depression. It is likely that medication will be needed, too.

If the first antidepressant tried does not do the job, better results may be obtained by switching to another medication, combining two antidepressants of different types, or combining an antidepressant with another medication that was not originally intended to treat depression, but that may boost the antidepressant's action. Because it may take a while for the full effects of medication to kick in, it also helps to stick with the treatment regimen for up to three months before concluding that it does not work.

When psychotherapy is used, studies have shown benefits from **cognitive-behavioral therapy** (CBT), which helps people change self-defeating thoughts and maladaptive behaviors, and **interpersonal therapy** (IPT), which helps people address interpersonal triggers for their symptoms. In addition, **psychodynamic therapy**, which stresses the impact of unconscious influences and past experiences on current behavior, may help people examine the psychological factors that maintain their depression over time.

A blend of CBT and IPT, called **cognitive behavioral analysis system of psychotherapy** (CBASP), is the first psychotherapy to be devised specifically for treating chronic depression. Research has yielded promising results. CBASP was developed by U.S. psychologist James P. McCullough Jr. (1936– ), a professor at Virginia Commonwealth University.

The theory behind this therapy is that depressed adults are stuck at an immature level of interpersonal functioning. They have become disconnected from the environment, so they do not perceive the consequences of their actions. Through a technique called situational analysis, people learn to recognize the effects of their behavior on others and use this information to change their maladaptive thoughts and behaviors.

When medication and psychotherapy don't provide enough relief, **electroconvulsive therapy** (ECT) may be considered. This treatment involves passing a carefully controlled electrical current through the person's brain, which induces a brief seizure that is thought to alter some of the electrochemical processes involved in brain functioning.

Another option is **vagus nerve stimulation**, which uses a small implanted device, similar to a pacemaker, to deliver mild electrical pulses to the vagus nerve. This nerve then transmits the pulses to the brain, targeting areas that affect mood and other symptoms of depression. Thanks to the growing number of treatments that are available, the odds of beating chronic depression are rising as well.

*See also:* Treatment-Resistant Depression

## Bibliography

American Psychiatric Association Work Group on Major Depressive Disorder. *Practice Guideline for the Treatment of Patients with Major Depressive Disorder.* 2nd ed. Washington, DC: American Psychiatric Publishing, 2000.

American Psychiatric Association. *Diagnostic and Statistical Manual of Mental Disorders.* 4th ed., text rev. Washington, DC: American Psychiatric Association, 2000.

Arnow, Bruce A., and Michael J. Constantino. "Effectiveness of Psychotherapy and Combination Treatment for Chronic Depression." *Journal of Clinical Psychology* 59 (2003): 893–905.

*Cognitive Behavioral Analysis System of Psychotherapy: Psychopathology and Treatment.* CBASP .org, http://www.cbasp.org/psy.htm.

Klein, Daniel N., and Neil J. Santiago. "Dysthymia and Chronic Depression: Introduction, Classification, Risk Factors, and Course." *Journal of Clinical Psychology* 59 (2003): 807–816.

Klein, Daniel N., Stewart A. Shankman, Peter M. Lewinsohn, Paul Rohde, and John R. Seeley. "Family Study of Chronic Depression in a Community Sample of Young Adults." *American Journal of Psychiatry* 161 (2004): 646–653.

Law, Bridget Murray. "Probing the Depression-Rumination Cycle." *Monitor on Psychology* (November 2005).

McCullough, James P. Jr. *Treating Chronic Depression with Disciplined Personal Involvement: Cognitive Behavioral Analysis System of Psychotherapy (CBASP).* New York: Springer, 2006.

McCullough, James P. Jr. *Treatment for Chronic Depression: Cognitive Behavioral Analysis System of Psychotherapy (CBASP).* New York: Guilford Press, 2003.

McCullough, James P. Jr., Daniel N. Klein, Frances E. Borian, Robert H. Howland, Lawrence P. Riso, Martin B. Keller, et al. "Group Comparisons of *DSM-IV* Subtypes of Chronic Depression: Validity of the Distinctions, Part 2." *Journal of Abnormal Psychology* 112 (2003): 614–622.

*Next Steps: Getting the Treatment You Need to Reach Real Recovery.* Depression and Bipolar Support Alliance, 2006, http://www.dbsalliance.org/pdfs/NextSteps.pdf.

Nolen-Hoeksema, Susan. "The Role of Rumination in Depressive Disorders and Mixed Anxiety/Depressive Symptoms." *Journal of Abnormal Psychology* 109 (2000): 504–511.

Thase, Michael E., and Susan S. Lang. *Beating the Blues: New Approaches to Overcoming Dysthymia and Chronic Mild Depression.* New York: Oxford University Press, 2004.

*Treatment-Resistant Depression: Explore Options When Depression Won't Go Away.* Mayo Clinic, August 29, 2007, http://www.mayoclinic.com/health/treatment-resistant-depression/DN00016.

**CHRONIC PAIN.**   Chronic pain is pain that persists for weeks, months, or even years. Acute pain is a normal sensation that serves a helpful purpose: It is the means by which the **nervous system** alerts a person to possible injury and prompts that person to take protective action. Although acute pain may be distressing, it is self-limiting. Chronic pain, in contrast, continues indefinitely and interferes with day-to-day functioning. As time wears on, the relentless pain can take a psychological toll, often bringing with it **stress** and depression.

In some cases, an initial mishap, such as a muscle strain or serious infection, sets chronic pain in motion. In other cases, there is an ongoing cause of lasting pain, such as arthritis or cancer. But still for other people, the source of chronic pain remains unknown. No obvious injury or illness can be found. Yet the suffering is all too evident.

By definition, pain is subjective. The International Association for the Study of Pain defines it as "an unpleasant sensory and emotional experience associated with actual or potential tissue damage, or described in terms of such damage." Depression, likewise, is a subjective experience associated with unpleasant emotional and sensory signals. Perhaps it is no surprise, then, that the two often go hand in hand.

Chronic pain can cause or intensify depression, and vice versa. People who are depressed have three times the average risk of developing chronic pain. And people in chronic pain have three times the average risk of developing mental and emotional symptoms, especially mood and **anxiety disorders**. The worse the pain and the more places it is felt, the more severe the psychological repercussions are apt to be.

The combination of chronic pain and depression can be quite disabling, interfering with personal relationships and curtailing activities at home, work, and school. Left untreated, pain slows **recovery** from depression, and depression makes it harder to stick with a pain rehabilitation program. As a result, having both conditions makes getting proper treatment for each doubly important.

***The Depression Connection.***   The link between chronic pain and depression is complex. Both conditions are associated with changes in thoughts, behavior, and brain function. And both can lead to social isolation and physical inactivity, which may cause the pain and depression to become worse.

On a psychological level, mental anguish may sometimes be expressed through physical pain. When depression comes first, headaches, stomachaches, and other forms of pain are common symptoms. When chronic pain comes first, it can cause considerable stress, which may trigger or worsen depression in some individuals. Even people who start out resilient and optimistic may find that constant pain chips away at their mood over time.

On a physiological level, the brain pathways that receive pain signals use **serotonin** and **norepinephrine**, two brain chemicals that play a big role in regulating mood. When there are abnormalities in these chemicals, both pain sensations and depressed feelings may be intensified.

**Substance P** is another naturally occurring chemical that may be involved in both pain and depression. This chemical helps transmit and amplify pain signals to and from the brain. Research indicates that excessive amounts of substance P may be released during emotional distress.

***Treatment Considerations.***   Chronic pain is a complicated problem. The treatment approach is individualized based on the type and severity of the pain as well the lifestyle, preferences, and overall health of the pain sufferer. Medications, physical therapy, occupational therapy, biofeedback, acupuncture, local electrical stimulation, and surgery are just some of the possible options.

**Antidepressants** are mainstays of treatment not only for depression, but also for some types of chronic pain, even when depression is not a factor. **Tricyclic antidepressants** (TCAs) are used to treat burning or searing pain caused by nerve damage. For some people, TCAs also help prevent **migraine** (a type of headache characterized by intense pulsing or throbbing pain in one area of the head) or relieve fibromyalgia (a disorder characterized by widespread muscle pain, multiple tender points, and fatigue). When it comes to treating pain, the most widely prescribed and best-studied TCA is amitriptyline. But other medications in this class also may be helpful.

Another group of antidepressants called **serotonin-norepinephrine reuptake inhibitors** may help control some types of pain as well. In addition, people with chronic pain who take **selective serotonin reuptake inhibitors** (SSRIs), a widely used type of antidepressant, often report feeling better. In the case of SSRIs, though, the effect may be due more to the lifting of depression than to direct relief of pain.

**Psychotherapy** and counseling may be beneficial for both chronic pain and depression. **Cognitive-behavioral therapy** in particular can help people learn to avoid fearful anticipation, control demoralizing thoughts, and change their behavior in adaptive ways.

*See also:* Physical Illness

**Further Information.**   American Chronic Pain Association, P.O. Box 850, Rocklin, CA 95677, (800) 533-3231, www.theacpa.org.

American Pain Foundation, 201 N. Charles Street, Suite 710, Baltimore, MD 21201, (888) 615-7246, www.painfoundation.org.

National Institute of Neurological Disorders and Stroke, P.O. Box 5801, Bethesda, MD 20824, (800) 352-9424, www.ninds.nih.gov.

National Pain Foundation, 300 E. Hampden Avenue, Suite 100, Englewood, CO 80113, www.nationalpainfoundation.org.

## Bibliography

American Psychiatric Association. *Diagnostic and Statistical Manual of Mental Disorders.* 4th ed., text rev. Washington, DC: American Psychiatric Association, 2000.

*Antidepressants: Another Weapon Against Chronic Pain.* Mayo Clinic, July 1, 2008, http://www .mayoclinic.com/health/pain-medications/PN00044.

"Depression and Pain." *Harvard Mental Health Letter* (September 2004).

*IASP Pain Terminology.* International Association for the Study of Pain, http://www.iasp -pain.org/AM/Template.cfm?Section=General_Resource_Links&Template=/CM/ HTMLDisplay.cfm&ContentID=3058.

*NINDS Chronic Pain Information Page.* National Institute of Neurological Disorders and Stroke, July 31, 2008, http://www.ninds.nih.gov/disorders/chronic_pain/chronic_pain.htm.

*Pain and Depression.* National Pain Foundation, March 27, 2008, http://www.nationalpainfoundation .org/MyTreatment/News_PainAndDepression.asp.

*Pain and Depression.* National Pain Foundation, March 27, 2008, http://www.nationalpainfoundation .org/MyTreatment/News_PainAndDepression2.asp.

*Pain: Hope Through Research.* National Institute of Neurological Disorders and Stroke, July 31, 2008, http://www.ninds.nih.gov/disorders/chronic_pain/detail_chronic_pain.htm.

*The Relationship Between Pain, Depression and Mood: An Interview with Rollin Gallagher, MD, MPH.* National Pain Foundation, June 4, 2008, http://www.nationalpainfoundation.org/ MyTreatment/News_PainAndDepression_GallagherInterview.asp.

**CINGULOTOMY.** A cingulotomy is a type of brain surgery that destroys a small amount of tissue in the **anterior cingulate cortex** (ACC). This region of the brain serves as an important interface between the brain's higher, more rational circuits and lower, more instinctive parts. Studies have found structural and functional abnormalities in the ACC of people with depression. In rare cases, individuals with very severe, persistent, and disabling depression may be treated with cingulotomy when all other treatment options have been exhausted.

During a cingulotomy, local anesthetic is first administered to numb the area. Then a small hole is made in the skull, and sophisticated technology is used to pinpoint an area of the brain very precisely. In some cases, a slender probe with an electrode on the tip is inserted, and an electrical current is passed through the electrode to burn away the targeted tissue.

In other cases, the tissue is destroyed using the gamma-knife method, which focuses intersecting beams of radiation on the area. Each beam by itself is too weak to do any damage. It is only at the spot where the beams converge that there is a strong enough effect to destroy tissue.

***Benefits and Risks.*** Research suggests that cingulotomy may be effective against severe depression in about one-third of patients—a respectable success rate considering the fact that these patients have not responded to any other approach. On the downside, multiple operations are sometimes needed before improvement is seen, and the procedure is not reversible if something goes awry.

When improvement occurs, a mood change is often evident soon after the surgery. Full **recovery** may take months, however. Little is known about the long-term effectiveness of the surgery, although there are reports of patients who remained much improved or fully recovered for years.

A cingulotomy is brain surgery, so it is has some serious risks that must be weighed carefully against the potential benefits. Possible surgical complications include bleeding in the brain, stroke, infection, and breathing problems. Temporary, mild confusion may occur right after the surgery, and long-lasting personality changes have occasionally been reported.

Irreversible brain surgery is not a step to be taken lightly. But for some people with crippling depression that does not respond to other treatments, cingulotomy may offer another chance at feeling better.

*See also:* Treatment of Depression

## Bibliography

*Brain Surgery.* National Library of Medicine, January 22, 2009, http://www.nlm.nih.gov/medline plus/ency/article/003018.htm.

Ford-Martin, Paula Anne. "Psychosurgery." *Gale Encyclopedia of Medicine.* Farmington Hills, MI: Gale Research, 1999.

*Gamma-Knife Radiosurgery.* Mayo Clinic, October 10, 2008, http://www.mayoclinic.com/health/gamma-knife-radiosurgery/MY00206.

Neimat, Joseph S., Clement Hamani, Peter Giacobbe, Harold Merskey, Sidney H. Kennedy, Helen S. Mayberg, et al. "Neural Stimulation Successfully Treats Depression in Patients with Prior Ablative Cingulotomy." *American Journal of Psychiatry* 165 (2008): 687–693.

Sabbatini, Renato M. E. "Modern Psychosurgery." *Brain and Mind Magaine* (June 1997).

Sachdev, Perminder S., and Jagdeep Sachdev. "Long-Term Outcome of Neurosurgery for the Treatment of Resistant Depression." *Journal of Neuropsychiatry and Clinical Neurosciences* 17 (2005): 478–485.

Shields, Donald C., Wael Asaad, Emad N. Eskandar, Felipe A. Jain, G. Rees Cosgrove, Alice W. Flaherty, et al. "Prospective Assessment of Stereotactic Ablative Surgery for Intractable Major Depression." *Biological Psychiatry* 64 (2008): 449–454.

Steele, J. Douglas, David Christmas, M. Sam Eljamel, and Keith Matthews. "Anterior Cingulotomy for Major Depression: Clinical Outcome and Relationship to Legion Characteristics." *Biological Psychiatry* 63 (2008): 670–677.

**CIRCADIAN RHYTHMS.** Circadian rhythms refer to the body's internal system for regulating physiological and behavioral cycles that repeat daily, such as the sleep-wake cycle. A disruption in circadian rhythms may contribute to various types of depression, including **seasonal affective disorder** (SAD) and **premenstrual dysphoric disorder** (PMDD).

Most circadian rhythms are governed by the body's internal "clock," which is located in a pair of pinhead-sized brain structures called the suprachiasmatic nucleus (SCN). Although tiny, these two structures combined contain about 20,000 nerve cells.

When light strikes the retina in the eye, it creates a signal that travels along the optic nerve to the SCN. From there, messages are sent to several areas of the brain. One of these areas is the pineal gland, which responds to the light signals by switching off production of a hormone called **melatonin**. When darkness falls, melatonin production switches back on again. This hormone has a mild drowsiness effect, and it also helps regulate other body functions tied to the sleep-wake cycle, such as body temperature, hormone secretion, urine production, and changes in blood pressure.

Because circadian rhythms are synchronized to sunlight and darkness, it is not a big conceptual jump to using very bright light from an artificial source to reset out-of-sync body rhythms. "Phase shifting" is the technical term for this process, which lies at the heart of a treatment called **light therapy.** The shift may involve either advancing rhythms (shifting the body cycle to an earlier clock time) or delaying rhythms (shifting the body cycle to a later clock time).

*The SAD Story.* SAD is a form of **major depression** in which symptoms start and stop around the same time each year, typically beginning in fall or winter and subsiding in spring. Research indicates that people with SAD may have abnormalities in their circadian rhythms. In many, the body's rhythms seem to be delayed by the late winter dawn. Exposure to bright light in the morning helps correct this problem, but bright light in the evening may make it worse.

Considerable evidence has been amassed to support a link between SAD and circadian rhythms, and light therapy is now a well-established treatment for the disorder. But contradictory findings have been reported as well. Not everyone with SAD has delayed circadian rhythms, for example. In addition, some studies have failed to find a clear link between improvement after light therapy and circadian phase shifting. This highlights the point that multiple factors probably play a role in causing SAD. Circadian rhythms may be important, but they are not the only contributing factor.

*The PMDD Connection.* PMDD is a mood disorder that begins in the week before the onset of a woman's menstrual period and subsides within a few days after her period starts. Scientists have speculated that changes in female sex **hormones** during the menstrual cycle may disrupt circadian rhythms in certain women. Supporting this idea, studies have found that such hormonal changes are linked to several physiological functions with a circadian pattern, and the effect on these body functions is different in women with PMDD than in women without the disorder. Among the functions affected are sleep EEG, body temperature, and production of melatonin and **cortisol** (a **stress** hormone).

Given these findings, researchers have wondered if light therapy could be helpful for PMDD, too. Preliminary studies suggest it might, but more research is needed before any firm conclusions can be drawn.

***Other Types of Depression.*** Circadian disruptions also might play a role in nonseasonal major depression—the familiar form of serious depression that involves being in a low mood nearly all the time and/or losing interest or enjoyment in almost everything. One compelling line of evidence comes from the observation that keeping people with major depression awake in a sleep clinic overnight often leads to a very rapid, if short-lived, improvement in their symptoms. It is still unclear exactly why this effect occurs. But animal research suggests that sleep deprivation may temporarily weaken the body's internal clock, which might make it easier to reset.

Researchers are now testing controlled sleep deprivation, called **wake therapy**, as a possible treatment for major depression. Although the benefits tend to disappear as soon as the person goes to sleep, one way to overcome this limitation may be to combine one or more sessions of wake therapy with light therapy, medication, and/or gradual changes in the person's bedtime.

This is an exciting time for research on the link between circadian rhythms and all types of depression. As more is learned, it is likely that more treatment options aimed at correcting circadian disruptions will be developed as well.

*See also:* Agomelatine

***Further Information.*** Society for Light Treatment and Biological Rhythms, www.sltbr.org.

## Bibliography

*Brain Basics: Understanding Sleep.* National Institute of Neurological Disorders and Stroke, May 21, 2007, http://www.ninds.nih.gov/disorders/brain_basics/understanding_sleep.htm.

Krasnik, Catherine, Victor M. Montori, Gordon H. Guyatt, Diane Heels-Ansdell, and Jason W. Busse for the Medically Unexplained Syndromes Study Group. "The Effect of Bright Light Therapy on Depression Associated with Premenstrual Dysphoric Disorder." *American Journal of Obstetrics and Gynecology* 193 (2005): 658–661.

Lam, Raymond W. and Anthony J. Levitt, eds. *Canadian Consensus Guidelines for the Treatment of Seasonal Affective Disorder.* Clinical & Academic Publishing, 1999.

Lewy, Alfred J., Bryan J. Lefler, Jonathan S. Emens, and Vance K. Bauer. "The Circadian Basis of Winter Depression." *Proceedings of the National Academy of Sciences of the USA* 103 (2006): 7414–7419.

Parry, Barbara L. and Ruth P. Newton. "Chronobiological Basis of Female-Specific Mood Disorders." *Neuropsychopharmacology* 25 (2001): S102-S108.

Wehr, Thomas A., Wallace C. Duncan Jr., Leo Sher, Daniel Aeschbach, Paul J. Schwartz, Erick H. Turner, et al. "A Circadian Signal of Change of Season in Patients with Seasonal Affective Disorder." *Archives of General Psychiatry* 58 (2001): 1108–1114.

Wirz-Justice, Anna, Francesco Benedetti, Mathias Berger, Raymond W. Lam, Klaus Martiny, Michael Terman, et al. "Chronotherapeutics (Light and Wake Therapy) in Affective Disorders." *Psychological Medicine* 35 (2005): 939–944.

Wirz-Justice, Anna. "Chronobiology and Psychiatry." *Sleep Medicine Reviews* 11 (2007): 423–427.

**CLINICAL DEPRESSION.** Clinical depression is an umbrella term that is sometimes used to describe any type of depression that is serious enough to need professional treatment. Often, the term is used in reference to **major depression**, a mood disorder that involves being in a low mood nearly all the time and/or losing interest or enjoyment in almost everything. In major depression, these feelings last for at least two weeks, are associated with several other symptoms, and lead to serious problems getting along in everyday life.

For some people, depression alternates with **mania**, an overly high mood. The pattern of cycling between very low and very high moods is known as **bipolar disorder**, and clinical depression also can include the depressive phase of this condition.

In addition, clinical depression can refer to **dysthymia**, a form of depression characterized by a down mood that is relatively mild but quite long-lasting. The mood is present most of the day, more days than not for at least two years, and it is associated with other symptoms.

***Other Forms of Clinical Depression.*** The criteria for diagnosing major depression, bipolar disorder, and dysthymia are laid out in the ***Diagnostic and Statistical Manual of Mental Disorders, Fourth Edition, Text Revision*** (*DSM-IV-TR*). It is not unusual for someone to feel depressed without meeting all the criteria for any of these disorders. Yet the person's depressed mood may still be causing enough distress or disruption in daily life that a mental health professional thinks treatment is advisable. In such situations, the *DSM-IV-TR* allows for other diagnoses to be made.

An "**adjustment disorder with depressed mood**" is the term used for a psychological reaction to a stressful situation that leads to more distress than would normally be expected or causes problems in the person's work, school, or social life. When the mood is depressed, the main manifestations include a low mood, frequent **crying**, or feelings of hopelessness. This diagnosis is only made when a person's symptoms don't meet the threshold for any of the disorders discussed above. But the person may still be clinically depressed in the sense that a professional thinks he or she would benefit from treatment.

A "**depressive disorder not otherwise specified**" is a catchall diagnostic term that is used when depression is serious enough to cause significant problems, but does not rise to the level needed to qualify as major depression, dysthymia, or an adjustment disorder. Some forms of depression lumped into this category—such as **premenstrual dysphoric disorder**, **minor depression**, and **recurrent brief depression**—may become diagnostic entities in their own right in the next edition of the *DSM*. In the meantime, professional treatment may still be warranted if the problems that result are serious enough.

*Bibliography*

American Psychiatric Association. *Diagnostic and Statistical Manual of Mental Disorders*. 4th ed., text rev. Washington, DC: American Psychiatric Association, 2000.
Frances, Allen, Michael B. First, and Harold Alan Pincus. *DSM-IV Guidebook*. Washington, DC: American Psychiatric Press, 1995.
Lewis, Carol. "The Lowdown on Depression." *FDA Consumer* (January-February 2003).

**CLINICAL PSYCHOLOGIST.** Psychologists are trained in the practice, research, or teaching of psychology, the science of the mind and behavior. Clinical psychologists specialize in the diagnosis and treatment of mental, emotional, and behavioral disorders. When making a diagnosis, clinical psychologists may interview patients, make behavioral assessments, and give tests that evaluate personality traits, intellectual abilities, and other psychological characteristics.

**Psychotherapy** is the dominant treatment approach used by clinical psychologists. However, some also provide other psychologically based treatments. Examples include cognitive rehabilitation, which helps people regain mental function after a brain injury or illness, and biofeedback, which helps people learn to control a normally involuntary body response (such as heart rate) by watching output from a device that continuously monitors the response.

***Debate Over Prescribing Authority.*** Historically, psychologists were not permitted to prescribe medication, although they often worked closely with psychiatrists and other medical doctors who did. That is still the case in most states, but it may be changing. New Mexico and Louisiana were the first states to pass laws allowing clinical psychologists with advanced training to prescribe medication. Those laws were implemented in 2005. Legislation giving qualified psychologists prescribing authority has also been proposed in other states.

The issue remains controversial. Proponents point to a shortage of psychiatrists. More than 70 percent of medications for treating mental, emotional, and behavioral disorders are prescribed by primary care doctors and other non-psychiatrist physicians, who typically have only limited training in this area. Clinical psychologists are among the most highly trained mental health professionals, and extra requirements for training and experience can be set for those seeking prescribing privileges. When it comes to safety, proponents note the good track records of prescribers such as optometrists, podiatrists, and advanced practice registered nurses.

Critics contend that the additional training provided to prescribing psychologists is not sufficient to ensure patient safety and prevent medication errors. They note that medications affect the whole body, and they worry that even specially trained psychologists may not be adequately prepared to deal with issues such as side effects and drug interactions. For now, this continues to be the subject of active debate. The outcome will be particularly relevant for people with depression, because medication, either alone or combined with psychotherapy, often plays a role in their treatment.

***Training and Credentials.*** A doctoral degree (PhD or PsyD) generally is required to work as an independent licensed clinical psychologist. The educational program for clinical psychologists includes coursework in normal and abnormal behavior and personality. Clinical psychologists-in-training also must complete a supervised clinical internship plus at least one year of postdoctoral supervised experience before they can practice independently.

### Other Types of Psychologists

Clinical psychologists are the ones most likely to be involved in the treatment of depression. However, two other types of psychologists also work directly with people who are experiencing problems.

#### Counseling Psychologists

These psychologists advise people on how to cope with problems of daily living. For instance, they may help people handle **stress,** resolve conflicts, deal with crises, and make vocational choices. Counseling psychologists often work in university counseling centers, hospitals, and private practices.

#### School Psychologists

These psychologists work with students in elementary and secondary schools. They address learning and behavior problems. School psychologists also may assess learning disabled or gifted students to help determine the best teaching strategies for them. In addition, school psychologists may advise parents and teachers on how to create a healthy, supportive environment.

Some psychologists go on to become board certified by the American Board of Professional Psychology. To obtain board certification, psychologists must pass an exam and meet eligibility requirements, such as having a doctoral degree and being licensed or certified by their state at the independent practice level. Among the specialties recognized by the board are clinical psychology and clinical child and adolescent psychology.

***Clinical Psychology in Action.*** Most clinical psychologists work in private practices, counseling centers, mental health clinics, or psychiatric hospitals. Others work in community agencies, rehabilitation programs, schools, and prisons. The American Psychological Association, with 148,000 members, is the largest professional society for psychologists in the world.

All states have licensing or certification requirements for clinical psychologists. In addition to meeting requirements for education, training, and experience, applicants must pass an exam. The Association of State and Provincial Psychology Boards is the organization for psychology licensing boards in the United States and Canada.

*See also:* Diagnosis of Depression; Treatment of Depression

***Further Information.*** American Board of Professional Psychology, 300 Drayton Street, 3rd Floor, Savannah, GA 31401, (800) 255-7792, www.abpp.org.

American Psychological Association, 750 First Street N.E., Washington, DC 20002, (800) 374-2721, www.apa.org, www.apahelpcenter.org, www.psychologymatters.org.

Association of State and Provincial Psychology Boards, P.O. Box 241245, Montgomery, AL 36124, (334) 832-4580, www.asppb.org.

## Bibliography

*About Clinical Psychology.* Society of Clinical Psychology (American Psychological Association Division 12), http://www.apa.org/divisions/div12/aboutcp.html.

Bureau of Labor Statistics. "Psychologists," in *Occupational Outlook Handbook, 2006–07 Edition.* Washington, DC: U.S. Department of Labor, 2005.

Yates, Deanna F., Jack G. Wiggins, Jeremy A. Lazarus, James H. Scully Jr., and Michelle Riba. "Should Psychologists Have Prescribing Authority?" *Psychiatric Services* 55 (2004): 1420–1426.

**CLINICAL SOCIAL WORKER.** Social workers are professionals trained to help individuals and families overcome social, health, and other practical problems. Clinical social workers assess and treat people with mental, emotional, or behavioral disorders. More than other mental health professionals, they often take on the dual roles of treatment provider and patient advocate. When appropriate, they may provide direct assistance with getting help from government agencies or lining up other community support services.

Clinical social workers frequently provide **psychotherapy**. Some also provide other psychological and social interventions. Examples include social rehabilitation, which helps individuals with mental disorders or disabilities achieve a higher level of social functioning through group activities, and crisis intervention, which helps people cope with the immediate aftermath of a traumatic event. In addition, some clinical social workers offer practical training in skills of everyday living.

***Training and Credentials.*** Clinical social workers must have at least a master's degree in social work (MSW) usually plus two years of supervised clinical experience. Some also hold professional credentials offered by the National Association of Social Workers (NASW). The best known of these is the Academy of Certified Social Workers (ACSW) credential, which requires not only a master's degree and post-degree experience, but also peer evaluations and continuing education. Other NASW credentials for clinical social workers include Diplomate in Clinical Social Work (DCSW), Qualified Clinical Social Worker (QCSW), and Clinical Social Worker in Gerontology (CSW-G).

***Clinical Social Work in Action.*** About 116,000 U.S. social workers have jobs in the mental health or **substance abuse** fields. Many work in hospitals, substance abuse treatment centers, military services, and government or nonprofit agencies. Some clinical social workers provide psychotherapy in private practice. NASW, with 150,000 members, is the largest professional society for social workers in the world.

All states have licensing, certification, or registration requirements for social workers. The Association of Social Work Boards is the organization for state boards that regulate the profession. This organization offers licensing exams in several categories, including clinical social work.

*See also:* Diagnosis of Depression; Treatment of Depression

***Further Information.*** Association of Social Work Boards, 400 S. Ridge Parkway, Suite B, Culpeper, VA 22701, (800) 225-6880, www.aswb.org.

National Association of Social Workers, 750 First Street N.E., Suite 700, Washington, DC 20002, (202) 408-8600, www.socialworkers.org, www.helpstartshere.org.

*Bibliography*

Bureau of Labor Statistics. "Social Workers," in *Occupational Outlook Handbook, 2006–07 Edition.* Washington, DC: U.S. Department of Labor, 2005.
*Mental Health.* National Association of Social Workers, http://www.socialworkers.org/pressroom/features/issue/mental.asp.

**CLINICAL TRIAL.** A clinical trial is a research study designed to answer specific questions about an investigational treatment. The trial follows a study plan, called a protocol, which outlines who participants will be, how tests and treatments will be carried out, the schedule for study events, and the length of the study. The goal of the protocol is twofold: to ensure that study questions are answered and to safeguard the health and welfare of participants.

Clinical trials are sponsored by pharmaceutical companies, government agencies, non-profit organizations, research foundations, and medical institutions. Participants are individuals who volunteer to take part and who meet the trial's eligibility criteria. These criteria specify in advance who is and who is not an appropriate participant based on relevant factors, such as age, gender, current health status, previous treatment history, and coexisting medical conditions. Some studies require that participants have a particular disorder, and others require that participants be healthy.

Participants who are enrolled, or signed up, for the study are assigned to a particular group. In a randomized study, these assignments are made randomly, or by chance. Participants may be placed in one of two or more treatment groups. Or they may be placed in a control group, which is a nontreatment group that is included for comparison's sake.

Placebo-controlled trials are often used to study drug treatments. The placebo is a dummy pill that looks like the real thing but does not contain an active ingredient. Researchers know that the expectation of feeling better after a treatment can itself be beneficial, a phenomenon known as the placebo effect. By comparing the treatment group to the placebo group, researchers can gauge how much of any improvement that is seen can be attributed to the treatment itself rather than to positive expectations.

***Volunteering to Participate.*** People volunteer to take part in clinical trials for a number of reasons. Some want to help others and do their part for medical progress. Others are interested in gaining access to experimental treatments that are not yet available to the general public. If it is a placebo-controlled trial, there is a chance they could wind up getting the placebo rather than the treatment. But even in that case, all participants, including controls, may be provided with careful medical monitoring and free, high-quality care.

On the downside, an experimental treatment, by definition, has not yet been fully tested. There is always a risk that it might be ineffective, or it might cause unpleasant or even dangerous side effects. Some studies also require considerable time, effort, and attention. For instance, participants might need to travel some distance to the study site, show up for multiple appointments, or stick to a complex treatment regimen.

Informed consent helps ensure that individuals who are thinking about signing up for a clinical trial have all the information they need to weigh the pros and cons. Potential volunteers are provided with a document that outlines their rights as study participants and the details of the study, including its purpose, duration, and required procedures. Volunteers must sign this document before participating in the trial. But even once they sign up, people may choose to withdraw from a trial at any time.

***Phases of Clinical Trials.*** New treatments go through four basic phases of research designed to assess their effectiveness and safety. The research questions and study design for clinical trials vary from one phase to the next. The discussion below explains the process for testing an experimental drug. A similar progression may be followed when testing other kinds of new treatments.

*Phase I Trials.* At this stage, an experimental drug that looks promising after preclinical lab and animal studies is tested for the first time in humans. About 20 to 100 healthy volunteers take part in Phase I trials. One goal is to evaluate the drug's safety, determine the safe dosage range, and identify side effects. Another goal is to study the drug's pharmacological properties, including how it is absorbed, distributed, metabolized, and excreted by the body. Phase I drug trials generally take six months to a year to complete.

*Phase II Trials.* In Phase II, the experimental drug is given to a larger number of volunteers—typically, 100 to 500—who have the targeted disease. The primary goal is to establish that the drug is effective for treating this condition. Researchers also continue assessing the drug's safety and watching for side effects. In addition, they determine the optimal dose strength and frequency. Phase II drug trials generally take six months to a year.

*Phase III Trials.* Drugs that make it this far are ready to be tested in randomized placebo-controlled trials involving substantially more patient volunteers—typically, 1000 to 5,000. The goal is to confirm the drug's effectiveness, monitor side effects, and compare the benefits and risks to those of standard treatments. Phase III drug trials generally take one to four years.

Once this phase is completed, if the drug has proved to be safe and effective, the pharmaceutical company can file a New Drug Application (NDA) with the Food and Drug Administration (FDA). The NDA includes all the data from preclinical testing and Phase I through III clinical trials along with additional information, such as manufacturing plans and proposed labeling. A typical NDA runs 100,000 pages or longer.

The NDA is then reviewed by the FDA to determine whether the drug should be cleared for marketing. It takes an average of a year and a half for the FDA to complete its review process. After that, if the drug is approved, it becomes available to the public.

*Phase IV Trials.* Data collection continues after the drug is on the market and being used by a much larger and more diverse pool of patients. In Phase IV trials, researchers may evaluate long-term safety or look more closely at how the medication works in particular groups of patients, such as **children** or **older adults**. Post-marketing clinical trials may go on for years.

*See also:* Randomized Controlled Clinical Trial

**Further Information.** CenterWatch, 100 North Washington Street, Suite 301, Boston, MA 02114, (866) 219-3440, www.centerwatch.com.

National Library of Medicine, 8600 Rockville Pike, Bethesda, MD 20894, (888) 346-3656, www.clinicaltrials.gov, www.pubmed.gov.

## Bibliography

*Glossary of Clinical Trials Terms.* National Library of Medicine, March 18, 2008, http://clinicaltrials .gov/ct2/info/glossary.

*Research and Development.* Pharmaceutical Research and Manufacturers of America, 2009, http://www.phrma.org/index.php?option=com_content&task=view&id=382&Itemid=119.

*Understanding Clinical Trials.* National Library of Medicine, September 20, 2007, http:// clinicaltrials.gov/ct2/info/understand.

*Volunteering for a Clinical Trial.* CenterWatch, http://www.centerwatch.com/clinical-trials/ volunteering.aspx.

## COGNITIVE BEHAVIORAL ANALYSIS SYSTEM OF PSYCHOTHERAPY.

Cognitive behavioral analysis system of psychotherapy (CBASP) is the first **psychotherapy** to be devised specifically for treating **chronic depression**—in other words, depression that lasts for two years or longer. CBASP was developed by U.S. psychologist James P. McCullough Jr. (1936– ), a professor at Virginia Commonwealth University. His theory is that depressed adults have become perceptually disconnected from the environment, so they do not perceive the effects of their actions on others. The primary goal of therapy is to help people recognize that their interpersonal behavior has consequences, and use this information to learn more adaptive ways of thinking and behaving.

CBASP blends elements of **cognitive-behavioral therapy** (CBT), which helps people change self-defeating thoughts and maladaptive behaviors, and **interpersonal therapy** (IPT), which helps people address interpersonal triggers for their symptoms. CBT and IPT are the best-validated psychotherapies for treating depression. When depression is long-lasting, several studies also support the treatment benefits of CBASP.

*The Preoperational Adult.* CBASP assumes that adults with chronic depression are stuck at an immature level of emotional, cognitive, and behavioral development. Their relationships with other people are typical of preoperational functioning, as described by Swiss psychologist Jean Piaget (1896–1980). During the preoperational stage, which usually corresponds to ages two through seven, children are focused on themselves and have little capacity for seeing the point of view of others. Because this is a pre-logical stage, they are also unable to grasp the logical connection between actions and consequences.

McCullough believes this description also applies to the personal relationships of adults with chronic depression. Like preoperational children, depressed adults may interact in a manner reminiscent of a recorded message, always saying and doing the same things regardless of the listener's reaction. According to McCullough, this faulty interaction style may cause and maintain poor relationships, which in turn may prolong symptoms of depression.

McCullough has proposed two pathways by which adults might wind up functioning at a level more appropriate for young children. In some cases, abuse, neglect, or trauma early in life may stunt development. As a result, children are unable to move past preoperational functioning in the social realm, and this leads to the early onset of chronic depression. In other cases, when depression strikes later in life, adults who had previously been functioning normally regress to a less mature way of seeing the world. CBASP is intended for people with both early-onset and later-onset depression.

***The Process at a Glance.*** The aim of CBASP is to help people see the link between their interpersonal behaviors and specific consequences. This goal is accomplished using a technique called situational analysis, through which clients learn to recognize the effects of their behavior on others. Clients can then use this information to change their maladaptive thoughts and actions.

One assumption of CBASP is that the kinds of interpersonal difficulties that occur in everyday life are also likely to crop up during therapy sessions. Therefore, one therapeutic technique is to teach clients how their interpersonal behavior is affecting the therapist. Toward that end, the therapist may use contingent personal responsivity—a response to the client's maladaptive behavior during a therapy session that focuses attention on the negative consequences and explores the reasons for the behavior. For example, if a client makes a derogatory remark, the therapist might respond, "When you said that, I felt attacked. Why do you want to attack what I'm doing?"

Another technique is an interpersonal discrimination exercise. The goal of this type of exercise is to help the client distinguish the therapist from significant others who have caused emotional hurt in the past. Eventually, the client sees that the relationship with the therapist is unique and can be used to learn new, more productive ways of interacting.

***Benefits for Depression.*** Research has generally supported the benefits of CBASP for treating chronic depression. In one study, 681 adults with chronic major depression were randomly assigned to receive an antidepressant, CBASP, or both. About half got better with either medication or CBASP alone. However, the combination of both was more effective than either treatment by itself.

In another study conducted at 12 psychiatric centers around the United States, people with chronic major depression who did not get better after 12 weeks of either medication or CBASP were switched to the other treatment. The switch from medication to CBASP or vice versa led to improvement in many people who had not responded to the first treatment that was tried.

*See also:* Treatment of Depression

***Further Information.*** Cognitive Behavioral Analysis System of Psychotherapy, www.cbasp.org.

## Bibliography

*Cognitive Behavioral Analysis System of Psychotherapy: Psychopathology and Treatment.* CBASP.org, http://www.cbasp.org/psy.htm.

Keller, Martin B., James P. McCullough, Daniel N. Klein, Bruce Arnow, David L. Dunner, Alan J. Gelenberg, et al. "A Comparison of Nefazodone, the Cognitive Behavioral-Analysis System of Psychotherapy, and Their Combination for the Treatment of Chronic Depression." *New England Journal of Medicine* 342 (2000): 1462–1470.

McCullough, James P. Jr. *Treating Chronic Depression with Disciplined Personal Involvement: Cognitive Behavioral Analysis System of Psychotherapy (CBASP)*. New York: Springer, 2006.

McCullough, James P. Jr. *Treatment for Chronic Depression: Cognitive Behavioral Analysis System of Psychotherapy (CBASP)*. New York: Guilford Press, 2003.

Schatzberg, Alan F., A. John Rush, Bruce A. Arnow, Phillip L. C. Banks, Janice A. Blalock, Frances E. Borian, et al. "Chronic Depression: Medication (Nefazodone) or Psychotherapy (CBASP) Is Effective When the Other Is Not." *Archives of General Psychiatry* 62 (2005): 513–520.

Swan, John S., and Alastair M. Hull. "The Cognitive Behavioural Analysis System of Psychotherapy: A New Psychotherapy for Chronic Depression." *Advances in Psychiatric Treatment* 13 (2007): 458–469.

**COGNITIVE-BEHAVIORAL THERAPY.**   Cognitive-behavioral therapy (CBT) is a form of **psychotherapy** that fuses two related treatment approaches: **cognitive therapy** and **behavioral therapy**. Cognitive therapy helps people recognize and change self-defeating thought patterns, and behavioral therapy helps people identify and change maladaptive behaviors. Each of these two approaches has been extensively studied and is well established as an effective treatment for depression in its own right. It is no surprise, then, that CBT has proved to be effective for depression as well.

CBT is not a single approach. Instead, it encompasses a number of different therapies that integrate cognitive and behavioral techniques. As a practical matter, most forms of cognitive therapy use not only cognitive strategies, but also behavioral ones. Examples include the cognitive therapy of U.S. psychiatrist **Aaron T. Beck** (1921– ) and the rational emotive behavior therapy of U.S. psychologist **Albert Ellis** (1913–2007).

One unifying theme in all these approaches is the premise that most cognitive, emotional, and behavioral responses are learned. Therefore, undesirable responses can be unlearned and replaced with more desirable ones. Clients acquire skills that facilitate this process—skills they can keep using to prevent or relieve depression long after formal therapy ends.

***The Process at a Glance.***   CBT is a goal-oriented approach to treatment. The client plays an active role in reformulating thoughts and practicing new behaviors. The therapist collaborates in this process, partnering with the client to set appropriate goals and develop specific plans for achieving them. Often, the therapist assigns homework, such as keeping a journal of thoughts and behaviors or following a schedule designed to increase participation in pleasant activities.

Therapist visits are structured, with a specific agenda for each session. Research has shown that a significant improvement in depression often can be seen in just 12 to 20 weeks. This relatively fast progress is due to the use of action-oriented techniques that put a premium on changing thoughts and behaviors, whether or not people ever understand the source of their old, unhelpful styles of thinking and behaving.

CBT is a time-limited approach, so clients are aware from the beginning that there will be a day in the not-too-distant future when formal therapy will end. To ensure that progress is maintained over the long term, follow-up appointments, known as booster sessions, may be scheduled. Typically, booster sessions might occur at three, six, and 12 months after the end of formal therapy, as well as at any time when symptoms flare up again.

***Benefits for Depression.***   The principles and practices of CBT are solidly grounded in research. There is strong evidence that CBT can be an effective treatment for depression. Some meta-analyses—analyses that pool the results from several previously published studies—have found that the effects of CBT are even more pronounced than those of **antidepressants**, but others have found that the results are comparable. CBT also compares favorably to other forms of psychotherapy, including **interpersonal therapy** (IPT), another well-validated treatment that focuses on addressing the interpersonal triggers for mental, emotional, and behavioral symptoms.

Some studies suggest that CBT may not work quite as well for people with the most severe depression, however. In the National Institute of Mental Health's Treatment of Depression Collaborative Research Program study, CBT was less effective than a medication called imipramine in severely depressed individuals, and there was also a trend for CBT to be less effective than IPT.

The benefits of CBT have been best studied in people with **major depression**, the form of the disorder that involves being in a low mood nearly all the time and/or losing interest or enjoyment in almost everything. These feelings last for at least two weeks, are associated with several other symptoms, and lead to significant impairment in the ability to function in everyday life. There is also some evidence that CBT is beneficial for treating **dysthymia**, a less intense but longer-lasting form of low mood. However, improvement may be somewhat smaller in people with dysthymia than in those with major depression.

The rise of CBT since the 1960s has dramatically changed the way depression is treated. In fact, CBT has become the gold standard against which other nonmedication treatments are measured. By teaching new ways of thinking and behaving, CBT helps people with depression break free of old, maladaptive thought and behavior patterns that are contributing to their illness.

*See also:* Dialectical Behavior Therapy; Treatment of Depression

***Further Information.*** Association for Behavioral and Cognitive Therapies, 305 7th Avenue, 16th Floor, New York, NY 10001, (212) 647-1890, www.abct.org.

National Association of Cognitive-Behavioral Therapists, P.O. Box 2195, Weirton, WV 26062, (800) 853-1135, www.nacbt.org.

## Bibliography

American Psychiatric Association Work Group on Major Depressive Disorder. *Practice Guideline for the Treatment of Patients with Major Depressive Disorder.* 2nd ed. Washington, DC: American Psychiatric Publishing, 2000.

Persons, Jacqueline B., Joan Davidson, and Michael A. Tompkins. *Essential Components of Cognitive-Behavior Therapy for Depression.* Washington, DC: American Psychological Association, 2001.

*What Is Cognitive-Behavioral Therapy?* National Association of Cognitive-Behavioral Therapists, http://www.nacbt.org/whatiscbt.htm.

**COGNITIVE FACTORS.**    Cognition refers to thinking skills, such as perceiving, conceiving, evaluating, reasoning, remembering, and imagining. These cognitive factors affect the way a person reacts to both external and internal cues. In someone who is genetically or biologically susceptible to depression, cognitive factors influence risk or resilience when confronted with **stress**.

Cognitive theories of depression assume that people's thoughts, beliefs, and interpretations color their **emotions** and behaviors. When trouble strikes, characteristic thinking patterns play a pivotal role in determining how strongly people react. Some people respond to a seemingly minor setback by falling into a deep, persistent depression, but others faced with greater trauma or tragedy weather the crisis without becoming depressed. Differences in thinking style help account for this apparent contradiction.

***Thoughts and Schemas.*** The cognitive model of depression proposed by U.S. psychiatrist **Aaron T. Beck** (1921– ) was integral to the development of **cognitive therapy**. This form of **psychotherapy**, now a well-established treatment for depression, helps people recognize and change self-defeating thought patterns that are contributing to their emotional and behavioral problems.

According to Beck, people with depression often experience streams of negative thoughts that pop up automatically and repeatedly. These thoughts involve viewing themselves, the world, and the future in an excessively negative light. Beck noted that people often cling to such self-defeating thoughts even in the face of objective evidence to the contrary. He attributed this tendency to relatively stable, underlying thought patterns, which he called schemas.

Beck theorized that such thought patterns act as mental filters, selectively directing attention toward stimuli that are congruent with a person's schemas. Common schemas in depressed individuals include themes of loss, separation, worthlessness, failure, and rejection. As a result, people with depression have a cognitive bias toward processing information that reinforces these themes.

When a depressive schema is activated by a relevant stressor, depression may ensue. Once a person becomes depressed, a tendency to see only the worst in oneself, other people, and the world just perpetuates and intensifies the dark mood. The goal of cognitive therapy is to break this vicious cycle and help people assess their thoughts more accurately. Over time, a lasting shift in thinking style may occur, making people less prone to a repeat bout of depression in the future.

***Helplessness and Hopelessness.*** Another seminal idea is the concept of **learned helplessness**, which refers to a giving-up reaction stemming from exposure to unpleasant events that are beyond the individual's control. The theory of learned helplessness was developed by U.S. psychologist **Martin E. P. Seligman** (1942– ) in the 1960s and 1970s.

According to this theory, one thing that helps determine whether people become depressed when under stress is the extent to which they believe themselves to have control over the situation. Those who believe they have the power to improve their lot are apt to keep trying to improve things. In contrast, those who believe they are powerless are apt to give up and sink into depression.

Although Seligman was clearly onto something important, the original formulation of learned helplessness was too simplistic to explain all the complexities of human behavior. In a later refinement of the theory, Seligman emphasized the mediating role of explanatory style—people's habitual way of explaining negative events to themselves. Seligman focused on three dimensions of explanatory style: permanence (how long the negative event or its cause will last), pervasiveness (how broad its effects are), and personalization (how much people blame themselves).

The explanatory style most closely linked to depression is **pessimism**. Seligman noted that pessimists tend to see a bad event as something that will last a long time and undermine everything they do, and they blame themselves for it. This downbeat view engenders hopelessness, low self-esteem, and in some people, full-blown depression.

Further elaboration of Seligman's model resulted in hopelessness theory, developed by U.S. psychologist Lyn Y. Abramson (1950– ). According to this theory, a pessimistic or negative thinking style contributes to hopelessness, and that in turn leads to specific symptoms such as **sadness**, apathy, lack of energy, slowed-down behavior, delayed reaction times, sleep problems, trouble concentrating, negative thoughts, and suicide. Thus, hopelessness is an intermediate step between a depressive thinking style and depression itself.

***Consuming Mental Resources.***   One paradoxical finding is that people with depression often have problems with concentration and memory. Yet they focus all too readily on negative, hopeless thoughts, and they show enhanced recall of memories supporting their dark view of themselves and the world.

The resource allocation hypothesis is one effort to explain this finding. The assumption is that mental resources are finite, and the more spent on depressive thinking, the fewer that are available for other cognitive tasks. Along the same lines, the affective interference hypothesis assumes that people with depression are preoccupied with processing emotional material. Because most of their mental energy is aimed in that direction, their capacity for thinking in nonemotional terms is reduced.

***Reducing Cognitive Control.***   Among the most distressing aspects of depression is a tendency toward **rumination**—repetitive, passive thinking about negative feelings, distressing symptoms, and the dark side of life. Rumination is closely related to the irrationally negative thoughts described above, which tend to be brief, shorthand appraisals of a situation. Link several such thoughts together, and you have full-fledged rumination, which is a longer chain of repeated, negative thinking.

In people with depression, negative thoughts take on increased power. Overriding such strong responses and focusing attention elsewhere calls for great cognitive control. Rumination may result from reduced cognitive control as well as a decreased ability to block out depression-irrelevant material.

***Optimism and Humor.***   Most research to date has looked at how maladaptive thinking patterns serve as **risk factors** for depression. Yet a smaller, but growing, body of evidence shows that adaptive thoughts can foster resilience and serve as **protective factors**.

Optimism is the mirror image of pessimism. When confronted with one of life's hard knocks, optimists tend to believe that it is just a temporary setback and one-time event, and it is not their fault. In short, where pessimists put a negative spin on events and expect the worst, optimists do the reverse. Research has shown that an optimistic thinking style is associated with greater life satisfaction.

Several studies also have found a link between a good sense of humor and a reduced risk of depression. Researchers have noted that humor allows individuals to confront painful feelings and express strong emotions without personal discomfort. In this way, humor may help defuse stressful situations.

Certain types of humor may be more beneficial than others, however. Affiliative humor involves joking around, telling funny stories, saying witty things, and generally enjoying a good laugh with others. Self-enhancing humor involves looking at the light side of life and using humor to feel better, but self-defeating humor involves using humor in an excessively self-disparaging way and allowing oneself to be the butt of others' jokes. A study of 418 college students found a link between fewer depressive symptoms and higher levels of affiliative and self-enhancing humor as well as lower levels of self-defeating humor.

*See also:* Causes of Depression

## Bibliography

Abramson, Lyn Y., Gerald I. Metalsky, and Lauren B. Alloy. "Hopelessness Depression: A Theory-Based Subtype of Depression." *Psychological Review* 96 (1989): 358–372.

Beck, Aaron, T., A. John Rush, Brian F. Shaw, and Gary Emery. *Cognitive Therapy of Depression.* New York: Guilford Press, 1979.

Chang, Edward C., and Lawrence J. Sanna. "Optimism, Pessimism, and Positive and Negative Affectivity in Middle-Aged Adults: A Test of a Cognitive-Affective Model of Psychological Adjustment." *Psychology and Aging* 16 (2001): 524–531.

Hugelshofer, Daniela S., Paul Kwon, Robert C. Reff, and Megan L. Olson. "Humour's Role in the Relation Between Attributional Style and Dysphoria." *European Journal of Personality* 20 (2006): 325–336.

Joormann, Jutta. "Cognitive Aspects of Depression." In *Handbook of Depression.* 2nd ed., by Ian H. Gotlib and Constance L. Hammen, eds., 298–321. New York: Guilford Press, 2009.

Nezu, Arthur M., Christine M. Nezu, and Sonia E. Blissett. "Sense of Humor as a Moderator of the Relation Between Stressful Events and Psychological Distress: A Prospective Analysis." *Journal of Personality and Social Psychology* 54 (1988): 520–525.

Schou, I., Ø. Ekeberg, and C. M. Ruland. "The Mediating Role of Appraisal and Coping in the Relationship Between Optimism-Pessimism and Quality of Life." *Psycho-oncology* 14 (2005): 718–727.

Seligman, Martin E. P. *Helplessness: On Depression, Development, and Death.* San Francisco: W. H. Freeman, 1975.

Seligman, Martin E. P. *Learned Optimism.* New York: Alfred A. Knopf, 1991.

**COGNITIVE THERAPY.**   Cognitive therapy is a form of **psychotherapy** that helps people recognize and change self-defeating thought patterns. In practice, it often is combined with **behavioral therapy**, which focuses on helping people identify and change maladaptive behaviors. This therapeutic hybrid, known as **cognitive-behavioral therapy** (CBT), is one of the best-validated forms of treatment for depression.

The underlying premise of cognitive therapy is that people's feelings and behavior are based largely on how they think about themselves and the world. When their habitual style of thinking is maladaptive, it can cause or maintain emotional and behavioral problems.

For example, some people tend to overgeneralize. They start with a single event ("I made a mistake this time") and generalize too broadly to a range of situations ("I never do anything right"). Such thinking not only promotes negative feelings, but also discourages positive action. People who believe they are doomed to future failure, for example, have little incentive to work toward a better outcome. Their belief becomes a self-fulfilling prophesy, which just strengthens their habit of thinking about themselves and the world in an overly pessimistic and irrational manner.

Cognitive Distortions

People's thinking patterns can contribute to their depression. Below are examples of common distortions in characteristic thinking style that can give rise to dysfunctional automatic thoughts. These thoughts in turn may lead to unpleasant emotions and maladaptive behavior.

| Distorted Thinking Style | Triggering Event | Dysfunctional Thought |
|---|---|---|
| All-or-none thinking | You get third place in a contest. | "I am a total loser." |
| Catastrophizing | You experience a setback at work. | "My career is over." |
| Discounting the positive | You get an A in a class. | "It doesn't count; the class was easy." |
| Fortune telling | You don't try a sport that looks fun. | "I'll make a fool of myself." |
| Mind reading | A busy salesclerk is curt with you. | "She thinks I'm a loser." |
| Overgeneralizing | The person you have been dating breaks up with you. | "I'll never find love." |

***Historical Roots.***   Cognitive therapy aims to help people interrupt this vicious cycle and instill more adaptive patterns of thinking. Two pioneers who have played key roles in developing cognitive therapy are U.S. psychiatrist **Aaron T. Beck** (1921– ) and U.S. psychologist **Albert Ellis** (1913–2007).

*Beck's Cognitive Therapy.*   Beck's approach to cognitive therapy, introduced in the early 1960s, grew directly out of his search for a better way to understand and treat depression. While studying and working with depressed individuals, Beck noticed that they often experienced what he called automatic thoughts—streams of negative thoughts that pop up spontaneously. Beck also discovered that these automatic thoughts seemed to fall into three main categories: negative thoughts about themselves, the world, and the future.

Beck began helping clients with depression identify and evaluate their automatic thoughts. He found that, in the process, clients learned to appraise situations more realistically. That ability, in turn, helped them manage their emotions and behavior more effectively. The process of identifying and analyzing unrealistically negative thoughts and replacing them with more realistic ones became the cornerstone of cognitive therapy.

Beck's evidence-based approach was groundbreaking. It was the first time a scientist had used systematic research to demonstrate the effectiveness of any form of psychotherapy for treating depression.

*Ellis's Rational Emotive Behavior Therapy.*   A second approach to cognitive therapy was developed by Ellis starting in the late 1950s. Rational emotive behavior therapy (REBT)—originally called rational emotive therapy—is based on the premise that intense emotions make it hard to think clearly, which can lead to behavior that is irrational and dysfunctional. When people are depressed, they may take small slights too personally, blow minor setbacks out of proportion, and become less tolerant of day-to-day hardships and hassles.

According to Ellis, people in distress often engage in an internal dialogue based on implicit, irrational assumptions. In REBT, therapists actively confront clients with their most pernicious beliefs and prod clients to challenge such beliefs. By disputing irrational thinking in this way, REBT helps people break the hold of distorted beliefs, allowing for the development of more adaptive thoughts and behaviors.

***The Process at a Glance.***   Cognitive therapy is a time-limited, structured approach to treating depression and other emotional and behavioral disorders. The goal is to help people formulate more accurate interpretations of various situations, which leads to a shift in their thinking and consequently to a change in their feelings and behavior. Clients play an active role in reformulating their thoughts and thereby gaining control over their symptoms.

Therapists likewise are active participants in cognitive therapy. Their style may range from gentle guidance to more vigorous confrontation, but the aim is always to establish a helpful alliance with clients. The goal is not to inculcate a fixed set of beliefs about what is rational. Instead, rationality is defined by what works for a given person.

Beck has described five basic steps in the therapy process: (1) monitoring habitual negative thoughts, (2) recognizing the connection between these thoughts and associated feelings and behavior, (3) examining the evidence for and against the negative thoughts, (4) substituting more realistic thoughts for the unrealistically negative ones, and (5) identifying and changing the dysfunctional beliefs that underlie the distorted thinking.

*Initial Phase.*   During the first session, the client and therapist work together to decide what the specific goals of therapy will be. Within a couple of sessions, the therapist often has a rough idea of how long it will take to reach those goals. Some clients with mild, short-term problems need just six to eight sessions. Other clients with longstanding problems need 12 to 20 sessions or more.

At the outset, many cognitive therapists also ask their clients to fill out a questionnaire, such as the **Beck Depression Inventory**, designed to assess mood. The questionnaire can be repeated at regular intervals to give both the therapist and the client an objective way of measuring progress.

*Intermediate Phase.* As treatment continues, each therapy session often begins by having the client assess how his or her mood compares to previous weeks. Then the client and therapist talk about what has happened since the last visit and decide which problem to address in the current session. The focus is on present issues in the client's life rather than past experiences.

Once the target problem has been identified, the therapist guides the client in finding solutions by using problem-solving techniques and assessing the accuracy of thoughts about the situation. The client and therapist then discuss how best to put what was learned to practical use during the coming week. Homework exercises may be assigned.

*Termination Phase and Booster Sessions.* Unless the client is in crisis, early sessions usually are scheduled a week apart. As the client starts to feel better, though, the length of time between visits may be extended first to two weeks, then to three weeks or longer. By tapering off gradually, the client is able to practice newly learned strategies while the therapist is still available for guidance and support.

Follow-up appointments, known as booster sessions, may be scheduled to ensure that progress is maintained over the long haul. Typically, booster sessions might occur at three, six, and 12 months after the end of formal therapy as well as at any time when symptoms start to flare up again.

***Benefits for Depression.*** The more effort people put into cognitive therapy, the more benefit they are likely to get out of the experience. Most notice some improvement in their symptoms within three to four weeks if they attend sessions regularly and do their homework assignments between therapist visits.

Cognitive therapy, either used alone or fused with behavioral therapy in CBT, has been studied extensively. Taken as a whole, research shows that the benefits for mild to moderate depression are at least equal to—and in some cases, greater than—those of **antidepressants**. For more severe depression, cognitive therapy may be most helpful when combined with drug therapy.

Research also indicates that booster sessions may help keep symptoms of depression from coming back once therapy is completed. Cognitive therapy teaches people skills they can use for a lifetime. By calling upon the strategies they have learned in therapy, people can recognize, challenge, and reverse the unduly negative beliefs that perpetuate their depression.

*See also:* Mindfulness-Based Cognitive Therapy; Treatment of Depression

***Further Information.*** Academy of Cognitive Therapy, 260 South Broad Street, 18th Floor, Philadelphia, PA 19102, (267) 350-7683, www.academyofct.org.

Albert Ellis Institute, 45 East 65th Street, New York, NY 10065, (800) 323-4738, www.albertellisinstitute.org.

Association for Behavioral and Cognitive Therapies, 305 7th Avenue, 16th Floor, New York, NY 10001, (212) 647-1890, www.abct.org.

Beck Institute for Cognitive Therapy and Research, One Belmont Avenue, Suite 700, Bala Cynwyd, PA 19004, 610) 664-3020, www.beckinstitute.org.

National Association of Cognitive-Behavioral Therapists, P.O. Box 2195, Weirton, WV 26062, (800) 853-1135, www.nacbt.org.

*Bibliography*

American Psychiatric Association Work Group on Major Depressive Disorder. *Practice Guideline for the Treatment of Patients with Major Depressive Disorder.* 2nd ed. Washington, DC: American Psychiatric Publishing, 2000.

Beck, Aaron, T., A. John Rush, Brian F. Shaw, and Gary Emery. *Cognitive Therapy of Depression.* New York: Guilford Press, 1979.

Burns, David D. *Feeling Good: The New Mood Therapy.* New York: Avon Books, 1999.

Millon, Theodore. *Masters of the Mind: Exploring the Story of Mental Illness from Ancient Times to the New Millennium.* New York: John Wiley and Sons, 2004.

Persons, Jacqueline B., Joan Davidson, and Michael A. Tompkins. *Essential Components of Cognitive-Behavior Therapy for Depression.* Washington, DC: American Psychological Association, 2001.

**COMORBIDITY.**   Comorbidity refers to the presence of two or more illnesses in the same person at the same time. The coexisting conditions are apt to influence each other in ways that affect the course and outcome of both. Depression often exists side by side with other mental and physical illnesses, and in this situation, getting a correct diagnosis and proper treatment for both conditions is doubly important.

More than half of people with depression have a comorbid anxiety disorder, such as **generalized anxiety disorder**, **panic disorder**, **post-traumatic stress disorder**, or **obsessive-compulsive disorder**. Other mental disorders that may coexist with depression include **substance abuse**, **eating disorders**, **attention-deficit hyperactivity disorder**, and **borderline personality disorder**. Many of these disorders can themselves produce symptoms that are similar to those of depression, so disentangling the effects of comorbid mental disorders can be a challenge. An experienced mental health professional can help sort out multiple problems, which is the first step toward finding effective solutions.

Depression also is common in people with serious physical illnesses, such as **heart disease**, **stroke**, **cancer**, **human immunodeficiency virus** (HIV) infection, **diabetes**, **Parkinson's disease**, and **multiple sclerosis**. People who have depression along with another **physical illness** tend to have more severe symptoms of both conditions. They also tend to incur higher medical costs and have more difficulty adapting to physical impairment. In such individuals, treating depression can help improve the outcome of the physical illness, too.

*See also:* Anxiety Disorders; Dual Diagnosis; Physical Illness

*Bibliography*

*Comorbidity: Addiction and Other Mental Illnesses.* National Institute on Drug Abuse, December 2008, http://www.drugabuse.gov/PDF/RRComorbidity.pdf.

*What Illnesses Often Co-exist with Depression?* National Institute of Mental Health, January 30, 2009, http://www.nimh.nih.gov/health/publications/depression/what-illnesses-often-co-exist-with-depression.shtml.

**COMPLEMENTARY AND ALTERNATIVE MEDICINE.**   Complementary and alternative medicine (CAM) refers to a diverse group of health care practices that are not generally considered to be part of conventional medicine. A wide array of CAM treatments have been advocated for depression at one time or another. Among the best established are

**exercise**, **relaxation techniques**, **acupuncture**, **yoga**, and certain **dietary supplements**. Surveys indicate that people with depression are more likely to use CAM than the general public.

Some CAM therapies have scientific data supporting their use. By definition, though, this evidence is still limited or inconsistent. Once enough evidence is amassed confirming that a CAM therapy is safe and effective, it typically is accepted into standard practice and is no longer considered unconventional. A good example is **light therapy**, which was once an unconventional option but is now a standard treatment for **seasonal affective disorder**.

Technically speaking, complementary medicine is used along with conventional medicine in an effort to enhance the effects, provide further benefits, or reduce side effects. Alternative medicine is used instead of conventional medicine. The latter can be a risky choice when a CAM treatment that has not been studied in controlled scientific trials replaces a proven conventional treatment.

Integrative medicine combines conventional treatments with complementary therapies for which there is preliminary evidence of usefulness. For individuals who are interested in trying CAM options, this is often the best approach.

*See also:* Herbal Remedies; Meditation; Traditional Chinese Medicine

**Further Information.** National Center for Complementary and Alternative Medicine, 9000 Rockville Pike, Bethesda, MD 20892, (888) 644-6226, nccam.nih.gov.

## Bibliography

Ernst, Edzard, Julia I. Rand, and Clare Stevinson. "Complementary Therapies for Depression: An Overview." *Archives of General Psychiatry* 55 (1998): 1026–1032.

Jorm, Anthony F., Helen Christensen, Kathleen M. Griffiths, and Bryan Rodgers. "Effectiveness of Complementary and Self-Help Treatments for Depression." *Medical Journal of Australia* 176 (2002): S84-S96.

Unützer, Jürgen, Rruth Klap, Roland Sturm, Alexander S. Young, Tonya Marmon, Jess Shatkin, et al. "Mental Disorders and the Use of Alternative Medicine: Results From a National Survey." *American Journal of Psychiatry* 157 (2000): 1851–1857.

*What Is CAM?* National Center for Complementary and Alternative Medicine, February 2007, http://nccam.nih.gov/health/whatiscam/overview.htm.

Wu, Ping, Cordelia Fuller, Xinhua Liu, Hsin-Chien Lee, Bin Fan, Christina W. Hoven, et al. "Use of Complementary and Alternative Medicine Among Women with Depression: Results of a National Survey." *Psychiatric Services* 58 (2007): 349–356.

**CONDUCT DISORDER.** Conduct disorder is a behavioral disorder characterized by extreme, persistent difficulty with following the rules or behaving in a socially acceptable manner. It is usually first diagnosed before age 18. All **children** and **adolescents** test the rules now and then, but those with conduct disorder have a longstanding, seriously disruptive pattern of rule-breaking or antisocial behavior. Conduct disorder and depression sometimes occur side by side in troubled children and teens. In addition, young people with conduct disorder are at increased risk for developing depression later in life.

Children and teens with conduct disorder may bully others, get into fights, set fires, vandalize property, skip school, lie, steal, stay out all night, or run away from home. Their behavior puts them at risk for physical harm, poor grades, school expulsion, legal problems, risky sex, **substance abuse**, and unhealthy relationships. Young people with the disorder also have an increased risk of depression, suicidal thoughts, and attempted or completed **suicide**. Conduct disorder is sometimes referred to as a "disruptive behavior disorder," stressing the condition's unsettling effect on young people, their families, fellow students, the surrounding community, and society at large.

Reported rates of conduct disorder in young people vary from one percent to more than 10 percent, depending on the population surveyed and how the disorder is defined. The problem appears to be more common in boys than in girls, and more prevalent in cities than in rural areas.

When the first signs of conduct disorder appear before age 10, it is considered childhood-onset type. This early form of the disorder generally has a worse prognosis than adolescent-onset type, which begins at age 10 or later. Most people outgrow the problem behaviors as adults, but some continue to struggle with social and occupational problems. Among the latter group, many go on to meet the criteria for antisocial personality disorder, a condition characterized by a pervasive pattern of disregarding and violating the rights of others.

Treatment for conduct disorder typically includes **behavioral therapy**, a form of **psychotherapy** that helps people identify and change maladaptive behavior patterns. Equally important is appropriate treatment for any coexisting conditions, such as substance abuse, **anxiety disorders**, **attention-deficit hyperactivity disorder**, **learning disorders**, or oppositional defiant disorder (a behavioral disorder characterized by a long-lasting pattern of unusually frequent defiance, hostility, or lack of cooperation).

When depression is an issue, **cognitive-behavioral therapy**—which combines behavioral techniques with cognitive techniques for changing self-defeating thought patterns—may be helpful. **Antidepressants** are sometimes prescribed as well. For the best chance of success, treatment for coexisting depression and conduct disorder should involve the young person's doctor, therapist, school, and family working together as a coordinated team.

*Criteria for Diagnosis.* The symptoms of conduct disorder are defined by the ***Diagnostic and Statistical Manual of Mental***

---

### Treatment of Conduct Disorder

When people have both conduct disorder and depression simultaneously, both conditions need to be addressed for optimal improvement. Below are some of the main treatment options for conduct disorder.

#### *Family Behavioral Therapy*

Behavioral therapy is the primary tool for treating conduct disorder. Because family members may be more distressed by the problem behavior and motivated to see it change than the youngsters themselves, parents often play a pivotal role in treatment. Parents may be taught how to communicate expectations clearly, enforce rules effectively, reward positive behavior, and reduce family conflict.

#### *Medication*

Although there are no medications specifically approved to treat conduct disorder, drug therapy may be used to manage particular symptoms or coexisting conditions. Antidepressants, **lithium**, and **anticonvulsants** may help stabilize moods and reduce aggressiveness. Stimulants may help improve attention and decrease impulsivity. Clonidine, a blood pressure-lowering medicine, also may reduce aggressive or impulsive outbursts.

***Disorders, Fourth Edition, Text Revision***, a diagnostic guidebook published by the American Psychiatric Association and used by mental health professionals from many disciplines. The hallmark of the disorder is a longstanding, repeated pattern of behavior that violates other people's rights or age-appropriate social rules or expectations.

The problem behavior can be divided into four main categories: aggression toward people or animals, destruction of property, lying or theft, and serious infractions of the rules. To be diagnosed with conduct disorder, a young person must have displayed at least three of 15 specific behaviors (listed below) within the last year.

*Aggression toward People or Animals.* Examples include (1) frequently bullying, threatening, or intimidating others, (2) frequently starting physical fights, (3) using a weapon that has the potential to cause serious injury, such as a bat, broken bottle, knife, or gun, (4) being physically cruel to other people, (5) being physically cruel to animals, (6) committing theft while confronting a victim, such as in a mugging or armed robbery, and (7) forcing someone to have sex.

*Destruction of Property.* Examples include (8) deliberately setting fires with the intention of causing serious damage, and (9) deliberately destroying the property of others by some other means.

*Lying or Theft.* Examples include (10) breaking into another person's house, building, or car, (11) frequently lying to get things, gain favors, or avoid obligations, and (12) stealing without confronting a victim, such as in shoplifting or forgery.

*Serious Infractions of the Rules.* Examples include (13) often staying out at night despite parental rules against it, beginning before age 13, (14) running away from home overnight at least twice, or once if the child or teen stays away for a lengthy period, and (15) frequently skipping school, beginning before age 13.

***Relationship to Depression.*** Most children and teens with conduct disorder are probably reacting to distressing events and situations in their lives. Risk factors for the disorder include child abuse or neglect, family violence, parental mental illness, discord in the parents' relationship, separation from the parents without a good alternative caregiver, crowding, and poverty. The same types of stressors also may trigger or worsen depression in young people with a genetic tendency toward **mood disorders**.

Once both conduct disorder and depression are present, they may feed off each other. The constant upheaval caused by troubled behavior can magnify depression, and a continually down mood can make it harder to cope with daily challenges and focus on constructive change. Fortunately, treatment can help break this vicious cycle. The sooner it begins, the better, because behavior may be harder to change after it becomes ingrained.

*See also:* Comorbidity; Family Therapy

## Bibliography

American Psychiatric Association. *Diagnostic and Statistical Manual of Mental Disorders.* 4th ed., text rev. Washington, DC: American Psychiatric Association, 2000.

*Children's Mental Health Facts: Children and Adolescents with Conduct Disorder.* National Mental Health Information Center, April 2003, http://mentalhealth.samhsa.gov/publications/allpubs/CA-0010/default.asp.

Sanders, Lee M., Judith Schaechter, and Janet R. Serwint. "Conduct Disorder." *Pediatrics in Review* 28 (2007): 433–434.

Searight, H. Russell, Fred Rottnek, and Stacey L. Abby. "Conduct Disorder: Diagnosis and Treatment in Primary Care." *American Family Physician* 63 (2001): 1579–1588.

**CONTINUATION TREATMENT.**   Treatment for depression falls into three stages: acute, continuation, and maintenance. These stages apply to treatment with **antidepressants** and **psychotherapy** alike. During the continuation phase, the aim is to prevent a relapse—the return of symptoms from a prior episode that never fully resolved, even though the person got quite a bit better for a while.

Most people who have improved on an antidepressant should receive at least six months of continuation treatment. This typically involves seeing the prescribing doctor once or twice a month, which allows the doctor to monitor symptoms and side effects as well as make any necessary adjustments in dosage. With continuation of drug treatment, the risk of relapse is only 10 percent to 20 percent, versus 40 percent to 60 percent without continued care.

Many psychotherapists also gradually taper off treatment. After a successful course of weekly sessions, people may return for several sessions scheduled two to four weeks apart before therapy is ended completely.

During the continuation phase, functioning in everyday life continues to improve. The ultimate goal is to consolidate gains into a total remission—the resolution of symptoms to a level similar to that of healthy individuals.

*See also:* Acute Treatment; Maintenance Treatment

*Bibliography*

Kupfer, David J. "Acute Continuation and Maintenance Treatment of Mood Disorders." *Depression* 3 (1995): 137–138.

U.S. Department of Health and Human Services. *Mental Health: A Report of the Surgeon General.* Rockville, MD: U.S. Department of Health and Human Services, 1999.

**CONTINUUM OF CARE.**   In the mental health world, continuum of care refers to the complete range of treatment programs and services, which vary in intensity depending on the urgency and severity of an individual's symptoms. At one end of the continuum is outpatient treatment, the least restrictive and most flexible option. At the other end is **hospitalization**, which is reserved for the most severe or highest-risk cases. Options that fall in between include partial hospitalization, crisis residential treatment, and residential treatment centers.

In the best-case scenario, individuals with depression would have access to the full continuum of care. For the majority of people with depression, outpatient treatment might be all they ever need. But for those who would benefit from more intensive treatment, it would be available to help them through a severe episode or suicidal crisis. As treatment took hold and symptoms began to lessen, the individual could step down to a less intensive level of care.

In the real world, this scenario is not always realistic. The nearest facility might be far away, a treatment program might be full, or the cost might be prohibitive. Yet the more options that are available, the easier it is for treatment providers to custom-tailor mental health care to each individual's needs.

***Levels of Care.***   Below is a brief rundown of several treatment options. They are organized roughly from least intensive to most intensive. However, there is considerable variability in how treatment is delivered, which affects where any particular service or program would fall on the continuum.

*Outpatient Treatment.* Patients live at home and go to work or school as usual, but they occasionally see a doctor or therapist at an office or clinic. Each visit typically lasts 30 to 60 minutes. Depending on the patient's needs, the frequency of visits may range from a few times a week to once a month or less. This is the most common mode of treatment for depression.

*Partial Hospitalization.* This form of treatment, also called day hospital, may be provided at a hospital, school, or clinic. Patients spend at least four hours a day on treatment-related services, but they go home at night. A wide range of services—such as individual or **group therapy**, special education, job training, and therapeutic recreation—may be included.

*Crisis Residential Treatment.* Patients receive short-term, 24-hour care in a non-hospital setting. This approach may be an alternative for those who are experiencing a mental health crisis, but who do not require the full range of services found at a hospital. Stays typically last no more than two weeks.

### Residential Treatment Controversy

Since the early 1990s, hundreds of private RTCs for youth have sprung up, creating a billion-dollar industry serving 10,000 to 14,000 children and teenagers. Recently, nonprofit watchdog groups and government agencies have expressed concern about the overuse of RTCs. Research has established that community-based treatment and support is effective for most young people with mental and behavioral disorders. In contrast, there is little hard evidence for the effectiveness of the RTC approach.

Private RTCs go by a number of monikers, including "therapeutic boarding schools," "emotional growth academies," "behavior modification facilities" and "teen boot camps." Such programs are not regulated by the federal government in the United States, and many are not subject to state licensing or monitoring as mental health or educational facilities. A 2007 report to Congress by the Government Accountability Office found cases of serious abuse or neglect at some programs.

Although there are high-quality RTCs, there are also high-risk ones. The Federal Trade Commission recommends that parents who are considering RTC treatment for a child check out the program carefully, asking questions about state licensure, clinical director credentials, staff credentials and experience, employee background checks, pre-admission assessments, individualized treatment, academic curriculum, discipline policies, emergency procedures, family involvement, and total cost.

If a program makes claims about success rates, ask how success was measured. Also, look for accreditation by a reputable, independent organization, such as the Joint Commission (JACHO), Council on Accreditation (COA) or Commission on Accreditation of Rehabilitation Facilities (CARF).

*Residential Treatment Center.* In a residential treatment center (RTC), **children** or **adolescents** with severe mental and behavioral disorders live round-the-clock in a campus-like setting. The treatment is less specialized and intensive than in a hospital, but the stay may last many weeks or months. One concern is that gains made in an RTC may not carry over into life afterward without careful coordination between RTC staff and community schools and treatment providers. Unfortunately, such coordination is often lacking.

*Psychiatric Hospitalization.* Patients receive inpatient treatment in a facility that provides intensive, specialized care and close, 24-hour monitoring. Hospitalization may be helpful for those who pose to a threat to themselves or others, are behaving in a disoriented or destructive manner, require medication that must be closely monitored, or need round-the-clock care to become stabilized. A hospital stay for depression typically lasts no more than several days.

***Further Information.*** Alliance for the Safe, Therapeutic and Appropriate Use of Residential Treatment, University of South Florida, astart.fmhi.usf.edu.

American Association of Children's Residential Centers, 11700 W. Lake Park Drive, Milwaukee, WI 53224, (877) 332-2272, www.aacrc-dc.org.

American Hospital Association, One North Franklin, Chicago, IL 60606, (312) 422-3000, www.aha.org.

Association for Ambulatory Behavioral Healthcare, 247 Douglas Avenue, Portsmouth, VA 23707, (757) 673-3741, www.aabh.org.

Commission on Accreditation of Rehabilitation Facilities, 4891 E. Grant Road, Tucson, AZ 85712, (520) 325-1044, www.carf.org.

Council on Accreditation, 120 Wall Street, 11th Floor, New York, NY 10005, (212) 797-3000, www.coanet.org.

Joint Commission, One Renaissance Boulevard, Oakbrook Terrace, IL 60181, (630) 792-5000, www.jointcommission.org.

National Association of Psychiatric Health Systems, 701 13th Street N.W., Suite 950, Washington, DC 20005, (202) 393-6700, www.naphs.org.

National Association of Therapeutic Schools and Programs, 5272 River Road, Suite 600, Bethesda, MD 20816, (301) 986-8770, www.natsap.org.

## Bibliography

*A START.* Alliance for the Safe, Therapeutic and Appropriate Use of Residential Treatment, http://astart.fmhi.usf.edu/AStartDocs/factsheet.pdf.

*Considering a Private Residential Treatment Program for a Troubled Teen?* Federal Trade Commission, July 2008, http://www.ftc.gov/bcp/edu/pubs/consumer/products/pro27.pdf.

Evans, Dwight L., and Linda Wasmer Andrews. *If Your Adolescent Has Depression or Bipolar Disorder: An Essential Resource for Parents.* New York: Oxford University Press, 2005.

*Fact Sheet: Children in Residential Treatment Centers.* Bazelon Center for Mental Health Law, http://www.bazelon.org/issues/children/factsheets/rtcs.htm.

*Partial Hospitalization.* Association for Ambulatory Behavioral Healthcare, http://aabh.org/about-aabh/fast-facts.

*Residential Treatment Programs: Concerns Regarding Abuse and Death in Certain Programs for Troubled Youth.* GAO-08–146T. Washington, DC: U.S. Government Accountability Office, 2007.

*The Continuum of Care for Children and Adolescents.* American Academy of Child and Adolescent Psychiatry, September 2008, http://www.aacap.org/cs/root/facts_for_families/the_continuum_of_care_for_children_and_adolescents.

U.S. Department of Health and Human Services. *Mental Health: A Report of the Surgeon General.* Rockville, MD: U.S. Department of Health and Human Services, 1999.

**CORTICOTROPIN-RELEASING HORMONE.** Corticotropin-releasing hormone (CRH)—also known as corticotropin-releasing factor—is a hormone produced by the **hypothalamus**, part of the brain that acts as a command center for the **nervous system** and **endocrine system**. CRH plays a central role in the **hypothalamic-pituitary-adrenal axis**, a body system involved in the physiological **stress** response. CRH also is widely distributed in brain areas outside the hypothalamus. Overproduction of CRH is associated with depression.

Under normal circumstances, CRH serves a vital purpose, managing the internal response to stressful situations. One effect of CRH may be to put a person's guard up in the face of a threat, leading to extra vigilance, anxiety, or fear. CRH also sets off a physiological chain of events that includes the release of two other stress hormones: adrenocorticotropic hormone (ACTH) and **cortisol**. The latter arouses various body systems and gets them ready to cope with a threat. Later, it facilitates the body's return to a normal state.

When all goes well, this stress system is protective. But when the system becomes overactive, it is a classic case of too much of a good thing. Over 40 years ago, researchers discovered that many people with depression produce excessive cortisol, indicating an over-amped stress system. Since then, more specific studies have suggested that the problem may stem from abnormally high CRH activity.

***The Depression Connection.***   Researchers have found that some people with depression have higher levels of CRH in their cerebrospinal fluid, compared to both people with other mental disorders and healthy individuals. People with depression also may have an increase in the number of CRH-producing brain cells. And when scientists injected CRH into the brains of animals, they observed behavioral changes similar to those seen in depressed humans, such as decreased appetite and reduced sex drive.

Current **antidepressants** target other chemical messengers in the brain, especially **serotonin**. But one byproduct of their impact on serotonin may be to decrease CRH, which may contribute to their effectiveness. Scientists have speculated that drugs targeting CRH directly might be even more effective—potentially working faster, helping more people, and causing fewer side effects. The search for such CRH-blocking drugs is now underway, and some promising candidates have been identified.

***Early Life Stress.***   Scientists also are making headway in understanding why CRH activity goes awry in the first place. Research shows that extreme stress and trauma early in childhood can have a lasting impact. In animals, severe stress early in life leads to increased CRH production in adulthood. In humans, a history of childhood physical or sexual abuse is associated with both increased CRH levels and a greater risk of depression as adults.

It seems that experiencing extreme stress at a young age, when brain pathways are still developing, may affect CRH-producing brain cells in a way that leads to long-term overactivity. This overactivity, in turn, may create a super-sensitive stress response, in which brain cells react strongly to even mild threats.

In one study of 49 women, researchers induced mild stress by having them take part in a public speaking and mental arithmetic task in front of an audience. Depressed women with a history of child abuse had a six times greater increase in ACTH levels after the task, compared to nondepressed women with no such history. In the long run, living in an exaggerated state of high alert could take a toll on the mind and body, with one possible consequence being depression.

*See also:* Hormones

---

### Freud and CRH

CRH was not discovered until 1981. Yet its discovery and the research that ensued helped validate some core concepts put forth by Austrian psychiatrist **Sigmund Freud** (1856–1939) decades before. Freud believed that childhood events helped shape later psychological experiences, and studies have shown that extreme childhood stress can lead to increased CRH activity that lasts into adulthood. CRH overactivity, in turn, is associated with depression. Thus, scientists finally have a physiological explanation for how early trauma and later depression might be connected.

*Bibliography*

Belmaker, R. H., and Galila Agam. "Major Depressive Disorder." *New England Journal of Medicine* 358 (2008): 55–68.

*Brain Facts: A Primer on the Brain and Nervous System.* 6th ed. Washington, DC: Society for Neuroscience, 2008.

*Depression and Stress Hormones.* Society for Neuroscience, http://www.sfn.org/index.cfm?pagename =brainBriefings_depressionAndStressHormones.

Evans, Dwight L., and Linda Wasmer Andrews. *If Your Adolescent Has Depression or Bipolar Disorder: An Essential Resource for Parents.* New York: Oxford University Press, 2005.

Gabbard, Glen O., and Tanya J. Bennett. "Psychoanalytic and Psychodynamic Psychotherapy for Depression and Dysthymia." In *The American Psychiatric Publishing Textbook of Mood Disorders,* by Dan J. Stein, David J. Kupfer and Alan F. Schatzberg, eds., 389–404. Washington, DC: American Psychiatric Publishing, 2006.

Gillespie, Charles F., and Charles B. Nemeroff. "Hypercortisolemia and Depression." *Psychosomatic Medicine* 67 (2005): S26-S28.

Heim, Christine, D. Jeffrey Newport, Stacey Heit, Yolanda P. Graham, Molly Wilcox, Robert Bonsall, et al. "Pituitary-Adrenal and Autonomic Responses to Stress in Women After Sexual and Physical Abuse in Childhood." *JAMA* 284 (2000): 592–597.

**CORTISOL.**    Cortisol is a hormone made by the adrenal cortex—the outer part of the adrenal glands. Levels of this hormone vary throughout the day. They peak right before dawn, preparing the body to wake up, eat, and become active. Cortisol also is released as part of the body's **stress** response, arousing various body systems and getting them ready to cope with a threat. People with depression often have an overactive stress response and abnormally high levels of cortisol in their blood.

Cortisol belongs to the family of **hormones** known as glucocorticoids, so named because they affect the metabolism of glucose (blood sugar). When a stressful situation is first encountered, glucocorticoids help put the body on alert. They mobilize glucose, the body's main source of energy, moving it from storage sites into the bloodstream. These hormones also increase cardiovascular tone to prepare the body for action, and they delay long-term body processes that are not essential in a crisis, such as digestion, growth, and reproduction.

Later, glucocorticoids help the body recover from stress and return to its normal state. At this point, the hormones promote glucose replenishment and efficient cardiovascular function.

Glucocorticoids play a vital role in health. But when hormone levels stay too high for too long, they can strain the built-in mechanisms for maintaining a healthy balance in body systems.

***The Depression Connection.***    Depression may be one consequence of prolonged exposure to excessive cortisol. One way to assess whether the body is producing too much cortisol is with a **dexamethasone suppression test** (DST). This test involves taking an oral dose of dexamethasone, a synthetic glucocorticoid. Blood is then drawn the next day so that cortisol can be measured.

Normally, when there is enough cortisol present, the body cuts back on producing the hormone rather than continuing to pump out even more. Because dexamethasone is a chemical cousin of cortisol, it should have the same effect, suppressing cortisol production. But this suppression fails to occur in about half of the most severely depressed people, indicating that their bodies are making more cortisol than they need.

In general, studies have shown that depressed and nondepressed individuals both have elevated levels of blood cortisol immediately after mild stress. But cortisol levels often stay high in people with depression rather than falling back to normal as they do in healthy individuals. This difference tends to be more obvious in the afternoon, and it is most pronounced in **older adults** and those with severe depression.

The adrenal glands may be enlarged in people with depression, too, which is another sign of cortisol overproduction. The good news is that all these changes—adrenal enlargement, high blood cortisol, and nonsuppression on the DST—tend to go back to normal after depression has been successfully treated.

*See also:* Endocrine System; Hypothalamic-Pituitary-Adrenal Axis

## Bibliography

Belmaker, R. H., and Galila Agam. "Major Depressive Disorder." *New England Journal of Medicine* 358 (2008): 55–68.

*Brain Facts: A Primer on the Brain and Nervous System.* 6th ed. Washington, DC: Society for Neuroscience, 2008.

Burke, Heather M., Mary C. Davis, Christian Otte, and David C. Mohr. "Depression and Cortisol Responses to Psychological Stress: A Meta-anaylsis." *Psychoneuroendocrinology* 30 (2005): 846–856.

Gillespie, Charles F., and Charles B. Nemeroff. "Hypercortisolemia and Depression." *Psychosomatic Medicine* 67 (2005): S26-S28.

**COUPLES THERAPY.**    Couples therapy—also known as marital therapy—is a form of **psychotherapy** in which the therapist treats both partners in a committed relationship at the same time. The goal is to resolve conflicts and improve support between the partners as well as to treat individual problems that affect the relationship. For example, both partners might be having trouble expressing their feelings, and one might also be suffering from depression. Working with the couple both jointly and individually, the therapist guides the partners in resolving these problems and reducing interpersonal **stress**. This type of treatment is typically provided by a **marriage and family therapist**.

In many cases, couples therapy can help rebuild a damaged relationship. In other cases, the partners may decide they will each be better off if they split up. Either can be a valid therapeutic outcome if it helps the partners understand the relationship better and make well-informed decisions about the future.

Sometimes specific events—such as an extramarital affair or the loss of a job—can set off problems in a relationship. Other times, communication and intimacy break down more gradually. Left to fester, a dysfunctional relationship can give rise to anger, loneliness, anxiety, and **sadness**. In people who are prone to depression, the stress of a troubled relationship may trigger a new episode or make an ongoing bout worse.

Depression, in turn, can test even a healthy relationship. People who are depressed often withdraw from others, lose interest in sex, stop taking care of themselves, and become gloomy or irritable. Although such behaviors are symptoms of an illness, not intentional slights to the partner, that distinction does not make them any easier to live with.

In couples therapy, the partners work with a therapist to build on the strengths and shore up the weaknesses of their relationship. They often focus on developing specific skills, such as communication, negotiation, and problem solving. When one partner has full-blown depression, the marriage and family therapist sometimes collaborates with other treatment providers, who may treat the depression with individual therapy and/or medication.

***Couples Therapy for Depression.*** Research has found a strong link between relationship discord and the onset and course of depression. Once one or both partners are depressed, couples tend to express more criticism, hostility, and overprotection toward one another. As a result, the relationships of people with depression are often—but not always—characterized by considerable stress.

A recent study by Swiss researchers included 60 couples, each of which had one partner with depression. One-third of the depressed individuals were treated with **cognitive-behavior therapy** (CBT) and one-third with **interpersonal therapy** (IPT)—two well-established treatments for depression. The remaining third were treated along with their partners using coping-oriented couples therapy (COCT). Like individual CBT, COCT teaches strategies to identify and change maladaptive patterns of thinking and behaving. However, the focus in COCT is mainly on strategies that improve communication within the couple and enhance the support each partner offers the other.

In this study, couples therapy was as effective as individually-oriented CBT and IPT in reducing the depressed partner's symptoms of depression. But unlike CBT and IPT, COCT also reduced the amount of criticism directed toward the depressed individual by the partner.

The results of other studies have been similar. A review of eight studies found that couples therapy and individual therapy were about equally effective for treating depression. Couples therapy had an advantage, though, when it came to reducing the severity and persistence of relationship distress. With this in mind, couples therapy might be a good choice when relationship problems are a major issue for someone with depression.

*See also:* Family Therapy; Relationship Issues; Treatment of Depression

***Further Information.*** American Association for Marriage and Family Therapy, 112 S. Alfred Street, Alexandria, VA 22314, (703) 838-9808, www.aamft.org.

## Bibliography

Barbato, Angelo, and Barbara B. D. D'Avanzo. "Marital Therapy for Depression." *Cochrane Database of Systematic Reviews* 2 (2009): art. no. CD004188.

Beach, Steven R. H., Deborah J. Jones, and Kameron J. Franklin. "Marital, Family, and Interpersonal Therapies for Depression in Adults." In *Handbook of Depression.* 2nd ed., by Ian H. Gotlib and Constance L. Hammen, eds., 624–641. New York: Guilford Press, 2009.

Bodenmann, Guy, Bernard Plancherel, Steven R. H. Beach, Kathrin Widmer, Barbara Gabriel, Nathalie Meuwly, et al. "Effects of Coping-Oriented Couples Therapy on Depression: A Randomized Clinical Trial." *Journal of Consulting and Clinical Psychology* 76 (2008): 944–954.

*Marriage Counseling: Working Through Relationship Problems.* Mayo Clinic, November 15, 2007, http://www.mayoclinic.com/health/marriage-counseling/MH00104.

**CREATIVITY.** Creativity—the ability to produce novel works or ideas that display originality and imagination—is often reputed to go hand in hand with emotional suffering. Research suggests that this reputation may be deserved, particularly among those whose creativity takes an artistic bent. Several studies have found that writers, artists, and other creative individuals are more likely than average to have **major depression** or **bipolar disorder**.

Such disorders seem to be more common in people from artistic fields than in creative people from other fields, such as science and business. Within the arts, there is evidence that poets—especially female poets—are more likely than other writers and artists to show signs of a mood disorder or die by **suicide**. This tendency has been nicknamed the "Sylvia Plath Effect," after the acclaimed U.S. poet who took her own life in 1963.

Depressed Poets Society

Several of the most beloved poets in the English language are thought to have suffered from serious bouts of depression. Below is a partial list, which reads like the syllabus from English Lit 101.

| | Born | Died | Nationality |
|---|---|---|---|
| William Cowper | 1731 | 1800 | British |
| Thomas Chatterton* | 1752 | 1770 | British |
| Percy Bysshe Shelley | 1792 | 1822 | British |
| Edgar Allan Poe | 1809 | 1849 | U.S. |
| Emily Dickinson | 1830 | 1886 | U.S. |
| Vachel Lindsay* | 1879 | 1931 | U.S. |
| Sara Teasdale* | 1884 | 1933 | U.S. |
| Edna St. Vincent Millay | 1892 | 1950 | U.S. |
| Hart Crane* | 1899 | 1932 | U.S. |
| Randall Jarrell* | 1914 | 1965 | U.S. |
| Anne Sexton* | 1928 | 1974 | U.S. |
| Sylvia Plath* | 1932 | 1963 | U.S. |

*Died by suicide

One possible explanation is that the distorted thinking that characterizes depression is readily transferable to poetry. Consider a type of thought distortion known as magnification, in which some aspect of a situation is overstated. This error in thinking is closely related to hyperbole, a literary device in which exaggeration is used for emphasis or effect.

**Links to Depression.** At first blush, the link between depression and creativity may seem counterintuitive, because depression saps energy, motivation, and concentration. And in fact, there is evidence that creative individuals may be more productive once their depression lifts. Even for a poet, treatment for depression can be beneficial.

But why does the link exist in the first place? One theory states that creativity and depression are connected via a third factor: **rumination**, which is a tendency toward repetitive, passive thinking about negative feelings and the dark side of life. People with depression are prone to this type of thinking. Their rumination may generate lots of thoughts, which, in turn, may give rise to artistic ideas in those with creative

**"What Is a Poet?"**

Danish philosopher Søren Kierkegaard (1813–1855), who was himself prone to depression, eloquently described the relationship between poetry and emotional suffering in his book *Either/Or* (1843): "What is a poet? An unhappy man who hides deep anguish in his heart, but whose lips are so formed that when the sigh and cry pass through them, it sounds like lovely music."

tendencies. So the same people who get the blues to the point of depression are also the ones who are likely to self-reflect on their blues and write songs about them.

The relationship probably cuts both ways. The artistic process involves deep introspection, and it often entails thinking about distressing emotions and disturbing subject matter. This introspective turn of mind may fuel rumination, which, in turn, may contribute to depression in those prone to mood disorders.

*See also:* Cognitive Factors; Melancholia; Mood Disorders

## Bibliography

Akinola, Modupe, and Wendy Berry Mendes. "The Dark Side of Creativity: Biological Vulnerability and Negative Emotions Lead to Greater Artistic Creativity." *Personality and Social Psychology Bulletin* 34 (2008): 1677–1686.

Andreasen, N. C. "Creativity and Mental Illness: Prevalence Rates in Writers and Their First-Degree Relatives." *American Journal of Psychiatry* 144 (1987): 1288–1292.

Bailey, Deborah Smith. "The 'Sylvia Plath' Effect." *Monitor on Psychology* (November 2003): 42–43.

Jamison, Kay Redfield. *Touched with Fire: Manic-Depressive Illness and the Artistic Temperament.* New York: Free Press, 1993.

Kaufman, James C. "The Sylvia Plath Effect: Mental Illness in Eminent Creative Writers." *Journal of Creative Behavior* 35 (2001): 37–50.

Kierkegaard, Søren. Alastair Hannay, trans. Victor Eremita, ed. *Either/Or: A Fragment of Life.* New York: Penguin Books, 1992.

Maisel, Eric. *The Van Gogh Blues: The Creative Person's Path Through Depression.* Novato, CA: New World Library, 2002.

Thomas, Katherine M., and Marshall Duke. "Depressed Writing: Cognitive Distortions in the Works of Depressed and Nondepressed Poets and Writers." *Psychology of Aesthetics, Creativity, and the Arts* 1 (2007): 204–218.

Verhaeghen, Paul, Jutta Joormann, and Rodney Khan. "Why We Sing the Blues: The Relation Between Self-Reflective Rumination, Mood, and Creativity." *Emotion* 5 (2005): 226–232.

**CRYING.**   Crying frequently or easily is considered a classic symptom of depression. The ***Diagnostic and Statistical Manual of Mental Disorders, Fourth Edition, Text Revision***, the bible of the mental health field, mentions tearfulness as one possible outward sign of a depressed mood. Many tests designed to screen for depression also include questions about crying. Yet although the link between crying and depression seems intuitive, surprisingly little is known about it.

Two main theories exist. The dominant theory posits a linear relationship between crying and depression. In a nutshell, it states that the more depressed people are, the more frequently they are apt to cry. Most screening tests that ask about crying—such as the **Center for Epidemiologic Studies Depression Scale**, the **Zung Self-Rating Depression Scale**, and the **Edinburgh Postnatal Depression Scale**—assume this type of linear relationship.

The competing theory holds that increased crying may occur in mild to moderate depression, but an inability to cry often typifies more severe depression. In explaining how to score the **Hamilton Depression Rating Scale**, for example, test developer **Max Hamilton** (1912–1988) noted that some severely depressed individuals "go beyond weeping." The **Beck Depression Inventory**-II assumes this type of nonlinear relationship.

Which theory is correct? Not enough research has been done to answer the question definitively. One pilot study found that people with various forms of depression reported crying more frequently and easily than a matched group of nondepressed individuals. But within the depressed group, no clear pattern of a linear or nonlinear relationship emerged.

***Why Cry?*** Shedding emotional tears is a peculiarly human trait. Several possible explanations for emotional crying have been put forth. English naturalist Charles Darwin (1809–1882) considered crying a universal distress signal. This led to the view that the purpose of crying is to communicate the need for help and elicit care, comfort, and support from others.

Austrian psychiatrist **Sigmund Freud** (1856–1939), on the other hand, regarded crying as a way to discharge negative feelings and reduce internal tension. This led to the view of crying as cathartic—in other words, capable of letting out strong, pent-up emotions.

A third viewpoint, not mutually exclusive with the other two, focuses on the physiological benefits of crying. Experimental data suggest that crying may stimulate activity in the parasympathetic **nervous system**, the branch of the nervous system that conserves energy and resources when the body is relaxed. Parasympathetic activation helps counter an overactive **stress** response, promoting a healthier balance among the body's systems. Tears also may help remove waste products from the body that build up during emotional stress.

***Gender Issues.*** In the general population, **women** are more prone to crying than men. There is some evidence that depression may mute this difference, increasing how frequently and readily men shed tears. Nevertheless, in a society where "big boys don't cry," weeping is generally associated with being female.

Since many tests for depression include questions about crying, this could skew the results toward labeling more women as depressed. Some experts have called for eliminating crying as an indicator of depression, since using it as a diagnostic sign may promote gender bias.

*See also:* Emotion; Sadness

*Bibliography*

American Psychiatric Association. *Diagnostic and Statistical Manual of Mental Disorders.* 4th ed., text rev. Washington, DC: American Psychiatric Association, 2000.

Hamilton, Max. "A Rating Scale for Depression." *Journal of Neurology, Neurosurgery and Psychiatry* 23 (1960) 56–62.

Romans, Sarah E., and Rose F. Clarkson. "Crying as a Gendered Indicator of Depression." *Journal of Nervous and Mental Disease* 196 (2008): 237–243.

Rottenberg, Jonathan, Annemarie Cevaal, and Ad J. J. M. Vingerhoets. "Do Mood Disorders Alter Crying? A Pilot Investigation." *Depression and Anxiety* 25 (2008): E9–E15.

Rottenberg, Jonathan, James J. Gross, Frank H. Wilhelm, Sadia Najmi, and Ian H. Gotlib. "Crying Threshold and Intensity in Major Depressive Disorder." *Journal of Abnormal Psychology* 111 (2002): 302–312.

Vingerhoets, A. J. J. M., J. Rottenberg, A. Cevaal, and J. K. Nelson. "Is There a Relationship Between Depression and Crying? A Review." *Acta Psychiatrica Scandinavica* 115 (2007): 340–351.

**CULTURAL FACTORS.** Culture refers to the distinctive customs, values, beliefs, art, language, and lore of a group of people. Depression does not observe cultural lines, occurring in individuals around the globe. International research has found that depression can be identified in every country and culture where it has been studied. However, the way a particular culture conceptualizes depression affects how it is experienced, diagnosed, and treated.

Several hundred studies of culture and depression have been published in the last two decades. One goal has been to investigate whether Western ideas about depression generalize to other cultural contexts. In some cases, the answer is yes. For example, certain risk factors for depression—including female gender, life **stress**, and low **socioeconomic status**—have shown remarkable consistency across diverse cultures.

In other cases, though, the results have shown more cross-cultural variation. Generally speaking, depression is associated with **sadness**, joylessness, anxiety, tension, and lack of energy. But the emphasis placed on certain of these symptoms, and the other symptoms that go along with them, vary considerably from culture to culture.

***Individual versus Interpersonal Focus.***    The Western view of depression, reflected in the ***Diagnostic and Statistical Manual of Mental Disorders, Fourth Edition, Text Revision*** (*DSM-IV-TR*), stresses the uniqueness and autonomy of the individual. This viewpoint places a premium on personal goals, values, and preferences. Healthy functioning is defined in terms of enhancing the self and maintaining positive self-regard. Conversely, depression is often described in terms of a sense of worthlessness and the inability to feel personal pleasure—symptoms that deviate from important cultural norms.

In East Asian cultures, by comparison, individuals are apt to be viewed as interdependent and defined by their relationship to the group. Healthy functioning involves viewing the self critically, avoiding interpersonal conflict, and preserving social harmony. More significance may be attached to depressive symptoms such as social withdrawal and failure to meet interpersonal obligations—symptoms with greater salience in that culture.

A case in point is self-enhancement—a bias toward seeing oneself as better than others. In the United States, healthy individuals show a tendency toward self-enhancement, but those who are depressed are less likely to see themselves this way. Thus, it might seem that self-criticism is a negative thing. But in Asia, self-criticism is often socially approved as a path to improving oneself. Within this context, a self-critical attitude is considered a good thing, and the link to depression disappears.

***Psychological versus Physical Symptoms.***    Westerners tend to think of mental illnesses, such as depression, as fundamentally different from physical ones. This division is evident in the way health care is provided within two separate systems: medical care and mental health care. Although Western diagnostic criteria for depression include both psychological and physical symptoms, primary importance is attached to two psychological ones: a low mood and lack of pleasure.

In many non-Western cultures, however, mind and body are viewed not as distinct entities, but rather as a single unit. When describing their distress, individuals in these cultures may not distinguish between mental and physical pain. The bodily side of depression may be more obvious in this context.

Consider a Chinese syndrome known as *shenjing shuairuo* (also called neurasthenia, or "nervous weakness"). It is characterized by physical and mental fatigue, dizziness, headaches, other aches and pains, trouble concentrating, difficulty sleeping, and memory loss. Other possible symptoms include digestive problems, sexual dysfunction, irritability, and excitability. Although physical symptoms are relatively prominent, there are also many psychological features. Some, but by no means all, people with this condition would meet *DSM-IV-TR* criteria for **major depression**.

A Common Language for Distress

A cultural idiom of distress refers to a conventional way of talking about distress that is shared by local members of the same culture. Below are some cultural idioms that may sometimes be applied to depression-like symptoms. But keep in mind: There is not a one-to-one correspondence between these culture-specific syndromes and major depression. Although some individuals identified as having these syndromes might meet DSM-IV-TR criteria for major depression, many others would not.

| Geographic Area | Cultural Idiom | Typical Symptoms |
|---|---|---|
| Caribbean (Latinos), Latin America, Latin Mediterranean | *Ataque de nervios* ("attack of nerves") | Crying spells, suicidal gestures, uncontrollable shouting, trembling, verbal or physical aggression, a warm feeling in the chest rising to the head, seizure-like or fainting episodes; often occurs in reaction to a stressful event affecting the family |
| China | *Shenjing shuairuo* (neurasthenia, or "nervous weakness") | Physical and mental fatigue, dizziness, headaches, other aches and pains, trouble concentrating, difficulty sleeping, memory loss, digestive problems, sexual dysfunction, irritability, excitability |
| Ecuador | *Pena* ("suffering") | Crying spells, inability to feel pleasure, trouble concentrating, social withdrawal, sleep and appetite disturbances, digestive symptoms, heart pain; may serve as an appeal to others to make restitution after a personal loss |
| Korea | *Hwa-byung* ("anger syndrome") | Unpleasant mood, trouble sleeping, fatigue, lack of appetite, feeling of tightness in the chest, panic, fear of impending death, indigestion, palpitations, aches and pains |
| United States (Latinos), Latin America | **Susto** ("soul loss") | Sadness, lack of motivation to do anything, appetite disturbances, sleep problems, feelings of low self-worth, muscle aches and pains, headaches, stomachaches, diarrhea |
| West Africa | *Brain fag* | Trouble thinking and concentrating, memory problems, head or neck pain, blurred vision; occurs in students as a result of academic stress |

***Implications for Treatment.*** Culture helps shape the experience and meaning of depression, so it is important for mental health professionals to consider culture when making a diagnosis and developing a treatment plan. This involves noting the cultural identity and preferred language of the individual. For immigrants or ethnic minorities, it also involves noting the degree of identification and involvement with both the culture of origin and the host culture.

Mental health professionals should also be aware of cultural explanations of the individual's illness. Depending on the culture, explanations might center around physical illness, "nerves," bad luck, or spirit possession. To succeed in a multicultural setting, professionals need to show sensitivity to and respect for such alternative perspectives.

Where screening and diagnosis are concerned, it is not always enough to simply translate a test into a new language. The test's validity must also be established in the new context. Several popular screening tests for depression have proved to be useful across a range of cultures, including the **Beck Depression Inventory** and **Zung Self-Rating Depression Scale**. In addition, several culture-specific measures of depression have been developed, such as the Vietnamese Depression Scale, Amritsar Depression Inventory (for Punjabi-speaking individuals in India), and Primary Care Anxiety and Depression Scale (for Arabic-speaking individuals in the United Arab Emirates).

Where treatment is concerned, cultural factors play a role in determining the most appropriate treatment for a particular individual. Some individuals may be unwilling to take **antidepressants** for depression, due to a belief that the condition is primarily interpersonal or spiritual in nature. Others may be hesitant to take part in forms of **psychotherapy** that require disclosing personal thoughts and feelings or family problems, due to a belief that such matters should not be discussed with a stranger.

At the same time, mental health professionals may not be knowledgeable about treatment approaches outside the Western tradition. Yet such approaches may be more acceptable to non-Western patients, and in some cases there is limited scientific evidence to support their use. For example, preliminary research shows that **acupuncture** and **yoga** may be beneficial for some people with depression. A treatment plan that integrates non-Western and Western therapies is sometimes the best option.

*See also:* African Americans; American Indians and Alaska Natives; Asian Americans and Pacific Islanders; Environmental Factors; Ethnicity; Hispanic Americans

***Further Information.*** National Center for Cultural Competence, Georgetown University Center for Child & Human Development, Box 571485, Washington, DC 20057, (800) 788-2066, www11.georgetown.edu/research/gucchd/nccc.

## Bibliography

American Psychiatric Association. *Diagnostic and Statistical Manual of Mental Disorders.* 4th ed., text rev. Washington, DC: American Psychiatric Association, 2000.

Chentsova-Dutton, Yulia E., and Jeanne L. Tsai. "Understanding Depression Across Cultures." In *Handbook of Depression.* 2nd ed., by Ian H. Gotlib and Constance L. Hammen, eds., 363–385. New York: Guilford Press, 2009.

Kirmayer, Laurence J., and G. Eric Jarvis. "Depression Across Cultures." In *The American Psychiatric Publishing Textbook of Mood Disorders,* by Dan J. Stein, David J. Kupfer and Alan F. Schatzberg, eds., 699–715. Washington, DC: American Psychiatric Publishing, 2006.

Nezu, Arthur M., Christine Maguth Nezu, Jill Friedman, and Minsun Lee. "Assessment of Depression." In *Handbook of Depression.* 2nd ed., by Ian H. Gotlib and Constance L. Hammen, eds., 44–68. New York: Guilford Press, 2009.

**CYCLOTHYMIA.** Cyclothymia—also known as cyclothymic disorder—is similar to **bipolar disorder** in that people cycle back and forth between unusually high and unusually low moods. The mood swings are less pronounced, however. In cyclothymia, people alternate between a high mood that is less extreme than full-blown **mania** and a low mood that is less disabling than **major depression**.

Yet the symptoms of cyclothymia still cause real distress and disruption, in part because they are so persistent, lasting at least two years in adults. Although most people with cyclothymia can function in everyday life, they are not at their best. The unpredictable shifts in mood can cause problems in relationships and with daily routines at home, work, or school.

The highs of cyclothymia can lead to poor judgment and risky behavior with serious consequences. The lows can leave people feeling dispirited, hopeless, and worn out. These mood swings can be difficult to handle without professional help. Fortunately, treatment with medications and **psychotherapy** can help people with cyclothymia stay on a more even keel.

Because cyclothymia is a chronic condition, it requires treatment that is long-term—perhaps even lifelong. With proper care, the frequency and severity of highs and lows can be reduced, allowing for a more stable and enjoyable life. Plus, treatment may help keep cyclothymia from turning into more severe bipolar disorder.

***Criteria for Diagnosis.*** The symptoms of cyclothymia are defined by the ***Diagnostic and Statistical Manual of Mental Disorders, Fourth Edition, Text Revision*** (*DSM-IV-TR*), a diagnostic guidebook published by the American Psychiatric Association and widely used by mental health professionals from many disciplines. According to the *DSM-IV-TR*, people with cyclothymia alternate between numerous bouts of hypomania, which is milder than full-fledged mania, and numerous bouts of depressive symptoms, which are milder than major depression.

The symptoms of cyclothymia may let up from time to time, but they are never gone for more than two straight months. This pattern continues over the course of at least two years in adults, or one year in children and adolescents. During the first couple of years that a person is ill, the symptoms never worsen to the point of qualifying as either bipolar disorder or major depression. If they do, the person is diagnosed with one of those other disorders rather than cyclothymia. After that, it is possible for someone to be diagnosed with both cyclothymia and either bipolar disorder or major depression at the same time, assuming the criteria for both disorders are met.

Although the symptoms of cyclothymia are relatively mild, that does not mean they are harmless. In fact, for mood swings to be considered cyclothymia, they must lead to significant distress or cause problems in daily life.

*Hypomanic Episodes.* Hypomania is characterized by an unusually high, grandiose, or irritable mood that lasts for at least four days. When the person's mood is high or grandiose, at least three of the following symptoms must be present: (1) inflated self-esteem or exaggerated ideas about oneself, (2) decreased need for sleep, (3) increased talkativeness or a feeling of pressure to keep talking, (4) racing thoughts or abrupt changes of topic when speaking, (5) easy distractibility, (6) increased activity or restlessness, and (7) excessive involvement in pleasurable but high-risk activities, such as reckless driving, unsafe sex, or spending sprees. If the person's mood is only irritable, at least four of these seven symptoms must occur.

Although the person's mood is clearly different from usual, the change is not drastic enough to seriously impair functioning, necessitate hospitalization, or lead to psychotic symptoms. In fact, the milder burst of energy associated with hypomania may feel good to the person and lead to an outpouring of creativity or productivity. Even when family and friends come to recognize the mood shifts as a problem, the person may deny that anything is wrong. Yet left untreated, hypomania can lead to hostile behavior, strained relationships, poor judgment, and ill-advised or dangerous actions with lasting consequences. It also sometimes turns into full-blown mania or switches into major depression.

*Depressive Episodes.* The depressive symptoms seen in cyclothymia are similar to those seen in major depression. They include (1) a down mood, (2) loss of interest in daily activities, (3) weight gain or weight loss, (4) trouble sleeping or oversleeping, (5) restless activity or slowed-down movements, (6) constant tiredness or lack of energy, (7) feelings of worthlessness or inappropriate guilt, (8) difficulty concentrating or making decisions, and (9) recurring thoughts of death or **suicide**. Although the person's mood is obviously different from well periods, the symptoms don't rise to the level of major depression. There are fewer than five of them, they last less than two weeks, or they are not severe enough to be disabling.

***Causes and Risk Factors.*** Cyclothymia is estimated to occur in up to one percent of the population at some point in their lives. That number could be an underestimate, however, because the disorder is not widely publicized, and it often may go undiagnosed or misdiagnosed. Cyclothymia typically starts in adolescence or young adulthood, and it strikes about the same number of men and women.

People with close family members who have cyclothymia or bipolar disorder may have an increased risk of developing cyclothymia themselves. This suggests that **genetic factors** play a role in causing the disorder.

But genes aren't the full story. **Environmental factors**, such as high **stress** and major life changes, may trigger or worsen cyclothymia. **Substance abuse** may contribute to the disorder as well.

***Treatment of Cyclothymia.*** From 15 percent to 50 percent of people with cyclothymia eventually go on to develop bipolar disorder. Treatment helps reduce this risk as well as even out erratic moods and unpredictable behavior. The main treatment options are medications and psychotherapy.

The most commonly prescribed medications for cyclothymia are **mood stabilizers**, which help keep moods steadier. **Lithium**, the oldest and best-known mood-stabilizing drug, is generally the first-choice treatment for hypomania. But another group of medications called **anticonvulsants**, originally developed to help prevent seizures, also may be used to help regulate moods.

**Antidepressants** usually are not prescribed unless they are combined with a mood stabilizer. Even then, the decision to take one of these medications needs to be carefully weighed, because in people with cyclothymia, antidepressants may sometimes trigger a sudden switch to dangerous mania.

Psychotherapy can help people with cyclothymia understand their condition and get along better in daily life. One type of psychotherapy that may be particularly helpful is **cognitive-behavioral therapy** (CBT), in which people learn to recognize and change dysfunctional thought and behavior patterns that are contributing to their illness. Through CBT, people can become more attuned to situations that trigger their mood swings and develop effective strategies for coping with these situations.

*See also:* Mood Disorders

## Bibliography

American Psychiatric Association. *Diagnostic and Statistical Manual of Mental Disorders.* 4th ed., text rev. Washington, DC: American Psychiatric Association, 2000.

*Cyclothymia (Cyclothymic Disorder).* Mayo Clinic, April 18, 2008, http://www.mayoclinic.com/health/cyclothymia/DS00729.

Totterdell, Peter, and Stephen Kellett. "Restructuring Mood in Cyclothymia Using Cognitive Behavior Therapy: An Intensive Time-Sampling Study." *Journal of Clinical Psychology* 64 (2008): 501–518.

**CYTOCHROME P450 TEST.**   The cytochrome P450 (CYP450) test is a genetic lab test that predicts how a person's body will process certain drugs, including most **antidepressants**. The test evaluates genes from the CYP450 family, which produce enzymes that the body needs to break down and use many medications. Variations in these genes may cause people to metabolize a medication too slowly, leading to side effects, or too quickly, reducing the effectiveness.

Although there are general guidelines for doctors on prescribing antidepressants, finding the best medication for a specific patient often takes some trial and error. The CYP450 test can help predict which antidepressants are most likely to be safe and effective for a given individual, based on that person's metabolism. This may give doctors a better chance of prescribing the right antidepressant at the right dosage, taking some of the guesswork out of treating depression.

So far, CYP450 testing has been used mainly for research purposes. However, a test for clinical use, called the AmpliChip P450 Genotyping Test, was approved by the Food and Drug Administration (FDA) in 2004. As this article was being written, the test was not yet widely available, and it was not covered by most major insurance plans. But the hope is that it will usher in a new era of more personalized prescribing that helps reduce risks and optimize benefits.

***How the Test Is Done.***   The CYP450 is a simple blood test. Blood is drawn from a vein in the person's arm and sent to a laboratory for testing.

At the lab, genotyping—testing to determine a person's genetic makeup—is carried out. In this case, the testing looks for variants in a few genes that produce CYP450 enzymes. The test itself makes use of a DNA microarray. The microarray is similar to a computer microchip, but instead of tiny circuits, it contains millions of tiny DNA molecules.

***What the Results Mean.***   Based on the results of the CYP450 test, people are classified as normal, intermediate, slow, and ultra-rapid metabolizers.

*Normal Metabolizers.*   These individuals process certain antidepressants normally. They may be more likely to benefit from the medications and have fewer side effects than people who do not metabolize drugs as well.

*Intermediate Metabolizers.*   These individuals have at least one tested gene that does not function as it should. They may not process certain antidepressants as well as normal metabolizers do.

*Slow Metabolizers.*   These individuals process certain antidepressants more slowly than normal. The medications may build up in the body, increasing the risk of side effects.

*Ultra-rapid Metabolizers.*   These individuals process certain antidepressants more quickly than normal. The medications may be eliminated from the body too soon, before they have a chance to work effectively.

***From Promise to Practice.***   One big drawback to antidepressant treatment is that it takes weeks for the full effects to be felt. If the dosage needs to be adjusted or the medication needs to be switched, it takes even longer. In theory, the CYP450 test could reduce this time lag by helping doctors make better treatment choices.

But there are hurdles to be overcome before use of the test becomes standard practice. A 2007 report from the federal Agency for Healthcare Research and Quality noted a paucity of large, high-quality studies showing whether the test actually leads to better outcomes in the real world.

The AmpliChip CYP450 test looks for variants of two genes thought to be especially important in drug metabolism. Yet there are actually more than 50 different CYP450 genes, and more than one CYP450 enzyme may be involved in the metabolism of a specific antidepressant. In addition, several factors other than these enzymes affect how drugs are used by the body.

The more important these factors are, the less helpful CYP450 testing will be. At present, such testing may be most useful for people who show unusual resistance or sensitivity to antidepressants at normal doses.

*See also:* Genetic Factors

## Bibliography

*Cytochrome P450 (CYP450) Genotyping Test.* Mayo Clinic, May 30, 2008, http://mayoclinic.com/health/cyp450-test/MY00135.

*FDA Clears First of Kind Genetic Lab* Test. Food and Drug Administration, December 23, 2004, http://www.fda.gov/bbs/topics/news/2004/new01149.html.

Lynch, Tom, and Amy Price. "The Effect of Cytochrome P450 Metabolism on Drug Response, Interactions, and Adverse Effects." *American Family Physician* 76 (2007) 391–396.

Matchar, David B., and Mugdha Thakur. "Is Genetic Testing for Cytochrome P450 Polymorphisms Ready for Implementation?" *American Family Physician* 76 (2007): 348, 351.

Matchar, David B., Mugdha E. Thakur, Iris Grossman, Douglas C. McCrory, Lori A. Orlando, David C. Steffens, et al. *Testing for Cytochrome P450 Polymorphisms in Adults with Non-psychotic Depression Treated with Selective Serotonin Reuptake Inhibitors (SSRIs): Evidence Report/Technology Assessment No. 146.* Rockville, MD: Agency for Healthcare Research and Quality, 2007.

McAlpine, Donald E., Dennis J. O'Kane, John L. Black, and David A. Mrazek. "Cytochrome P450 2D6 Genotype Variation and Vanlafaxine Dosage." *Mayo Clinic Proceedings* 82 (2007): 1065–1068.

*The Cytochrome P450 Genetic Test.* Mayo Clinic, http://www.mayoclinic.org/depression/cytochrome.html.

# D

**DAWN SIMULATION.**  Dawn simulation is an experimental treatment for **seasonal affective disorder** (SAD), a form of **major depression** in which symptoms start and stop around the same time each year. Typically, the symptoms begin in fall or winter, a pattern that seems to be tied to shorter days with less sunlight. As the days lengthen again in spring, the symptoms improve. The aim of dawn simulation is to artificially mimic the light conditions of a spring dawn while it is still winter.

To do this, a timer gradually turns on a lamp in the person's bedroom early in the morning, before the natural winter dawn occurs. The lamp emits light that is much less intense than what is used for conventional **light therapy**, a well-established treatment for SAD. It starts at less than 1 lux, simulating starlight, and gradually increases to about 300 lux, simulating sunrise under tree cover. In contrast, conventional light therapy uses light that is about 10,000 lux.

The light gradually brightens during the last hour and a half to two hours of sleep. It is set to go off at the person's wake-up time. One big advantage of dawn simulation is that it is a passive treatment, requiring no special effort once the lamp is put in place. Because the lamp has a diffuser, it creates a wide field of illumination that can reach the person in different sleep positions. (An ordinary lamp set to turn on early may not work due to its narrow illumination field.)

***Benefits for Depression.***  Dawn simulation was first described in 1989 by a research team led by U.S. psychologist Michael Terman (1943– ), a professor in the psychiatry department at Columbia University. In several subsequent studies, it has been shown to relieve symptoms of SAD. For instance, in one study, 95 people with SAD were randomly assigned to one of three groups: dawn simulation, standard light therapy, or a placebo treatment (dim red light). Their symptoms were rated over the next six weeks by a psychiatrist who did not know which treatment they were getting. Those in the dawn simulation group showed greater improvement than those in both other groups.

Research indicates that dawn simulation affects **circadian rhythms**, the body's internal system for regulating physiological and behavioral cycles that repeat daily, such as the sleep-wake cycle. In particular, it suppresses production of **melatonin**, a hormone secreted by the pineal gland in response to darkness. Disturbances in circadian rhythms and in the timing of melatonin secretion may play a role in SAD, so these effects help explain how the treatment might work. But more research is still needed to confirm the depression-lifting potential of dawn simulation.

*Bibliography*

Avery, David H., Derek N. Eder, Mary Ann Bolte, Carla J. Hellekson, David L. Dunner, Michael V. Vitiello, et al. "Dawn Simulation and Bright Light in the Treatment of SAD: A Controlled Study." *Biological Psychiatry* 50 (2001): 205–216.

*Frequently Asked Questions at CET.* Center for Environmental Therapeutics, 2007, http://www.cet .org/q-and-a.htm.

Golden, Robert N., Bradley N. Gaynes, R. David Ekstrom, Robert M. Hamer, Frederick M. Jacobsen, Trisha Suppes, et al. "The Efficacy of Light Therapy in the Treatment of Mood Disorders: A Review and Meta-analysis of the Evidence." *American Journal of Psychiatry* 162 (2005): 656–662.

Terman, Michael, and Jiuan Su Terman. "Controlled Trial of Naturalistic Dawn Simulation and Negative Air Ionization for Seasonal Affective Disorder." *American Journal of Psychiatry* 163 (2006): 2126–2133.

Terman, Michael, and Jiuan Su Terman. "Light Therapy for Seasonal and Non-seasonal Depression: Efficacy, Protocol, Safety, and Side Effects." *CNS Spectrums* 10 (2005): 647–663.

Terman, Michael, David Schlager, Stephen Fairhurst, and Bill Perlman. "Dawn and Dusk Simulation as a Therapeutic Intervention." *Biological Psychiatry* 25 (1989): 966–970.

**DEEP BRAIN STIMULATION.**   Deep brain stimulation (DBS) is a treatment in which electrodes are surgically implanted in the brain, where they stimulate the targeted area with electrical impulses. This technique is already a standard treatment for **Parkinson's disease** and some other neurological conditions that cause uncontrollable movements. It is now being tested as a possible option for **treatment-resistant depression** when **antidepressants** and **psychotherapy** do not provide enough relief. The use of DBS for treating depression is still considered experimental, though. Because it is the most invasive form of **brain stimulation** used for depression, it is also somewhat controversial.

Interest in DBS for depression grew out of an unexpected observation: Some people with conditions such as Parkinson's disease who underwent DBS found that their mood improved. Subsequent research in a small number of patients with treatment-resistant depression has yielded promising enough results to warrant further study.

Based on evidence to date, mood symptoms may decrease or go away in some people with depression who receive DBS. But others, especially those who have been depressed for years, may not get better. Additional research on safety and effectiveness is needed.

***Surgical Procedure.***   DBS actually requires two surgical procedures: brain surgery to implant the electrodes and chest surgery to implant a battery-operated device similar to a pacemaker near the collarbone. This device is connected to the electrodes by wires that run under the skin of the shoulder, neck, and head. It sends electrical signals to the electrodes, which in turn stimulate the brain. The stimulation is usually continuous, 24 hours a day.

For the brain surgery part, local anesthetic is used to numb the area, and a small hole is made in the skull. Then sophisticated imaging technology guides the surgeon in implanting electrodes in both sides of the brain. The patient stays awake and able to talk to the surgeon, which helps ensure that the right areas of the brain have been located. Because the brain itself does not generate pain signals, the process is not painful.

For the chest surgery part, the patient is put in a sleep-like state with general anesthesia. A device called a neurostimulator is placed in the chest area and connected to the electrodes with wires.

A week or so after surgery, the neurostimulator is turned on in the doctor's office with a magnetic controller. The patient is given a handheld magnet that can be used to turn it off at home if necessary.

Periodic follow-up visits to the doctor are required to make sure the neurostimulator continues working properly and does not shift out of place. The stimulation can be adjusted to maximize effectiveness and minimize side effects over time. When necessary, the neurostimulator can be replaced or removed in a simple surgical procedure.

***Effects on the Brain.***   Researchers still are not sure exactly how DBS might work for relieving depression. However, the area where the electrodes are implanted, called the subgenual **anterior cingulate cortex** (ACC), is thought to be overactive in many depressed individuals, and DBS may decrease activity there. In addition, it may reset the activity level of several other parts of the brain that are connected to the subgenual ACC.

Interestingly, while still in the operating room, patients often say they feel as if something negative has suddenly been taken away when the surgeon stimulates the electrode sites. Patients may describe a sense of relief, the lifting of a dark cloud, or the disappearance of an empty feeling. If questioned, they also may talk about being interested in getting back to activities, when previously they were disinterested and inactive.

After surgery, patients may experience more subtle and gradual improvement once the neurostimulator is turned on. It may take several weeks before the full benefits are felt.

***Risks and Side Effects.***   DBS involves brain surgery, so it is has some serious risks that must be weighed carefully against the potential benefits. Possible complications of the surgery itself include bleeding in the brain, stroke, infection, heart problems, nausea, breathing problems, and scarring. Possible side effects of the treatment include bleeding in the brain, infection, seizure, confusion, unwanted mood changes, movement disorders, lightheadedness, dizziness, insomnia, tingling in the face or limbs, and device malfunction.

Although DBS is still an experimental treatment for depression, it has a good track record with other conditions. The electrodes are usually well tolerated, with no significant changes in the surrounding brain tissue. Although the treatment might prove useful for some with severe, hard-to-treat depression, it is not yet widely available for that purpose.

*See also:* Treatment of Depression

## Bibliography

*Deep Brain Stimulation for Treatment-Resistant Depression: An Expert Interview with Helen S. Mayberg, MD.* Medscape, January 5, 2006, http://www.medscape.com/viewarticle/520659.

*Deep Brain Stimulation.* American Association of Neurological Surgeons, April 2007, http://www.neurosurgerytoday.org/what/patient_e/deep%20brain%20stimulation.asp.

*Deep Brain Stimulation.* Mayo Clinic, July 31, 2008, http://www.mayoclinic.com/health/deep-brain-stimulation/MY00184.

Mayberg, Helen S., Andrews M. Lozano, Valerie Voon, Heather E. McNeely, David Seminowicz, Clement Hamani, et al. "Deep Brain Stimulation for Treatment-Resistant Depression." *Neuron* 45 (2005): 651–660.

Tye, Susannah J., Mark A. Frye, and Kendall H. Lee. "Disrupting Disordered Neurocircuitry: Treating Refractory Psychiatric Illness with Neuromodulation." *Mayo Clinic Proceedings* 84 (2009): 522–532.

**DEMENTIA SYNDROME OF DEPRESSION.**   Dementia syndrome of depression (DOD)—also known as pseudodementia—refers to an impairment in memory and thinking abilities that is caused by depression. It mimics other types of dementia, such as the mental impairment caused by **Alzheimer's disease** or **stroke**. Unlike these other forms of dementia, however, DOD disappears once the depression is treated.

DOD has never held a place in the official nomenclature for mental disorders. Nevertheless, the fact that depression can masquerade as dementia has been recognized for many years, and DOD is often discussed in medical texts. The symptoms of DOD, such as memory loss and disorientation, are quite real. And like other symptoms of depression, they are associated with changes in brain chemistry and function.

The defining difference between DOD and true dementia is the potential for reversing mental deficits caused by depression. Therefore, one litmus test for DOD is whether a person gets better when treated with **antidepressants**. Beyond that, behavioral clues and psychological tests can help health care professionals identify DOD. People with the condition tend to be very distressed by memory lapses and mental confusion, even when they show only slight impairment on objective tests. Their ability to perform tasks of similar difficulty also may vary widely in testing. In addition, other symptoms of depression are present.

***DOD or Alzheimer's?*** Just because people have symptoms of both depression and dementia at the same time does not automatically mean they have DOD. Depression also is common in people who have true Alzheimer's disease. To differentiate DOD from Alzheimer's dementia, health care professionals look for telltale signs.

Compared to Alzheimer's dementia, DOD tends to come on more quickly. The mental deficits are often less severe in DOD, and they generally involve fewer areas of thinking ability. For example, unlike people with true Alzheimer's, those with DOD usually do not develop impairments in language skills.

*Bibliography*

Brown, Walter A. "Pseudodementia: Issues in Diagnosis." *Psychiatric Times* (April 9, 2005).

Busby, Charlotte, and Alistair Burns. "Differential Diagnosis of Dementia." In *Principles and Practice of Geriatric Psychiatry,* 2nd ed., by John R.M. Copeland, Mohammed T. Abou-Saleh and Dan G. Blazer, eds., 293–296. New York: John Wiley and Sons, 2002.

**DEPRESSED MOOD.** A **depressed mood** is often described as feeling sad, empty, hopeless, helpless, or being down in the dumps. The predisposition to respond emotionally in this way lasts for hours, days, or longer. One of the most common reasons that people seek mental health care is a depressed mood they cannot shake.

A depressed mood can occur in a wide range of mental disorders. It is a prominent feature of **major depression**, **dysthymia**, **bipolar disorder**, **cyclothymia**, **adjustment disorder with depressed mood**, and **schizoaffective disorder**. In addition, a depressed mood can be associated with dementia (a decline in mental abilities caused by one of several disorders affecting the brain, such as Alzheimer's disease or stroke), another general medical condition, or **substance abuse** and withdrawal.

The presence of a depressed mood does not necessarily mean someone has a disorder that requires professional treatment. An occasional bout of "the blues" is a normal part of everyday experience. But when the depressed mood causes significant distress or interferes with the ability to get along in daily life, it may be a sign that something more serious is going on.

*See also:* Dysphoria

*Bibliography*

American Psychiatric Association. *Diagnostic and Statistical Manual of Mental Disorders.* 4th ed., text rev. Washington, DC: American Psychiatric Association, 2000.

First, Michael B., Allen Frances, and Harold Alan Pincus. *DSM-IV Handbook of Differential Diagnosis.* Washington, DC: American Psychiatric Press, 1995.

**DEPRESSION AND BIPOLAR SUPPORT ALLIANCE.** The Depression and Bipolar Support Alliance (DBSA; formerly the National Depressive and Manic Depressive Association) is a national, nonprofit group dedicated to providing information and support to people with **mood disorders**, including **major depression** and **bipolar disorder**. Founded in 1985, the DBSA now has a network of more than 400 chapters and about 1,000 **support groups** across the United States serving approximately 70,000 people every year.

The DBSA publishes educational materials about mood disorders written for the general public. In addition, the group advocates in Washington, D.C., on behalf of people with mood disorders, speaking out on issues such as research funding, **insurance parity**, and patient confidentiality. Other activities include holding an annual conference and sponsoring surveys on issues of importance to those living with or providing treatment for depression and bipolar disorder.

*Further Information.* Depression and Bipolar Support Alliance, 730 N. Franklin Street, Suite 501, Chicago, IL 60610, (800) 826-3632, www.dbsalliance.org, www.peersupport.org, www.facingus.org.

*Bibliography*

*About the Depression and Bipolar Support Alliance (DBSA).* Depression and Bipolar Support Alliance, January 22, 2008, http://www.dbsalliance.org/site/PageServer?pagename=dbsa_aboutdbsa.

**DEPRESSIVE DISORDER NOT OTHERWISE SPECIFIED.** "Depressive disorder not otherwise specified" (NOS) is a catchall term that is used when depression is serious enough to cause problems but does not fulfill the criteria for any established disorder. To make a diagnosis, mental health professionals use the ***Diagnostic and Statistical Manual of Mental Disorders, Fourth Edition, Text Revision*** (*DSM-IV-TR*). But this manual does not cover every possible manifestation of depression, so the authors included the NOS category to give professionals more latitude for making a diagnosis and prescribing treatment even when all the criteria for **major depression**, **dysthymia**, or an **adjustment disorder with depressed mood** are not met.

Some of the cutoff points in the *DSM-IV-TR*—for example, the requirements that major depression must involve at least five symptoms and last at least two weeks—are largely arbitrary. Also, to avoid having too many false positives—false identifications of a disorder as being present when it actually is not—the thresholds are set fairly high. This means there inevitably will be some false negatives—failures to detect a disorder that actually is present. As a result, people may fall short of the *DSM-IV-TR* criteria for depressive disorders and still have symptoms that warrant diagnosis and treatment.

That is where the NOS category comes in handy, offering treatment providers an option for making a diagnosis based partly on clinical judgment. Some forms of depression currently lumped into this category—such as **premenstrual dysphoric disorder**, **minor depression**, and **recurrent brief depression**—may become diagnostic entities in their own right in the next edition of the *DSM*. In the meantime, the *DSM-IV-TR* designation for people with these conditions is depressive disorder NOS.

*See also:* Clinical Depression

*Bibliography*

American Psychiatric Association. *Diagnostic and Statistical Manual of Mental Disorders.* 4th ed., text rev. Washington, DC: American Psychiatric Association, 2000.

Frances, Allen, Michael B. First, and Harold Alan Pincus. *DSM-IV Guidebook.* Washington, DC: American Psychiatric Press, 1995.

**DEPRESSIVE PERSONALITY DISORDER.**   Depressive personality disorder (DPD) is a term that is sometimes used to describe a long-lasting and wide-ranging pattern of depressive thoughts and behaviors. This pattern begins by early adulthood and occurs in all or most settings. It is one of the proposed new diagnoses being considered for inclusion in the next edition of the *Diagnostic and Statistical Manual of Mental Disorders,* a diagnostic guide published by the American Psychiatric Association and used by mental health professionals from many disciplines.

Each of us has our own set of cognitive traits, emotional patterns, and behavioral styles that make up our personality. The nature of our personality colors how we see the world and shapes our thoughts, feelings, and actions in a fairly consistent way. But healthy people have enough flexibility to adapt to the normal stresses and strains of life, and they are able to form satisfying relationships. People with personality disorders, in contrast, have such a rigid view of the world that they are unable to cope with changes and challenges, and they often have great trouble dealing with others.

People with DPD, in particular, are constantly glum and overly serious. They never seem to let their hair down and have fun, and they lack a sense of humor. Those with DPD may feel as if they are unworthy of being happy, and they may have a deep sense of inadequacy. Because they tend to be as harshly critical of others as they are of themselves, relationships are difficult. People with DPD are often quiet, introverted, and unassertive. They also tend to brood and worry, dwelling on pessimistic thoughts.

DPD differs from the ordinary unhappiness and self-criticism that everyone experiences from time to time. The traits associated with DPD cast a dark cloud over an individual's life that follows that person through the years and across a wide range of situations.

***Historical Roots.***   The concept of a personality pattern based on low-level depression has a long history. As far back as 1921, German psychiatrist Emil Kraepelin (1856–1926), who pioneered the modern classification system of mental disorders, described something he called "depressive temperament." People with this temperament tended to be gloomy, serious, guilt-ridden, and self-reproaching, starting at a young age and lasting throughout their lives. Kraepelin believed that such traits reflected an inherited temperament.

In the late 1950s, another German psychiatrist, Kurt Schneider (1887–1967), described "depressive psychopathy." The term conveys the same sense of overriding gloom that Kraepelin had recognized. Schneider believed that people with depressive psychopathy take pride in their suffering. They tend to be gloomy, pessimistic, serious, unable to relax, quiet, skeptical, duty-bound, self-doubting, and awash in worries.

Yet despite this history, there is still active debate about whether DPD is really a distinct condition. In particular, critics have noted the strong similarities between DPD and **dysthymia**, a mental disorder characterized by a down mood that is relatively mild but quite persistent. However, dysthymia often manifests itself in physical symptoms (such as changes in sleep, appetite, and energy level), and DPD is defined by personality traits and mental symptoms (such as brooding, **pessimism**, and low self-esteem). Several studies have shown that fewer than half of people with DPD meet the criteria for dysthymia, and vice versa.

***Criteria for Diagnosis.*** Like all personality disorders, DPD is characterized by an enduring pattern of thinking, feeling, and behaving that differs markedly from societal norms. This pattern is inflexible, which helps explain why it is maladaptive, because people with personality disorders find it difficult to adapt to the changing demands of their environment. The disorder also is pervasive, affecting all or most areas of personal functioning. The dysfunctional pattern emerges by adolescence or early adulthood and is relatively stable over time. It leads to emotional distress and/or problems getting along in daily life.

What sets DPD apart from other personality disorders is the specific constellation of symptoms and traits that typify it. People with DPD have at least five of the following: (1) a mood that is usually dominated by dejection, gloominess, joylessness, or unhappiness, (2) a self-concept that centers around inadequacy, worthlessness, and low self-esteem, (3) an attitude toward the self that is critical, blaming, and derogatory, (4) an attitude toward others that is negative, critical, and judgmental, (5) a tendency to brood and worry, (6) a tendency to feel guilty or remorseful, and (7) pessimism.

***Treatment of DPD.*** Personality disorders can be challenging to treat, but recognizing the problem is the first step toward managing it. Treatment typically involves individual, group, or family **psychotherapy**. In general, therapy can help people take responsibility for the unhappiness in their lives and find more effective ways of responding. Common goals of therapy include building better relationships, becoming more mentally flexible, and reducing patterns of thinking and behaving that interfere with everyday activities. Among the approaches sometimes used to treat personality disorders are **cognitive-behavioral therapy**, **dialectical behavior therapy**, and **psychodynamic therapy**.

Not surprisingly, some people with DPD go on to have an episode of **major depression**. When that happens, **antidepressants** may be prescribed to treat the depression. Getting proper treatment and sticking with it are especially important if major depression occurs, because having DPD is predictive of less improvement in depressive symptoms.

*See also:* Personality Factors

## Bibliography

American Psychiatric Association. *Diagnostic and Statistical Manual of Mental Disorders.* 4th ed., text rev. Washington, DC: American Psychiatric Association, 2000.

*Factsheet: Personality Disorders.* Mental Health America, November 8, 2006, http://www.nmha.org/go/information/get-info/personality-disorders.

Frances, Allen, Michael B. First, and Harold Alan Pincus. *DSM-IV Guidebook.* Washington, DC: American Psychiatric Press, 1995.

Laptook, Rebecca S., Daniel N. Klein, and Lea R. Dougherty. "Ten-Year Stability of Depressive Personality Disorder in Depressed Outpatients." *American Journal of Psychiatry* 163 (2006): 865–871.

*Personality Disorders.* Mayo Clinic, September 11, 2006, http://mayoclinic.com/health/personality-disorders/DS00562.

Phillips, Katharine A., John G. Gunderson, Robert M.A. Hirschfeld, and Lauren E. Smith. "A Review of the Depressive Personality." *American Journal of Psychiatry* 147 (1990): 830–837.

Ryder, Andrew G., Michael Bagby, and Deborah R. Schuller. "The Overlap of Depressive Personality Disorder and Dysthymia: A Categorical Problem with a Dimensional Solution." *Harvard Review of Psychiatry* 10 (2002): 337–352.

Silverstein, Marshall L. *Disorders of the Self: A Personality-Guided Approach.* Washington, DC: American Psychological Association, 2007.

Yen, Shirley, Meghan E. McDevitt-Murphy, and M. Tracie Shea. "Depression and Personality." In *The American Psychiatric Publishing Textbook of Mood Disorders,* by Dan J. Stein, David J. Kupfer, and Alan F. Schatzberg, eds., 673–686. Washington, DC: American Psychiatric Publishing, 2006.

**DEXAMETHASONE SUPPRESSION TEST.** The dexamethasone suppression test (DST) is a lab test that measures the ability of dexamethasone, a synthetic hormone, to suppress the release of **cortisol**, a natural hormone that plays a key role in the body's **stress** response. The test has been used in numerous studies exploring the link between depression and stress. These studies have shown that dexamethasone often fails to suppress cortisol as it should in people with severe depression.

Under normal circumstances, the brain responds to a stressful situation by stimulating the pituitary gland to release adrenocorticotropic hormone (ACTH). This hormone travels to the adrenal glands, located just above the kidneys, where it triggers the release of cortisol. The cortisol, in turn, arouses various body systems and gets them ready to cope with whatever threat is at hand.

The level of cortisol in the blood affects how much ACTH is released by the pituitary. The more cortisol is present, the less ACTH is released, which keeps the adrenal glands from continuing to pump out even more cortisol. Because dexamethasone is a man-made cousin of cortisol, it normally has the same effect, lowering ACTH levels and thus leading to decreased cortisol in the blood.

***How the Test Is Done.*** The test procedure may vary somewhat. Typically, though, a person takes a low dose of dexamethasone by mouth at 11:00 p.m. The next day, a health care provider draws blood one to three times, starting at 8:00 a.m. Cortisol levels in the blood samples are then measured.

***What the Results Mean.*** Using the test procedure described above, a cortisol level below 1.8 mcg/dl is considered normal. Anything above that level is a sign that the body is not suppressing cortisol but instead is continuing to release it. Some—but not all—people with untreated depression show nonsuppression on the DST. Nonsuppression is most common in people with severe depression, including those with **psychotic depression**. It occurs in about half of those with severe symptoms.

DST status before treatment for depression does not predict how well treatment will work. But people who are still nonsuppressors after treatment are more likely to relapse than those who are not.

As a research tool, the DST has provided important insights into the biology of depression. But as a test for diagnosing depression in clinical practice, it has proved less useful. Its ability to distinguish depression from other disorders is low, because DST nonsuppression also can be caused by other medical illnesses, various medications, and malnutrition.

*See also:* Hypothalamic-Pituitary-Adrenal Axis

*Bibliography*

Belmaker, R.H., and Galila Agam. "Major Depressive Disorder." *New England Journal of Medicine* 358 (2008): 55–68.

*Dexamethasone Suppression Test.* National Library of Medicine, March 18, 2008, http://www.nlm.nih .gov/medlineplus/ency/article/003694.htm.

Gillespie, Charles F., and Charles B. Nemeroff. "Hypercortisolemia and Depression." *Psychosomatic Medicine* 67 (2005): S26-S28.

Seidman, Stuart N. "Psychoneuroendocrinology of Mood Disorders." In *The American Psychiatric Publishing Textbook of Mood Disorders,* by Dan J. Stein, David J. Kupfer and Alan F. Schatzberg, eds., 117–130. Washington, DC: American Psychiatric Publishing, 2006.

**DIABETES.**   Diabetes is a disorder of metabolism—the way the body uses digested food for energy and growth. When not controlled, diabetes can lead to a host of serious complications, including heart disease, stroke, vision loss, kidney failure, nerve damage, amputations, pregnancy problems, and birth defects. Several studies also have shown that diabetes doubles the risk of depression, and the risk only gets higher as more complications arise.

During digestion, most food is broken down into a form of sugar called glucose. This glucose passes into the bloodstream and is carried around the body, where a hormone called insulin helps move the glucose from blood into the cells. In healthy individuals, the pancreas automatically produces the right amount of insulin for this purpose. In people with diabetes, though, either the pancreas produces little or no insulin or the cells do not use it properly. Either way, glucose builds up in the blood and eventually passes out of the body in urine, robbing the body of its primary energy source.

When blood glucose stays too high for too long, it can harm almost every part of the body. Depression just magnifies the problem, increasing the risk of poor glucose control and diabetes complications. One reason is that depression saps people's energy and motivation, making it harder to practice good health habits and stick to a diabetes treatment plan. Depression also leads to social isolation, and support from others is often a crucial factor affecting people's ability to control their diabetes.

Fortunately, both depression and diabetes can be managed with proper treatment and good self-care. When their mood improves, people tend to do a better job of following a diabetes treatment plan. And when diabetes improves, people generally find it easier to feel upbeat and hopeful about the future. It is a classic win-win situation.

*The Depression Connection.*   Researchers are still trying to untangle the complex relationship between diabetes and depression. It is common for people with diabetes to worry about the disease's effect on their personal life, the cost of medical care, and the possibility of future complications. The **stress** of living with such worries may trigger or worsen depression in vulnerable individuals.

In addition, there may be a physiological connection between the two conditions. Several changes in brain anatomy and function have been linked to chronic stress and repeated exposure to stress **hormones**. Increased levels of stress hormones also are associated with insulin resistance, in which muscle, fat, and liver cells do not use insulin as they should.

**Brain imaging** studies have shown that the **hippocampus**—a brain structure that plays a role in learning, emotion, and memory—tends to be smaller in people with stress-related disorders, including depression. Studies also have found hippocampal decreases in cell division and in the creation of new brain cells as a consequence of high blood glucose. Interestingly, these diabetes-related decreases can be reversed by **antidepressants**.

*Treatment Considerations.*   In the United States, about five percent to 10 percent of diagnosed diabetes is type 1, a form of the disease in which the **immune system** attacks and destroys insulin-producing cells in the pancreas. People with type 1 diabetes must take daily insulin to survive. Healthy eating, physical activity, and close monitoring of blood glucose levels also play an important role in treatment.

About 90 percent to 95 percent of Americans with diabetes have type 2, a form of the disease that is often associated with older age and obesity. Diet, exercise, and blood glucose monitoring are the basic management tools for type 2 diabetes. Many people with this form of the disease also take diabetes pills and/or insulin to help keep their blood glucose under control.

When people with diabetes also have depression, **psychotherapy**, antidepressants, or both can help relieve their mood symptoms and promote better self-care. Research has shown that getting appropriate treatment for depression can improve blood glucose control as well.

If antidepressants are prescribed, **selective serotonin reuptake inhibitors** are often the treatment of choice. Two other types of antidepressants—**tricyclic antidepressants** and **monoamine oxidase inhibitors**—can interfere with glucose metabolism, so they are not usually prescribed for people with diabetes.

*See also:* Physical Illness

***Further Information.*** American Diabetes Association, 1701 N. Beauregard Street, Alexandria, VA 22311, (800) 342-2383, www.diabetes.org.

Juvenile Diabetes Research Foundation International, 120 Wall Street, New York, NY 10005, (800) 533-2873, www.jdrf.org.

National Diabetes Education Program, One Diabetes Way, Bethesda, MD 20814-9692, (888) 693-6337, ndep.nih.gov.

National Institute of Diabetes and Digestive and Kidney Diseases, Building 31. Room 9A06, 31 Center Drive, MSC 2560, Bethesda, MD 20892, (301) 496-3583, www.niddk .nih.gov.

*Bibliography*

Anderson, Ryan J., Ray E. Clouse, Kenneth E. Freedland, and Patrick J. Lustman. "The Prevalence of Comorbid Depression in Adults with Diabetes: A Meta-analysis." *Diabetes Care* 24 (2001): 1069–1078.

Boland, Robert. "Depression in Medical Illness (Secondary Depression)." In *The American Psychiatric Publishing Textbook of Mood Disorders,* by Dan J. Stein, David J. Kupfer, and Alan F. Schatzberg, eds., 639–652. Washington, DC: American Psychiatric Publishing, 2006.

de Groot, Mary, Ryan Anderson, Kenneth E. Freedland, Ray E. Clouse, and Patrick J. Lustman. "Association of Depression and Diabetes Complications: A Meta-analysis." *Psychosomatic Medicine* 63 (2001): 619–630.

*Diabetes at Work: What's Depression Got to Do with It?* National Diabetes Education Program, 2008, http://www.diabetesatwork.org/DiabetesResources/DepressionCaseStudy.cfm.

*Diabetes Overview.* National Institute of Diabetes and Digestive and Kidney Diseases, September 2006, http://diabetes.niddk.nih.gov/dm/pubs/overview.

*Frequently Asked Questions: Diabetes-Related Health Concerns.* Centers for Disease Control and Prevention, July 12, 2007, http://www.cdc.gov/diabetes/faq/concerns.htm.

National Institute of Mental Health. *Breaking Ground, Breaking Through: The Strategic Plan for Mood Disorders Research.* Bethesda, MD: National Institute of Mental Health, 2003.

Reagan, Lawrence P., Claudia A. Grillio, and Gerado G. Piroli. "The As and Ds of Stress: Metabolic, Morphological and Behavioral Consequences." *European Journal of Pharmacology* 585 (2008): 64–75.

*Recognizing and Handling Depression for People with Diabetes.* American Diabetes Association, 2004, http://professional.diabetes.org/UserFiles/File/Make%20the%20Link%20Docs/CVD%20Toolkit/ 15-Depression.pdf.

Talbot, France, and Arie Nouwen. "A Review of the Relationship Between Depression and Diabetes in Adults: Is There a Link?" *Diabetes Care* 23 (2000): 1556–1562.

**DIAGNOSIS OF DEPRESSION.** Diagnosis refers to the process of identifying a disorder by its signs and symptoms. The first step to getting appropriate treatment for depression is accurate diagnosis of the disorder. Life would be simpler if a blood test or brain scan could definitely identify who has depression and who does not. Unfortunately, it is not that easy. To determine whether someone has depression, a mental health care provider must evaluate a person's symptoms and make an informed judgment about whether they meet the diagnostic criteria laid out in the ***Diagnostic and Statistical Manual of Mental Disorders, Fourth Edition, Text Revision***.

First, though, a medical exam may be done to rule out other possible causes for the symptoms. Certain medical conditions and medications can cause the same symptoms as depression. To check for such problems, the physician asks about a person's medical history and performs a physical exam, which may include measuring height and weight, checking blood pressure and temperature, listening to the heart and lungs, and examining the abdomen. In some cases, lab tests may be ordered as well.

If no medical cause is found, the physician may do a mental health evaluation or refer the person to a mental health professional for further assessment. The most important part of the evaluation is a diagnostic interview, which involves asking about symptoms, including when they started, how long they have lasted, how severe they are, whether they have occurred before, and if so, how they were treated and how well the treatment worked. Other questions address family history of mental illness, daily lifestyle, alcohol or drug use, and any thoughts of **suicide**.

In addition to the oral interview, written questionnaires may be used to assess the severity of symptoms. Common tests include the **Beck Depression Inventory**, **Center for Epidemiologic Studies Depression Scale**, **Inventory of Depressive Symptomatology**, and **Zung Self-Rating Depression Scale**. For young people, the **Children's Depression Inventory** or **Reynolds Adolescent Depression Scale** may be used. For older adults, the **Geriatric Depression Scale** may be given. By themselves, questionnaires are not sufficient for making a diagnosis, but they may add useful information to what is learned in the interview.

At times, other people close to the patient, such as a parent or caregiver, may be asked to answer questions or fill out questionnaires as well. Input from others is especially helpful when the patient is a child, or when the patient is an adult with very severe depression symptoms or another medical condition that makes communication difficult.

*See also:* Screening Tests

## Bibliography

*Depression (Major Depression): Tests and Diagnosis.* Mayo Clinic, February 14, 2008, http://mayoclinic .com/health/depression/DS00175/DSECTION=tests-and-diagnosis.

Evans, Dwight L., and Linda Wasmer Andrews. *If Your Adolescent Has Depression or Bipolar Disorder: An Essential Resource for Parents.* New York: Oxford University Press, 2005.

*How Is Depression Detected and Treated?* National Institute of Mental Health, January 30, 2009, http://www.nimh.nih.gov/health/publications/depression/how-is-depression-detected-and -treated.shtml.

Yonkers, Kimberly A., and Jacqueline A. Samson. "Mood Disorders Measures." In *Handbook of Psychiatric Measures,* 2nd ed., by A. John Rush Jr., Michael B. First, and Deborah Blacker, eds., 499–528. Washington, DC: American Psychiatric Publishing, 2008.

**DIAGNOSTIC AND STATISTICAL MANUAL OF MENTAL DISORDERS, FOURTH EDITION, TEXT REVISION.** The *Diagnostic and Statistical Manual of Mental Disorders, Fourth Edition, Text Revision* (*DSM-IV-TR*) is a diagnostic guidebook published by the American Psychiatric Association (APA) and used by mental health professionals from many disciplines. In addition to guiding clinical practice, the *DSM-IV-TR* is used to define and identify mental disorders for research, administrative, and educational purposes. The classification system has been adopted not only in the United States, but also worldwide, and the latest version of the manual has now been translated into 22 languages.

The *DSM-IV-TR* was developed to provide a convenient shorthand among mental health care providers. When one health care professional diagnoses a patient with major depressive disorder, for example, other providers immediately know that the person is troubled by a long-lasting low mood and/or a loss of interest in once-enjoyed activities.

***Organization of the Manual.*** Each disorder in the *DSM-IV-TR* is defined by a list of diagnostic criteria. The accompanying text provides further elaboration. It also discusses associated features, and when applicable, lab test results that can help when making a diagnosis. Age-, gender- and culture-specific features, prevalence rates, family patterns, and the typical course of the illness are described as well. Finally, the text provides guidelines on differentiating the disorder in question from other mental and physical conditions that can produce similar symptoms.

No information about the causes or treatment of disorders is given, however. When it comes to mental disorders, these are generally more controversial subjects, so their exclusion has helped secure widespread acceptance of the manual. The downside to this approach is that people with the same diagnosis do not necessarily share the same causal factors and therefore may not respond to the same treatment regimen.

The APA stresses that the *DSM-IV-TR* is nothing more than a compilation of current knowledge about how symptoms cluster together. That knowledge base is constantly growing. Over the coming decades, the classification system is likely to undergo a radical overhaul to make it more useful for guiding treatment decisions as the causes of mental disorders become better understood.

***History of the DSM.*** The first *Diagnostic and Statistical Manual* was published in 1952. Subsequent editions included the *DSM-II* (1968), *DSM-III* (1980), *DSM-III-R* (1987), and *DSM-IV* (1994). A text revision of the *DSM-IV*, known as the *DSM-IV-TR*, was published in 2000. However, it is considered a minor revision rather than a major update, because it was mainly the descriptive text that was changed rather than the all-important diagnostic criteria.

The first edition of the manual was intended not only as a diagnostic guidebook, but also as a tool for collecting hospital statistics—hence, the word "statistical" in the title. Although the current edition still gives codes for the disorders that are used for record keeping, the primary purpose is now diagnostic. The original title has been retained for historical reasons, however.

When the first two editions of the manual were published, there was not much scientific evidence available about mental disorders. As a result, the early versions were based largely on expert opinion. Starting with the *DSM-III,* however, the manual has become increasingly research-based. New diagnoses are now added only if there is enough hard evidence to allow for an objective assessment of the pros and cons of their inclusion. Nevertheless, the number of listed disorders has mushroomed from about 100 in the first edition to about 300 in the latest one.

*Depression, Then and Now.* The changing criteria for **major depression** provide a good example of how the *DSM* has evolved over the decades since its inception. In the first edition of the *DSM*, this disorder was called depressive reaction. The term "reaction" was used throughout the manual, a reflection of the then-prevalent view of mental disorders as an individual reaction to psychological, social, and biological factors. The underlying mechanisms for mental disorders were described in terms that reflected the influence of psychoanalytic theory as developed by **Sigmund Freud** and refined by others in the first half of the twentieth century.

In a depressive reaction as defined by the *DSM-I*, a low mood and poor self-esteem were seen as a means of allaying the anxiety triggered by a loss. The severity of the depression was thought to be determined in part by the extent of the individual's ambivalence toward the lost person or object.

> ### Another Classification System
>
> The *DSM* classification system isn't the only kid on the block. *The International Classification of Diseases, Ninth Edition, Clinical Modification (ICD-9-CM)* is a system devised by the World Health Organization (WHO) for categorizing diseases. The *ICD-9-CM* is currently the coding system used by the U.S. government for tracking diseases and deaths, and it is also used by health care professionals when billing for services. The *DSM-IV-TR* assigns ICD-9-CM codes to its disorders to simplify record keeping for mental health care providers.
>
> A tenth edition of the ICD was endorsed by the 43rd World Health Assembly in 1990 and began being implemented by WHO member states in 1994. It is currently being adapted for use in the United States. At the time this was written, however, the U.S. switchover to ICD-10 codes had not yet occurred.

In the *DSM-IV-TR*, the term used for major depression is major depressive disorder. The definition reflects the current trend to describe symptom clusters rather than presumed causes. Major depressive disorder is defined by the presence of five or more symptoms, at least one of which is a depressed mood or a loss of interest or pleasure in almost everything. The symptoms must last at least two weeks and cause serious problems getting along in daily life.

*Looking Ahead: DSM-V.*   Publication of the next edition of the *DSM* is scheduled for 2011 at the earliest. However, preplanning for the forthcoming revision began as far back as 1999.

One issue that is being explored is the relationship between major depression and **generalized anxiety disorder** (GAD), a disorder characterized by constant worry over a number of different things. In the *DSM-IV-TR*, major depression is grouped with **mood disorders**, but GAD is grouped with **anxiety disorders**. Yet depression and anxiety often go hand in hand in the real world. In fact, research indicates that more than 70 percent of people who have had GAD also meet the criteria for major depression at some point in their lives.

At a 2007 planning conference, the consensus was that major depression and GAD are closely related disorders. The majority of conference participants took the position that differences between the two conditions were small enough to justify a change in classification. One suggestion was the creation of a new category of distress disorders that would include both major depression and GAD. The years ahead will tell how this issue is ultimately resolved.

*See also:* Diagnosis of Depression; Reactive Depression

**Further Information.**   American Psychiatric Association, 1000 Wilson Boulevard, Suite 1825, Arlington, VA 22209, (888) 357-7924, www.psych.org, www.dsmivtr.org, www.dsm5.org.

*Bibliography*

*About the International Classification of Diseases, Tenth Revision, Clinical Modification (ICD-10-CM).* National Center for Health Statistics, August 2, 2007, http://www.cdc.gov/nchs/about/otheract/icd9/abticd10.htm.

American Psychiatric Association. *Diagnostic and Statistical Manual of Mental Disorders.* Washington, DC: American Psychiatric Association, 1952.

American Psychiatric Association. *Diagnostic and Statistical Manual of Mental Disorders.* 4th ed., text rev. Washington, DC: American Psychiatric Association, 2000.

*DSM-V Timeline.* American Psychiatric Association, http://www.dsm5.org/timeline.cfm.

First, Michael B. *Depression and Generalized Anxiety Disorder Research Planning Conference.* American Psychiatric Association, http://dsm5.org/conference6.cfm.

Frances, Allen, Michael B. First, and Harold Alan Pincus. *DSM-IV Guidebook.* Washington, DC: American Psychiatric Press, 1995.

*Frequently Asked Questions About DSM.* American Psychiatric Association, http://www.dsmivtr.org/2–1faqs.cfm.

*International Classification of Diseases (ICD).* World Health Organization, http://www.who.int/classifications/icd/en/index.html.

Moffitt, Terrie E., HonaLee Harrington, Avshalom Caspi, Julia Kim-Cohen, David Goldberg, Alice M. Gregory, et al. "Depression and Generalized Anxiety Disorder: Cumulative and Sequential Comorbidity in a Birth Cohort Followed Prospectively to Age 32 Years." *Archives of General Psychiatry* 64 (2007): 651–660.

**DIALECTICAL BEHAVIOR THERAPY.**   Dialectical behavior therapy (DBT) is an offshoot of **cognitive-behavioral therapy**, which focuses on helping people change maladaptive thought and behavior patterns. DBT adds two new elements to the mix: acceptance strategies, which let people know that they are acceptable just as they are, and dialectical strategies, which help people find a comfortable balance between the need for acceptance and the need for change.

DBT was originally developed by U.S. psychologist Marsha Linehan (1943– ) to treat people who were suicidal. It soon evolved into a treatment for those with **borderline personality disorder** (BPD), a condition characterized by pervasive instability in moods, relationships, self-image, and behavior. Many people with BPD also suffer from **major depression**. Intentional **self-injury** is common as well, and about 10 percent of those with the disorder die by **suicide**.

DBT is now the best-studied treatment for BPD. In people with BPD, studies have shown that the therapy can reduce depressive symptoms, suicide attempts, self-injury, and hospitalizations. But the coping skills it teaches apply to life situations that are not the exclusive province of any single mental disorder, so researchers have begun adapting it to the treatment of other conditions, including major depression.

***Acceptance and Dialectics.***   The acceptance piece of DBT grew out of Linehan's frustration with conventional CBT. In the late 1970s, she was attempting to use CBT to treat women with histories of repeated suicide attempts. Linehan noted that many of the women reported feeling invalidated by CBT's incessant focus on change. As a result, they got angry or gave up, and they often dropped out of therapy before much headway had been made.

To address this problem, acceptance strategies were added to the procedure. These strategies let clients know that they are accepted as they are and their behavior makes real sense in some way. Therapists also point out to clients when their thoughts, feelings, and behavior are perfectly normal. This helps clients discover that they are capable of sound judgment and able to learn when and how to trust themselves.

Although self-acceptance is a big step forward, change is still crucial for getting and staying well. To this end, traditional CBT techniques, such as skills training and homework assignments, are used. Yet there is a natural tension between the need to accept oneself right now and the need to work toward a better life in the future.

That is where dialectical strategies come in. Dialectics refers to the process of weighing conflicting ideas with the intention of resolving apparent contractions. Besides helping people balance acceptance and change, dialectical strategies can help them find a happy medium between passionate feelings and logical thoughts.

**The Process at a Glance.**    The overriding goal of DBT is to help people create lives that they feel are truly worth living. The exact form taken by that goal varies from person to person. For some it might mean finishing school, and for others it might mean finding a romantic partner. But one thing all clients have in common is the need to bring problem behaviors under control, with the most urgent priority given to problems that are life-threatening.

The DBT process is organized into stages, and within each stage into targets—behaviors that are the current focus of therapeutic attention. The orderly progression through stages and targets helps keep therapy from bogging down in one crisis after another.

*Stage 1.*    Starting out, the objective is to move from being out of control to being in control. The initial target of treatment is suicidal or self-harming behavior. The second target is behavior that interferes with therapy, such as poor attendance. The third target is behavior that severely affects the person's quality of life, such as depression, anxiety, **eating disorders**, **substance abuse**, social isolation, or neglect of medical problems.

Several modes of treatment are used. In one-on-one sessions with a therapist, clients work on identifying and addressing factors that are causing and maintaining their problems. Skills training, often provided in a group, helps clients learn to build healthy relationships, understand their emotions, and tolerate emotional pain without resorting to self-destructive behavior. Clients also learn how to focus more on the here and now, so they can stop worrying about the future and obsessing about the past. Telephone coaching may be provided to support clients as they strive to apply what they have learned in therapy sessions to real-life situations at home. To date, most research on DBT has looked at Stage 1 treatment goals.

*Stage 2.*    The objective of this stage is to move from being emotionally shut down to experiencing emotions fully. By this point, clients are in control of their behavior, but they still may be suffering inside. Therapy helps them learn how to experience their emotions in a healthy way without feeling overwhelmed.

Many people with BPD also have **post-traumatic stress disorder** (PTSD), an anxiety disorder that develops after exposure to a traumatic event. Symptoms include reexperiencing the trauma, emotional numbing, avoidance behavior, and increased arousal. This is the stage at which any symptoms of PTSD are addressed.

*Stage 3.*    The objective of this stage is to achieve an ordinary life, complete with normal happiness and unhappiness. Clients work to solve problems in everyday living, such as interpersonal conflicts and job dissatisfaction. Some continue seeing a DBT therapist, and others switch to a different type of therapist or counselor. Still others take a break from formal therapy, using the skills they have learned to tackle problems on their own.

**Benefits for Depression.**    One preliminary study that adapted DBT for use in people with **treatment-resistant depression** found promising results. In the study, 24 people with hard-to-treat depression were randomly assigned to either get 16 weekly sessions of DBT or be put on a waiting list. Those in the DBT group showed greater improvement in their symptoms.

Another small study applied DBT to the treatment of depression in **older adults**. The 34 participants, most of whom had longstanding problems, were randomly assigned to get 28 weeks of either medication alone or medication plus DBT skills training and telephone coaching. The results showed that adding DBT led to increased benefits. More research is needed to clarify what role DBT might play in relieving the symptoms of depression, especially when other treatments have been tried without success.

*See also:* Psychotherapy; Treatment of Depression

***Further Informtion.***   Behavioral Tech, 2133 Third Avenue, Suite 205, Seattle, WA 98121, (206) 675-8588, www.behavioraltech.org.

## Bibliography

*About Dialectical Behavior Therapy.* University of Washington Behavioral Research and Therapy Clinics, 2006, http://depts.washington.edu/brtc/about/dbt.

American Psychiatric Association. *Diagnostic and Statistical Manual of Mental Disorders.* 4th ed., text rev. Washington, DC: American Psychiatric Association, 2000.

*Borderline Personality Disorder.* National Institute of Mental Health, June 26, 2008, http://www.nimh .nih.gov/health/publications/borderline-personality-disorder.shtml.

*Borderline Personality Disorder: A Costly, Severe Mental Illness.* National Education Alliance for Borderline Personality Disorder, February 2008, http://www.borderlinepersonalitydisorder.com/documents/ BPDBriefingPaperDraft_607Feb08.pdf.

*DBT Resources: What Is DBT?* Behavioral Tech, http://behavioraltech.org/resources/whatisdbt.cfm.

*Dialectical Behavior Therapy Frequently Asked Questions.* Behavioral Tech, http://behavioraltech.org/ downloads/dbtFaq_Cons.pdf.

Dimeff, Linda A., and Kelly Koerner, eds. *Dialectical Behavior Therapy in Clinical Practice: Applications Across Disorders and Settings.* New York: Guilford Press, 2007.

Dimeff, Linda, and Marsha M. Linehan. "Dialectical Behavior Therapy in a Nutshell." *California Psychologist* 34 (2001): 10–13.

Harley, Rebecca, Susan Sprich, Steven Safren, Michelle Jacobo, and Maurizio Fava. "Adaptation of Dialectical Behavior Therapy Skills Training Group for Treatment-Resistant Depression." *Journal of Nervous and Mental Disease* 196 (2008): 136–143.

Linehan, Marsha M. *Cognitive Behavioral Treatment of Borderline Personality Disorder.* New York: Guilford Press, 1993.

Lynch, Thomas R., Jennifer Q. Morse, Tamar Mendelson, and Clive J. Robins. "Dialectical Behavior Therapy for Depressed Older Adults." *American Journal of Geriatric Psychiatry* 11 (2003): 33–45.

Lynch, Thomas R., Jennifer S. Cheavens, Kelly C. Cukrowicz, Steven R. Thorp, Leslie Bronner, and John Beyer. "Treatment of Older Adults with Co-Morbid Personality Disorder and Depression: A Dialectical Behavior Therapy Approach." *International Journal of Geriatric Psychiatry* 22 (2007): 131–143.

Marra, Thomas. *Depressed and Anxious: The Dialectical Behavior Therapy Workbook for Overcoming Depression and Anxiety.* Oakland, CA: New Harbinger, 2004.

**DIATHESIS-STRESS MODEL.**   The term "diathesis" refers to an inherent susceptibility to a disease. According to the diathesis-stress model, a disease such as depression develops when a genetic or biological predisposition is coupled with a stressful situation, which triggers or exacerbates symptoms of illness. Some researchers also include psychological predisposition on the diathesis side of the equation. This view of depression, now widely accepted, lies at the heart of much current theory, research, and practice.

It seems clear that **stress** sets off many episodes of depression, but it also seems equally clear that not everyone is affected the same way. One person might fall into a debilitating, unshakable depression after a personal setback, but another person who goes through the same thing might bounce back in a matter of weeks. Inherent vulnerabilities explain why different people have different thresholds for developing depression or another stress-related disorder.

According to this model, the lower a person's intrinsic susceptibility to developing depression, the more extrinsic stress is needed to cause the disease. Until this critical point is reached, the person may function normally, and the potential for becoming depressed stays hidden.

*See also:* Causes of Depression; Environmental Factors; Genetic Factors

## Bibliography

Goodman, Sherryl H., and Sarah R. Brand. "Depression and Early Adverse Experiences." In *Handbook of Depression.* 2nd ed., by Ian H. Gotlib and Constance L. Hammen, eds., 249–274. New York: Guilford Press, 2009.

Needles, Douglas J., and Lyn Y. Abramson. "Positive Life Events, Attributional Style, and Hopelessness: Testing a Model of Recovery From Depression." *Journal of Abnormal Psychology* 99 (1990): 156–165.

Nemade, Rashmi, Natalie Staats Reiss, and Mark Dombeck. *Current Understandings of Major Depression: Diathesis-Stress Model.* El Paso Mental Health and Mental Retardation, http://info.epmhmr.org/poc/view_doc.php?type=doc&id=12998&cn=5.

**DIET.**    Diet refers to all the foods and beverages a person consumes. Food is the fuel that powers the body, and the quality of that fuel affects energy, health, and sometimes mood. The right mix of vitamins, minerals, fiber, amino acids, and fatty acids promotes optimal mental and physical functioning. In addition, the right balance of carbohydrates, proteins, and fats reduces the risk of many diseases.

People with depression may especially need the increased energy and enhanced brain function that come from a healthful, varied diet. A diet rich in fruits, vegetables, whole grains, and fish helps keep moods on a more even keel. Eating regular, evenly spaced meals also may help prevent sharp spikes and dips in blood glucose (sugar) as well as related peaks and valleys in energy, concentration, and mood.

In contrast, excessive amounts of sugar or **caffeine** may contribute to mood instability. Different people react differently to foods containing these substances. But for those who are sensitive, the foods may worsen mood swings, nervousness, and anxiety. **Alcohol** is another substance that can have a negative impact on moods. It can worsen depression, exacerbate sleep problems, and make treatment less effective.

***The Downside of Saturated Fat.***    Saturated fat is yet another example of a food component that may be harmful to brain health when eaten in excess. This type of fat, which is usually solid at room temperature, comes from animal sources and a few plant oils (such as palm oil, palm kernel oil, and coconut oil).

Saturated fat raises blood levels of cholesterol, which makes it bad for cardiovascular health. Studies indicate that eating high levels of saturated fat may hinder brain function as well. When researchers fed rats a diet in which 40 percent of daily calories came from

> ### Food for Thought
>
> These diet tips may help manage depression.
>
> #### Look for Negative Patterns
> Keep a daily journal of what you eat and drink, and how you feel. After several days, look back through the journal for any patterns. If you notice that certain foods seem to cause mood swings, try avoiding them for a week or two and see if your mood improves.
>
> #### Be Ready for Food Cravings
> Some people with depression have cravings for sweets, which can lead to unwanted weight gain. If this is a problem, keep healthy, naturally sweet foods—such as fruit and low-fat yogurt—on hand. Also, plan ways to distract yourself when cravings strike, such as taking a mini-walk or cleaning the house.
>
> #### Avoid Extreme Eating Habits
> **Eating disorders** can coexist with depression, and when this happens, it is important that both conditions be treated. Consult your doctor if you experience drastic changes in weight, either up or down. Also, talk to your doctor or therapist if you severely restrict your diet or binge on large amounts of food, then purge by self-induced vomiting.

saturated fat—a diet comparable to what some Americans eat—the animals performed poorly on tests of memory and learning.

*The Upside of Antioxidants.* Antioxidants are examples of food components that may be as good for the brain as they are for the rest of the body. These substances help prevent or repair damage to cells. They act by slowing or preventing the oxidative process—in other words, oxygen damage—that is caused by molecules called free radicals. Examples of antioxidant substances include beta-carotene, lutein, lycopene, selenium, and vitamins A, C, and E. Such substances are found in many foods, including fruits, vegetables, nuts, grains, and some meats, poultry, and fish.

Antioxidants may help prevent heart disease and diabetes, and they also may improve immune function and perhaps lower the risk for infection and cancer. In addition, they may help protect brain cells from free radicals. When researchers fed strawberries, blueberries, or spinach—three high-antioxidant foods—to aging rats every day for two months, the diet improved communication between the rats' brain cells.

*Depression-Fighting Nutrients.* Some nutrients have been singled out for specific benefits in helping keep depression at bay. For example, B vitamins, such as **folate** and **vitamin B12**, help break down an amino acid called homocysteine in the body. Homocysteine is then converted into **S-adenosyl-L-methionine** (SAMe), a compound that helps form chemical messengers in the brain. These brain chemicals include **serotonin** and **dopamine**, both of which are thought to play important roles in depression.

**Omega-3 fatty acids**—beneficial fats found in fish, shellfish, and organ meats—may help protect against depression as well. The strongest evidence for this effect comes from clinical trials in which people with mood disorders were randomly assigned to receive either an omega-3 supplement or a placebo (dummy pill). A recent analysis that pooled the results from 10 previous clinical trials found that omega-3 supplements significantly improved depressive symptoms.

*See also:* Dietary Supplements

*Further Information.* American Dietetic Association, 120 S. Riverside Plaza, Suite 2000, Chicago, IL 60606-6995, (800) 877-1600, www.eatright.org.

Center for Food Safety and Applied Nutrition, Food and Drug Administration, 5100 Paint Branch Parkway, College Park, MD 20740, (888) 723-3366, www.cfsan.fda.gov.

Center for Nutrition Policy and Promotion, U.S. Department of Agriculture, 3101 Park Center Drive, Room 1034, Alexandria, VA 22302, (888) 779-7264, www.mypyramid.gov.

Food and Nutrition Board, Institute of Medicine, U.S. National Academies, 500 Fifth Street N.W., Washington DC 20001, (202) 334-2352, www.iom.edu.

Food and Nutrition Information Center, National Agricultural Library, U.S. Department of Agriculture, 10301 Baltimore Avenue, Beltsville, MD 20705, (301) 504–5414, www.nutrition.gov.

## Bibliography

*Antioxidants.* National Library of Medicine, http://www.nlm.nih.gov/medlineplus/antioxidants .html.

Bickford, Paula C., Thomas Gould, Lori Briederick, Kathy Chadman, Amber Pollock, David Young, et al. "Antioxidant-Rich Diets Improve Cerebellar Physiology and Motor Learning in Aged Rats." *Brain Research* 866 (2000): 211–217.

*Diet and the Brain.* Society for Neuroscience, March 2003, http://www.sfn.org/skins/main/pdf/ BrainBriefings/BrainBriefings_Mar2003.pdf.

*Dietary Guidelines for Americans 2005.* U.S. Department of Health and Human Services and U.S. Department of Agriculture, http://www.healthierus.gov/dietaryguidelines.

*Dietary Supplement Fact Sheet: Folate.* National Institutes of Health Office of Dietary Supplements, August 22, 2005, http://ods.od.nih.gov/factsheets/folate.asp.

*Dietary Supplement Fact Sheet: Vitamin B12.* National Institutes of Health Office of Dietary Supplements, April 26, 2006, http://ods.od.nih.gov/factsheets/vitaminb12.asp.

Folstein, Marshal, Timothy Liu, Inga Peter, Jennifer Buel, Lisa Arsenault, Tammy Scott, et al. "The Homocysteine Hypothesis of Depression." *American Journal of Psychiatry* 164 (2007): 861–867.

*Food and Mood.* Depression and Bipolar Support Alliance, 2005, http://www.dbsalliance.org/ pdfs/foodmoode2.pdf.

Greenwood, C.E., and G. Winocur. "Learning and Memory Impairment in Rats Fed a High Saturated Fat Diet." *Behavioral and Neural Biology* 53 (1990): 74–87.

Lin, Pao-Yen, and Kuan-Pin Su. "A Meta-analytic Review of Double-Blind, Placebo-Controlled Trials of Antidepressant Efficacy of Omega-3 Fatty Acids." *Journal of Clinical Psychiatry* 68 (2007): 1056–1061.

*Saturated Fats.* American Heart Association, January 2009, http://www.americanheart.org/presenter .jhtml?identifier=3045790.

Somers, Elizabeth. *Food and Mood: The Complete Guide to Eating Well and Feeling Your Best.* 2nd ed. New York: Owl Books, 1999.

*What Is an Antioxidant?* American Dietetic Association, September 14, 2006, http://www.eatright .org/cps/rde/xchg/ada/hs.xsl/home_9660_ENU_HTML.htm.

**DIETARY SUPPLEMENTS.** Dietary supplements are products—such as vitamins, minerals, and herbs sold in pill form—that are intended to augment a person's **diet**. Several types of supplements have shown promise in reducing the risk of developing depression, including **folate**, **vitamin B12**, **omega 3 fatty acids**, **melatonin**, **S-adenosyl-L-methionine** (SAMe), and **St. John's wort**.

In the United States, the Dietary Supplement Health and Education Act of 1994 defines a dietary supplement as a product containing one or more dietary ingredients or their constituents. Such ingredients include vitamins, minerals, amino acids, and herbs or other botanicals (plants or plant parts used for their scent, flavor, or therapeutic properties).

The product is meant to be taken by mouth as a pill, capsule, tablet, or liquid, and it is not intended to be used as a conventional food or a meal replacement.

Some supplements may promote optimal health or help ensure that people get adequate amounts of essential nutrients. However, supplements do not go through the same rigorous testing for safety and effectiveness as medications do. They are not meant to replace drug therapy or other proven treatments for people with health conditions, including depression. They are also no substitute for the variety of foods needed for a healthful diet.

People who suspect that they might be depressed should see a health care provider for professional diagnosis and treatment. When considering a dietary supplement, they should talk to their provider about how best to work it into their overall treatment plan.

***Government Regulation.*** The U.S. Food and Drug Administration (FDA) regulates dietary supplements, but as foods rather than drugs. The requirements for marketing foods are much less stringent than those for medications. In particular, supplement makers do not have to prove that their product is safe and effective, the way drug companies do. Consequently, scientific evidence supporting the benefits of supplements for depression and other conditions is generally limited and sometimes nonexistent.

Supplement manufacturers also do not have to prove their product's quality. The FDA does not analyze the content of supplements, and companies are only required to meet the manufacturing standards for foods, which are not as strict as those for drugs. As a result, what is in a supplement bottle does not always match what is on the label. In some cases, supplements might contain the active ingredient in a higher or lower amount than stated, or even a different ingredient altogether.

Some supplement makers use the terms "standardized," "verified," or "certified" on their labels. However, these terms are not defined by U.S. law, so they do not guarantee product quality or consistency.

If the FDA determines that a supplement is unsafe once it is on the market, only then can the agency take action. Possible actions include issuing a warning or requiring that a product be pulled from the marketplace.

***Buying and Using Supplements.*** Although the U.S. government does not test or rate dietary supplements, a few nongovernmental organizations offer seals of approval, which indicate that a product has passed independent quality testing. These seals do not guarantee safety or effectiveness, but they do provide some assurance that a product contains the ingredients listed on its label and does not have harmful levels of contaminants. Among the organizations that provide testing programs are ConsumerLab.com (www.consumerlab.com), NSF (www.nsf.org), and the U.S. Pharmacopeia (www.usp.org).

Like medications, supplements have chemical and biological activity in the body. Some may cause side effects, and others may interact harmfully with certain medications. For example, when combined with certain **antidepressants**, a popular herbal supplement called St. John's wort may increase side effects such as nausea, anxiety, headache, and confusion.

To be on the safe side, people should talk to a health care provider before taking a dietary supplement. This is particularly important for those who (1) have a chronic health condition, (2) take any medication, (3) plan to have surgery, (4) are pregnant or breastfeeding, or (5) are considering giving a supplement to a child.

Supplement users should not exceed the dose given on the label unless told to do so by a health care provider. If any unexpected reactions occur, they should stop the supplement and contact their doctor.

*See also:* Herbal Remedies

***Further Information.*** Center for Food Safety and Applied Nutrition, Food and Drug Administration, 5600 Fishers Lane, Rockville, MD 20857, (888) 463-6332, www.cfsan .fda.gov/~dms/supplmnt.html.

International Bibliographic Information on Dietary Supplements, National Institutes of Health Office of Dietary Supplements and U.S. Department of Agriculture National Agricultural Library, grande.nal.usda.gov/ibids.

Office of Dietary Supplements, National Institutes of Health, 6100 Executive Boulevard, Room 3B01, MSC 7517, Bethesda, MD 20892, (301) 435-2920, ods.od.nih.gov.

*Bibliography*

*Dietary Supplements: Background Information.* National Institutes of Health Office of Dietary Supplements, April 12, 2006, http://ods.od.nih.gov/factsheets/DietarySupplements.asp.

*Frequently Asked Questions (FAQ).* National Institutes of Health Office of Dietary Supplements, August 8, 2008, http://ods.od.nih.gov/Health_Information/ODS_Frequently_Asked_Questions .aspx.

*What's in the Bottle? An Introduction to Dietary Supplements.* National Center for Complementary and Alternative Medicine, February 2007, http://nccam.nih.gov/health/bottle.

**DOPAMINE.** Dopamine is a neurotransmitter—a chemical messenger within the brain—that is essential for movement and also influences motivation, the perception of reality, and the ability to experience pleasure. Dopamine levels seem to fall during depression and rise during **mania** in people who cycle back and forth between the two extremes. Depression also is a side effect of certain diseases (such as **Parkinson's disease**) and medications (such as the blood pressure drug reserpine) that reduce the brain's dopamine supply.

Despite these connections, the study of dopamine's relationship to depression has historically been overshadowed by research on two other neurotransmitters: **serotonin** and **norepinephrine**. These neurotransmitters are the targets of most current **antidepressants**, but such medications do not work equally well for everyone. In an effort to expand the understanding of depression and the effectiveness of treatments, scientists have recently begun taking a closer look at the role played by dopamine.

There are four main dopamine pathways in the brain. Dopamine-producing cells in the ventral tegmental area (VTA) connect to the cortex, which is the seat of higher mental functions such as concentration and memory, and to the limbic area, which is involved in reward, motivation, and the experience of pleasure. Dopamine-producing cells in the substantia nigra connect to the striatum, which is involved in the planning and execution of movement. And dopamine-producing cells in the **hypothalamus** connect to the pituitary gland, which secretes several different **hormones** that regulate the activity of the rest of the **endocrine system**.

***Transmitting a Message.*** To convey a message from one brain cell to another, dopamine is first released by a sending cell into the synapse—the tiny gap between a cell and its neighbor. After crossing the gap, dopamine binds with a matching receptor on the receiving cell. Scientists have identified two families of dopamine **receptors**, divided into a total of five subtypes.

Once dopamine has delivered its message, in some parts of the brain, it is carried back into the cell that originally released it by a protein complex called a dopamine **transporter**. In other parts of the brain, dopamine is removed from the synapse by norepinephrine transporters. The process by which it is reabsorbed into the sending cell is called **reuptake**.

This whole system is dynamic. The density of some kinds of dopamine receptors and the number of dopamine transporters is increased or decreased based on how much dopamine is present.

***Malfunctioning Reward System.*** One of the cardinal symptoms of depression is the inability to experience pleasure. Dopamine plays a critical role in feelings of pleasure and reward, so it stands to reason that inadequate dopamine might be related to this symptom. And in fact, researchers have found reduced levels of dopamine-related chemicals in people with severe depression, both in cerebrospinal fluid and in brain regions that are involved in mood and motivation.

Interestingly, when people with severe depression are given an amphetamine—a stimulant drug that boosts dopamine—they report liking it more than either those with milder depression or healthy individuals. One possible explanation: To compensate for low levels of dopamine associated with severe depression, cells increase the density of dopamine receptors and decrease the number of dopamine transporters. These adjustments let them make the best possible use of what little dopamine is available. But when extra dopamine suddenly floods the brain as a result of the drug, there are more receptors to receive it as well as fewer transporters to carry it out of the synapse. As a result, reaction to the drug is heightened. This finding could help explain why **substance abuse** is so common in people with depression.

*See also:* Monoamine Hypothesis; Neurotransmitters

*Bibliography*

Dailly, Eric, Franck Chenu, Caroline E. Renard, and Michel Bourin. "Dopamine, Depression and Antidepressants." *Fundamental and Clinical Pharmacology* 18 (2004): 601–607.
Dunlop, Boadie W., and Charles B. Nemeroff. "The Role of Dopamine in the Pathophysiology of Depression." *Archives of General Psychiatry* 64 (2007): 317–337.
Robinson, Donald S. "The Role of Dopamine and Norepinephrine in Depression." *Primary Psychiatry* 14 (2007): 21–23.

**DOUBLE DEPRESSION.** Double depression is a term that is sometimes used for the situation in which a person simultaneously meets the diagnostic criteria for both **dysthymia** and **major depression**. Dysthymia is characterized by a down mood that is relatively mild but quite persistent, lasting for at least two years. During that period, symptoms tend to wax and wane. At times, they may become intense and numerous enough to qualify as a full-blown episode of major depression superimposed on the dysthymia.

Major depression is characterized by being in a low mood nearly all the time and/or losing interest or enjoyment in almost everything. For major depression to be diagnosed, this mood is only required to last for two weeks. But major depression is associated with a wider range of emotional, mental, physical, and behavioral symptoms than dysthymia, and the symptoms sometimes reach severely disabling or suicidal proportions.

Double depression is not a formal diagnosis. Instead, a person would be diagnosed as having both dysthymia and major depression at the same time. This seems to imply that they are two separate conditions. However, it is more likely that they are different phases in a single condition, in which depression goes through peaks and valleys of severity.

Indeed, researchers have found few distinctions in type of symptoms, family history, and treatment response between those with double depression, dysthymia, and chronic major depression. This calls into question the value of distinguishing between these conditions.

For practical purposes, it may be more useful to differentiate between **chronic depression** of any kind and non-chronic major depression.

## Bibliography

American Psychiatric Association. *Diagnostic and Statistical Manual of Mental Disorders*. 4th ed., text rev. Washington, DC: American Psychiatric Association, 2000.

Frances, Allen, Michael B. First, and Harold Alan Pincus. *DSM-IV Guidebook*. Washington, DC: American Psychiatric Press, 1995.

Klein, Daniel N., and Neil J. Santiago. "Dysthymia and Chronic Depression: Introduction, Classification, Risk Factors, and Course." *Journal of Clinical Psychology* 59 (2003): 807–816.

Klein, Daniel N., Stewart A. Shankman, and Suzanne Rose. "Ten-Year Prospective Follow-Up Study of the Naturalistic Course of Dysthymic Disorder and Double Depression." *American Journal of Psychiatry* 163 (2006): 872–880.

McCullough, James P. Jr., Daniel N. Klein, Frances E. Borian, Robert H. Howland, Lawrence P. Riso, Martin B. Keller, et al. "Group Comparisons of *DSM-IV* Subtypes of Chronic Depression: Validity of the Distinctions, Part 2." *Journal of Abnormal Psychology* 112 (2003): 614–622.

Thase, Michael E., and Susan S. Lang. *Beating the Blues: New Approaches to Overcoming Dysthymia and Chronic Mild Depression*. New York: Oxford University Press, 2004.

**DUAL DIAGNOSIS.**    Dual diagnosis refers to the situation in which an individual suffers from both a drug or **alcohol** problem and another mental disorder, such as depression. A person with a dual diagnosis has two separate illnesses, each of which can affect the course and outcome of the other. To recover fully, the person needs appropriate treatment for both conditions.

Depression is one mental disorder that frequently occurs in tandem with **substance abuse** and addiction. Other mental disorders that often are found in dually diagnosed individuals include **bipolar disorder**, schizophrenia, and **anxiety disorders**. All told, over one-third of alcohol abusers and more than half of drug abusers have a mental disorder as well.

At times, the mental disorder starts first. In a vain attempt to relieve mental suffering, the person may turn to alcohol or drugs. Mental health professionals sometimes call this "self-medication." But although the person might feel better temporarily, the improvement never lasts for long. Meanwhile, the alcohol or drug use may create its own set of emotional, social, medical, and legal problems. As problems continue to mount, the substance use may escalate to abuse and eventually addiction. By this point, the individual has two conditions rather than one, both of which need attention.

At other times, the alcohol or drug use comes first. As the person's problems become more severe, they may cause severe stress—and that, in turn, may trigger mental health issues in vulnerable individuals. Alcohol or drug use also can directly cause some mental, emotional, or behavioral symptoms by affecting the chemistry and function of the brain.

***Getting Dual Treatment.***    A dual diagnosis calls for dual treatment. The two major treatment options for depression are **psychotherapy** and **antidepressants**. Psychotherapy is unlikely to be very useful while a person is under the influence, and antidepressants may interact harmfully with alcohol or other drugs. This helps explain why getting treatment for substance abuse or addiction is vital to **recovery** not only from the drug or alcohol problem, but also from coexisting depression.

Often, substance abuse treatment and depression treatment are provided by two different sets of professionals working in different settings. Collaboration by the mental health care providers—for instance, through regular meetings and shared progress reports—helps ensure that the treatments mesh well. But the logistics of getting to two sets of appointments and following two treatment plans puts an added burden on dually diagnosed individuals. It is no wonder that some are tempted to give up one treatment or the other.

To overcome this obstacle, the trend today is toward more integration of services. In this model, mental health care providers who are cross-trained in both substance abuse treatment and mental health care develop a single treatment plan addressing both concerns. Therapeutic techniques aimed at improving both conditions are combined in the same provider visit.

Although integrated treatment is often more convenient, it is not necessarily more effective. A collaborative treatment strategy can be very helpful, too. The key is making sure that both the drug or alcohol problem and the depression are adequately treated, regardless of where that is done.

*See also:* Comorbidity; Substance-Induced Mood Disorder

**Further Information.** Double Trouble in Recovery, P.O. Box 245055, Brooklyn, NY 11224, (718) 373-2684, www.doubletroubleinrecovery.org.

Dual Recovery Anonymous, P.O. Box 8107, Prairie Village, KS 66208, (877) 883–2332, www.draonline.org.

## Bibliography

*Co-occurring Disorders: Integrated Dual Disorders Treatment.* National Mental Health Information Center, http://mentalhealth.samhsa.gov/cmhs/communitysupport/toolkits/cooccurring/consumers.asp.

*Definitions and Terms Relating to Co-occurring Disorders.* Substance Abuse and Mental Health Services Administration, 2006, http://coce.samhsa.gov/cod_resources/PDF/DefinitionsandTerms-OP1.pdf.

*Dual Diagnosis and Recovery.* Depression and Bipolar Support Alliance, December 22, 2006, http://www.dbsalliance.org/site/PageServer?pagename=about_publications_dualdiag.

*Factsheet: Dual Diagnosis.* Mental Health America, September 23, 2008, http://www.nmha.org/go/information/get-info/co-occurring-disorders/dual-diagnosis.

**DYSPHORIA.**   Dysphoria—from the Greek *dysphoros,* meaning "hard to bear"—is an unpleasant mood characterized by feelings such as sadness, **irritability**, or anxiety. A mood is a sustained emotion that colors a person's whole view of the world. When the mood is dysphoric, it creates a distressing outlook that can diminish a person's quality of life. An exaggerated degree of dysphoria is the hallmark of **major depression**, which involves feeling sad or dejected almost all the time or losing interest in almost everything.

The current concept of dysphoria is notably broad and vague. In theory, it can apply to any mood that creates distress or discomfort. In practice, it is often applied more narrowly. Some writers primarily use the term to describe a mood characterized by depressive feelings, such as sadness and despair. Others use it to describe a mood state that combines feeling sad or unhappy with being easily provoked to annoyance or anger.

One common application of the term is in the name of **premenstrual dysphoric disorder** (PMDD), a mood disorder that begins in the week before the onset of a woman's menstrual period and subsides within a few days after her period starts. PMDD is not yet a formal diagnostic entity in the ***Diagnostic and Statistical Manual of Mental Disorders, Fourth Edition, Text Revision***, the bible of mental health professionals. However, it has been proposed for inclusion in the manual's next edition. The proposed definition of PMDD takes a broad view of dysphoria, including moods that are marked by depression, anger, or anxiety.

*Bibliography*

American Psychiatric Association. *Diagnostic and Statistical Manual of Mental Disorders.* 4th ed., text rev. Washington, DC: American Psychiatric Association, 2000.

Starcevic, Vladan. "Dysphoric About Dysphoria: Towards a Greater Conceptual Clarity of the Term." *Australasian Psychiatry* 15 (2007): 9–13.

**DYSTHYMIA.** Dysthymia—also known as dysthymic disorder—is a mental disorder characterized by a down mood that is relatively mild but quite persistent. The mood is present most of the day, more days than not for at least two years, and it is associated with other changes in emotions, thoughts, and behavior. Overall, the symptoms are not as intense as those of **major depression**. But because dysthymia lasts so long, the cumulative impact can be at least as great.

To understand how this works, think of the difference between chronic allergies and a bad case of the flu. The flu, like a bout of major depression, is more dramatic and severe. But over time, the allergies, like dysthymia, wear away at a person's well-being. The nagging symptoms may take an even bigger toll on the person's quality of life in the long run.

As time passes, people with dysthymia may feel as if their symptoms are the norm for them. They may say, "I've always been this way" or "This is just how I am." When asked if anything is wrong, they may not mention the symptoms unless prompted. The sense of apathy, low self-concept, constant tiredness, and other problems have become so much a part of their day-to-day existence that they no longer think of them as being out of the ordinary.

Yet dysthymia is not something that just has to be endured. The same types of treatment used for more severe depression also can help with dysthymia. Even people who have felt down and despairing for years usually can start to feel better, often in a matter of weeks.

***Criteria for Diagnosis.*** The symptoms of dysthymia are defined by the ***Diagnostic and Statistical Manual of Mental Disorders, Fourth Edition, Text Revision*** (*DSM-IV-TR*), a diagnostic guidebook published by the American Psychiatric Association and widely used by mental health professionals from many disciplines. According to the *DSM-IV-TR*, people with dysthymia feel sad or down in the dumps. This **depressed mood** lasts for at least two years. In children and adolescents, the mood may be more irritable, and it only needs to last one year for a diagnosis of dysthymia to be made.

In addition to a depressed mood, people with dysthymia have two or more of the symptoms listed below. These symptoms may occasionally let up, but they are never gone for more than two months at a time. Although the symptoms are not as intense as those of major depression, they still cause distress or create problems in everyday life.

*Changes in Appetite.* Some people with dysthymia lose their appetite. Others go to the opposite extreme and overeat.

*Changes in Sleep.* Dysthymia may lead to insomnia, which refers to difficulty falling or staying asleep. In other cases, it leads to hypersomnia, which refers to oversleeping or excessive daytime sleepiness.

*Lack of Energy.* People with dysthymia may feel tired nearly all the time, or they may feel as if all their energy has been sapped.

*Low Self-Esteem.* A poor self-concept is common among those with dysthymia. They may see themselves as incapable or uninteresting, or they may feel as if they have failed to live up to others' expectations.

*Impaired Thinking.* People with dysthymia may have trouble concentrating, or they may find it difficult to make decisions.

*Feelings of Hopelessness.*    Dysthymia often leads to a sense of hopelessness. People with the disorder may see life as bland and monotonous, and they may find it difficult to muster up much interest in anything.

***Causes and Risk Factors.***    About six percent of people have dysthymia at some point in their lives. In children and adolescents, the disorder occurs about equally in both sexes. However, in adults, women are two to three times more likely than men to develop dysthymia.

**Genetic factors** may increase some people's risk of becoming depressed. Those with dysthymia are more likely than individuals without the disorder to have a close relative with either dysthymia or major depression. A family history of depression is especially common among those who develop dysthymia as children or adolescents, suggesting that the early-onset form of the disease may have a more pronounced genetic contribution.

A genetic predisposition is not destiny, however. It is just a susceptibility that may lie dormant until activated by life **stress**. When dysthymia begins in childhood or adolescence, it is often associated with early trauma, such as parental rejection or child abuse. In contrast, when dysthymia begins in old age, it is often associated with health problems or major losses.

***Course of the Illness.***    Dysthymia that begins at a young age may have a different set of causal factors than when it begins later in life. The symptoms also may vary, with children and adolescents apt to feel irritable and cranky as well as depressed. Thus, it seems that early dysthymia and later dysthymia may be different variants of the disorder.

In recognition of this fact, the *DSM-IV-TR* divides dysthymia into two distinct categories: early onset, with symptoms that begin before age 21, and late onset, with symptoms that begin at age 21 or older. Those with early-onset dysthymia are more likely than those with the late-onset form to eventually develop full-blown major depression at some point.

Without treatment, dysthymia can maintain its grip on a person's mind for many years or even decades. As few as 10 percent of people with dysthymia recover on their own within any given year. However, professional help can greatly improve those odds. With proper treatment, even people who have been depressed for years may start to feel more upbeat and motivated and begin acting more social and engaged in daily life.

*Double Depression.*    Major depression is similar to dysthymia, but generally more intense. It involves being in a low mood nearly all the time and/or losing interest or enjoyment in almost everything. For a diagnosis of major depression to be made, the down mood is only required to last for two weeks, rather than the two years required for dysthymia. But major depression is associated with a wider range of emotional, mental, physical, and behavioral symptoms. At times, the symptoms of major depression can reach severely disabling or suicidal proportions.

Most people with dysthymia go through periods where their dark mood deepens into full-fledged major depression. In fact, about three-quarters of those with dysthymia develop major depression within five years. **Double depression** is a term that is sometimes used for the situation in which a person simultaneously meets the criteria for both dysthymia and major depression.

Rather than being two distinct conditions, dysthymia and major depression may be different phases of a single condition in which depression waxes and wanes, often in response to stressful events. During the worst periods, more symptoms are present, causing greater disruption in daily life. During milder periods, the symptoms are fewer and less disabling, and they may even go away for several weeks. But until the dysthymia lifts completely, the person is never free of depression for more than a couple of months at a time.

A Matter of Degree

Dysthymia and major depression have many symptoms in common. The two conditions are differentiated mainly by the symptoms' number, frequency, duration, and intensity. These differences are highlighted in the chart below.

|  | **Dysthymia** | **Major Depression** |
|---|---|---|
| Defining Symptoms | Depressed mood | Depressed mood and/or loss of interest or pleasure in nearly all activities |
| Associated Symptoms | Poor appetite or overeating | Poor appetite or overeating |
|  | Sleep problems or oversleeping | Sleep problems or oversleeping |
|  | Low energy or fatigue | Low energy or fatigue |
|  | Trouble concentrating or making decisions | Trouble concentrating or making decisions |
|  | Feelings of low self-esteem | Feelings of worthlessness |
|  | Sense of hopelessness | Recurring thoughts of death or **suicide** |
|  |  | Restless activity or slowed-down movements |
| Number of Symptoms (Defining + Associated) | Minimum of three | Minimum of five |
| Frequency of Symptoms | Majority of days | Nearly every day |
| Duration of Symptoms | At least two years (at least one year in children and adolescents) | At least two weeks |
| Intensity of Symptoms | Mild to moderate | Mild to severe |
| Interspersed Periods of Normal Mood | Last up to two months | Rare |

*Treatment of Dysthymia.* The majority of people with dysthymia feel much better after treatment. For many, it is a revelation to discover what feeling good is like after so many years of living under a dark cloud. The main treatment options are **psychotherapy**, **antidepressants**, or a combination of both. After two months, half of those who get either psychotherapy or antidepressants alone have fully recovered. When both treatments are combined, the odds of a full **recovery** jump to 85 percent.

Two forms of psychotherapy that have proved effective are **cognitive-behavioral therapy**, which helps people change self-defeating thoughts and maladaptive behaviors, and **interpersonal therapy**, which helps people address interpersonal triggers for their symptoms. Psychotherapy may be a particularly good option for those who have suffered a recent loss or trauma or who believe their problems stem from life stress.

Antidepressants, taken alone or combined with psychotherapy, may be recommended for those who are unable to get any pleasure at all out of life or whose depression is becoming more severe. In addition, antidepressants may be the first choice for individuals who have responded well to these medications in the past. Studies have shown that the various types of antidepressants are about equally effective for treating dysthymia.

*See also:* Chronic Depression; Clinical Depression; Mood Disorders; Unipolar Depression

*Bibliography*

American Psychiatric Association. *Diagnostic and Statistical Manual of Mental Disorders.* 4th ed., text rev. Washington, DC: American Psychiatric Association, 2000.

Burton, S.W., and H.S. Akiskal, eds. *Dysthymic Disorder.* London: Gaskell, 1990.

Frances, Allen, Michael B. First and Harold Alan Pincus. *DSM-IV Guidebook.* Washington, DC: American Psychiatric Press, 1995.

Klein, Daniel N., and Neil J. Santiago. "Dysthymia and Chronic Depression: Introduction, Classification, Risk Factors, and Course." *Journal of Clinical Psychology* 59 (2003): 807–816.

Klein, Daniel N., Stewart A. Shankman, and Suzanne Rose. "Ten-Year Prospective Follow-Up Study of the Naturalistic Course of Dysthymic Disorder and Double Depression." *American Journal of Psychiatry* 163 (2006): 872–880.

Lima, M.S., J. Moncrieff and B.G.O. Soares. "Drugs Versus Placebo for Dysthymia (Review)." *Cochrane Database of Systematic Reviews* 2 (2005): art. no. CD001130.

Thase, Michael E., and Susan S. Lang. *Beating the Blues: New Approaches to Overcoming Dysthymia and Chronic Mild Depression.* New York: Oxford University Press, 2004.

# E

**EATING DISORDERS.** Eating disorders are psychological conditions characterized by serious disturbances in eating behavior. People with eating disorders go to one extreme or the other, either severely restricting what they eat or binging on very large amounts. Some binge, then attempt to compensate by means such as self-induced vomiting or laxative abuse. Eating disorders frequently occur alongside other mental disorders, including depression. Untreated depression, in turn, makes it harder to recover from an eating disorder.

Two main types of eating disorders are recognized by the ***Diagnostic and Statistical Manual of Mental Disorders, Fourth Edition, Text Revision*** (*DSM-IV-TR*), a diagnostic guidebook published by the American Psychiatric Association and used by mental health professionals from many disciplines. These two disorders are called anorexia nervosa and bulimia nervosa.

Anorexia nervosa is characterized by an obsession with being thin, sometimes to the point of deadly self-starvation. Even though underweight, individuals with anorexia are terrified of weight gain, and they may severely restrict what they eat. Malnutrition can lead to death by cardiac arrest. People with anorexia are also at high risk for **suicide**, and having depression at the same time raises the risk further. Other physical health risks associated with anorexia include heart problems, electrolyte imbalances, anemia, bone loss, menstrual irregularities in females, decreased testosterone in males, lung problems, digestive disorders, and kidney damage.

Bulimia nervosa is characterized by bouts of binging and purging. During these bouts, people eat large amounts of food in a short time and feel as if their eating is out of control. Then they try to make up for the eating binge by purging themselves of the extra calories. Unlike those with anorexia, individuals with bulimia tend to be normal weight or even a little overweight. But the two groups share an intense fear of weight gain and a warped view of their own bodies. Purging through means such as repeated vomiting or misuse of laxatives can lead to health problems, such as electrolyte imbalances, digestive disorders, tooth damage, and mouth sores.

Binge-eating disorder is a third condition that is getting more attention lately. In the *DSM-IV-TR*, it falls into a catchall category called "eating disorder not otherwise specified," but it may become a disorder in its own right in the next edition of the manual. This disorder is characterized by the same type of eating binges seen in bulimia. However, the binges are not followed by purging, which means that those with binge-eating disorder are often overweight or obese. Obesity, in turn, is linked to numerous health risks, including **heart disease, stroke, diabetes**, certain types of **cancer**, osteoarthritis, respiratory problems, and liver and gallbladder disease.

People with eating disorders often start out eating just a little more or less than usual. At some point, though, their eating behavior spirals out of control. Most often, the eating problem escalates during **adolescence** or young adulthood, but it can start earlier or later. **Women** and girls are more likely to develop eating disorders than men and boys. When depression complicates the picture, it is vital to get help for both conditions.

*Criteria for Diagnosis.* The symptoms of eating disorders are defined by the *DSM-IV-TR.* Anorexia and bulimia are established diagnoses. Provisional criteria for binge-eating disorder are given in an appendix, which describes disorders that are being considered for future inclusion in the manual.

*Anorexia Nervosa.* People with anorexia refuse to maintain a healthy body weight, to the point where their weight falls below 85% of normal for someone of their height and age. Yet despite being underweight, they have an intense fear of gaining weight or getting fat, and they have a seriously distorted view of their body's shape or size. They may weigh or measure themselves often, or they may check in mirrors frequently for any perceived signs of fat. Adolescent girls and women with anorexia stop having their menstrual periods.

There are two subtypes of anorexia. In the restricting subtype, which is more common, people lose weight by severely limiting what they eat, going on food fasts, and/or exercising to an extreme. In the purging subtype, people lose weight through self-induced vomiting or the misuse of laxatives, enemas, or diuretics.

*Bulimia Nervosa.* Individuals with bulimia go on

---

### Treatment of Eating Disorders

When people have both an eating disorder and depression simultaneously, both conditions need to be addressed. Below are some of the main treatment options for eating disorders.

#### Nutritional Counseling
The goal of this treatment is to help people learn about a nutritious **diet** and develop healthier eating habits. People with binge-eating disorder may benefit from a weight-loss program.

#### Hospitalization
People with anorexia who refuse to eat may need a hospital-based feeding program as a first step. **Hospitalization** may also be recommended for people with other serious medical problems associated with an eating disorder. Facilities with specialized eating disorder programs generally offer more intensive treatment over longer periods of time.

#### Psychotherapy
**Cognitive-behavioral therapy** (CBT)—in which people address maladaptive patterns of thinking and behaving—is one form of **psychotherapy** that has been used successfully to treat eating disorders. CBT is also a proven therapy for depression. In addition to one-on-one treatment, **family therapy** and **group therapy** are often helpful.

#### Medications
Various medications may help people control the urge to binge and purge or manage a preoccupation with food and diet. When antidepressants or anti-anxiety medications are prescribed, they may help with not only the eating disorder, but also depression or anxiety.

repeated eating binges, during which they eat an unusually large amount in a short time and feel as if they cannot stop eating or control what they eat. These binges are followed by inappropriate behavior intended to prevent weight gain. Most commonly, this involves self-induced vomiting. Other methods of compensating for overeating include the misuse of laxatives, enemas, or diuretics.

This pattern of binging and purging repeats itself at least twice a week, on average, over a period of at least three months. People with bulimia also tend obsess about their body weight and shape. They often fear gaining weight, want desperately to lose weight, or are intensely unhappy with their shape or size.

*Binge-Eating Disorder.*   Binge-eating disorder is characterized by repeated episodes of excessive, out-of-control eating. These episodes have three or more of the following features: (1) eating more rapidly than normal, (2) eating until feeling uncomfortably full, (3) eating a large amount when not feeling physically hungry, (4) eating alone due to embarrassment over how much one is eating, or (5) feeling depressed, disgusted, or very guilty about overeating. Such eating binges cause serious distress. They occur at least twice a week, on average, over a period of at least six months.

***Relationship to Depression.***   Changes in appetite and weight are common symptoms of depression. These symptoms are different from the extreme eating behavior that typifies an eating disorder. But depression and eating disorders can exist side by side and make each other worse. In such cases, getting treatment for both conditions can provide the best chance at **recovery**.

Some factors that contribute to eating disorders may play a role in depression as well. For example, people with eating disorders may have low self-esteem, perfectionism, impulsive behavior, family conflicts, or relationship problems. The **stress** rising from such issues might trigger or worsen depression in susceptible individuals.

In addition, there is some evidence that a brain chemical called **serotonin** may influence eating disorders because of its role in regulating food intake. Serotonin also is thought to play a pivotal role in mood, and **antidepressants** that affect serotonin activity are sometimes used to treat not only depression, but also eating disorders.

*See also:* Comorbidity

***Further Information.***   Academy for Eating Disorders, 111 Deer Lake Road, Suite 100, Deerfield, IL 60015, (847) 498-4274, www.aedweb.org.

National Association for Anorexia Nervosa and Associated Disorders, Box 7, Highland Park, IL 60035, (847) 831-3438, www.anad.org.

National Eating Disorders Association, 603 Stewart Street, Suite 803, Seattle, WA 98101, (800) 931-2237, www.nationaleatingdisorders.org.

*Bibliography*

American Psychiatric Association. *Diagnostic and Statistical Manual of Mental Disorders.* 4th ed., text rev. Washington, DC: American Psychiatric Association, 2000.

*Anorexia Nervosa.* Mayo Clinic, December 20, 2007, http://www.mayoclinic.com/health/anorexia/DS00606.

Berkman, Nancy D., Kathleen N. Lohr, and Cynthia M. Bulik. "Outcomes of Eating Disorders: A Systematic Review of the Literature." *International Journal of Eating Disorders* 40 (2007): 293–309.

*Binge Eating Disorder.* National Institute of Diabetes and Digestive and Kidney Diseases, June 2008, http://win.niddk.nih.gov/publications/binge.htm.

*Eating Disorders.* Mayo Clinic, January 15, 2008, http://www.mayoclinic.com/health/eating-disorders/DS00294.

*Eating Disorders.* National Institute of Mental Health, February 11, 2009, http://www.nimh.nih.gov/health/publications/eating-disorders/complete-index.shtml.

*Eating Disorders: The Myths.* Academy for Eating Disorders, http://www.aedweb.org/public/the-myths.cfm.

Franko, Debra L., and Pamela K. Keel. "Suicidality in Eating Disorders: Occurrence, Correlates, and Clinical Implications." *Clinical Psychology Review* 26 (2006): 769–782.

*Overweight and Obesity: Introduction.* Centers for Disease Control and Prevention, March 24, 2009, http://www.cdc.gov/nccdphp/dnpa/obesity/index.htm.

**ECONOMIC IMPACT.**   Depression places a heavy burden on affected individuals, their families, their communities, and society as a whole. Although the human toll is incalculable, scientists and economists have attempted to estimate the economic cost. The sheer magnitude of the economic impact is staggering, reaching $53 billion annually by one often-cited estimate.

Direct treatment costs account for 23 percent of that figure. Such costs include expenditures for items such as outpatient care, medication, hospitalization, and residential treatment. Economic costs from increased mortality due to suicide account for another 15 percent. However, the lion's share of costs—62 percent—are for economic losses associated with reduced productivity at work. These losses are due not only to missed workdays, but also to depression-related impairment on the job.

Several factors help explain why depression exacts such as massive toll. It is one of the most common long-term diseases in the labor force. It has an earlier age of onset than most other chronic diseases, typically starting during the late teens or early twenties, and it often recurs throughout the working years. Its symptoms, such as lack of motivation and low energy, interfere directly with educational attainment and work performance. And despite the availability of effective treatments, only a minority of people receive adequate treatment for a sufficient length of time.

Yet there are hopeful signs, too. A sophisticated simulation based on dozens of studies found that providing a minimal level of enhanced care for employee depression could save employers more than $2,800 per 1,000 workers over five years. In this model, enhanced care was assumed to include a one-time depression screening for all employees as well as telephone care management for those identified as possibly having depression. Even though enhanced care would initially increase use of mental health services, the simulation predicted it would ultimately save employers money by reducing costs associated with absenteeism and employee turnover.

*Bibliography*

Wang, Philip S., Amanda Patrick, Jerry Avorn, Francisca Azocar, Evette Ludman, Joyce McCulloch, et al. "The Costs and Benefits of Enhanced Depression Care to Employers." *Archives of General Psychiatry* 63 (2006): 1345–1353.

Wang, Philip S., and Ronald C. Kessler. "Global Burden of Mood Disorders." In *The American Psychiatric Publishing Textbook of Mood Disorders,* by Dan J. Stein, David J. Kupfer, and Alan F. Schatzberg, eds., 55–67. Washington, DC: American Psychiatric Publishing, 2006.

Wang, Philip S., Gregory Simon, and Ronald C. Kessler. "The Economic Burden of Depression and the Cost-Effectiveness of Treatment." *International Journal of Methods in Psychiatric Research* 12 (2003): 22–33.

**EDINBURGH POSTNATAL DEPRESSION SCALE.** The Edinburgh Postnatal Depression Scale (EPDS) is a self-report questionnaire designed to screen for **postpartum depression**, a form of depression in which the symptoms begin within the first several months after giving birth. The EPDS was introduced in 1987 by British psychiatrist John L. Cox and his colleagues. Unlike most other depression rating scales, this one is specifically geared to detecting depression in new mothers.

Many popular screening tests for depression ask about symptoms such as fatigue and loss of sleep. But because such feelings are almost universal among new mothers, they are not useful for differentiating postpartum women who are depressed from those who are not, so they do not appear on the EPDS. On the other hand, women with postpartum depression often report feeling scared or panicked—a symptom that is included on the EPDS but does not appear on most other depression rating scales.

The EPDS, which takes five to 10 minutes to complete, is a 10-item questionnaire. Each item has four possible responses that describe the severity of a particular symptom. The test is designed to help doctors and nurses identify new mothers who might have postpartum depression. Those women can then be referred for a complete diagnostic evaluation. An EPDS score alone is not sufficient for making a diagnosis.

***Pros and Cons of the EPDS.*** Both health care providers and postpartum women seem to find the EPDS easy to use. On the surface, it appears to be a valuable tool. However, the scale has not been as thoroughly studied as some other measures of depression. More research is needed to establish its reliability, the extent to which the results obtained on the test are consistent and repeatable.

The scale's validity—its ability to discriminate depression from other disorders—has been better studied. The EPDS does an acceptable job of singling out postpartum women with either **major depression** or **minor depression**. Major depression involves being in a low mood nearly all the time and/or losing interest or enjoyment in almost everything. These feelings last for at least two weeks and are associated with several other symptoms. Minor depression is similar, but less pervasive; that is, it produces the same kind of associated symptoms, but fewer of them. Either form of depression can occur in women during the postpartum period.

*See also:* Diagnosis of Depression

*Bibliography*

Cox, J. L., J. M. Holden, and R. Sagovsky. "Detection of Postnatal Depression: Development of the 10-Item Edinburgh Postnatal Depression Scale." *British Journal of Psychiatry* 150 (1987): 782–786.

Cox, John, and Jeni Holden. *Perinatal Mental Health: A Guide to the Edinburgn Postnatal Depression Scale.* London: Royal College of Psychiatrists, 2003.

Dew, Mary Amanda, Galen E. Switzer, Larissa Myaskovsky, Andrea F. DiMartini, and Marianna I. Tovt-Korshynska. "Rating Scales for Mood Disorders." In *The American Psychiatric Publishing Textbook of Mood Disorders,* by Dan J. Stein, David J. Kupfer, and Alan F. Schatzberg, eds., 69–97. Washington, DC: American Psychiatric Publishing, 2006.

Yonkers, Kimberly A., and Jacqueline A. Samson. "Mood Disorders Measures." In *Handbook of Psychiatric Measures,* 2nd ed., by A. John Rush Jr., Michael B. First, and Deborah Blacker, eds., 499–528. Washington, DC: American Psychiatric Publishing, 2008.

**ELECTROCONVULSIVE THERAPY.** Electroconvulsive therapy (ECT) is a treatment that involves passing a carefully controlled electrical current through a person's brain to induce a brief seizure. It is thought to alter some of the electrochemical processes that affect **mood**. ECT has proved to be a very effective treatment for depression, even in many cases where other treatments have been tried and failed. Yet more than 70 years after its introduction, ECT remains a controversial procedure that is used mainly after other options have been exhausted.

ECT may be considered for people with depression when other treatments have been ineffective or when medications might cause serious adverse effects. Because ECT acts more rapidly than other treatments, it may also be considered for people with urgent symptoms, such as suicidal impulses, refusal to eat, or psychotic delusions and hallucinations.

ECT is one of the best-researched treatments in the annals of psychiatry, and study after study has shown that it is the most effective and fastest-acting therapy for depression. Modern methods of administering ECT are much gentler and safer than those of days past, when so-called "shock therapy" earned its bad reputation. Today, although there are still risks associated with ECT, the treatment's negative image is largely undeserved.

For some individuals battling severe, hard-to-treat depression, ECT may be the only treatment that works. And for those with intense thoughts of **suicide**, it may sometimes be a literal lifesaver.

*A Brief History of ECT.* Electric eels and fish were used to treat headaches and mental illness in ancient times. In the 1930s, the therapeutic use of electricity was revived by Italian psychiatrists **Ugo Cerletti** (1877–1963) and Lucino Bini (1908–1964). While studying **epilepsy**, Cerletti and Bini realized that electricity could bring on a seizure. Other researchers at the time were experimenting with the use of medications to induce seizures, which seemed to reduce symptoms of schizophrenia. Cerletti and Bini decided to try using electricity for the same purpose. After testing the technique on dogs, they administered the first ECT treatment to a human patient with schizophrenia in 1938.

The Italian psychiatrists had some success with the new treatment, and their reports created a stir in the psychiatric community. By the 1940s, ECT had spread from Europe to the United States. By the 1950s, it had become one of the standard treatments used for depression in hospitalized patients.

Yet there was a dark side to ECT's sudden rise to popularity. In the early days, high doses of electricity were administered without the anesthesia and muscle relaxants that are standard procedure today. The result could be broken or dislocated bones, serious memory loss, or occasionally even death. Over the decades, technical refinements reduced the risks, but they could not erase the treatment's harsh history.

---

**ECT on the Screen**

Movie portrayals of ECT have helped shape public opinion of the treatment. Since ECT's film debut in *The Snake Pit* (1948), the treatment has been depicted or discussed in a number of movies, including *One Flew Over the Cuckoo's Nest* (1975), *Frances* (1982), and *Shine* (1996).

In some films, ECT has been sensationalized for horror or played cheap laughs. In others, it has simply been portrayed inaccurately. For instance, people undergoing ECT are often shown fully awake, even though general anesthesia has been a routine part of the procedure since the 1950s. Such portrayals might seem like harmless fictions, but they may discourage people from using a potentially life-changing treatment or contribute to the **stigma** associated with mental health care.

*Public Backlash.* Starting in the 1960s, the tide of public opinion began to turn against ECT. This was due in part to the treatment's tainted past and in part to a cultural backlash against psychiatry. Books such as Ken Kesey's novel *One Flew Over the Cuckoo's Nest* (1962) portrayed psychiatry in general and ECT in particular as institutional tools for quashing nonconformist behavior. The 1975 film of the same title, which became a blockbuster hit, helped cement ECT's negative image.

In the 1970s and early 1980s, public hostility to ECT was so great that California passed a law against it. The procedure fell out of favor among medical professionals as well, and it was no longer a routine part of the curriculum for psychiatrists in training.

*Renewed Interest.* The rehabilitation of ECT's public image began with a National Institutes of Health Consensus Development Conference on the subject in 1985. The conference panel found that "not a single controlled study has shown another form of treatment to be superior to ECT in the short-term management of severe depressions."

In the years since, ECT has regained a place in the psychiatrist's armamentarium, but it never reclaimed its former glory. What was once a first-choice treatment is now viewed as a treatment of last resort.

*Treatment Procedure.* Before the first ECT session, patients undergo a medical assessment, which usually includes a medical history, physical exam, and electrocardiogram (ECG) as well as basic blood tests. Several medical conditions increase the chance of serious complications from ECT, so the medical risks must be carefully evaluated.

The procedure itself takes about 10 to 15 minutes, although additional time is needed for preparation and recovery. Patients typically get two or three treatments per week for two to four weeks. Some are hospitalized, but others receive ECT on an outpatient basis.

Before ECT, anesthesia is administered to keep the patient unconscious and pain-free during the procedure. A muscle relaxant also is given to prevent violent physical convulsions during the seizure. A blood pressure cuff may be put around one forearm or ankle to prevent the muscle relaxant from reaching that hand or foot. By watching for movement

---

### The Eagleton Affair

In the summer of 1972, Democratic presidential candidate George McGovern selected Missouri senator Thomas Eagleton (1929–2007) to be his vice presidential running mate. Eighteen days later, Eagleton stepped down as a candidate under intense pressure from party leaders and McGovern's staff. This dramatic turn of events was driven by the revelation that Eagleton had previously been hospitalized three times for depression and treated twice with ECT.

Today, the relevance of Eagleton's past illness and the appropriateness of his fellow politicians' response are still being discussed. The debacle raised profound questions about societal attitudes toward mental illness. McGovern and his advisors feared that Eagleton's history of depression and ECT would damage the campaign's image, and several major U.S. newspapers also urged Eagleton to take himself out of contention. But the pundits may have badly misjudged public reaction. A poll by *Time* magazine found that over three-quarters of those surveyed said Eagleton's medical history would not affect their vote.

McGovern eventually suffered a landslide defeat in the presidential race. Meanwhile, Eagleton went on to enjoy a successful career, serving in the U.S. Senate until 1987 and practicing law after that. McGovern was later quoted as saying that he regretted Eagleton's withdrawal, noting that he and his inner circle knew little about mental illness at the time.

there, the doctor can tell when the seizure occurs. In addition, a mouth guard may be inserted to provide extra protection for the teeth and tongue.

Electrode pads, each about the size of a silver dollar, are placed on the head. After the anesthesia takes effect, a small amount of electrical current is passed through the electrodes to the brain. This produces a seizure—a sudden change in electrical activity within the brain—that usually lasts 30 to 90 seconds. The change in activity shows up on an electroencephalogram (EEG), a test that measures and graphs brain waves.

Just a few minutes later, the effects of the anesthesia and muscle relaxant start wearing off. Upon coming out of anesthesia, the person may experience temporary confusion that typically lasts from a few minutes to several hours.

***Benefits for Depression.*** About 80 percent of those who receive a full course of treatment with ECT improve—an excellent result in light of the fact that many of these individuals have especially hard-to-treat depression. Most patients start feeling better by the second or third treatment, and the full benefits are felt within four to 12 sessions received over the course of a few weeks. In contrast, it takes several weeks to feel the full effects of **antidepressants**.

Experts differ in their recommendations about the use of antidepressants during the ECT treatment period. Some believe medication should be avoided during this period to reduce the risk of adverse effects, but others believe combining the two may boost the benefits. In one recent study, the effectiveness of ECT was substantially increased by taking an antidepressant at the same time. The effect on cognitive side effects, such as memory loss, was favorable for one antidepressant, but not for another.

Although ECT can help most people with depression feel better in the short term, more than 80 percent will have another episode of depression within six months if they do not receive ongoing care. **Maintenance treatment** with antidepressants reduces the relapse rate. For those who still relapse or who cannot tolerate medication, ECT treatments may be continued over a longer period. As time goes on, the interval between the treatments is gradually increased until they are spaced about a month apart.

***Risks and Side Effects.*** Right after an ECT treatment, people may experience some temporary confusion. They may not know where they are or why. This mental fog usually clears in a matter of minutes to hours. But the more ECT treatments someone has had, the longer the confusion may last, and occasionally it persists for days.

Memory loss is one of the biggest concerns with ECT. Some people experience retrograde amnesia—difficulty remembering events that occurred before the treatment. Others have trouble recalling things that happened during the treatment period or even after ECT is over. Fortunately, most memory problems go away within a few months. Permanent memory loss is relatively rare.

On the day of ECT, some people experience headache, jaw pain, muscle aches, nausea, or vomiting. During the treatment, heart rate and blood pressure also increase, and in rare cases, that may lead to serious heart complications. Although ECT does have risks and side effects, they must be weighed against the very real risks of disabling or suicidal depression, especially when there are no other viable treatment options.

*See also:* Brain Stimulation; Magnetic Seizure Therapy; Treatment of Depression; Treatment-Resistant Depression

## Bibliography

*A Scientific Odyssey: People and Discoveries—Electroshock Therapy Introduced.* PBS, 1998, http://www.pbs.org/wgbh/aso/databank/entries/dh38el.html.

American Academy of Child and Adolescent Psychiatry. "Practice Parameter for Use of Electroconvulsive Therapy with Adolescents." *Journal of the American Academy of Child and Adolescent Psychiatry* 43 (2004): 1521–1539.

Clymer, Adam. "Thomas F. Eagleton, 77, a Running Mate for 18 Days, Dies." *New York Times* (March 5, 2007).

*Electroconvulsive Therapy.* Mayo Clinic, July 11, 2008, http://www.mayoclinic.com/health/electroconvulsive-therapy/MY00129.

*Factsheet: Electroconvulsive Therapy (ECT).* Mental Health America, http://www.nmha.org/go/information/get-info/treatment/electroconvulsive-therapy-ect.

Fink, Max, and Michael Alan Taylor. "Electroconvulsive Therapy: Evidence and Challenges." *JAMA* 298 (2007): 330–332.

Hirshbein, Laura, and Sharmalie Sarvananda. "History, Power, and Electricity: American Popular Magazine Accounts of Electroconvulsive Therapy, 1940–2005." *Journal of the History of the Behavioral Sciences* 44 (2008): 1–18.

Kellner, Charles H., Rebecca G. Knapp, Georgios Petrides, Teresa A. Rummans, Mustafa M. Husain, Keith Rasmussen, et al. "Continuation Electroconvulsive Therapy vs Pharmacotherapy for Relapse Prevention in Major Depression: A Multisite Study From the Consortium for Research in Electroconvulsive Therapy (CORE)." *Archives of General Psychiatry* 63 (2006): 1337–1344.

Kesey, Ken. *One Flew Over the Cuckoo's Nest.* New York: Viking Press, 1962.

National Institutes of Health Office of Medical Applications of Research. "Electroconvulsive Therapy." *National Institutes of Health Consensus Development Conference Statement* 5 (1985):1–23.

Pandya, Mayur, Leopoldo Pozuelo, and Donald Malone. "Electroconvulsive Therapy: What the Internist Needs to Know." *Cleveland Clinic Journal of Medicine* 74 (2007): 679–685.

Sackeim, Harold A., Elaine M. Dillingham, Joan Prudic, Thomas Cooper, W. Vaughn McCall, Peter Rosenquist, et al. "Effect of Concomitant Pharmacotherapy on Electroconvulsive Therapy Outcomes: Short-Term Efficacy and Adverse Effects." *Archives of General Psychiatry* 66 (2009): 729–737.

Shorter, Edward. "The History of ECT: Unsolved Mysteries." *Psychiatric Times* (February 1, 2004).

"The Campaign: McGovern's First Crisis—The Eagleton Affair." *Time* (August 7, 1972).

Walter, Garry, and Andrew McDonald. "About to Have ECT? Fine, but Don't Watch It in the Movies: The Sorry Portrayal of ECT in Film." *Psychiatric Times* (June 1, 2004).

**ELECTROENCEPHALOGRAPHY.** Electroencephalography (EEG) is a painless, noninvasive test that monitors electrical activity in the brain. Small, flat metal discs, called electrodes, are attached to the scalp. These electrodes are connected to wires, which lead to a machine that amplifies and graphs the brain's electrical activity. Over the years, advances have been made in EEG technology, increasing its ability to record activity from the whole head at once. This allows scientists to compare the relative position and strength of electrical activity in different parts of the brain.

Within brain cells, information is carried by electrical impulses. The electrical activity goes on all the time, even during sleep. On an EEG readout, all that activity shows up as a pattern of wavy lines. These lines are a graphic representation of brain waves—spontaneous, rhythmic electrical impulses arising from different parts of the brain.

*The Depressed Brain.* EEG testing is used to help diagnose several **neurological disorders**, including **epilepsy**, brain tumors, traumatic brain injuries, encephalitis (inflammation of the brain), and sleep disorders. It is not yet possible to diagnose depression with an EEG. But in research settings, certain EEG findings are more common in depressed individuals than in those without the disorder.

For example, several studies have found a link between depressive symptoms and an unequal level of activity between the two sides of the front part of the cortex. Most, but not all, of these studies have shown reduced left frontal activity or increased right frontal activity when the brain is at rest. Some researchers have suggested that this particular pattern of brain activity might be a preexisting risk factor that makes people vulnerable to becoming depressed when something stressful happens.

Abnormalities have also been found in studies where EEGs were done while depressed individuals were sleeping. Such sleep abnormalities are more common in people with severe symptoms, including those with **psychotic depression** and **melancholic depression**.

In addition, certain EEG patterns have been linked to antidepressant response. More research still needs to be done, but it is hoped that EEG testing might one day help professionals choose the most effective treatment for an individual with depression.

***How the Test Is Done.*** An EEG can be done at a doctor's office, hospital, or testing facility. Prior to the test, the person must avoid caffeine and certain medications. When it is time for the EEG, a technician measures the person's head and marks where the electrodes will go. Then the electrodes are attached using a special paste or extremely fine needles. In some cases, an elastic cap fitted with electrodes is used instead. Once the electrodes are in place, the procedure typically takes 30 to 60 minutes.

First, a very low electrical current is sent through the electrodes, and baseline brain activity is recorded. During much of the remaining time, the person rests in a comfortable position. At specific points, however, the person might be exposed to various stimuli, such as a bright or flashing light, loud noise, or certain drugs. The person also might be asked to perform simple tasks, such as opening and closing the eyes, breathing deeply, reading a paragraph, or looking at a picture. The electrodes pick up any resulting changes in electrical activity.

EEGs also may be done in a sleep lab while the person is sleeping. In such cases, the person is sometimes given a sedative first to make it easier to relax. Performing an EEG during sleep generally takes at least three hours.

Once testing is done, the effects of any sedative need time to wear off. Otherwise, there are no side effects. A doctor trained to analyze EEGs interprets the readout and sends the results to the doctor who ordered the test.

*See also:* Sleep Disturbances

## Bibliography

American Psychiatric Association. *Diagnostic and Statistical Manual of Mental Disorders.* 4th ed., text rev. Washington, DC: American Psychiatric Association, 2000.

*Baylor Study Uses EEG to Help Those Suffering From Depression.* Baylor University, June 6, 2006, http://www.bcm.edu/news/item.cfm?newsID=638.

*EEG (Electroencephalogram).* Mayo Clinic, May 21, 2009, http://www.mayoclinic.com/health/eeg/MY00296.

Hunter, Aimee M., Andrew F. Leuchter, Melinda L. Morgan, and Ian A. Cook. "Changes in Brain Function (Quantitative EEG Cordance) During Placebo Lead-In and Treatment Outcomes in Clinical Trials for Major Depression." *American Journal of Psychiatry* 163 (2006): 1426–1432.

Mathias, Robert. *The Basics of Brain Imaging.* National Institute on Drug Abuse, November/December 1996, http://www.nida.nih.gov/NIDA_notes/NNVol11N5/Basics.html.

*Neurological Diagnostic Tests and Procedures.* National Institute of Neurological Disorders and Stroke, May 15, 2009, http://www.ninds.nih.gov/disorders/misc/diagnostic_tests.htm.

Thibodeau, Ryan, Randall S. Jorgensen, and Sangmoon Kim. "Depression, Anxiety, and Resting Frontal EEG Asymmetry: A Meta-analytic Review." *Journal of Abnormal Psychology* 115 (2006): 715–729.

**ELLIS, ALBERT (1913–2007).** Albert Ellis was a U.S. psychologist who developed the first discrete form of **cognitive therapy**. This type of **psychotherapy** helps people recognize and change self-defeating thought patterns that contribute to their emotional and behavioral problems. Ellis' signature approach, originally called rational emotive therapy, is now known as rational emotive behavior therapy (REBT). It teaches people how to modify and replace irrational thoughts with more rational ones, leading to more effective ways of feeling and behaving.

REBT is an action-oriented method of coping with psychological problems, including depression, and enhancing personal growth. It focuses on current beliefs rather than past experiences. Therapists work closely with clients to uncover the individual beliefs—composed of attitudes, expectations, and personal rules—that contribute to their emotional distress.

Once these beliefs have been identified, REBT helps clients reformulate them into more sensible, realistic ones. Therapists encourage clients to challenge their most pernicious beliefs by engaging in behavior that runs counter to them. By disputing irrational beliefs in this manner, REBT helps people break free of distorted thought patterns and adopt more rational behavior.

As one of the founders of cognitive therapy, Ellis had a major impact on modern psychology. In fact, a 1982 article in *American Psychologist* ranked him as the second most influential psychotherapist at the time. In the twenty-first century, his ideas continue to exert a powerful influence.

***Early Career Highlights.*** Born in Pittsburgh and raised in New York City, Ellis suffered from a kidney disorder as a child that turned his attention from sports to books. As a young man, he earned a degree in business administration and worked as a personnel manager while dreaming of a career as a novelist. When that career failed to materialize, he set his sights on becoming a nonfiction author instead.

Writing about sexuality and relationships, Ellis discovered an interest in family and sex counseling. He entered the clinical psychology program at Columbia University, completing his doctorate in 1947. After graduation, Ellis received additional training in psychoanalysis, a form of long-term psychotherapy originated by **Sigmund Freud** (1856–1939). Psychoanalysis stresses the importance of unconscious wishes and childhood events in shaping current experiences. It generally requires several sessions per week, and the psychoanalyst plays a relatively passive role. But Ellis soon discovered that his clients progressed just as quickly when he saw them weekly rather than daily, and they improved even faster when he assumed a more active role as therapist, offering his interpretations and advice.

By the mid-1950s, Ellis had given up psychoanalysis in favor of his own therapeutic technique, which involved confronting people with their irrational beliefs and persuading them to adopt more rational thinking instead. His first book on REBT, titled *How to Live with a Neurotic*, was published in 1957. Two years later, Ellis founded the Institute for Rational Living, where he taught his principles to other therapists.

***Major Concepts in REBT.*** REBT holds that intense negative emotions—such as depression, rage, and panic—not only cause unhappiness, but also disrupt people's ability to manage their lives. Under the influence of such emotions, people's quality of thinking may deteriorate and become unrealistic. Those suffering from depression, for instance, may take things too personally, view minor setbacks as major catastrophes, or blame others for their own mistakes. REBT helps people think more realistically about their personal circumstances. This, in turn, helps restore their emotional balance.

## Stoic Roots of REBT

"Men are disturbed not by things, but by the principles and notions which they form concerning things."—Greek philosopher Epictetus (AD 55–ca. AD 135) in *The Enchiridion*.

Ellis has said that REBT owes at least as much to the ancient Greek philosopher Epictetus as to Sigmund Freud. Epictetus belonged to a school of philosophy known as Stoicism, which held that the wise man should be free of passion—governed not by emotion, but by reason. The Stoics believed that this approach to life provided a buffer against the vagaries of misfortune, because reason was under the individual's control. REBT, likewise, focuses on rationality as an antidote to **stress** and depression.

The basic steps of REBT are often referred to as the ABCDE technique. In brief, an Activating event leads to an irrational Belief, which brings about inappropriate behavioral Consequences. In therapy, Disputing the belief results in various beneficial Effects, including more rational thinking, appropriate feelings, and desirable behaviors.

***Ellis in Perspective.*** Ellis became known for his irreverent attitude and straight-talking persona as much as his groundbreaking ideas. A prolific lecturer and writer, he promoted REBT largely through workshops for other therapists and self-help books for the general public. Ellis was neither a researcher nor an academician. Yet his approach had a profound impact on mainstream psychology.

Among other things, Ellis demonstrated that thoughts and beliefs are more accessible and controllable than psychoanalysis had maintained. He also showed that therapy can be effective by focusing on present-day problems rather than past experiences. Although these principles are widely accepted now, they were revolutionary when Ellis first wrote about them. Today cognitive therapy is a dominant force within psychotherapy in general and the treatment of depression in particular.

***Further Information.*** Albert Ellis Institute, 45 East 65th Street, New York, NY 10065, (800) 323-4738, www.albertellisinstitute.org.

## Bibliography

*A Sketch of Albert Ellis.* Albert Ellis Institute, http://www.albertellisinstitute.org/aei/albert_ellis_bio.html.

Ellis, Albert. *How to Stubbornly Refuse to Make Yourself Miserable about Anything (Yes, Anything!).* Rev. ed. New York: Kensington Publishing, 2006.

Kaufman, Michael T. "Albert Ellis, 93, Influential Psychotherapist, Dies." *New York Times* (July 25, 2007).

Millon, Theodore. *Masters of the Mind: Exploring the Story of Mental Illness from Ancient Times to the New Millennium.* New York: John Wiley and Sons, 2004.

Sheehy, Noel, Antony J. Chapman, and Wendy Conroy, eds. "Ellis, Albert," in *Biographical Dictionary of Psychology.* New York: Routledge, 2002.

Smith, Darrell. "Trends in Counseling and Psychotherapy." *American Psychologist* 37 (1982): 802–809.

**EMOTION.**    An emotion is a subjective feeling state that occurs in response to a personally meaningful event or situation. Examples of emotions include **sadness**, fear, disgust, surprise, and anger. The specific emotion that is felt is determined by the meaning of the event. For example, if the event involves a loss, sadness is likely to ensue, but if the event is perceived as threatening, fear is likely to result.

In addition to feelings, emotions have behavioral and physiological responses associated with them. Each response in itself may not be limited to just one emotion; for example, an increased heart rate is a common feature of many strong emotions, including joy, anger, fear, and guilt. Nevertheless, researchers have found that certain clusters of behaviors and bodily changes are linked to particular emotions across a range of cultures. For example, sadness is typified by **crying**, withdrawing, tensing muscles, feeling cold, a faster heartbeat, and the sensation of a lump in the throat.

***Timeless Perspectives on Emotion.*** The nature of emotion has long been the stuff of literature and philosophy. More recently, it also has been the subject of innumerable studies in psychology. Many ideas about emotion that were first put forth decades or centuries ago still figure prominently in modern concepts.

*Cognitive Viewpoint.* The ancient Greek philosopher Aristotle (384 BC–322 BC) attributed emotions to mental appraisals of events. He observed that anger is prompted by undeserved slights, fear by danger, and shame by disgraceful deeds. This idea is echoed in the work of U.S. psychologist Richard Lazarus (1922–2002), who argued that a person's appraisal of the harms and benefits inherent in a situation is what determines the emotions that result. For example, an appraisal of irrevocable loss leads to sadness, and an appraisal of reasonable progress toward achieving a personal goal leads to happiness.

*Evolutionary Viewpoint.* English naturalist Charles Darwin (1809–1882), whose theory of natural selection became the foundation of modern studies of evolution, believed that emotions were adaptive behaviors that tended to increase the chance of survival. In recent times, U.S. psychiatrist Randolph M. Nesse (1948– ) has argued that the best way to advance the scientific understanding of emotions is by developing evolutionary explanations for the specific roles they serve. For instance, Nesse has suggested that happiness arises out of situations that increase evolutionary fitness (for example, being loved, getting pregnant, having children), and sadness arises out of situations that decrease fitness (for example, illness, loss of a friend, death of a family member).

*Physiological Viewpoint.* U.S. philosopher and psychologist William James (1842–1910) noted that the commonsense way of looking at emotion was to believe that the perception of a situation leads to an emotion, which then leads to various physical changes, such as an increase in heart rate and muscle tension. James, however, believed that this sequence

> **Darwin on Frowning**
>
> In his classic book *The Expression of the Emotions in Man and Animals* (1872), Darwin had this to say about lowering of the corners of the mouth created by the *depressores anguli oris* muscle: "The expression of low spirits, grief or dejection, due to the contraction of this muscle has been noticed by every one who has written on this subject. To say that a person is 'down in the mouth,' is synonymous with saying that he is out of spirits."

was wrong. He argued that outward actions and inward physiological changes actually precede the emotional response. Modern research has debunked the notion that bodily changes always come first, but they sometimes may. U.S. psychologist Carroll E. Izard (1923– ) has suggested that facial expressions send signals from the muscles and skin of the face to the brain that play a major role in generating emotions. Supporting research shows that exaggerating or inhibiting facial expressions associated with pain may increase or decrease painful sensations.

*Neurological Viewpoint.* U.S. physiologist Walter Cannon (1871–1945) pointed out several flaws in James' theory, including the fact that different emotions often are associated with similar bodily changes. As an alternate theory, he proposed that the perception of a situation as threatening leads to arousal of a brain structure called the **hypothalamus**, and this structure, in turn, simultaneously triggers emotional and physiological responses. Cannon believed that the physiological changes were designed to prepare the body to fight or flee. Later researchers have continued to explore the brain structures involved in emotion. For example, Estonian-born U.S. physiological psychologist Jaak Panksepp (1943– ) has identified several emotional command circuits in the brain. For one circuit associated with panic, loneliness, and grief, key brain areas include the **anterior cingulate cortex**, dorsomedial thalamus, dorsal periaqueductal gray, bed nucleus of the stria terminalis, and preoptic area. Key changes in brain chemicals include the activation of **glutamate** and **corticotropin-releasing hormone** as well as the inhibition of opioids, oxytocin, and prolactin.

*Psychoanalytic Viewpoint.* Austrian neurologist and psychiatrist **Sigmund Freud** (1856–1939) believed that emotions are complex states involving conflicts, early experiences, personality traits, and defense mechanisms. Following in Freud's footsteps, U.S. psychoanalyst Charles Spezzano has argued that emotions provide information about unconscious drives and motives. They are also adaptive; for instance, people are born with the capacity to feel depressed as a means of motivating withdrawal from hopeless situations.

**The Emotional Feedback Loop.** Feelings don't exist in a vacuum. Within a given individual, they are part of a feedback system that also includes thoughts and actions. This system relates to the outside world as well. It may be activated by an outside situation, and the resulting feelings, thoughts, and behaviors may lead to outward consequences.

To see how this works, consider the example of sadness. The stimulus that sets off the emotional chain of events is often a significant personal loss; for instance, a breakup with a lover or an argument with a friend. The loss may trigger thoughts of abandonment, which in turn may lead to specific feelings of sadness along with general signs of physiological arousal, such as a faster heartbeat and muscle tension. These changes might trigger crying, and the crying might elicit sympathy in others, who may then be moved to offer help and support. Viewed from this perspective, it is easy to see how an emotion such as sadness might serve a useful purpose.

Theorists who have taken an evolutionary stance, such as U.S. psychologist Robert Plutchik (1927–2006), look for the adaptive advantage conferred by an emotion. In the case of sadness, it might be the replacement of or symbolic reconnection with what has been lost through the nurturing of others.

**Emotion, Mood, and Personality.** Emotions and moods are closely related. A **mood** is a general predisposition to respond emotionally in a certain way that lasts for hours, days, or longer. An emotion, in contrast, is a shorter-lived and more specific response to a given situation. In other words, emotions fluctuate like the weather, but moods are more sustained and pervasive, like the climate.

Sadness is an emotion, for example. **Dysphoria** is an unpleasant mood that may be characterized by persistent sadness. **Major depression** is a mood disorder in which dysphoria is exaggerated to the point where it causes serious distress or significant problems in daily life.

*Personality Traits and Defense Mechanisms.* Personality traits are relatively stable, consistent, and long-lasting inner characteristics that help define a particular person's unique way of adjusting to life. Plutchik argued that, when an emotion persists over time or is repeated frequently, it may come to be seen as a personality trait. Thus, someone who is consistently sad may be described as having a gloomy personality.

Defense mechanisms are unconscious psychological reactions that protect a person from the anxiety that would otherwise be aroused by emotional conflicts or stressful situations. Plutchik theorized that defense mechanisms are ways of dealing with emotions. Sadness, for instance, may elicit a defense mechanism known as compensation, in which a person unconsciously emphasizes a strength in one area to offset a real or imagined weakness in another. This defense mechanism, which can be used to compensate for a loss, often has positive consequences, although it can be maladaptive if taken to an extreme.

There is still much to be learned about the nature and functions of emotion. But it seems clear that emotions are a central part of the human experience and have a major impact on virtually every aspect of life.

*See also:* Evolutionary Perspective

## Bibliography

"Emotion." *Encyclopedia Britannica Online,* 2008, http://www.britannica.com/eb/article-9106029.

Darwin, Charles. *The Expression of the Emotions in Man and Animals.* New York: Oxford University Press, 1998.

Keller, Matthew C., and Randolph M. Nesse. "The Evolutionary Significance of Depressive Symptoms: Different Adverse Situations Lead to Different Depressive Symptom Patterns." *Journal of Personality and Social Psychology* 91 (2006): 316–330.

Oatley, Keith. "Emotions," in Wilson, Robert A., and Frank C. Keil, eds. *The MIT Encyclopedia of the Cognitive Sciences.* Cambridge, MA: MIT Press, 1999.

Plutchik, Robert. *Emotions and Life: Perspectives from Psychology, Biology, and Evolution.* Washington, DC: American Psychological Association, 2003.

**EMOTION-FOCUSED THERAPY.** Emotion-focused therapy (EFT) is a form of **psychotherapy** that stresses the role of emotional processing as a vehicle for positive change. The idea that working through painful emotions can help a person feel better is as old as psychotherapy. However, the development of a research-based treatment focused specifically on emotional change is still a relatively new idea. In studies to date, EFT seems to hold promise as a treatment for depression.

The underlying premise of EFT is that **emotion** is a basic aspect of human functioning. Therefore, emotional change is a valid target for therapy. EFT has been presented as an alternative to two other, better-studied treatments: **cognitive-behavioral therapy** (CBT), which focuses on changing self-defeating thoughts and behaviors, and **interpersonal therapy** (IPT), which focuses on improving people's ability to interact with others. Cognitive, behavioral, and interpersonal factors clearly play a role in depression. But proponents of EFT contend that an emotional structure underlies all these factors, and permanent change is best achieved by tackling emotions directly.

***Historical Roots.*** EFT is considered a type of humanistic therapy, a form of psychotherapy that aims to foster personal growth through direct experience. One leading figure in the early days of the humanistic movement was U.S. psychologist Carl Rogers (1902–1987), who introduced client-centered therapy in the 1940s. According to Rogers, a therapist sets the stage for client growth by providing understanding, acceptance, and respect. A key technique is reflection of feeling, in which the therapist makes statements that distill the essence of what the client has expressed, helping the client gain a clearer picture of his or her true self. As therapy progresses, the client resolves conflicts, reorganizes values, and learns to better interpret feelings and thoughts.

Another influential figure from the same period was Frederick (Fritz) S. Perls (1893–1970). His gestalt therapy focuses on the totality of a client's functioning and relationships in the present, rather than experiences in the past. An underlying assumption of gestalt therapy is that healthy people organize their experiences into well-defined needs, to which they respond effectively. Those with psychological disorders, in contrast, do not appropriately organize their experiences or address their own needs. In gestalt therapy, active techniques, such as role playing, are used to elicit spontaneous feelings, enhance self-awareness, and promote personal growth.

Originally called process experiential therapy, EFT integrates features from both these older approaches. Like client-centered therapy, it stresses an empathetic relationship between client and therapist. Like gestalt therapy, it emphasizes an active, task-focused approach to treatment.

*Greenberg's Model of Depression.*    EFT is the brainchild of South African-born Canadian psychologist Leslie S. Greenberg (1945– ), a professor at York University in Toronto. According to Greenberg, depression has a powerful effect on the emotional structure of the self. Depressed individuals experience not only a decrease in feelings of interest, pleasure, and joy, but also an increase in sadness, anger, anxiety, and shame.

Human beings are complex systems, however. Within any given person, depression is experienced not only on an emotional level, but also on cognitive, behavioral, social, and physiological levels. One basic premise of EFT is that these levels are closely interconnected, and a change in one is likely to reverberate through the others.

Another premise of EFT is that depression often is rooted in negative emotional memories from the past. Current stressful situations may trigger depression, but it is unresolved memories of earlier life experiences that actually fuel it. For instance, a woman may be stressed by going through a divorce, but it is the emotional memories of a parent's death 20 years earlier that pitch her into full-blown depression.

**The Process at a Glance.**    At the outset of therapy, people with depression typically feel closed off from their emotions. They may experience a sense of weakness or powerlessness as a result, and they often struggle to put their feelings into words. Learning to better articulate their inner experience helps them confront and ultimately conquer the emotions that feed their depression.

From the perspective of EFT, people's lives are viewed as being profoundly shaped by emotional experiences and memories. One goal of therapy is to promote emotional processing by bringing painful emotional memories into awareness. By reflecting upon these memories, clients become better able to distinguish between what is currently going on in their lives and what happened in the past. This allows them to make better choices for the present, and the new, positive experiences that result gradually transform old, maladaptive emotional patterns into more adaptive ones.

A related goal of therapy is to enhance emotional intelligence—the ability to recognize and use emotional information to solve problems and manage behavior. Emotion itself is seen as a potentially constructive force that can be channeled in beneficial directions.

In EFT, the concerns of the client dictate the focus of the therapy. The therapist assumes a supportive, helping role. On one hand, if a client feels overwhelmed by high emotion, the therapist can be a soothing presence, helping the client manage those strong feelings. On the other hand, if a client's level of emotional arousal is too low, the therapist can help the client tap into more emotion in a productive way.

***Benefits for Depression.*** EFT appears to be most appropriate for people whose depression is mild to moderate. In studies to date, those who responded best to the therapy were not disabled by their depression. They were still able to get along in the world—working, going to school, raising children.

Research on EFT is still limited, however. Three small studies of an EFT program for depression, originally called process experiential therapy, found promising results. In one study, 66 depressed adults took part in weekly sessions of either EFT or CBT for 16 weeks. Most outcomes were equivalent for the two treatments, although the EFT group reported a greater decrease in interpersonal problems than the CBT group. More studies such as this one are needed to show whether EFT really can hold its own next to more established treatments for depression, including CBT.

*See also:* Treatment of Depression

***Further Information.*** Emotion-Focused Therapy, www.emotionfocusedtherapy.org.

## Bibliography

Elliott, Robert, and Leslie S. Greenberg. "Process-Experiential Psychotherapy." In *Humanistic Psychotherapies,* by David J. Cain and Julius Seeman, eds., 279–306. Washington, DC: American Psychological Association, 2001.

Greenberg, Leslie S., and Antonio Pascual-Leone. "Emotion in Psychotherapy: A Practice-Friendly Research Review." *Journal of Clinical Psychology* 62 (2006): 611–630.

Greenberg, Leslie S., and Jeanne C. Watson. *Emotion-Focused Therapy for Depression.* Washington, DC: American Psychological Association, 2006.

Greenberg, Leslie S. *Emotion-Focused Therapy: Coaching Clients to Work Through Their Feelings.* Washington, DC: American Psychological Association, 2002.

Pos, Alberta E., Leslie S. Greenberg, Rhonda N. Goldman, and Lorne M. Korman. "Emotional Processing During Experiential Treatment of Depression." *Journal of Consulting and Clinical Psychology* 71 (2003): 1007–1016.

Watson, Jeanne C., Laurel B. Gordon, Lana Stermac, Freda Kalogerakos, and Patricia Steckley. "Comparing the Effectiveness of Process-Experiental with Cognitive-Behavioral Psychotherapy in the Treatment of Depression." *Journal of Consulting and Clinical Psychology* 71 (2003): 773–781.

Watson, Jeanne C., Rhonda N. Goldman, and Leslie S. Greenberg. *Case Studies in Emotion-Focused Therapy of Depression: A Comparison of Good and Poor Outcome.* Washington, DC: American Psychological Association, 2007.

**EMPLOYEE ASSISTANCE PROGRAM.** Employee assistance programs (EAPs) are employer-sponsored programs that provide information, support, and referral services to workers and family members who are having problems with daily living or emotional well-being. The goal is to help employees get help for such problems so they can stay productive and on the job. Depression is the third-most common issue that brings employees to their EAP, outranked only by family crises and **stress**.

EAP services are usually free, but the range of services offered and number of visits allowed may be limited. An EAP counselor can usually screen for mental disorders and **substance abuse**. However, people who need in-depth diagnosis and treatment may be referred elsewhere.

An EAP may be either part of or separate from employer-sponsored health insurance. In either case, EAP visits are confidential. Information discussed with an EAP counselor is not shared with the employer.

***Further Information.*** Employee Assistance Professionals Association, 4350 North Fairfax Drive, Suite 410, Arlington, VA 22203, (703) 387-1000, www.eapassn.org.

Employee Assistance Society of North America, 2001 Jefferson Davis Highway, Suite 1004, Arlington, VA 22202, (703) 416-0060, www.easna.org.

*Bibliography*

*Factsheet: Depression in the Workplace.* Mental Health America, http://www.mentalhealthamerica.net/ go/information/get-info/depression/depression-in-the-workplace.

*Health Insurance: Provision of Mental Health and Substance Abuse Services.* National Mental Health Information Center, January 2003, http://mentalhealth.samhsa.gov/publications/allpubs/insurance.

*What Is EAP?* Employee Assistance Society of North America, 2007, http://www.easna.org/what -is-epa.html.

**ENDOCRINE SYSTEM.** The endocrine system is a network of glands that produce and secrete **hormones**, chemicals that travel around the body in the bloodstream and have effects on distant organs or tissues. Along with the **nervous system**, the endocrine system regulates body activities. Glitches in the system can lead to a wide range of problems, including depression.

The endocrine and nervous systems are the major communication pathways throughout the body. The actions of these two systems complement each other perfectly. The nervous system acts through electrical impulses and chemical messengers known as **neurotransmitters**. The effects are localized and brief, measured in seconds. The endocrine system, in contrast, acts through hormones. The effects are more generalized and longer-lasting, persisting anywhere from minutes to weeks.

These two systems are not as distinct as they might sound, however. There is considerable interaction and overlap between them. Many hormones have specialized binding sites, called **receptors**, in the brain, through which they influence mood, emotion, and behavior.

***The System at a Glance.*** There are two main types of glands: exocrine and endocrine. Exocrine glands, such as sweat or salivary glands, make substances that are discharged from the body. In contrast, the glands of the endocrine system make hormones that are used inside the body; hence, the Greek prefix "endo," meaning within.

The endocrine glands and organs produce and store hormones to be used as needed. When the time comes, hormones are released into the bloodstream and carried to specific targets in the body. There they may have a variety of effects, such as helping control energy use, growth, development, reproduction, and the body's response to **stress**. Hormones also help maintain the internal balance of body systems, called homeostasis.

The glands that make up the endocrine system include the pineal gland, pituitary gland, thyroid, parathyroid, adrenal glands, pancreas, thymus, ovaries, and testes. Part of the brain known as the **hypothalamus** is also considered an endocrine gland because it secretes a number of important hormones.

Of all the glands, the pituitary warrants special mention. Sometimes called the "master gland," it secretes hormones that influence almost every other gland in the body. If the pituitary produces too much or too little of a hormone, the target gland may respond in kind, leading to a hormonal imbalance.

***Hyperactive Stress Hormones.*** In some people, depression is linked to an overactive stress response. A hormonal cascade sets the exaggerated response in motion. The hypothalamus produces excessive **corticotropin-releasing hormone**. That stimulates the pituitary to overproduce a stress hormone called adrenocorticotropic hormone. And that, in turn, causes the adrenal glands to release too much of another stress hormone called **cortisol**.

The net effect of this chain of events is to arouse various body systems, getting them ready to cope with a threat or rise to a challenge. In a short-term crisis, this is a highly adaptive response. But when the stress response stays activated for a long time, it affects the body much like constant revving affects an engine. The wear and tear can take a toll, and depression is one possible consequence.

*See also:* Hypothalamic-Pituitary-Adrenal Axis

**Further Information.** American Association of Clinical Endocrinologists, 245 Riverside Avenue, Suite 200, Jacksonville, FL 32202, (904) 353-7878, www.aace.com.

Endocrine Society, 8401 Connecticut Avenue, Suite 900, Chevy Chase, MD 20815, (888) 363-6274, www.endo-society.org.

Hormone Foundation, (800) 467-6663, www.hormone.org.

National Endocrine and Metabolic Diseases Information Service, 6 Information Way, Bethesda, MD 20892-3569, (888) 828-0904, www.endocrine.niddk.nih.gov.

*Bibliography*

*Introduction to the Endocrine System.* National Cancer Institute, http://training.seer.cancer.gov/module _anatomy/unit6_1_endo_intro.html.

*The Endocrine System: Diseases, Types of Hormones and More.* Hormone Foundation, http://www .hormone.org/endo101.

*The Endocrine System: Endocrine Glands and Types of Hormones.* Hormone Foundation, http://www.hormone.org/Endo101/page2.cfm.

*The Wired Brain: Advanced.* Canadian Institute of Neurosciences, Mental Health and Addiction, http://thebrain.mcgill.ca/flash/a/a_01/a_01_cr/a_01_cr_fon/a_01_cr_fon.html.

*The Wired Brain: Intermediate.* Canadian Institute of Neurosciences, Mental Health and Addiction, http://thebrain.mcgill.ca/flash/i/i_01/i_01_cr/i_01_cr_fon/i_01_cr_fon.html.

**ENDORPHINS.** Endorphins are **neurotransmitters**—chemical messengers within the brain. They are classified as endogenous opioids, which means they are substances produced by the body that have mood-elevating and pain-relieving effects similar to those of morphine. Researchers have found that some people with depression show abnormal patterns of endorphin activity.

Mu-opioid **receptors** are specialized sites on cells that bind to and react with endorphins. One **brain imaging** study of mu-opioid receptors by University of Michigan researchers included 14 women with **major depression** and 14 healthy women of the same age and educational level. The women were asked to recall a very sad event from their lives while lying in a positron emission tomography (PET) scanner. They also had their brains imaged during a neutral emotional state. Some, but not all, of the depressed women showed exaggerated responses in the mu-opioid system.

The researchers speculated that this might have been part of a larger dysfunction in the body's response to **stress**. Other research has shown that some people with depression have an overactive stress response, which causes them to react strongly to the slightest provocation.

*Bibliography*

Kennedy, Susan E., Robert A. Koeppe, Elizabeth A. Young, and Jon-Kar Zubieta. "Dysregulation of Endogenous Opioid Emotion Regulation Circuitry in Major Depression in Women." *Archives of General Psychiatry* 63 (2006): 1199–1208.

Society for Neuroscience. *Brain Facts: A Primer on the Brain and Nervous System.* 6th ed. Washington, DC: Society for Neuroscience, 2008.

**ENVIRONMENTAL FACTORS.**   Depression is thought to be caused by a mixture of genetic, biological, psychological, and environmental factors. The latter are factors outside the person that influence that individual's functioning and behavior. A large body of evidence shows that both everyday life **stress** and once-in-a-lifetime **traumatic events** may trigger or worsen depression in susceptible individuals. A smaller number of studies suggest that certain types of **pollution** may cause neurological damage that increases the chance of becoming depressed.

Social and **cultural factors** can have a big impact on mental health as well. Consider low **socioeconomic status** (SES), which is associated with a higher-than-average rate of depressive symptoms. People from the lowest rung on the economic ladder are at risk for stressful situations, such as job loss, money problems, unsafe neighborhoods, and social discrimination. The resulting stress may play into depression. In addition, people who lack economic resources may have trouble getting good mental health care when they need it, making it less likely that depression will be diagnosed promptly and treated effectively.

Although environmental factors are undoubtedly important, the fact remains that most people who are faced with hardship and stress do not become depressed. Conversely, some people who are depressed seem to all outward appearances to be living the good life. Genetic and biological factors may influence how strongly people react to life stress or how likely they are to wind up in risky situations. Characteristic thinking patterns and personality styles also may mediate the complex interplay between nature and nurture.

*See also:* Adjustment Disorder with Depressed Mood; Causes of Depression; Diathesis-Stress Model; Genetic Factors; Relationship Issues; School Issues; Workplace Issues

*Bibliography*

Beseler, Cheryl L., Lorann Stallones, Jane A. Hoppin, Michael C. R. Alavanja, Aaron Blair, Thomas Keefe, et al. "Depression and Pesticide Exposures Among Private Pesticide Applicators Enrolled in the Agricultural Health Study." *Environmental Health Perspectives* 116 (2008): 1713–1719.

Monroe, Scott M., George M. Slavich, and Katholiki Georgiades. "The Social Environment and Life Stress in Depression." In *Handbook of Depression.* 2nd ed., by Ian H. Gotlib and Constance L. Hammen, eds., 340–360. New York: Guilford Press, 2009.

Norris, Fran H. *Range, Magnitude, and Duration of the Effects of Disasters on Mental Health: Review Update 2005.* Research Education Disaster Mental Health, March 2005, http://www.redmh.org/research/general/REDMH_effects.pdf.

Siefert, Kristine, Phillip J. Bowman, Colleen M. Heflin, Sheldon Danziger, and David R. Williams. "Social and Environmental Predictors of Maternal Depression in Current and Recent Welfare Recipients." *American Journal of Orthopsychiatry* 70 (2000): 510–522.

**EPILEPSY.**   Epilepsy is a brain disorder that produces brief disturbances in the normal pattern of electrical charges passing between nerve cells in the brain and going out to all parts of the body. In epilepsy, this pattern is disrupted by short bursts of high-intensity electrical activity, called seizures. These bursts can affect a person's emotions, sensations, and behavior. In some, but not all cases, they lead to convulsions, muscle spasms, and loss of consciousness.

Depression is the most common mental disorder that coexists with epilepsy. Prevalence estimates vary depending on how depression is defined, but when standardized methods are used, about 29 percent of people with epilepsy have **major depression**. For these individuals, depression can greatly diminish their quality of life, frequently even more than seizures do. People with untreated depression tend to have more health problems than those who are not depressed, and the **suicide** rate among people with epilepsy is substantially higher than in the general population.

Too often, though, depression goes unrecognized, perhaps because patients and even doctors consider it a "normal" reaction to the burden of having a chronic disorder. Some also think of depression as being "part of epilepsy" and therefore not something requiring special attention. As a result, about half of people with epilepsy who are also depressed are never treated for depression.

But it does not have to be this way. By seeking proper diagnosis and treatment for depression, people with epilepsy can take a big step toward making their lives easier and more enjoyable.

***The Depression Connection.*** Scientists are still sorting out the complex relationship between depression and epilepsy. Certainly, having a chronic disorder can be stressful, and **stress** can trigger depression in some people. In addition, there is evidence that people who feel as if epilepsy controls their lives may have an increased risk of depression.

But beyond these psychological links, there also seems to be a physiological connection between the two conditions. This connection may be due in part to shared brain regions. Also, abnormalities in the brain chemicals **serotonin** and **norepinephrine** have been implicated in both disorders.

For some people, mood changes are clearly linked to the timing of seizures, consistently occurring before, during, or after. But for others, they are not, and in such cases, depression may be tied to the place inside the brain where seizures originate. A seizure that arises from an emotion center may be more likely to produce a change in mood.

Then there is the chicken-and-egg question. Most people assume that epilepsy comes first, giving rise to depression in susceptible individuals. But the relationship cuts both ways. When depression comes first, it increases the risk of later developing epilepsy by up to seven-fold.

***Diagnostic Challenges.*** Some people with epilepsy who are depressed meet all the diagnostic criteria for major depression. Others,

---

### Anticonvulsants and Depression

Some medications used to treat epilepsy can cause depression as a side effect. The best-known example is phenobarbital. But other anticonvulsants—medications taken to prevent seizures—can have this effect as well. Taking several medications for epilepsy may just make the problem worse, and when medications are cut back, the mood frequently improves.

On the flip side, newer anticonvulsants are sometimes actually prescribed to even out mood swings in people with **bipolar disorder**. Gaining better control over seizures also is crucial for reducing stress and enhancing overall well-being. On balance, then, the benefits of epilepsy medications generally far outweigh their risks. But people taking anticonvulsants should let their doctor know about any side effects, including depression. In many cases, the doctor may be able to adjust the treatment regimen to reduce unwanted effects.

however, have periods of depression that never rise to this level, yet cause serious problems. And still others have low moods that look quite different from classic depression, yet respond to **antidepressants**.

To overcome these hurdles, health care professionals have devised a system for classifying the unique forms of depression that occur in epilepsy. This system is based on the relationship of depressive symptoms to ictal, or seizure, phases.

*Preictal Depression.* Depression precedes the seizure by hours to days, often lifting once the seizure arrives. Typical symptoms include **irritability**, poor tolerance for frustration, hyperactivity, and aggressive behavior in children.

*Ictal Depression.* Depressive symptoms occur as part of the seizure itself. The depression comes on swiftly, unrelated to anything in the environment. Typical symptoms include guilt, inability to feel pleasure, and suicidal thoughts. Often these symptoms are followed by a brief loss of awareness.

*Postictal Depression.* Depression comes on after a seizure and lasts for hours to days. Anxiety often occurs at the same time. Many people with this pattern also have atypical symptoms of depression between seizures.

*Interictal Dysphoric Disorder.* Bouts of depression between seizures often have an unusual pattern of symptoms, with a low mood, lack of energy, pain, and trouble sleeping intermixed with feelings of elation, irritability, fear, and anxiety. Such symptoms can occur in various combinations. They tend to last from hours to a few days and often recur interspersed with depression-free periods.

***Treatment Considerations.*** Most people with epilepsy can become seizure-free by taking anticonvulsant medication. Others can reduce the frequency and intensity of their seizures. When medication is not enough, options include surgery and **vagus nerve stimulation** (VNS). The latter uses a small implanted device to deliver mild electrical pulses to the vagus nerve, which connects the brain to the heart, lungs, and digestive tract. Although it is still unclear exactly how this works, most people who try VNS have fewer seizures.

For those whose depression is limited to very brief episodes before or during seizures, getting epilepsy under better control may be all it takes to boost their mood. For others with depression, though, specific treatment for the depressed mood is needed.

**Psychotherapy** can help people gain a firmer grasp on thoughts and behaviors that are contributing to their depression. Antidepressants may be prescribed as well. Antidepressants lower the seizure threshold, making it slightly easier for a seizure to occur. These medications also can interact with **anticonvulsants**, affecting how both drugs work. It may take a few tries to find the best medications and dosages for a given person. Overall, though, antidepressants can often be beneficial.

VNS targets areas of the brain that affect mood, and it also influences the activity of brain chemicals such as serotonin and norepinephrine. As a result, VNS is used not only for hard-to-control epilepsy, but also for depression that does not respond to standard treatments. When other options fail, VNS may offer some relief for both conditions.

*See also:* Mood Disorder Due to a General Medical Condition; Neurological Disorders; Physical Illness

***Further Information.*** American Epilepsy Society, 342 N. Main Street, West Hartford, CT 06117, (860) 586-7505, www.aesnet.org.

Epilepsy Foundation, 8301 Professional Place, Landover, MD 20785, (800) 332-1000, www.epilepsyfoundation.org.

National Institute of Neurological Disorders and Stroke, P.O. Box 5801, Bethesda, MD 20824, (800) 352-9424, www.ninds.nih.gov.

## Bibliography

Barry, John J., Alan B. Ettinger, Peggy Friel, Frank C. Gilliam, Cynthia L. Harden, Bruce Hermann, et al. "Consensus Statement: The Evaluation and Treatment of People with Epilepsy and Affective Disorders." *Epilepsy and Behavior* 13 (2008): S1–S29.

Blumer, Dietrich, Georgia Montouris, and Keith Davies. "The Interictal Dysphoric Disorder: Recognition, Pathogenesis, and Treatment of the Major Psychiatric Disorder of Epilepsy." *Epilepsy and Behavior* 5 (2004): 826–840.

Boland, Robert. "Depression in Medical Illness (Secondary Depression)." In *The American Psychiatric Publishing Textbook of Mood Disorders,* by Dan J. Stein, David J. Kupfer, and Alan F. Schatzberg, eds., 639–652. Washington, DC: American Psychiatric Publishing, 2006.

*Curing Epilepsy: The Promise of Research.* National Institute of Neurological Disorders and Stroke, October 6, 2008, http://www.ninds.nih.gov/disorders/epilepsy/epilepsy_research.htm.

*Depession and Epilepsy.* Epilepsy Foundation, http://www.epilepsyfoundation.org/answerplace/Medical/related/Depression/epilepsy.cfm.

*Frequently Asked Questions.* Epilepsy Foundation, http://www.epilepsyfoundation.org/answerplace/faq.cfm.

*Issues with Medicines.* Epilepsy Foundation, http://www.epilepsyfoundation.org/about/related/depression/medicines.cfm.

Kanner, Andres M. "Depression in Epilepsy Is Much More Than a Reactive Process." *Epilepsy Currents* 3 (2003): 202–203.

*Next Steps: Getting the Treatment You Need to Reach Real Recovery.* Depression and Bipolar Support Alliance, 2006, http://www.dbsalliance.org/pdfs/NextSteps.pdf.

*NINDS Epilepsy Information Page.* National Institute of Neurological Disorders and Stroke, October 6, 2008, http://www.ninds.nih.gov/disorders/epilepsy/epilepsy.htm.

Seethalakshmi, R., and Ennapadam S. Krishnamoorthy. "Depression in Epilepsy: Phenomenology, Diagnosis and Management." *Epileptic Disorders* 9 (2007): 1–10.

*Treatment for Depression.* Epilepsy Foundation, http://www.epilepsyfoundation.org/about/related/depression/treatment.cfm.

*Vagus Nerve Stimulation Therapy.* Epilepsy Foundation, http://www.epilepsyfoundation.org/answerplace/Medical/treatment/vns.

**ESTROGEN.** Estrogen is a hormone that is produced chiefly by the ovaries, although smaller amounts are made by the adrenal glands and other tissues. The hormone plays a pivotal role in female puberty and menstruation, but it also has non-reproductive functions. Fluctuations in estrogen levels during the menstrual cycle and over the lifespan may disrupt brain chemicals that affect mood, increasing the risk of depression in susceptible **women**.

Although estrogen is mainly known as a female sex hormone, men also make small amounts. Men do not experience dramatic changes in estrogen levels the way women do, however. Scientists have long noted that women's risk of depression seems to rise considerably at times when **hormones** are in flux.

There are three main forms of estrogen: estradiol, estriol, and estrone. Estradiol, secreted mainly by the ovaries but also made by the adrenal glands and testes, is the most potent form of estrogen. In women, normal levels of estradiol support ovulation, conception, and pregnancy. The hormone also helps promote healthy bones and regulate cholesterol levels. Estriol, produced in the placenta, is the major estrogen in pregnancy. Estrone, obtained from the adrenal glands and also made in fatty tissue, is the major estrogen in women after **menopause**.

***The Female Experience.*** In 2002, the Women's Health Initiative, a major research program looking at health issues in menopausal women, halted an arm of the study in which women were taking hormone replacement therapy consisting of estrogen plus progesterone. The researchers announced startling results in these women: an increased risk of breast cancer, heart disease, stroke, blood clots, and urinary incontinence. The announcement had an immediate impact. Physicians stopped prescribing the therapy, and many women who were already on the hormones abruptly stopped taking them.

Within two months, doctors noticed a new trend. Middle-aged women with a history of depression who had been fine while taking hormones began to feel depressed again shortly after stopping hormone therapy. When their depression came back, symptoms reappeared in an average of just three weeks, even in women who had been well for several years. It was not clear whether the resurgence of symptoms was due to lower hormone levels per se or to the sudden drop in hormones. But what was clear was the powerful effect that estrogen can exert on women's moods.

*Changing Estrogen Levels.*    Before puberty, girls and boys have similar rates of depression. But at puberty, a gender gap emerges, and from then on, women are twice as likely as men to become depressed. Female hormones fluctuate dramatically around the time of puberty, childbirth, and menopause. It is probably no coincidence that these are also occasions when depression is more likely to occur.

Of course, estrogen is not the only thing changing at these times. Other biological, social, and cultural factors are undoubtedly important as well. All these factors may interact to raise the risk of developing depression at various stages in a woman's life.

Monthly fluctuations related to the menstrual cycle also may contribute to premenstrual mood swings in some women. Estrogen early in the cycle constructs synapses, the gaps between neurons where messages are exchanged, and the withdrawal of estrogen later in the cycle tears these synapses down.

**The Depression Connection.**    In the brain, estrogen may boost the activity of chemicals such as **serotonin** and **norepinephrine**, which are thought to play key roles in depression. Estrogen also stimulates the production of enzymes that facilitate the transmission of chemical messages in the brain as well as **receptors** that receive the messages.

In the late 1970s and early 1980s, analyses of brain tissue from newborn mice showed that estrogen promoted the growth of **neurons**, tree-shaped nerve cells that transmit chemical messages. The hormone sprouted the cells' branch-like receiving extensions, called dendrites. It also enhanced the growth of the cells' trunk-like sending extensions, called axons.

More recent research has shown that estrogen can also promote new connections between neurons in mature animals. This suggests that it may help the adult brain process information. And in fact, studies indicate that the hormone may have beneficial effects on memory in both healthy women without functioning ovaries and postmenopausal women with Alzheimer's disease.

Studies have shown that estradiol by itself can sometimes relieve depression during the transitional period leading up to menopause. In women with hard-to-treat depression, some researchers have combined estrogen with **antidepressants** when either treatment alone was not enough.

*See also*: Endocrine System; Postpartum Depression; Premenstrual Dysphoric Disorder

*Bibliography*

*Depression in Women: Understanding the Gender Gap.* Mayo Clinic, September 6, 2008, http://www.mayoclinic.com/health/depression/MH00035.

*Estrogen.* American Association for Clinical Chemistry, May 15, 2006, http://www.labtestsonline.org/ understanding/analytes/estrogen/sample.html.

*Estrogen's Influence on the Brain.* Society for Neuroscience, http://www.sfn.org/index.cfm?pagename =brainBriefings_estrogensInfluenceOnTheBrain.

*Menopausal Hormone Replacement Therapy Use and Cancer: Questions and Answers.* National Cancer Institute, October 5, 2007, http://www.cancer.gov/cancertopics/factsheet/Risk/menopausal-hormones.

Stahl, Stephen M. *Effects of Estrogen on the Central Nervous System.* Clinical Neuroscience Research Center (San Diego) and University of California-San Diego, http://www.psychiatrist.com/pcc/ brainstorm/br6205.htm.

Stahl, Stephen M. *Estrogen Makes the Brain a Sex Organ.* Clinical Neuroscience Research Center (San Diego) and University of California-San Diego, http://www.psychiatrist.com/pcc/brainstorm/ br5810.htm.

Stewart, Donna E., Danielle E. Rolfe, and Emma Robertson. "Depression, Estrogen, and the Women's Health Initiative." *Psychosomatics* 45 (2004): 445–447.

**ETHNICITY.**    Ethnicity refers to an individual's membership in a particular social group that shares a collective identity based on history, culture, language, and sometimes religion. This concept is a bit different from race, a social group defined largely by ancestry, geographical origins, and physical features, such as skin color. But as society has become more aware of social factors, such as political heritage, that underlie racial divisions, the distinctions between ethnicity and race have become blurred. The two terms are now often used synonymously or combined in the hybrid term "race/ethnicity."

Evidence on the relative prevalence of depression in different ethnic groups is mixed. For example, most studies have found that **African Americans** have lower rates of depression than their white counterparts, but some have found equivalent or even higher rates.

One reason for such contradictory results may be that many studies have failed to distinguish clearly between different types of depression. A large, nationally representative survey found a higher lifetime prevalence of **major depression** in white individuals than in African Americans and Mexican Americans. However, the pattern was reversed for **dysthymia**, a milder but very long-lasting depressive disorder.

Another study found that Native Hawaiian youth were less likely than white youth to be diagnosed with depression or dysthymia, but more likely to be diagnosed with disruptive behavior disorders. This finding may partly reflect genuine ethnic variations in prevalence. But it also may partly reflect differences in how symptoms are interpreted by mental health care providers depending on the ethnicity of the patient.

Overall, any small ethnic differences in prevalence are dwarfed by a larger truth: Depression cuts across all

### Racism and Discrimination

Racism and discrimination refer to beliefs, attitudes, and practices that denigrate individuals or groups because of their ethnic group membership or physical characteristics, such as skin color. Being the target of racism and discrimination is stressful in itself, and it also may contribute to lower **socioeconomic status** and limited social opportunities. The resulting **stress**, in turn, may trigger depression in some vulnerable individuals. However, there is no evidence that living with racism and discrimination, as unpleasant and unfair as that may be, can cause full-blown depression in those who are not already susceptible to the disorder.

social categories. Although ethnic and **cultural factors** may influence how people experience the disorder and the type of care they receive, such factors do not necessarily have a major impact on who becomes depressed in the first place.

***Disparities in Mental Health Care.*** Once a disorder such as depression is present, the findings on ethnic disparities in treatment have been more consistent. Most studies have found lower treatment rates for ethnic minorities than for white Americans. There are several possible explanations for this difference.

*Stigma and Mistrust.* The **stigma** attached to **mental illness** discourages some people from seeking help. Ethnic minorities in the United States tend to hold attitudes toward mental illness that are at least as negative as those held by their white counterparts, and sometimes even more unfavorable. As a group, ethnic minorities also tend to be mistrustful of mental health services—another factor that may deter individuals from getting appropriate treatment.

*Culture and Language.* Cultural misunderstandings and language differences are important barriers, hindering communication between patients and mental health care providers. Consider the fact that there is no word for "depressed" in the languages of some **American Indians and Alaska Natives**. That fact does not preclude members of these groups from becoming depressed, but it does make communicating about the disorder more of a challenge.

*Lack of Access.* Lack of access to high-quality services is another major barrier to mental health care. Compared to other ethnic groups, a higher proportion of African Americans and **Hispanic Americans** are either uninsured or covered by Medicaid, a joint federal and state program that provides medical assistance for some people with low incomes and limited resources.

*Clinician Bias.* Finally, mental health professionals are not immune to the same kinds of prejudice and stereotyping that permeate the rest of society. Although such attitudes may be less overt today than in the past, they still may exert a subtle influence on diagnosis and treatment. One study found that white therapists rated the videotape of an African American patient with depression more negatively than they did the tape of a white patient with the same symptoms.

Even positive stereotypes can be detrimental. For instance, the stereotype of Asian Americans as being free of problems may cause health care providers to miss signs of distress. Ethnicity is a core part of a person's identity, so it should not be overlooked. But it also should not be allowed to overshadow the individual differences that make each person so wonderfully unique.

*See also:* Asian Americans and Pacific Islanders

***Further Information.*** National Center for Cultural Competence, Georgetown University Center for Child & Human Development, Box 571485, Washington, DC 20057, (800) 788-2066, www11.georgetown.edu/research/gucchd/nccc.

Office of Minority Health, U.S. Department of Health and Human Services, P.O. Box 37337, Washington, D.C. 20013, (800) 444-6472, www.omhrc.gov.

## Bibliography

Berndt, Julia, and Cara James. *The Effects of the Economic Recession on Communities of Color.* Kaiser Family Foundation, July 2009, http://www.kff.org/minorityhealth/upload/7953.pdf.

Bhopal, R. "Glossary of Terms Relating to Ethnicity and Race: For Reflection and Debate." *Journal of Epidemiology and Community Health* 58 (2004): 441–445.

Jenkins-Hall, K., and William P. Sacco. "Effect of Client Race and Depression on Evaluations by White Therapists." *Journal of Social and Clinical Psychology* 10 (1991): 322–333.

Nguyen, Ly, Larke N. Huang, Girlyn F. Arganza, and Qinghong Liao. "The Influence of Race and Ethnicity on Psychiatric Diagnoses and Clinical Characteristics of Children and Adolescents in Children's Services." *Cultural Diversity and Ethnic Minority Psychology* 13 (2007): 18–25.

Riolo, Stephanie A., Tuan Anh Nguyen, John F. Greden, and Cheryl A. King. "Prevalence of Depression by Race/Ethnicity: Findings From the National Health and Nutrition Examination Survey III." *American Journal of Public Health* 95 (2005): 998–1000.

Simpson, Sherri M., Laura L. Krishnan, Mark E. Kunik, and Pedro Ruiz. "Racial Disparities in Diagnosis and Treatment of Depression: A Literature Review." *Psychiatric Quarterly* 78 (2007): 3–14.

U.S. Department of Health and Human Services. *Culture, Race, and Ethnicity: A Supplement to Mental Health: A Report of the Surgeon General.* Rockville, MD: U.S. Department of Health and Human Services, 2001.

**EVOLUTIONARY PERSPECTIVE.**    Evolution refers to a change in inherited traits that is passed down to successive generations of an organism. The change is accomplished largely through natural selection, the process by which those organisms best adapted to their environment are more likely to survive and reproduce, thus passing along their genetic characteristics. Many evolutionary psychologists argue that transient **sadness** or a slightly down **mood** serve an adaptive role that can help ensure survival under certain circumstances.

Opinions vary when it comes to more severe depression. Some see it as a case where a normal, healthy adaptation has been taken to an abnormal, unhealthy extreme. Others believe that even severe depression has an adaptive function.

Regardless of severity, the characteristics of a depressed mood include low motivation, lack of energy, and loss of interest. The passive behavior arising from these characteristics might sound self-defeating, but it could be helpful to people in situations where active striving is likely to result in emotional loss, bodily harm, or wasted effort. Therefore, by inhibiting action, depression may confer an advantage in situations where a more active response might well be dangerous or futile.

***Evolutionary Theories of Depression.***    Much has been written about the biological and environmental factors that lead to depression. But evolutionary theorists try to explain why people have the capacity for becoming depressed in the first place. Possible roles for depression include communicating a need for help, minimizing risk in social situations, disengaging from unreachable goals, and conserving energy and resources for situations that are most likely to pay off.

*Communicating a Need for Help.*    U.S. psychologist Robert Plutchik (1927–2006) noted that sadness is often brought on by the loss of someone or something important. This loss may lead to **crying**, a sad facial expression, and other distress signals. Such signals, in turn, may arouse sympathetic feelings in other people, who may then offer help and support. In this view, depression is a persistent distress signal that constantly seeks to elicit helpful behavior from others. The problem is that it involves feeling distressed all the time. In addition, when distress signals continue too long, they may drive away others rather than attract help.

*Minimizing Risk in Social Situations.*    This theory states that depressed moods evolved to minimize social risk. Ideally, a person's value to society outweighs the burden that individual puts on others. But at times, social burden equals or exceeds social value, and the individual is in danger of being excluded from social interactions that are critical for survival. In such situations, a down mood may decrease the risk of exclusion. First it heightens sensitivity to being devalued and thus at risk of becoming an outcast. Then it leads to depressed behavior, which decreases the individual's desire for resources, such as food and sex, and signals others that the person is no threat. Such behavior reduces the person's burden on society, tipping the value-burden balance in a more favorable direction.

*Disengaging from Unreachable Goals.* According to this view, the most depressing situations are ones in which people pursue goals they cannot achieve. A low mood is nature's way of making people give up on such goals before too much time and energy have been wasted. Full-blown depression may set in when someone fails to give up on an unattainable goal, either because the goal is too personally important or because the individual sees no way out of the situation.

*Conserving Energy and Resources.* A depressed mood may also occur when a person's efforts yield a low rate of return. U.S. psychiatrist Randolph M. Nesse (1948– ) has proposed that a down mood discourages wasted energy and resources in situations that are unlikely to result in a payoff. In this way, resources are conserved for times when effort has a better chance of being rewarded.

*See also:* Emotion

*Bibliography*

Allen, Nicholas B., and Paul B. T. Badcock. "The Social Risk Hypothesis of Depressed Mood: Evolutionary, Psychosocial and Neurobiological Perspectives." *Psychological Bulletin* 129 (2003): 887–913.

Keller, Matthew C., and Randolph M. Neese. "The Evolutionary Significance of Depressive Symptoms: Different Adverse Situations Lead to Different Depressive Symptom Patterns." *Journal of Personality and Social Psychology* 91 (2006): 316–330.

Neese, Randolph M. "Is Depression an Adaptation?" *Archives of General Psychiatry* 57 (2000): 14–20.

Plutchik, Robert. *Emotions and Life: Perspectives From Psychology, Biology, and Evolution.* Washington, DC: American Psychological Association, 2003.

Snibbe, A. C. "Evolutionary Psychology: Examining the Origins of the Murderous, the Melancholic and the Miffed." *Monitor of Psychology* 35 (2004): 24.

**EXERCISE.** Exercise is one of the cornerstones of health and wellness. Done frequently and consistently, it can help strengthen muscles and bones, maintain a healthy weight, and reduce the risk for cardiovascular disease, type 2 diabetes, and certain cancers. Other benefits of regular physical activity include enhanced mental health and a decreased risk of developing depression.

Research has shown that physically active people tend to have better self-esteem and more positive moods than those who are sedentary. More active individuals also tend to report having a higher quality of life. Plus, studies have found that regular physical activity can help keep mental skills—such as thinking, learning, and judgment—sharp as people age.

***Two Types of Exercise.*** Two important types of exercise are aerobic physical activity and muscle-strengthening physical activity.

*Aerobic Exercise.* Aerobic physical activity (also called cardio training or endurance exercise) involves moving the large muscles of the arms and/or legs in a rhythmic manner for a sustained period. This type of exercise raises people's heart rate and makes them breathe harder. Aerobic activity improves heart and lung fitness. Examples include brisk walking, running, cycling, lap swimming, and doubles tennis.

Moderate-intensity aerobic activity involves working hard enough to get the heart beating a little faster and break a sweat. People exercising at moderate intensity are able to talk, but are too winded to sing a song. According to the Centers for Disease Control and Prevention (CDC), most adults need at least 150 minutes of moderate-intensity aerobic activity every week. Ideally, this should be spread out over several days. Within a single day, it can be broken up into bouts of no less than 10 minutes each.

Vigorous-intensity aerobic activity involves working hard enough to get the heart beating quite a bit faster. People exercising at a vigorous intensity are not able to say more than a few words without pausing to catch their breath. Those who are fit and healthy enough may choose to do at least 75 weekly minutes of vigorous-intensity activity, such as running or fast cycling, in place of moderate-intensity exercise.

*Muscle-Strengthening Exercise.* Muscle-strengthening physical activity (also called weight training or resistance exercise) involves doing things that increase the strength, power, mass, and endurance of skeletal muscles.

One way to strengthen the muscles is by training with dumbbells, barbells, weight machines, or resistance bands. Other ways include practicing **yoga**, doing exercises that use body weight for resistance (such as sit-ups and push-ups), and doing heavy chores (such as digging and shoveling). The CDC recommends doing muscle-strengthening activities on two or more days a week that work all the major muscle groups (legs, hips, back, abdomen, chest, shoulders, and arms).

### Two-For-One Exercise

The term mind/body exercise is sometimes used to describe activities that combine physical movement with mental focus and controlled breathing. Examples include yoga, tai chi, and Pilates. On a physical level, such activities may enhance strength, balance, flexibility, and overall health. On a psychological level, they may help reduce stress, increase mind/body awareness, and instill a sense of enhanced well-being.

***Working Out Depression.*** Research has shown that doing aerobic activity or a mix of aerobic and muscle-strengthening activities, three to five times a week for at least 30 minutes at a time, can lead to significant improvements in mental health. Some scientific evidence suggests that even lower levels of activity may be beneficial.

A recent analysis of 25 studies that used exercise to treat depression found moderate improvement in symptoms overall. When exercise was compared to **antidepressants** or **cognitive-behavioral therapy**, the benefits were similar. Results of studies that included follow-up periods suggest that exercise needs to be continued long-term to maintain the initial improvement in mood.

Researchers still are not sure exactly how exercise boosts mood, but several possibilities have been suggested. Exercise may serve as a welcome diversion from negative thoughts. The mastery of new skills also may offer a much-needed lift to people's confidence. When exercise is done with others, the social contact may be therapeutic as well.

On a physiological level, exercise may raise levels of mood-enhancing brain chemicals, including **endorphins**. It also may reduce blood levels of the stress hormone **cortisol**, which tend to be elevated in people with depression. In addition, exercise releases muscle tension, improves sleep, and increases body temperature, which may have a calming effect.

More recent studies suggest that exercise may stimulate the creation of new nerve cells in the brain, a process known as neurogenesis. It also may lead to the release of small proteins in the brain—such as **brain-derived neurotrophic factor** (BDNF)—that are needed for the growth and survival of specific groups of brain cells. BDNF affects brain cells related to chemicals that are involved in depression, such as **serotonin** and **dopamine**.

***Further Information.*** American College of Sports Medicine, P.O. Box 1440, Indianapolis, IN 46206-1440, (317) 637-9200, www.acsm.org.

American Council on Exercise, 4851 Paramount Drive, San Diego, CA 92123, (858) 279-8227, www.acefitness.org.

Centers for Disease Control and Prevention; Division of Nutrition, Physical Activity and Obesity; 4770 Buford Highway N.E.; MS/K-24; Atlanta GA 30341; (800) 232-4636, www.cdc.gov/physicalactivity.

President's Council on Physical Fitness and Sports, 200 Independence Avenue S.W., Room 738-H, Washington, DC 20201, (202) 690-9000, www.fitness.gov.

## Bibliography

Blumenthal, James A., Michael A. Babyak, P. Murali Doraiswamy, Lana Watkins, Benson M. Hoffman, Krista A. Barbour, et al. "Exercise and Pharmacotherapy in the Treatment of Major Depressive Disorder." *Psychosomatic Medicine* 69 (2007): 587–596.

*Depression and Anxiety: Exercise Eases Symptoms.* Mayo Clinic, October 23, 2007, http://www .mayoclinic.com/health/depression-and-exercise/MH00043.

*Exercise (Physical Activity), Mental Health and Mental Ability.* American Heart, http://www.american heart.org/presenter.jhtml?identifier=4550.

*How Much Physical Activity Do Adults Need?* Centers for Disease Control and Prevention, December 17, 2008, http://www.cdc.gov/physicalactivity/everyone/guidelines/adults.html.

Mead, Gillian E., Wendy Morley, Paul Campbell, Carolyn A. Greig, Marion McMurdo, and Debbie A. Lawlor. "Exercise for Depression (Review)." *Cochrane Database of Systematic Reviews* 4 (2008): art. no. CD004366.

*Physical Activity and Health.* Centers for Disease Control and Prevention, December 3, 2008, http://www.cdc.gov/physicalactivity/everyone/health/index.html.

*Tai Chi.* American Cancer Society, November 1, 2008, http://www.cancer.org/docroot/ETO/ content/ETO_5_3X_Tai_Chi.asp.

## F

**FAMILY THERAPY.** Family therapy is a treatment approach that brings together multiple members of a family for **psychotherapy** sessions. The goal is to address relationship problems between individual family members and change dysfunctional behavior patterns of the family unit as a whole. This form of treatment is typically provided by a **marriage and family therapist**.

In family therapy, the family is the "patient." However, that does not mean everyone has to sit down together for every session. At times, the therapist meets with all the family members at once, but at other times, the therapist might meet with specific members individually. Common goals include helping the family resolve problems and helping individual members share thoughts and emotions. Other issues that may be explored include family roles, rules, and expectations.

When one person in a family has depression, the whole family is affected. Depression itself can lead to symptoms—such as withdrawal, disinterest, or irritability—that cause relationship conflicts. In turn, depression can be worsened or prolonged by relationship **stress**.

Family therapy is often used in the treatment of depression, and it frequently seems to be helpful. However, a recent analysis of published studies found insufficient evidence to determine how family therapy stacks up against individual therapy for depression. More research is needed to settle that question.

*Types of Family Therapy.* There are numerous approaches to family-oriented therapy, a few of which are briefly described below. These approaches may be used alone. But when one member of a family has full-blown depression, family therapy may also be combined with individual therapy and/or medication.

*Attachment-Based Family Therapy.* This approach is based on the tenet that extreme family conflict, harsh criticism, lack of emotional rapport, and child abuse or neglect can break the attachment bonds between parents and children. As a result, children may not develop critical coping skills, leaving them vulnerable to stress and depression. The goal of this type of therapy is to mend broken bonds by addressing the underlying causes. It has shown promise as a treatment for depressed **adolescents**.

*Behavioral Family Therapy.* Like individual **behavioral therapy**, this approach is rooted in the principles of learning. The goal is to identify and change maladaptive behavior patterns that are contributing to family problems. Typically, the focus is on the parent-child relationship. The parent learns to use behavioral consequences and rewards to strengthen positive behaviors and weaken negative ones.

*Cognitive-Behavioral Family Therapy.*    Individual **cognitive-behavioral therapy** (CBT) is one of the best-validated treatments for depression. It focuses on identifying and changing dysfunctional patterns of thinking as well as behaving. CBT techniques have been adapted to treating family problems and teaching parenting skills. In one study of depressed mothers with children who were behaving disruptively, cognitive-behavioral family therapy was compared to behavioral family therapy. Initially, both treatments were equally effective at reducing both the mothers' depression and the children's disruptive behavior. But six months after therapy ended, families who got cognitive-behavioral treatment were doing better.

*Object Relations Family Therapy.*    This approach is a variation on **psychodynamic therapy**. Family problems are seen as resulting from a mismatch between a person's unconscious assumptions about how another family member ought to be in a relationship and how that family member actually is. Often, members of a family are locked into a system of mutually mismatched projections. The goal is to develop insight into these dynamics, leading to a more realistic perspective.

*Structural Family Therapy.*    In this approach, problems are thought to arise from an inappropriate family structure and organization. Relationships are conceptualized in terms of distance, falling on a continuum between enmeshed and disengaged. Troubled families tend to fall at one of these extremes. They also tend to have faulty boundaries between parents, children, and the extended family. The goal of therapy is to reorganize the family so that it comes closer to the ideal structure.

*See also:* Couples Therapy; Relationship Issues; Treatment of Depression

***Further Information.***    American Association for Marriage and Family Therapy, 112 S. Alfred Street, Alexandria, VA 22314, (703) 838-9808, www.aamft.org.

## Bibliography

Cottrell, David, and Paula Boston. "Practitioner Review: The Effectiveness of Systemic Family Therapy for Children and Adolescents." *Journal of Child Psychology and Psychiatry* 43 (2002): 573–586.

Diamond, Gary M., Guy S. Diamond, and Aaron Hogue. "Attachment-Based Family Therapy: Adherence and Differentiation." *Journal of Marital and Family Therapy* 33 (2007): 177–191.

*Family Therapy: Healing Family Conflicts.* Mayo Clinic, October 10, 2007, http://www.mayoclinic.com/health/family-therapy/HQ00662.

*Frequently Asked Questions on Marriage and Family Therapists.* American Association for Marriage and Family Therapy, 2002, http://www.aamft.org/faqs/index_nm.asp.

Henken, H. T., M. J. H. Huibers, R. Churchill, K. Restifo, and J. Roelofs. "Family Therapy for Depression (Review)." *Cochrane Database of Systematic Reviews* 3 (2007): art. no. CD006728.

Sanders, Matthew R., and Margaret McFarland. "Treatment of Depressed Mothers with Disruptive Children: A Controlled Evaluation of Cognitive Behavioral Family Intervention." *Behavior Therapy* 31 (2000): 89–112.

**FIVE-FACTOR MODEL.**    The five-factor model is an influential theory of personality proposed by U.S. psychologists Robert R. McCrae and Paul T. Costa Jr. The theory posits that personality has five major factors: Openness to Experience, Conscientiousness, Extraversion,

Agreeableness, and Neuroticism (OCEAN). Individuals vary along a continuum on each of these factors, with most people falling in between the two extremes. The makeup of an individual's personality may affect that person's vulnerability to becoming depressed.

The five-factor model was derived from linguistic analyses of personality-related adjectives as well as research using self-report questionnaires. Data from these studies were analyzed using a statistical procedure called factor analysis, which boils down large data sets to the smallest number of concepts (factors) required to explain the pattern of relationships in the data.

To assess the five domains of personality, Costa and McCrae developed a questionnaire called the NEO Personality Inventory. (NEO was originally short for Neuroticism Extraversion Openness, the only three factors measured on the first version of the test.) The latest incarnation, called the NEO PI-R, was introduced in 1992. With 240 items that are rated on a five-point scale, it takes about 20 to 40 minutes to complete.

***Five Factors of Personality.*** In this model, the five personality domains are thought to be relatively stable throughout adult life. Based on studies analyzing personality-related adjectives from different languages across diverse cultures, they are also considered universal. In addition, research indicates that the five factors and their component traits are least partly inherited. Following is a brief description of each factor.

*Openness to Experience.* This factor is characterized by an appreciation for new experiences and a willingness to consider novel ideas. It includes openness to fantasy, aesthetics, feelings, actions, ideas, and values.

*Conscientiousness.* This factor deals with the persistence, organization, and motivation needed to work toward goals. It includes competence, order, dutifulness, achievement striving, self-discipline, and deliberation.

*Extraversion.* This factor addresses the quantity and intensity of social interactions as well as the capacity for joy. It includes warmth, gregariousness, assertiveness, activity, excitement seeking, and positive emotions.

*Agreeableness.* This factor deals with the quality of social interactions along a continuum from compassion to antagonism. It includes trust, straightforwardness, altruism, compliance, modesty, and tender-mindedness.

*Neuroticism.* This factor reflects a tendency toward negative emotions and psychological distress. It includes depression, anxiety, hostility, self-consciousness, impulsiveness, and vulnerability to stress.

***Personality and Depression.*** Depression is a complex condition with multiple causes. Some people with a family history of depression or a personal history of trauma become depressed, but others do not. Personality may be one thing that helps determine how a given person responds to such genetic or environmental pressures.

On the face of it, the personality factor that seems most closely tied to depression is Neuroticism. In one particularly compelling study, researchers in Sweden sent a questionnaire that measured Neuroticism and Extraversion to a large number of same-sex twins in the early 1970s. Over 25 years later, researchers interviewed more than 20,000 of these twins and assessed their lifetime history of **major depression**. High Neuroticism scores were strongly associated with the risk for depression later in life. Further analyses showed that this association was largely due to the close relationship between Neuroticism and genetic risk for depressive illness.

Some facets of Openness to Experience may contribute to depression as well. One study found that Openness to Fantasy was associated with an increased risk of depression, but Openness to Actions had the opposite effect.

*See also:* Personality Factors

*Bibliography*

Acton, G. Scott. "Five-Factor Model." *Great Ideas in Personality,* July 2001, http://www.personality research.org/bigfive.html.

Carillo, J. M., N. Rojo, M. L. Sánchez-Bernardos, and M. D. Avia. "Openness to Experience and Depression." *European Journal of Psychological Assessment* 17 (2001): 130–136.

Jacobs, Nele, Gunter Kenis, Frenk Peeters, Catherine Derom, Robert Vlietinck, and Jim van Os. "Stress-Related Negative Affectivity and Genetically Altered Serotonin Transporter Function: Evidence of Synergism in Shaping Risk of Depression." *Archives of General Psychiatry* 63 (2006): 989–996.

Kendler, Kenneth S., Margaret Gatz, Charles O. Gardner, and Nancy L. Pedersen. "Personality and Major Depression: A Swedish Longitudinal, Population-Based Twin Study." *Archives of General Psychiatry* 63 (1996): 1113–1120.

Kling, Kristen C., Carol D. Ryff, Gayle Love, and Marilyn Essex. "Exploring the Influence of Personality on Depressive Symptoms and Self-Esteem Across a Significant Life Transition." *Journal of Personality and Social Psychology* 85 (2003): 922–932.

McDermut, Wilson, and Mark Zimmerman. "Personality Disorders, Personality Traits, and Defense Mechanisms Measures." In *Handbook of Psychiatric Measures,* 2nd ed., by A. John Rush Jr., Michael B. First, and Deborah Blacker, eds., 687–729. Washington, DC: American Psychiatric Publishing, 2008.

Millon, Theodore. *Masters of the Mind: Exploring the Story of Mental Illness from Ancient Times to the New Millennium.* New York: John Wiley and Sons, 2004.

*NEO Personality Inventory-Revised (NEO PI-R).* Psychological Assessment Resources, 2005, http://www3.parinc.com/products/product.aspx?Productid=NEO-PI-R.

Piedmont, Ralph L. *Test Review: The NEO PI-R.* Association for Assessment in Counseling and Education, May 3, 2001, http://aac.ncat.edu/newsnotes/y97fall.html.

**FLUOXETINE.** (Brand names: Prozac, Sarafem.) Fluoxetine is one of a widely prescribed class of **antidepressants** called **selective serotonin reuptake inhibitors** (SSRIs). These medications increase the brain's available supply of **serotonin**, a chemical messenger that helps regulate mood, sleep, appetite, and sexual drive. As an early drug in the class, fluoxetine—better known by the brand name Prozac—was heavily promoted by its maker, Eli Lilly. Upon being approved for sale in the United States in 1987, the medication was heralded as a major breakthrough in the **treatment of depression**. Compared to other drugs that help people feel better, fluoxetine was portrayed as safe and non-addictive. Although the claims were at times overstated, fluoxetine has in many ways lived up to its reputation, offering the same effectiveness as older antidepressants with fewer severe side effects.

A number of newer antidepressants have since appeared on the U.S. market. Yet fluoxetine remains extremely popular, with prescriptions totaling more than 23 million in 2008. It is still among the best studied and most versatile of all psychiatric medications.

Fluoxetine has been approved by the Food and Drug Administration (FDA) for the treatment of **major depression** both in adults and in young people ages eight to 18. It has also been approved for treating **obsessive-compulsive disorder**, **panic disorder**, and bulimia.

Eli Lilly's exclusive patent on Prozac expired in 2001, so fluoxetine is now available in generic form, too. In addition, it is sold under the brand name Sarafem as a treatment for **premenstrual dysphoric disorder**. A combination product containing fluoxetine and olanzapine (an antipsychotic medication) is marketed under the brand name Symbyax for use in both **treatment-resistant depression** and the depressive phase of **bipolar disorder**.

*A Brief History of Fluoxetine.*   The development of SSRIs in general, and fluoxetine in particular, hinged on the discovery of a physiological process called **reuptake**—the reabsorption of a chemical messenger such as serotonin back into the nerve cell that originally released it. By the late 1960s, scientists had described the production, release, and reuptake of serotonin. They soon realized that blocking serotonin reuptake was one way of regulating how much of the chemical was available for use.

In 1972, researchers at Eli Lilly identified a compound, dubbed LY110140, which selectively blocked serotonin reuptake. Two years later, they published the first lab studies on the compound, and the results looked promising. In 1975, the compound was christened with the generic name fluoxetine, and the following year, an Investigational New Drug application was filed with the FDA. This was the crucial first step toward starting clinical trials to determine the safety and measure the effectiveness of the still-experimental drug in humans.

By 1983, all the requisite clinical trials had been completed, and a New Drug Application was submitted to the FDA seeking approval to market fluoxetine. Results from the trials filled more than 100 volumes of two-inch binders, and the bureaucratic process for reviewing this mound of data was cumbersome. It took another four years before fluoxetine was approved for sale in the United States.

Contrary to popular belief, fluoxetine was not the first SSRI antidepressant. That distinction goes to zimelidine, introduced in Europe in 1982. But zimelidine was withdrawn from the market due to troublesome side effects, and an aggressive marketing campaign by Eli Lilly turned the public spotlight onto fluoxetine.

*Prozac and Pop Culture.*   Even fluoxetine's most ardent supporters could hardly have anticipated the buzz that soon built around the new drug, however. It quickly became one of the most talked about medicines in history. A photo of the green-and-yellow capsule graced the cover of *Newsweek* (March 26, 1990), and the phrase "on Prozac" became synonymous with acting upbeat and peppy.

A memoir titled *Prozac Nation* (1994), by a young U.S. writer named Elizabeth Wurtzel, offered a frank look at the author's struggles with depression and Prozac's role in her recovery. Wurtzel's influential book, as well as innumerable other media accounts, helped secure Prozac's status as a pop culture icon.

Previous antidepressants had made do with hard-to-pronounce names that almost no one could remember. In contrast, the catchy name Prozac soon entered the national lexicon, as apt to be tossed around at a dinner party as in a doctor's office. In the words of a *Newsweek* article published the same year as Wurtzel's memoir, Prozac had become "as familiar as Kleenex and as socially acceptable as spring water."

Riding this wave of popularity, Prozac did not just conquer the existing market for antidepressants. It created an entirely new one among folks who would never have considered taking an antidepressant before. In 1975, annual U.S. sales of all antidepressants totaled a few hundred million dollars. Two decades later, in 1995, annual U.S. sales of Prozac alone reached the $2 billion mark.

*Benefits and Proper Use.*   Studies indicate that from 55 percent to 70 percent of people who take fluoxetine have the severity of their symptoms cut by at least half—a response rate comparable to that for other antidepressants. Unlike the others, though, fluoxetine is the only antidepressant that has gone through the extensive testing to be specifically approved for treating depression in **children**.

Consumers looking for convenience may appreciate Prozac Weekly, which has to be taken just once a week. Those concerned about cost may want to consider the lower-cost generic versions of fluoxetine.

## "Cosmetic Psychopharmacology"

In *Listening to Prozac* (1993), U.S. psychiatrist and bestselling author Peter D. Kramer pondered the possibility of using Prozac to not only treat depression sufferers, but also help healthy individuals who simply want a cheerier disposition:

> But I wondered whether we were ready for "cosmetic psychopharmacology." It was my musings about whether it would be kosher to medicate a patient like Tess in the absence of depression that led me to coin the phrase. Some people might prefer pharmacologic to psychologic self-actualization. Psychic steroids for mental gymnastics, medicinal attacks on the humors, antiwallflower compound—these might be hard to resist. Since you only live once, why not do it as a blonde? Why not as a peppy blonde? Now that questions of personality and social stance have entered the arena of medication, we as a society will have to decide how comfortable we are with using chemicals to modify personality in useful, attractive ways. We may mask the issue by defining less and less severe mood states as pathology, in effect saying, "If it responds to an antidepressant, it's depression." Already, it seems to me, psychiatric diagnosis had been subject to a sort of "diagnostic bracket creep"—the expansion of categories to match the scope of relevant medications . . .
>
> When one pill at breakfast makes you a new person, or makes your patient, or relative, or neighbor a new person, it is difficult to resist the suggestion, the visceral certainty, that who people are is largely biologically determined. I don't mean that it is impossible to escape simplistic biological materialism, but the drama, the rapidity, the thoroughness of drug-induced transformation make simplicity tempting. Drug responses provide hard-to-ignore evidence for certain beliefs—concerning the influence of biology on personality, intellectual performance, and social success—that heretofore we as a society have resisted. When I saw the impact of medication on patients' self-concept, I came to believe that even if we tried to understand these matters completely, new medications would redraw our map of those parts of the self that are biologically responsive, so that we would arrive, as a culture, at a new consensus about the human condition.

"Makeover," from Listening to Prozac by Peter D. Kramer, copyright © 1993 by Peter D. Kramer. Used by permission of Viking Penguin, a division of Penguin Group (USA) Inc.

It can take four to five weeks, and sometimes longer, to feel the full benefits of fluoxetine. Once people start feeling better, they should still continue taking their medication for as long as prescribed to help keep symptoms from coming back.

***Risks and Side Effects.***    About seven percent to 14 percent of people who start taking fluoxetine end up stopping it due to side effects—a discontinuation rate similar to that for other SSRIs and newer antidepressants. Possible side effects include nervousness, nausea, sexual problems, dry mouth, sore throat, drowsiness, weakness, uncontrollable shaking, loss of appetite, weight loss, and excessive sweating. Although such effects are often mild and short-lived, they are occasionally more bothersome and persistent.

**Serotonin syndrome** is a rare but potentially life-threatening drug reaction that can occur when serotonin levels build up to dangerously high levels in the body. This most often occurs when people combine two drugs that each raise serotonin levels. For example, it might happen if fluoxetine is combined with another antidepressant or with certain **migraine** medications, prescription pain relievers, over-the-counter cough medicines, or **St. John's wort** supplements. To prevent problems, people taking fluoxetine should be sure to tell their doctor about any medicines or supplements they are using.

Antidepressants can save lives by reducing depression and thus decreasing the risk of **suicide**. In a small number of children, **adolescents**, and young adults, however, taking antidepressants may actually lead to worsening mood symptoms or increased suicidal thoughts and behavior. Patients taking fluoxetine—or parents of younger patients—should be alert for any suicidal thoughts and actions or unusual changes in mood and behavior. If such symptoms occur, they should contact their doctor right away.

*See also:* Antidepressants and Suicide

### Bibliography

*Antidepressant Medicines: A Guide for Adults with Depression.* Agency for Healthcare Research and Quality, August 2007, http://effectivehealthcare.ahrq.gov/repFiles/AntidepressantsConsumer Guide.pdf.

*Antidepressants: Comparing Effectiveness, Safety, and Price.* Consumer Reports, 2009, http://www.consumerreports.org/health/resources/pdf/best-buy-drugs/Antidepressants_update.pdf.

Eli Lilly. *Medication Guide: Prozac (Fluoxetine Hydrochloride) Pulvule, Oral Solution, Weekly Capsule.* 2009 ver. Food and Drug Administration, http://www.fda.gov/downloads/Drugs/DrugSafety/ucm088999.pdf.

*Fluoxetine.* National Library of Medicine, March 1, 2009, http://www.nlm.nih.gov/medlineplus/druginfo/meds/a689006.html.

Gupta, Sanjay. "If Everyone Were on Prozac . . ." *Time* (January 1, 2003).

Holmes, Stanley, John F. Lauerman, and Jeanne Gordon. "The Culture of Prozac: How a Treatment for Depression Became as Familiar as Kleenex and as Socially Acceptable as Spring Water." *Newsweek* (February 7, 1994).

Kramer, Peter D. *Listening to Prozac.* New York: Viking Penguin, 1993.

Moore, Anna. "Eternal Sunshine." *Guardian.co.uk* (May 13, 2007).

"2008 Top 200 Generic Drugs by Total Prescriptions." *Drug Topics,* 2009, http://drugtopics.modern medicine.com/drugtopics/data/articlestandard//drugtopics/222009/599844/article.pdf.

Wong, David T., Kenneth W. Perry and Frank P. Bymaster. "The Discovery of Fluoxetine Hydrochloride (Prozac)." *Nature Reviews Drug Discovery* 4 (2005): 764–774.

Wurtzel, Elizabeth. *Prozac Nation: Young and Depressed in America—A Memoir.* New York: Riverhead Books, 1994.

**FOLATE.** Folate is a B vitamin that occurs naturally in food, although folic acid is the synthetic form of folate found in **dietary supplements** and added to fortified food products. This vitamin is needed for the proper synthesis of **serotonin**, **dopamine**, and **norepinephrine**—chemical messengers in the brain that are thought to play key roles in depression. One sign of folate deficiency is depressive symptoms. About one third of people with **major depression** have low folate levels.

Scientists are still studying how folate might affect mood. Folate and other B vitamins help break down an amino acid called homocysteine in the body. Homocysteine is then converted into **S-adenosyl-L-methionine** (SAMe), a compound that helps form chemical messengers in the brain. Folate also helps produce tetrahydrobiopterin, another compound needed to make serotonin.

When B vitamin levels are low, homocysteine can build up in the blood. High blood levels of homocysteine are associated with an increased risk of **stroke**. And stroke-related damage in certain areas of the brain may be one reason for the high rate of depression seen in stroke survivors.

The cause-and-effect relationship could go both ways, though. People with depression might fail to get enough folate due to loss of appetite and a poor **diet**. In addition, **alcohol** interferes with the absorption of folate and increases the excretion of folate by the kidneys, so alcohol abuse may be a risk factor for both depression and folate deficiency.

Besides metabolizing homocysteine and helping maintain a healthy brain, folate has other critical functions in the body. It helps produce and maintain new cells, making it especially important during pregnancy and infancy. When women consume enough of the vitamin before and during pregnancy, it reduces the risk of major birth defects of the brain and spine, called neural tube defects. Both children and adults also need folate to produce normal red blood cells and avoid anemia. Plus, folate helps prevent changes in DNA that may lead to cancer.

***Benefits for Depression.***   Low folate levels have been linked to poor response to **selective serotonin reuptake inhibitors** (SSRIs), a widely prescribed type of antidepressant. In one study of 213 people with depression, those who had low levels of folate in their blood before starting an SSRI were less likely to feel better after eight weeks of treatment than those who started with normal levels of folate.

Conversely, studies have shown that augmenting antidepressant treatment with folate leads to greater improvements than the antidepressant alone. It is unclear whether this holds true for people who start out with normal folate levels or only for those with a folate deficiency. Also, some evidence suggests that adding folate may benefit women with depression but not men. More research is needed to sort out these findings.

***Sources of Folate.***   The Recommended Dietary Allowance (RDA) for folate is given in dietary folate equivalents (DFEs) to allow for the fact that synthetic folic acid is more readily absorbed than natural folate. One DFE equals 1 microgram of food folate or 0.6 micrograms of folic acid from supplements and fortified foods. The RDA is 400 DFEs for adults of both sexes, except during pregnancy and breastfeeding, when the daily requirement rises.

Daily Folate Requirement

| Age | Dietary Folate Equivalents (µg)* |
|---|---|
| Birth–6 months | 65** |
| 7–12 months | 80** |
| 1–3 years | 150 |
| 4–8 years | 200 |
| 9–13 years | 300 |
| 14 years and up | 400 |
| Pregnancy | 600 |
| Breastfeeding | 500 |

*1 DFE = 1 µg food folate = 0.6 µg folic acid

** The Institute of Medicine (IOM) of the U.S. National Academies is the scientific body that establishes dietary guidelines for nutrients. For infants, the IOM has set Adequate Intake levels rather than RDAs. This is done when the scientific evidence is insufficient to set a firm RDA, so guidelines instead give the nutrient intake that is assumed to be adequate based on the best available information.

Good food sources of natural folate include leafy green vegetables, such as spinach and turnip greens; fruits, such as oranges and cantaloupe; and dried beans and peas. In the United States, the Food and Drug Administration also requires the addition of folic acid to enriched breads, cereals, flour, cornmeal, pasta, rice, and other grain products. Thanks to this fortification program, most Americans now get enough folate/folic acid from their diet. Folic acid also is available in supplements and multivitamins.

***Side Effects and Cautions.*** Taking too much folic acid can trigger **vitamin B12** deficiency, and permanent nerve damage may result if the deficiency is not corrected. For adults, the upper limit for safe folic acid intake is 1,000 micrograms daily. Because the risk of a B12 deficiency rises with age, those ages 50 and older should talk to a doctor before taking a supplement that contains folic acid. At any age, it is advisable to choose a folic acid supplement that also contains B12.

Natural folate does not carry the same risk, and folate-rich foods also contain many other nutrients and fiber. A balanced diet containing plenty of fruits, vegetables, and beans is recommended for general health, and if it also helps decrease depression, that is a welcome bonus.

***Prescription L-Methoylfolate.*** Even people who get enough folate in their diet or folic acid in supplements may lack the enzymes needed to break down the vitamin properly. A prescription supplement called L-methylfolate may help such individuals. This is the only active form of folate that can cross the blood-brain barrier. Once inside the brain, L-methylfolate aids in the production of serotonin, dopamine, and norepinephrine.

Taking this prescription supplement may improve the benefits of **antidepressants** in people with depression who do not break down folate normally. Research indicates that many people with depression may have a specific genetic factor that impairs folate metabolism this way.

Few side effects have been reported in people taking L-methylfolate. When combined with antidepressants, possible benefits include greater improvements in mood, motivation, alertness, concentration, and sociability. People taking L-methylfolate may start to notice a difference within one to two weeks, although it may take four to six weeks to feel the full effects.

## Bibliography

Coppen, A. and J. Bailey. "Enhancement of the Antidepressant Action of Fluoxetine by Folic Acid: A Randomised, Placebo Controlled Trial." *Journal of Affective Disorders* 60 (2000): 121–130.

*Deplin: A First Choice Depression Augmentation.* Pamlab, 2008, http://www.deplin.com.

*Dietary Supplement Fact Sheet: Folate.* National Institutes of Health Office of Dietary Supplements, August 22, 2005, http://ods.od.nih.gov/factsheets/folate.asp.

Farah, Andrews. "The Role of L-Methylfolate in Depressive Disorders." *CNS Spectrums* 14 (2009): 2–7.

Fava, M., J. S. Borus, J. E. Alpert, A. A. Nierenberg, J. F. Rosenbaum, and T. Bottiglieri. "Folate, Vitamin B12, and Homocysteine in Major Depressive Disorder." *American Journal of Psychiatry* 154 (1997): 426–428.

*Folic Acid.* Centers for Disease Control and Prevention, http://www.cdc.gov/ncbddd/folicacid.

Folstein, Marshal, Timothy Liu, Inga Peter, Jennifer Buel, Lisa Arsenault, Tammy Scott, et al. "The Homocysteine Hypothesis of Depression." *American Journal of Psychiatry* 164 (2007): 861–867.

Kelly, Christopher B., Anne P. McDonnell, Timothy G. Johnston, Claran Mulholland, Stephen J. Cooper, Dorothy McMaster, et al. "The MTHFR C677T Polymorphism Is Associated with Depressive Episodes in Patients from Northern Ireland." *Journal of Psychopharmacology* 18 (2004): 567–571.

Miller, Alan L. "The Methylation, Neurotransmitter, and Antioxidant Connections Between Folate and Depression." *Alternative Medicine Review* 13 (2008): 216–226.

Stahl, Stephen M. "Novel Therapeutics for Depression: L-Methylfolate as a Trimonoamine Modulator and Antidepressant-Augmenting Agent." *CNS Spectrums* 12 (2007): 739–744.

Taylor, M. J., S. Carney, J. Geddes, and G. Goodwin. "Folate for Depressive Disorders (Review)." *Cochrane Database of Systematic Reviews* 2 (2003): art. no. CD003390.

**FREUD, SIGMUND (1856–1939).** Sigmund Freud was an Austrian neurologist and psychiatrist who developed psychoanalysis, which is both a major set of ideas and a school of **psychotherapy** based upon those concepts. Psychoanalytic theory stresses the influence of unconscious drives and wishes on behavior. It also emphasizes the central role of childhood events in shaping later experiences.

Freud viewed depression as hostility turned inward, a reaction rooted in the loss of someone for whom the person has intensely ambivalent feelings. To mitigate the sense of loss, the person takes on one or more characteristics of the lost individual. But because the lost individual is viewed with mixed feelings, hostility that once would have been directed outward is now directed inward toward the newly adopted characteristics. The result is harsh self-criticism, which sets the stage for depression.

Psychoanalysis continues to be practiced today as an intensive, long-term approach to psychotherapy and personal growth. In addition, it has given rise to **psychodynamic therapy**, a shorter-term, more results-oriented treatment based on psychoanalytic theory.

Freud himself continues to capture the imagination as well. From quips and jokes

---

### "My Present Distaste for Life"

Freud himself was no stranger to dark moods. In 1923, Freud was stricken by twin tragedies: the diagnosis of oral cancer as well as the death of his beloved four-year-old grandson Heinele. Writing in *Freud: A Life for Our Time* (1988), biographer Peter Gay describes the emotional fallout:

> He thought that his own illness intensified the shock he was feeling, but he felt worse about his grandson than about himself. "Don't try to live for ever," he wrote, quoting Bernard Shaw's preface to *The Doctor's Dilemma*, "you will not succeed." The end came on June 19. After Heinele, his "dear child" died, Freud, the man without tears, wept. When in mid-July, Ferenczi, self-centered and a little obtuse, inquired why Freud had not congratulated him on his fiftieth birthday, Freud replied that he would not have omitted this courtesy to a stranger. But he did not think he was exacting any kind of revenge. "Rather, it is connected with my present distaste for life. I have never had a depression before, but this now must be one." This is a remarkable statement: since Freud had been recurrently afflicted with depressive moods, this bout must have been exceptionally severe. "I am still being tormented in my snout," he told Eitingon in mid-August, "and obsessed by impotent longing for the dear child." He described himself as now a stranger to life and a candidate for death. Writing to his cherished lifelong friend Oscar Rie, he confessed that he could not get over the loss of the boy. "He meant the future to me and thus has taken the future away with him."

From *Freud: A Life for Our Time* by Peter Gay. Copyright © 1988 by Peter Gay. Used by permission of W.W. Norton & Company, Inc.

to movie and literary references, Freud holds a prominent place in the iconography of Western culture. He is an easy figure to lampoon, thanks to his focus on hidden sexual meanings in even the most innocuous situations. In the popular mind, the caricature of Freud threatens to overshadow the reality of the man and his groundbreaking accomplishments.

***Early Career Highlights.*** Freud was born in Freiberg, Moravia (now Příbor, Czech Republic), but his family moved to Vienna three years later. After entering the University of Vienna at age 17, Freud received his medical degree there in 1881. While a student, Freud began working in a physiology laboratory, and he went on to publish articles about neurology, the branch of medicine that studies the **nervous system**.

Soon after graduation, though, Freud decided to prepare himself for a career as a physician rather than a scientist. The decision was motivated in part by the prevalence of anti-Semitism, which meant that his opportunities for advancement in the academic world would be limited by his Jewish heritage.

Freud began training at the General Hospital of Vienna. In 1885, he traveled to Paris, where he spent 17 weeks studying under Jean Martin Charcot (1825–1893). The imminent French neurologist was an expert on hysteria, a disorder characterized by symptoms such as paralysis, seizures, or deafness that appear to be neurological in origin, but for which no physical cause can be found. Charcot was able to demonstrate a link between hysteria and hypnosis, the induction of a trance-like state in which a person is more susceptible to suggestion. This link implied that the mind rather than the nerves might be responsible for certain mental illnesses. The experience whetted Freud's interest in psychological disorders.

***Birth of Psychoanalysis.*** After his return from Paris, Freud began a clinical practice. He also struck up a collaboration with Josef Breuer (1842–1925), an eminent Austrian neurologist. Breuer told Freud about a female patient he had treated, dubbed Anna O. in the literature, who developed a variety of hysterical symptoms. Breuer found that letting his patient talk about how her symptoms began seemed to provide some relief from them, a treatment he called "the talking cure." In 1895, Freud and Breuer jointly published a book titled *Studies on Hysteria*, which described the case of Anna O. The book's publication is often considered to mark the founding of psychoanalysis.

This book is also noteworthy because it introduced a new treatment method called free association, in which patients freely express whatever random thoughts come to mind as a way of accessing unconscious material. Free association became a hallmark of psychoanalytic technique. It seemed to be an auspicious beginning. Within two years, however, Freud and Breuer had gone their separate ways, largely due to Freud's increasing focus on unresolved sexual issues as the source of psychological problems.

Later psychoanalysts underwent analysis of their personalities by someone else as part of their training. As the first psychoanalyst, Freud was forced to analyze himself, which he did mainly by interpreting the content of his dreams to reveal their hidden meanings. The result was a book titled *The Interpretation of Dreams*, published in 1899 but given a publication date of 1900. This book is regarded by many as Freud's greatest literary masterpiece, and dream analysis became another core technique of psychoanalysis.

***Core Psychoanalytic Concepts.*** After the break with Breuer, Freud continued to elaborate his theory of psychosexual development. According to the theory, sexuality exists in some form from infancy onward. Sexual energy, known as the libido, is concentrated in different organs as development progresses, giving rise to the oral, anal, phallic, latency, and genital stages. Each stage has its own characteristic erotic activities as well as a lasting impact on personality formation.

During the phallic stage around age three, Freud posited that boys experience castration anxiety, and girls experience penis envy. Freud believed another hallmark of this stage to be the Oedipus complex, the erotic feelings that a boy feels toward his mother, accompanied by rivalry with and hostility toward his father. Such notions of childhood sexuality offended many contemporaries, and Freud labored in relative isolation for a time.

But by the first decade of the twentieth century, Freud's reputation was growing. His inner circle now included several disciples who became significant figures in their own right, including Otto Rank (1884–1939), Carl Jung (1875–1961), and **Karl Abraham** (1877–1925).

*Three-Part Structure of Personality.* Psychoanalytic theory was expanding as well. In later years, Freud described a three-part structure of personality. The ego, in this view, is the component of personality that deals with the outside world and its practical demands. The id is the part that contains the biological drives of sex and aggression. And the super-ego is the part that contains the person's learned standards of right and wrong. Freud believed that a healthy ego channels id-based needs in directions that are consistent with superego values.

There is often tension among these personality components, however. Freud described defense mechanisms that the ego uses to protect itself against the resulting internal conflict. For example, repression is the mechanism by which anxiety-provoking thoughts, memories, or impulses are pushed out of conscious awareness and into the unconscious mind. Freud held that the unconscious mind is largely a repository for repressed material.

***View of Depression.*** Freud's first description of the psychological basis for depression appeared in his 1917 essay "Mourning and Melancholia." He further refined his ideas in the 1923 book *The Ego and the Id.*

Freud believed that depression, like mourning, arises from the loss of someone or something that is valued. Consider a man whose wife has died. In normal mourning, the man gradually reclaims the psychic energy invested in his wife as he comes to terms with her death over time. The man is then free to redirect that energy elsewhere. But in depression, which Freud called melancholia, the energy is never freed up, and problems persist as a result.

Not all losses are this obvious, but they can still have lasting effects. The person who has suffered a loss, real or imagined, is angered and hurt. Those feelings are directed at the most convenient target: characteristics of the lost individual that the person left behind has taken on. The anger often takes the form of bitter self-reproach,

---

### Freud on Melancholy

In his classic essay "Mourning and Melancholy" (1917), Freud had this to say about the relationship between grief and depression:

> Mourning is regularly the reaction to the loss of a loved person, or to the loss of some abstraction which has taken the place of one, such as fatherland, liberty, an ideal, and so on. As an effect of the same influences, melancholia instead of a state of grief develops in some people, whom we consequently suspect of a morbid pathological disposition.

which arises from guilt over perceived inadequacies in the relationship with the lost individual.

When relationships end for reasons other than death, the person left behind may feel rejected or abandoned. Rage over being treated this way is focused on the internalized part of the lost loved one. Taken to an extreme, inwardly directed rage and aggression can lead to **suicide**.

***Freud in Perspective.***   With the Nazi rise to power in the 1930s, Freud's Jewish heritage once again became an issue. Freud was reluctant to leave Vienna even when Nazis occupied the city. But in 1938, after Nazi sympathizers searched his home and the Gestapo interrogated his daughter, Freud finally took his family to stay in London. He died there from cancer the following year.

The debate over his ideas continues to this day, however. Psychoanalytic theory proved to be one of the most influential scientific and cultural movements of the twentieth century. It also became one of the most controversial. In an article marking the 150th anniversary of Freud's birth, *Newsweek* magazine referred to him as "modern history's most debunked doctor."

One common criticism of psychoanalysis is that neither the psychological system itself nor the therapeutic techniques that grew out of it lend themselves readily to scientific verification. A second criticism is that Freud overstated the importance of sex, ascribing much of human behavior to sexual motives. A third criticism is that Freud tended to make sweeping generalizations based on the experiences of just a few patients.

For modern women, Freud's idea that females are driven by penis envy—the jealousy and sense of being handicapped that girls supposedly feel when they realize that they lack a penis—is blatantly offensive. Critics also have taken Freud to task for his belief that superego development is weaker in women, rendering them less morally capable than men.

Yet Freud highlighted the lasting impact of childhood events and the influence of hidden motives for behavior. These concepts, taken for granted today, were revolutionary in their time. In addition, by developing the first major school of psychotherapy, Freud showed that many mental disorders are amenable to psychological treatment. In this sense, he laid the groundwork for all other forms of psychotherapy that followed.

*See also:* Attachment Theory

## Bibliography

Adler, Jerry with Anne Underwood and Marc Bain. "Freud in Our Midst." *Newsweek* (March 27, 2006).

Busch, Frederic N., Marie Rudden, and Theodore Shapiro. *Psychodynamic Treatment of Depression.* Washington, DC: American Psychiatric Publishing, 2004.

"Freud, Sigmund." *Encyclopedia Britannica Online,* 2007, http://www.britannica.com/eb/article -9109419/Sigmund-Freud.

Gabbard, Glen O., and Tanya J. Bennett. "Psychoanalytic and Psychodynamic Psychotherapy for Depression and Dysthymia." In *The American Psychiatric Publishing Textbook of Mood Disorders,* by Dan J. Stein, David J. Kupfer, and Alan F. Schatzberg, eds., 389–404. Washington, DC: American Psychiatric Publishing, 2006.

Gay, Peter. *Freud: A Life for Our Time.* New York: W. W. Norton, 1988.

Goodwin, C. James. *A History of Modern Psychology.* New York: John Wiley and Sons, 1999.

Krapp, Kristine, ed. "Sigmund Schlomo Freud," in *Psychologists and Their Theories for Students.* Vol. 1. Detroit, MI: Thomson Gale, 2005.

Radden, Jennifer, ed. *The Nature of Melancholy: From Aristotle to Kristeva.* New York: Oxford University Press, 2000.

Schwartz, Arthur, and Ruth M. Schwartz. *Depression Theories and Treatments: Psychological, Biological, and Social Perspectives.* New York: Columbia University Press, 1993.

Sheehy, Noel, Antony J. Chapman, and Wendy Conroy, eds. "Freud, Sigmund," in *Biographical Dictionary of Psychology.* New York: Routledge, 2002.

*Sigmund Freud: Life and Work.* Romanian Association for Psychoanalysis Promotion, May 30, 2008, http://www.freudfile.org.

Viney, Wayne, and D. Brett King. *A History of Psychology: Ideas and Context.* Boston: Allyn and Bacon, 1998.

# G

**GAMMA-AMINO-BUTYRIC ACID.**   Gamma-amino-butyric acid (GABA) is a neurotransmitter—a chemical messenger within the brain—that has an inhibitory effect, making cells less excitable. GABA helps control muscle activity and plays a key role in the visual system. It also may help quell anxiety. Research suggests that **major depression** is associated with decreased GABA activity.

People with depression tend to have lower levels of GABA in their blood and cerebrospinal fluid than those without depression. **Brain imaging** studies of severely depressed individuals also have shown reduced levels of GABA in part of the brain called the occipital cortex.

Treatment for depression, on the other hand, may raise GABA levels. This effect has been shown with both **selective serotonin reuptake inhibitors** (a widely used type of antidepressant) and **electroconvulsive therapy** (a treatment in which a carefully controlled electrical current is passed through a person's brain to induce a brief seizure).

*Postpartum Depression.*   Recent animal research indicates that GABA might also help explain why some women become depressed after childbirth but others do not. **Postpartum depression** is full-blown depression that begins within six months of giving birth. To study this condition in the lab, researchers used genetically engineered mice that lacked a key component of GABA **receptors**, the specialized sites on cells that receive and react with GABA messages. The receptor component, called the delta subunit, had previously been shown to fluctuate conspicuously during pregnancy and the postpartum period. This led researchers to believe that it might have important behavioral effects.

After giving birth, female mice deficient in the delta subunit showed depression-like behavior and neglected their newborn pups. When these same mice were given a drug that restored GABA receptor function despite the lack of delta subunits, their behavior improved and pup mortality declined.

More research is needed to see whether the same thing happens in human mothers. But researchers speculate that human postpartum depression might be related to a similar problem with delta subunits. As a result, the GABA system in the brain might not be able to adapt the way it should to hormonal fluctuations during the postpartum period.

*See also:* Neurotransmitters

*Bibliography*

*Brain Basics: Know Your Brain.* National Institute of Neurological Disorders and Stroke, May 1, 2007, http://www.ninds.nih.gov/disorders/brain_basics/know_your_brain.htm.

Maguire, Jamie, and Istvan Mody. "GABA$_A$R Plasticity During Pregnancy: Relevance to Postpartum Depression." *Neuron* 59 (2008): 207–213.

*Mechanism for Postpartum Depression Found in Mice.* National Institute of Mental Health, July 30, 2008, http://www.nimh.nih.gov/science-news/2008/mechanism-for-postpartum-depression-found-in -mice.shtml.

Sanacora, Gerard, Graeme F. Mason, Douglas L. Rothman, and John H. Krystal. "Increased Occipital Cortex GABA Concentrations in Depressed Patients after Therapy with Selective Serotonin Reuptake Inhibitors." *American Journal of Psychiatry* 159 (2002): 663–665.

Sanacora, Gerard, Graeme F. Mason, Douglas L. Rothman, Fahmeed Hyder, James J. Ciarcia, Robert B. Ostroff, et al. "Increased Cortical GABA Concentrations in Depressed Patients Receiving ECT." *American Journal of Psychiatry* 160 (2003): 577–579.

Sanacora, Gerard, Ralitza Gueorguieva, Neill Epperson, Yu-Te Wu, Michael Appel, Douglas L. Rothman, et al. "Subtype-Specific Alterations of γ–Aminobutyric Acid and Glutamate in Patients with Major Depression." *Archives of General Psychiatry* 61 (2004): 705–713.

**GENERALIZED ANXIETY DISORDER.**   Generalized anxiety disorder (GAD) is an anxiety disorder characterized by excessive, uncontrollable worry and tension over a number of different things. Everyone feels anxious or worried at times. But those with GAD are consumed by incessant fretting that lasts for months or years and takes a serious toll on their quality of life. Adding to the misery is depression, which often occurs side by side with GAD. Research indicates that more than 70 percent of people who have had GAD also meet the criteria for **major depression** at some point in their lives.

People with GAD live in a constant state of concern over a variety of things, from their health and finances to their work and relationships. Sometimes just the thought of getting through the day is enough to set the worries off. And once the worries start, nothing seems to shake them, even though people with GAD may realize that their anxiety is more intense than the situation warrants.

GAD affects about 6.8 million U.S. adults, two-thirds of whom are women. The disorder can start at any age, although the years of highest risk are between childhood and middle age. Without treatment, the symptoms may wax and wane over years or decades, often getting worse during times of **stress**. Most people with GAD struggle with other mental health problems as well. Besides depression, conditions that often coexist with GAD include **substance abuse** and other **anxiety disorders.**

Fortunately, effective treatments are available. GAD is commonly treated with medication and/or **cognitive-behavioral therapy** (CBT), a type of **psychotherapy** that helps people identify and change maladaptive thought and behavior patterns. When depression occurs along with GAD, getting prompt, appropriate treatment is doubly important, because people with both conditions report greater impairment in their emotional, mental, physical, and functional well-being than those with major depression alone.

*Criteria for Diagnosis.*   The symptoms of GAD are defined by the ***Diagnostic and Statistical Manual of Mental Disorders, Fourth Edition, Text Revision*** (*DSM-IV-TR*), a diagnostic guidebook published by the American Psychiatric Association and widely used by mental health professionals from many disciplines. People with GAD worry excessively about a variety of everyday problems on more days than not for at least six months. Even though the worry and anxiety cause real distress or problems in daily

life, people find it very difficult to control them.

The nagging worry and
anxiety are accompanied by
signs of mental and physical
tension. Adults with GAD
have at least three of the following symptoms, and children
have at least one: 1) feeling
restless, keyed up or on edge,
(2) getting tired easily, (3) finding it hard to concentrate or
having one's mind go blank,
(4) having trouble falling or
staying asleep, or sleeping restlessly, (5) **irritability**, and
(6) muscle tension.

***Causes and Risk Factors.***
Because GAD and major
depression coexist so frequently,
researchers have looked for
common causes. Research indicates that the two disorders
may be influenced by some, if
not most, of the same **genetic
factors**. In other words, the
same genes that affect people's
likelihood of developing

### Treatment of GAD

When people have GAD and depression simultaneously,
both conditions need to be addressed during treatment.
Below are some of the main treatment options for GAD.

#### *Psychotherapy*

CBT helps people identify self-defeating thought and behavior patterns, and replace them with more constructive ones.
People may start by recording their thoughts and worries in a
number of situations. Working with a therapist later, people
can then evaluate how realistic their thoughts and worries are
and learn how to change unrealistic thinking.

#### *Medication*

**Selective serotonin reuptake inhibitors,** a widely prescribed class of antidepressants, can help relieve symptoms of anxiety as well as depression. Other types of
antidepressants that may be used to treat GAD include
**serotonin-norepinephrine reuptake inhibitors** and **tricyclic antidepressants.** In addition, two types of medications developed specifically to treat anxiety are available.
Benzodiazepines are mild sedatives that act quickly but
can be habit-forming if taken for more than a few weeks.
Buspirone is a different type of anti-anxiety medication
that takes longer to work but doesn't pose a risk of
dependence.

depression also may affect their chances of developing GAD. One possibility is that these genes
act by influencing a personality trait called neuroticism, characterized by ongoing emotional
instability and a tendency toward distress. Neuroticism, which is moderately inheritable, has been
linked to an increased risk of developing both major depression and GAD individually.

Shared **environmental factors** also may play a role. For example, abuse and neglect
early in life increase the risk of developing both anxiety and depression later. Some experts
hold that events involving a sense of danger are more prone to trigger anxiety, and those
involving a sense of loss are more prone to trigger depression. But as a practical matter,
many distressing events combine elements of both danger and loss.

Despite these commonalities, strong evidence also exists for fundamental differences in
underlying biology. For instance, the **amygdala**, a structure inside the brain that is involved
in emotional learning and the fear response, tends to be overactive at rest in people with
depression, but it is overactive only when symptoms are revved up in those with anxiety.
Also, depression is associated with a number of biochemical changes not found in GAD,
such as elevated blood levels of adrenocorticotropic hormone (ACTH) and **cortisol—
hormones** that play key roles in the body's stress response.

Finally, people with major depression and those with GAD have different types of **sleep
disturbances**. For example, only those with major depression generally develop a shorten-
ing of the time it takes after they fall asleep for the first period of rapid eye movement
(REM) sleep to begin.

***Relationship to Depression.*** In the past, it was believed that when GAD and major depression occurred together, GAD usually came first. However, more recent research has challenged this notion. When researchers studied over 1,000 New Zealanders from childhood to age 32, they found that 12 percent were diagnosed with both major depression and GAD as adults. In that group, anxiety was diagnosed before the major depression 37 percent of the time, but major depression was diagnosed first 34 percent of the time—almost as often. The two disorders were diagnosed at the same time in the remainder of cases.

Another longstanding belief that has been disputed lately is the assumption that major depression is more distressing and disabling than GAD. Overall, research indicates that the two disorders are roughly equivalent in their impact, and the two disorders together tend to be associated with more severe problems than either by itself. For instance, having both disorders is particularly common in people with chronic or recurrent disease.

In the *DSM-IV-TR*, major depression is classified as a mood disorder, while GAD is classified as an anxiety disorder. Some researchers have argued for a change in classification that would reflect the close relationship between the two conditions. At a 2007 planning conference for the next edition of the *DSM*, the majority of participants agreed that differences between the two conditions were small enough to justify such a change. One suggestion was the creation of a new category of distress disorders that would include both major depression and GAD. Time will tell whether this change is adopted.

*See also:* Comorbidity

***Further Information.*** Anxiety Disorders Association of America, 8730 Georgia Avenue, Suite 600. Silver Spring, MD 20910, (240) 485-1001, www.adaa.org.

## Bibliography

American Psychiatric Association. *Diagnostic and Statistical Manual of Mental Disorders*. 4th ed., text rev. Washington, DC: American Psychiatric Association, 2000.

*Anxiety Disorders*. National Institute of Mental Health, 2007, http://www.nimh.nih.gov/health/publications/anxiety-disorders/summary.shtml.

First, Michael B. *Comorbidity of Depression and Generalized Anxiety Disorder (June 20–22, 2007)*. American Psychiatric Association, http://www.psych.org/MainMenu/Research/DSMIV/DSMV/DSMRevisionActivities/ConferenceSummaries/ComorbidityofDepressionandGAD.aspx.

Foa, Edna B., and Linda Wasmer Andrews. *If Your Adolescent Has an Anxiety Disorder: An Essential Resource for Parents*. New York: Oxford University Press, 2006.

*Generalized Anxiety Disorder*. Mayo Clinic, September 11, 2007, http://www.mayoclinic.com/health/generalized-anxiety-disorder/DS00502.

Mittal, Dinesh, John C. Fortney, Jeffrey M. Pyne, Mark J. Edlung, and Julie L. Wetherell. "Impact of Comorbid Anxiety Disorders on Health-Related Quality of Life among Patients with Major Depressive Disorder." *Psychiatric Services* 57 (2006): 1731–1737.

Moffitt, Terrie E., HonaLee Harrington, Avshalom Caspi, Julia Kim-Cohen, David Goldberg, Alice M. Gregory, et al. "Depression and Generalized Anxiety Disorder: Cumulative and Sequential Comorbidity in a Birth Cohort Followed Prospectively to Age 32 Years." *Archives of General Psychiatry* 64 (2007): 651–660.

*When Worry Gets Out of Control: Generalized Anxiety Disorder*. National Institute of Mental Health, June 26, 2008, http://www.nimh.nih.gov/health/publications/generalized-anxiety-disorder.shtml.

**GENETIC FACTORS.**   Genes are the fundamental units of heredity in an organism. They are responsible for storing information about inherited characteristics and passing that information along from one generation to the next. Genes influence not only physical traits, such as height and weight, but also mental and behavioral characteristics, such as intelligence and **temperament**. Among other things, genes affect the risk of developing depression.

Simply having relatives with depression does not mean a particular individual is destined to have the disorder, however. A person's risk is also influenced by biological, psychological, and **environmental factors**. Even identical twins differ in their propensity toward depression and other mental disorders, as well as their personality traits and behavior patterns. In general, research shows that genes account for about half of these differences.

The completion of the Human Genome Project in 2003 was a landmark achievement in science. It identified all 20,500 human genes and mapped the 3 billion chemical bases that comprise human DNA (deoxyribonucleic acid). The project also led to major technological advances in genetic research. As a result, scientists are now making great strides in identifying the specific variations in genes that make each person unique. Some variations affect how the brain works, and a subset of those variations may affect how likely it is that a given person will develop depression.

Genetics by the Numbers

| The Human Body Contains | | What This Is |
| --- | --- | --- |
| 1 | Genome | The complete set of DNA instructions for a particular organism. DNA is the double-stranded molecule in cells that carries hereditary information. |
| 46 | Chromosomes | Tightly-packed bundles of DNA in the nucleus of each cell. Humans have 23 pairs of chromosomes. One chromosome in each pair comes from the mother; the other, from the father. |
| 20,500 | Genes | Pieces of DNA located in specific positions on particular chromosomes. Genes serve as the basic units of heredity. Most contain instructions for making a specific protein. |
| 3 Billion | Bases | The chemical building blocks of DNA. The information in DNA is stored as a code made up of four chemical bases: adenosine (A), thymine (T), cytosine (C) and guanine (G). |

Yet despite recent progress, scientists are just starting to sort out all the genetic influences on depression. So far, a number of genetic variations on several chromosomes have been linked to the disorder, but each one generally confers only a small amount of risk by itself. It seems to be the combined effect of multiple genes acting in concert with the environment that helps decide whether or not an individual becomes depressed. The same is true for many physical illnesses, such as **heart disease**, **diabetes**, and asthma. Genes are only part of a complex picture.

*A Family Affair.*   Scientists have long noted that depression tends to run in families. Research has shown that the disorder is two to four times more common in people who have a close relative with a mood disorder, compared to those with no such family history.

But as striking as that statistic is, it does not in itself prove a genetic connection. Close relatives not only share genes, but also tend to live in the same environment, have common experiences, and share many beliefs.

One classic way of disentangling nature and nurture is by doing twin studies. Identical twins have exactly the same genes, and fraternal twins have only half of their genes in common. Identical twin pairs are more likely than fraternal ones to both have depression. Even when identical twins are adopted by different families and raised separately, their risk is still increased. These findings provide strong evidence for a genetic link.

Yet when one identical twin develops the depression, the other twin does not inevitably follow suit. This fact shows that genes alone are not the whole story. In the general population, twin studies indicate that genes account for 40 percent to 50 percent of susceptibility to **major depression**. The other 50 percent to 60 percent is due to nongenetic factors.

Among people with major depression, three characteristics predict a greater increase in risk for their relatives: recurrent episodes, severe symptoms, and an early age of onset. This suggests that some forms of depression may have a larger genetic component than others.

***Candidate Genes.***   Modern research techniques allow scientists to single out specific genetic variations that may play a role in causing depression. Much work remains to be done before scientists understand exactly how these genes interact with each other and with environmental factors. But rapid progress is being made on an almost daily basis.

Below are just a few of the genes that have been suggested as possible contributors to depression. The first name given is the gene's formal symbol. Many genes also are known by the name of their gene product—a protein or other molecule that is produced using information contained in that gene. The gene product name is given in parentheses.

*SLC6A4 (Serotonin Transporter Gene).*   This is one of the best-studied genes with regard to depression. It encodes the serotonin **transporter**—a protein complex that carries a brain chemical called **serotonin** back into the cell that originally released it. By affecting the rate at which serotonin is absorbed back into the releasing cell, this gene influences how much serotonin is available for use by the brain. Deficits in serotonin are thought to be important in depression.

*TPH2 (Tryptophan Hydroxylase 2 Gene).*   This gene encodes an enzyme involved in serotonin production. The enzyme transforms a dietary amino acid called **tryptophan** into 5-hydroxytryptophan (5-HTP). Then 5-HTP is converted in the brain to 5-hydroxytryptamine (5-HT)—the chemical name for serotonin. A variation in this gene has been linked to depression in some people.

*BDNF (Brain-Derived Neurotrophic Factor Gene).*   This gene encodes a small protein involved in **neuroplasticity**, the brain's ability to modify connections between cells in order to better cope with new circumstances. In particular, this protein affects the neuroplasticity of brain cells related to chemicals that are thought to play a role in depression, including serotonin and **dopamine**.

*DBH (Dopamine Beta-Hydroxylase Gene).*   This gene encodes an enzyme that converts dopamine into **norepinephrine**, another brain chemical that has been implicated in depression. In people with major depression, some studies have linked variations in this gene to psychotic symptoms (severely distorted beliefs or perceptions that are out of touch with reality).

***Looking to the Future.***   In the future, it is hoped that genetic research will help identify subtypes of depression and develop targeted treatments for them. Even better, it is hoped that genetic testing will help identify high-risk individuals so preventive steps can be taken.

Consider recent research on genetic links to suicidal thinking among people taking an antidepressant for major depression. The most severe consequence of depression is **suicide**, and **antidepressants** help avert life-threatening suicidality—suicidal thoughts and behaviors. Ironically, though, a minority of people with depression actually experience an increase in suicidality when they start antidepressants.

In one study, DNA samples were taken from 1,915 depressed individuals being treated with **citalopram**. Tests on the samples pinpointed variations of two genes that increased the risk for suicidal thoughts. The two genes—GRIK2 (kainite receptor gene) and GRIA3 (AMPA receptor gene)—both encode components of the brain's **glutamate** system. Glutamate is a chemical messenger in the brain that increases the firing of nerve cells, and excessive glutamate may interfere with healthy brain function.

In the study, the odds of developing suicidal thoughts went up twofold in individuals with a certain GRIA3 variation, eightfold in those with a GRIK2 variation, and 15-fold in those with both. If future research bears out these findings, genetic testing might someday be used to identify high-risk individuals who need close monitoring when starting an antidepressant. This could help allay concerns related to taking medication.

It is just one example of the great promise of genetic research. Genes are not the sole cause of depression or determinant of treatment response, but they are certainly an important one. The more scientists learn about genetic contributors to depression, the closer they come to unraveling the mysteries of the disorder itself.

*See also:* Causes of Depression; Parental Depression; Tryptophan Hydroxylase Gene

**Further Information.**   Behavioral Genetics Association, www.bga.org.

Genetics Home Reference, National Library of Medicine, 8600 Rockville Pike, Bethesda, MD 20894, (888) 346-3656, ghr.nlm.nih.gov.

Human Genome Project, Genome Management Information System, Oak Ridge National Laboratory, 1060 Commerce Park, MS 6480, Oak Ridge, TN 37830, (865) 576-6669, genomics.energy.gov.

National Human Genome Research Institute, Building 31, Room 4B09, 31 Center Drive, MSC 2152, 9000 Rockville Pike, Bethesda, MD 20892, (301) 402-0911, www.genome .gov.

## Bibliography

*A Guide to Your Genome.* National Human Genome Research Institute, October 2007, http://www .genome.gov/Pages/Education/AllAbouttheHumanGenomeProject/GuidetoYourGenome07 .pdf.

*Ask the Doctors: What Is the Role of Genetics in Mood Disorders?* Depressive and Bipolar Support Alliance, August 28, 2006, http://www.dbsalliance.org/site/PageServer?pagename=empower _QA_geneticsquestion.

Berrettini, Wade. "Genetics of Bipolar and Unipolar Disorders." In *The American Psychiatric Publishing Textbook of Mood Disorders,* by Dan J. Stein, David J. Kupfer and Alan F. Schatzberg, eds., 235–247. Washington, DC: American Psychiatric Publishing, 2006.

*DBH.* National Library of Medicine, April 24, 2009, http://ghr.nlm.nih.gov/gene=dbh.

*Entrez Gene BDNF.* National Library of Medicine, April 24, 2009, http://ghr.nlm.nih.gov/locuslink=627.

*Entrez Gene SLC6A4.* National Library of Medicine, April 24, 2009, http://ghr.nlm.nih.gov/locuslink =6532.

*Entrez Gene TPH2.* National Library of Medicine, April 24, 2009, http://ghr.nlm.nih.gov/locuslink =121278.

Laje, Gonzalo, Silvia Paddock, Husseini Manji, A. John Rush, Alexander F. Wilson, Dennis Charney, et al. "Genetic Markers of Suicidal Ideation Emerging During Citalopram Treatment of Major Depression." *American Journal of Psychiatry* 164 (2007): 1530–1538.

Levinson, Douglas F. "Genetics of Major Depression." In *Handbook of Depression.* 2nd ed., by Ian H. Gotlib and Constance L. Hammen, eds., 165–186. New York: Guilford Press, 2009.

Schwartz, Arthur and Ruth M. Schwartz. *Depression Theories and Treatments: Psychological, Biological, and Social Perspectives.* New York: Columbia University Press, 1993.

*Talking Glossary of Genetic Terms.* National Human Genome Research Institute, http://www.genome.gov/glossary.cfm.

U.S. Department of Health and Human Services. *Mental Health: A Report of the Surgeon General.* Rockville, MD: U.S. Department of Health and Human Services, 1999.

**GERIATRIC DEPRESSION SCALE.** The Geriatric Depression Scale (GDS) is a self-report questionnaire specifically developed for assessing depression in people ages 65 and over. It is among the most commonly used **screening tests** for depression in this age group. Published in 1982, the scale was developed by U.S. psychologist T. L. Brink and U.S. psychiatrist Jerome Yesavage.

The GDS is composed of 30 easy-to-read questions about various symptoms of depression. Test takers answer yes or no to indicate how they have felt over the past week. Other screening tests often give considerable weight to physical symptoms, such as poor sleep, loss of appetite, lack of energy, and decreased interest in sex. Such symptoms are less helpful for detecting depression in later life, however, because many nondepressed **older adults** have these problems as well. The GDS downplays physical complaints, which makes it especially appropriate for use in the older age group.

The GDS has been translated from English into 26 other languages. In addition, a shortened version of the English GDS with only 15 questions is available. Researchers have found a strong correlation between scores on the short form and the long form in people who took both.

***Pros and Cons of the GDS.*** Research on the GDS has shown that it has high reliability, the extent to which the results obtained are consistent and repeatable. The test also performs well when it comes to validity, the degree to which it actually measures what it purports to measure. Good results have been obtained using the GDS in older adults living in both the community and nursing homes. In addition, the test has been shown to differentiate depressed and nondepressed older adults in groups of patients with arthritis and mild to moderate dementia—a decline in mental abilities caused by one of several disorders affecting the brain, such as Alzheimer's disease and stroke.

Many professionals consider the GDS to be the best depression screening test for older adults overall. However, it may not be appropriate for those with more severe dementia. For older adults whose mental abilities are seriously impaired, a test called the Cornell Scale for Depression in Dementia (CSDD) may be more useful, because it gathers information not from only the person being evaluated, but also from the caregiver.

*See also:* Diagnosis of Depression; Physical Illness

*Bibliography*

Brink, T. L., Jerome A. Yesavage, Owen Lum, Philip H. Heersema, Michael Adey, and Terrence L. Rose. "Screening Tests for Geriatric Depression." *Clinical Gerontologist* 1 (1982): 37–43.

*Geriatric Depression Scale.* Stanford University Aging Clinical Research Center, http://www.stanford.edu/~yesavage/GDS.html.

## Geriatric Depression Scale

1. Are you basically satisfied with your life?
2. Have you dropped many of your activities and interests?
3. Do you feel that your life is empty?
4. Do you often get bored?
5. Are you hopeful about the future?
6. Are you bothered by thoughts you can't get out of your head?
7. Are you in good spirits most of the time?
8. Are you afraid that something bad is going to happen to you?
9. Do you feel happy most of the time?
10. Do you often feel helpless?
11. Do you often get restless and fidgety?
12. Do you prefer to stay at home, rather than going out and doing new things?
13. Do you frequently worry about the future?
14. Do you feel you have more problems with memory than most?
15. Do you think it is wonderful to be alive now?
16. Do you often feel downhearted and blue?
17. Do you feel pretty worthless the way you are now?
18. Do you worry a lot about the past?
19. Do you find life very exciting?
20. Is it hard for you to get started on new projects?
21. Do you feel full of energy?
22. Do you feel that your situation is hopeless?
23. Do you think that most people are better off than you are?
24. Do you frequently get upset over little things?
25. Do you frequently feel like crying?
26. Do you have trouble concentrating?
27. Do you enjoy getting up in the morning?
28. Do you prefer to avoid social gatherings?
29. Is it easy for you to make decisions?
30. Is your mind as clear as it used to be?

This is the original scoring for the scale: One point for each of these answers. Cutoff: normal = 0–9; mild depressives = 10–19; severe depressives = 20–30.

| | | | | | |
|---|---|---|---|---|---|
| 1. no | 6. yes | 11. yes | 16. yes | 21. no | 26. yes |
| 2. yes | 7. no | 12. yes | 17. yes | 22. yes | 27. no |
| 3. yes | 8. yes | 13. yes | 18. yes | 23. yes | 28. yes |
| 4. yes | 9. no | 14. yes | 19. no | 24. yes | 29. no |
| 5. no | 10. yes | 15. no | 20. yes | 25. yes | 30. no |

### Source

Mood Assessment Scale. Stanford University Aging Clinical Research Center, http://www.stanford.edu/~yesavage/GDS.english.long.html. The GDS is in the public domain.

*Note:* This test is provided for informational purposes only. It cannot take the place of diagnosis by a qualified professional. If you think you or someone you love might be depressed, seek professional help without delay.

Snarski, Melissa, and Forrest Scogin. "Assessing Depression in Older Adults." In Qualls, Sara H. and Bob G. Knight, eds. *Psychotherapy for Depression in Older Adults,* 45–77. Hoboken, NJ: John Wiley and Sons, 2006.

Yesavage, Jerome A., T. L. Brink, Terence L. Rose, Owen Lum, Virginia Huang, Michael Adey, et al. "Development and Validation of a Geriatric Screening Scale: A Preliminary Report." *Journal of Psychiatric Research* 17 (1982–1983): 37–49.

Yonkers, Kimberly A., and Jacqueline A. Samson. "Mood Disorders Measures." In *Handbook of Psychiatric Measures,* 2nd ed., by A. John Rush Jr., Michael B. First, and Deborah Blacker, eds., 499–528. Washington, DC: American Psychiatric Publishing, 2008.

**GLIAL CELLS.**  Glial cells are specialized cells in the **nervous system** that nourish and support **neurons**, the cells that transmit information. Until recently, scientists relegated glial cells to second-string status, regarding them as little more than the glue holding neurons together. Lately, though, glial cells have started to gain more respect in their own right. At the same time, researchers have found that the number and density of glial cells in key parts of the brain are often substantially reduced in people with depression.

Some glial cells form myelin, an insulating sheath that surrounds certain axons, the sending branches on neurons. Other glial cells remove debris after neurons are injured or die. And still others direct the growth of axons during development or assist communication between neurons.

***Glia and Glutamate.***  Astrocytes, one type of glial cell, have been singled out for much of the attention. Studies show that astrocytes are more than mere passive players in the brain. They influence and possibly even direct the activity of neurons.

In the 1990s, experiments in petri dishes showed that increasing the calcium in astrocytes led to increased calcium in surrounding neurons, implying that the two cell types could communicate. Later studies in rats used tiny electrodes to measure electrical impulses in the brain. These studies showed that a calcium increase in astrocytes did indeed affect neuron activity. Most tested neurons slowed down their signaling, but a few sped it up.

Newer studies have focused on chemicals that allow astrocytes to communicate. After a rise in calcium, astrocytes release **glutamate**, an amino acid that acts as a chemical messenger in the brain. The communication goes both ways, with neurons releasing their own glutamate to talk back. The glutamate, in turn, may cause astrocytes to produce neurotrophic factors, small proteins needed for the growth and survival of specific groups of neurons.

It stands to reason that a decrease in the number of astrocytes would lead to a decline in neuron activity. Depression is linked to a decrease in glial cells in certain parts of the brain, including the ventromedial **prefrontal cortex** (PFC). This might explain why the ventromedial PFC tends to shrink and be relatively inactive in people with depression.

*See also:* Nervous System

*Bibliography*

*Astrocytes.* Society for Neuroscience, http://www.sfn.org/index.cfm?pagename=brainBriefings_astrocytes.

McNally, Leah, Zubin Bhagwagar, and Jonas Hannestad. "Inflammation, Glutamate, and Glia in Depression: A Literature Review." *CNS Spectrum* 13 (2008): 501–510.

*Parts of the Brain That Slow Down or Speed Up in Depression.* Canadian Institute of Neurosciences, Mental Health and Addiction, http://thebrain.mcgill.ca/flash/a/a_08/a_08_cr/a_08_cr_dep/a_08_cr_dep.html.

Rajkowska, Grazyna. "Anatomical Pathology." In *The American Psychiatric Publishing Textbook of Mood Disorders,* by Dan J. Stein, David J. Kupfer, and Alan F. Schatzberg, eds., 179–195. Washington, DC: American Psychiatric Publishing, 2006.

Society for Neuroscience. *Brain Facts: A Primer on the Brain and Nervous System.* 6th ed. Washington, DC: Society for Neuroscience, 2008.

**GLUTAMATE.**   Glutamate is a neurotransmitter—a chemical messenger within the brain—that has an excitatory effect, increasing the firing of nerve cells. Excessive glutamate activity may interfere with healthy brain function. Research has shown that people with depression tend to have high levels of glutamate in some areas of the brain.

Glutamate acts on **receptors** for N-methyl-d-aspartate (NMDA) and alpha-amino-3-hydroxy-5-methylisoxazole-4-propionic acid (AMPA). Stimulation of these receptors is helpful up to a point, playing a role in learning, memory, and the development of nerve cell connections. But just because some is good does not mean more is better. Overstimulation may lead to nerve cell dysfunction, damage, or death.

**Antidepressants** are thought to act partly by helping brain cells keep their sensitivity to glutamate in check. By lowering the cells' sensitivity, these medications may help keep excess glutamate from overwhelming key brain regions involved in depression.

*See also:* Genetic Factors; Glial Cells; Ketamine; Neurotransmitters

*Bibliography*

McNally, Leah, Zubin Bhagwagar, and Jonas Hannestad. "Inflammation, Glutamate and Glia in Depression: A Literature Review." *CNS Spectrums* 13 (2008): 501–510.

Sanacora, Gerard, Ralitza Gueorguieva, Neill Epperson, Yu-Te Wu, Michael Appel, Douglas L. Rothman, et al. "Subtype-Specific Alterations of γ–Aminobutyric Acid and Glutamate in Patients with Major Depression." *Archives of General Psychiatry* 61 (2004): 705–713.

*Selective Serotonin Reuptake Inhibitors (SSRIs).* Mayo Clinic, December 10, 2008, http://www.mayoclinic.com/health/ssris/MH00066.

Society for Neuroscience. *Brain Facts: A Primer on the Brain and Nervous System.* 6th ed. Washington, DC: Society for Neuroscience, 2008.

**GLYCOGEN SYNTHASE KINASE 3 BETA.**   Glycogen synthase kinase 3 beta (GSK3-beta) is an enzyme that plays a critical role inside brain cells, sending chemical signals that help regulate cell function. GSK3-beta is one link in a chain of physiological events set off by a deficiency in **serotonin**, an important chemical messenger in the brain. As such, scientists believe that GSK3-beta may be involved in serotonin-related forms of **mental illness**, including depression.

In a recent study from Duke University, scientists looked at the tryptophan hydroxylase 2 (TPH2) gene, which makes another enzyme needed for the production of serotonin. A mutation of the TPH2 gene has been linked to depression in some people, and mice genetically engineered to have a comparable mutation show a profound drop in serotonin levels. In the Duke study, as serotonin levels fell in such mice, GSK3-beta went into action.

The enzyme sent chemical signals to brain cells, and the mice developed depression- and anxiety-like behaviors. Compared to normal mice, they gave up struggling sooner when held back by their tails, and they were slower to emerge from dark hiding places to explore their surroundings. When scientists blocked GSK3-beta with either a chemical compound or genetic engineering, the abnormal behaviors went away, even though serotonin stayed low.

Currently, most **antidepressants** target serotonin, aiming to make more of it available in the brain. But this research suggests that future antidepressants could target GSK3-beta. The hope is that blocking GSK3-beta directly might potentially lead to antidepressants that work better and faster.

*See also:* Tryptophan Hydroxylase Gene

## Bibliography

Beaulieu, Jean-Martin, Xiaodong Zhang, Ramona M. Rodriguiz, Tatyana D. Sotnikova, Michael J. Cools, William C. Wetsel, et al. "Role of GSK3ß in Behavioral Abnormalities Induced by Serotonin Deficiency." *Proceedings of the National Academy of Sciences of the USA* 105 (2008): 1333–1338.

*Tomorrow's Antidepressants: Skip the Serotonin Boost?* National Institute of Mental Health, February 14, 2008, http://www.nimh.nih.gov/science-news/2008/tomorrows-antidepressants-skip-the-serotonin-boost.shtml.

**GOETHE, JOHANN WOLFGANG VON** (**1749–1832**). Johann Wolfgang von Goethe, one of the preeminent figures of German literature, left his mark on poetry, drama, fiction, and science. Today, his best-known work is *Faust*, a two-part epic poem and play. In his time, however, Goethe gained worldwide fame for his novel *The Sorrows of Young Werther* (1774), a tale of unrequited love that culminates in depression and **suicide**. The novel achieved notoriety when it inspired numerous copycat suicides among readers. It is still regarded as a seminal book in the literature of depression.

Goethe was an early leader of German Romanticism, a literary, artistic, and intellectual movement that originated in Europe during the late eighteenth century. Romanticism celebrated strong emotion as a source of aesthetic experience. Writers influenced by this movement often idealized mental suffering as a means of feeling more deeply and seeing more clearly.

*See also:* Melancholia

### "Source of All My Sorrow"

In *The Sorrows of Young Werther,* Goethe's lovesick protagonist recounts his downward spiral into suicidal depression:

> Witness, Heaven, how often I lie down in my bed with a wish, and even a hope, that I may never awaken again. And in the morning, when I open my eyes, I behold the sun once more, and am wretched. If I were whimsical, I might blame the weather, or an acquaintance, or some personal disappointment, for my discontented mind; and then this insupportable load of trouble would not rest entirely upon myself. But, alas! I feel it too sadly. I am alone the cause of my own woe, am I not? Truly, my own bosom contains the source of all my sorrow, as it previously contained the source of all my pleasure.

## Bibliography

Goethe, J. W. von. R. D. Boylan, trans. Nathen Haskell Dole, ed. *The Sorrows of Young Werther.* Gutenberg.org, January 2, 2009, http://www.gutenberg.org/files/2527/2527-h/2527-h.htm.

Goethe, Johann Wolfgang von. Burton Pike, trans. *The Sorrows of Young Werther.* New York: Random House, 2004.

Radden, Jennifer, ed. *The Nature of Melancholy: From Aristotle to Kristeva.* New York: Oxford University Press, 2000.

**GRIEF.**   Grief—also known as bereavement—refers to the intense sorrow and distress that are felt in response to a significant loss, usually the death of a loved one. Losing a loved one is one of the most stressful experiences anyone can go through. It is common for a grieving person to have many symptoms of depression, such as prolonged sadness, bouts of **crying**, trouble sleeping, poor appetite, and weight loss. In the days and weeks after the loss, the person also may find it nearly impossible to keep up with usual activities at home, work, or school.

Grief often brings up other feelings as well. In addition to sorrow, many people go through a period of emotional numbness. Others have periods of anger, disbelief, confusion, despair, or guilt. Everyone experiences grief a little differently, but many people are surprised by the intensity and persistence of their feelings and the swiftness with which these feelings may change.

At times, the emotional, mental, and physical responses to a loss may be numerous and disruptive enough to meet the criteria for **major depression**. But given the circumstances, these responses are often a normal, even healthy, reaction. They are a sign that the survivor is acknowledging and coming to terms with a very upsetting loss. A diagnosis of major depression isn't made unless the symptoms are unusually severe or hang on for at least two months.

*Signs of Complicated Grief.*   Although grieving is normal, the process can go awry. Some survivors are unable to move on with their lives, even after a period of months or years. Others try to avoid the pain of grief by denying their feelings. Ironically, these attempts at avoidance may just increase their pain in the long run by prolonging the process. When normal grieving does not occur or continues for months without letting up, it is often called complicated grief.

Symptoms of complicated grief include (1) continued disbelief in the death of the loved one, (2) memories of the deceased that constantly intrude into other thoughts, (3) fantasizing that the lost loved one is still present and watching, (4) constant yearning for the deceased that does not lessen over time, and (5) withdrawal from other people.

*Causes and Risk Factors.*   Complicated grief is not yet formally recognized as a diagnostic entity, and research on the subject is still evolving. As a result, estimates of how many people are affected vary widely, from 6% to 20% of bereaved individuals.

Certain factors seem to increase the risk of developing complicated grief. One risk factor is the loss of a loved one to a sudden, unexpected death or suicide. Complicated grief also may be more likely when the survivor had a very close or dependent relationship with the deceased or is not skilled at adapting to life changes. In addition, people may be predisposed to complicated grief by traumatic experiences in childhood, such as abuse or neglect.

*From Grief to Depression.*   What starts out as ordinary grief sometimes turns into major depression with a number of distressing or disabling symptoms, including unremitting sadness and/or loss of interest and pleasure in activities that were once enjoyed. Other symptoms of depression include changes in eating and sleeping habits, lack of energy, changes in activity level, trouble concentrating, feelings of worthlessness, and thoughts of **suicide**. When several of these symptoms occur together and last for months, it is time to seek help.

Although there are close similarities between ordinary grief and major depression, there are also telltale differences. For instance, many survivors feel guilt, justified or not, about

> ## Coping with a Loss
>
> Professional treatment is recommended for complicated grief or major depression. But there are also things you can do for yourself that help you work through the grief and cope with the **stress** of a devastating loss.
>
> ### Stay Socially Involved
> Although you may not feel like it at first, make an effort to stay connected with others whose company you enjoy. Your family and friends may offer you a shoulder to cry on, swap fond memories of the loved one, prompt you to get out of the house, or simply take your mind off the loss.
>
> ### Join a Support Group
> As time passes, you may find it comforting to share your experiences with other people who have gone through their own losses. Some support group members go on to form lasting friendships. As you begin to heal, you may take solace in repaying the favor by reaching out to others in need.
>
> ### Plan for Anniversaries
> Holidays, birthdays, and anniversaries are particularly likely to trigger painful memories. Plan ahead for these dates. Find positive, hopeful ways to remember your loved one; for instance, by planting a tree in the person's memory or by having family and friends write down their favorite memories of the loved one and collecting these anecdotes in a notebook.
>
> ### Take Care of Yourself
> Remind yourself that your loved one would not want you to neglect your own health. Eat a balanced diet, get enough rest, and find healthful ways to relax, such as taking up a hobby, joining a yoga class, or listening to soothing music. Get regular exercise, which helps relieve stress, depression, and anxiety. And avoid looking for a quick fix in alcohol or other drugs.

things they did around the time of a loved one's death. Continued, excessive guilt about other things is less common, though, and might be a sign of full-blown depression.

It is not unusual for survivors to have occasional thoughts of wishing they had died with the loved one or believing they would be better off dead now that the loved one is gone. But if these thoughts become frequent or turn into more specific suicidal impulses or plans, professional help should be sought immediately.

Many people have trouble keeping up with their usual routine in the wake of a loved one's death. Most begin slowly returning to their daily lives within two months, however. If problems continue without improvement, they could be a sign that full-fledged depression has set in.

Other signs that the grieving person might be seriously depressed include (1) constant preoccupation with thoughts of worthlessness, (2) a sense of moving and talking in slow motion, and (3) waking hallucinations of seeing the dead person or hearing the voice of the deceased.

*Treatment of Complicated Grief.*   People who sink into major depression after losing a loved one can benefit from the same treatments that help other depressed individuals. The main treatment options are **psychotherapy**, **antidepressants**, or both.

People who have suicidal thoughts or impulses should seek help immediately rather than waiting to see if these thoughts go away on their own with time. Those who feel totally overwhelmed or extremely distressed by their feelings may also want to see a therapist or counselor without delay.

Even when complicated grief does not rise to the level of a diagnosable mental disorder, counseling still may help reduce the suffering and resolve the grief. The painful feelings may not totally disappear, but they should gradually become less intense and more manageable.

*See also:* Support Groups; Treatment of Depression

**Further Information.**  Compassionate Friends, 900 Jorie Boulevard, Suite 78, Oak Brook, IL 60523, (877) 969-0010, www.compassionatefriends.org.

GriefNet, www.griefnet.org.

GriefShare, P.O. Box 1739, Wake Forest, NC 27588, (800) 395-5755, www.griefshare.org.

Hospice Foundation of America, 1621 Connecticut Avenue N.W., Suite 300, Washington, DC 20009, (800) 854-3402, www.hospicefoundation.org.

*Bibliography*

American Psychiatric Association. *Diagnostic and Statistical Manual of Mental Disorders.* 4th ed., text rev. Washington, DC: American Psychiatric Association, 2000.

*Complicated Grief.* Mayo Clinic, September 28, 2007, http://www.mayoclinic.com/health/complicated -grief/DS01023.

*Coping with Bereavement.* Mental Health American, March 12, 2007, http://www.nmha.org/go/ information/get-info/grief-and-bereavement/coping-with-loss.

*Major Depression and Complicated Grief.* American Cancer Society, January 8, 2008, http://www.cancer .org/docroot/MBC/content/MBC_4_1X_Major_DepressDep_and_Complicated_Grief.asp ?sitearea=MBC.

**GROUP THERAPY.**  Group therapy refers to **psychotherapy** that brings together several individuals with similar diagnoses or issues for sessions. Under the guidance of a therapist, group members interact with each other in an atmosphere of mutual respect and support. This not only helps develop social skills, but also helps enrich self-understanding and improve self-esteem.

Group therapy is sometimes incorporated into the treatment of depression, especially in settings such as hospitals, schools, and correctional facilities. Studies suggest that it can be a helpful alternative or adjunct to other treatment options, such as individual therapy and medication.

**Adolescent Coping with Depression Program.**  One group approach with proven effectiveness is the Adolescent Coping with Depression (CWD-A) program. This approach is rooted in **cognitive-behavioral therapy** (CBT), which helps people recognize and change maladaptive patterns of thinking and behaving. The CWD-A program targets problems typically experienced by **adolescents** with depression, such as irrationally negative thoughts, anxiety, poor social skills, and low participation in pleasant activities.

The program consists of 16 two-hour sessions conducted over an eight-week period. Each group is composed of up to 10 adolescents ages 13 through 17. Participants are taught skills that help them monitor their own moods, interact and communicate with others, restructure irrational thoughts, schedule activities, manage stress, resolve conflicts, and prevent relapses once they start feeling better. To encourage generalization of these skills to everyday life, participants are given homework assignments that are reviewed at the beginning of the next session.

The CWD-A program has been used with adolescents in a wide range of settings, including inner-city and rural areas. It has been implemented at schools, juvenile detention centers, and state correctional facilities. In large, randomized studies it has been shown to be an effective treatment for adolescent depression. It also has improved recovery rates in young people with coexisting **major depression** and **conduct disorder**—a behavioral disorder characterized by extreme, persistent difficulty with following the rules or behaving in a socially acceptable manner.

*See also:* Lewinsohn, Peter M.; Treatment of Depression

**Further Information.**   American Group Psychotherapy Association, 25 East 21st Street, 6th Floor, New York, NY 10010, (877) 668-2472, www.agpa.org.

## Bibliography

*Adolescent Coping with Depression (CWD-A).* SAMHSA National Registry of Evidence-Based Programs and Practices, July 2007, http://www.nrepp.samhsa.gov/programfulldetails.asp?PROGRAM_ID=124.

Clarke, Gregory N., Paul Rohde, Peter M. Lewinsohn, Hyman Hops, and John R. Seeley. "Cognitive-Behavioral Treatment of Adolescent Depression: Efficacy of Acute Group Treatment and Booster Sessions." *Journal of the American Academy of Child and Adolescent Psychiatry* 38 (1999): 272–279.

Clarke, Gregory, Peter Lewinsohn, and Hyman Hops. *Leader's Manual for Adolescent Groups: Adolescent Coping with Depression Course.* Portland, OR: Kaiser Permanente Center for Health Research, 1990.

Rohde, Paul, Gregory N. Clarke, David E. Mace, Jenel S. Jorgensen, and John R. Seeley. "An Efficacy/Effectiveness Study of Cognitive-Behavioral Treatment for Adolescents with Comorbid Major Depression and Conduct Disorder." *Journal of the American Academy of Child and Adolescent Psychiatry* 43 (2004): 660–668.

Rohde, Paul, John R. Seeley, Noah K. Kaufman, Gregory N. Clarke, and Eric Stice. "Predicting Time to Recovery Among Depressed Adolescents Treated in Two Psychosocial Group Interventions." *Journal of Consulting and Clinical Psychology* 74 (2006): 80–88.

# H

**HAMILTON DEPRESSION RATING SCALE.** The Hamilton Depression Rating Scale (HAM-D)—also known as the Hamilton Rating Scale for Depression (HRSD)—is an interview-based test administered by a mental health professional. It assesses the severity of symptoms in people who have already been diagnosed with **major depression**. The scale, developed by German-born British psychiatrist **Max Hamilton** (1912–1988) in the late 1950s, was first published in 1960. The original aim was to measure the effectiveness of **antidepressants** in controlled research. Today it remains the most widely used test of depression for this purpose.

The HAM-D also is used in clinical practice to evaluate the severity of symptoms before treatment. It may be repeated periodically to monitor the effect of treatment, and once symptoms are gone, to watch for their reappearance.

The test, which takes about 15 to 20 minutes to administer, consists of 17 items that are rated by a mental health professional based on a thorough interview of the client. The items are various symptoms of depression, such as a depressed mood, guilt, and suicidal thoughts and behavior. Each item is rated on a three-point or five-point scale indicating the severity of that symptom. The higher the total score is, the worse the depression.

Four additional items at the end of the scale provide further information about the client's condition, such as whether unusual symptoms are present. However, these last four items do not contribute to the total score on the scale.

***Pros and Cons of the HAM-D.*** The HAM-D has been the gold standard in antidepressant research for more than four decades. The scale itself also has been the subject of extensive study. Although several alternate versions have been published, including both lengthened and shortened forms, most studies evaluating the HAM-D have used the original 17-item format. In general, these studies have found that the scale is correlated with other measures of depression and distinguishes people with depression from those with other conditions. In addition, most studies have shown that different mental health professionals using the scale tend to come up with similar overall ratings for the same client.

One criticism of the original HAM-D is that it reflects a view of major depression that is now outmoded, because items on the scale only partially agree with currently accepted diagnostic criteria in the ***Diagnostic and Statistical Manual of Mental Disorders, Fourth Edition, Text Revision*** (*DSM-IV-TR*). Proponents of the HAM-D counter that the scale was never meant for diagnostic use the way *DSM-IV-TR* criteria are. Instead, the

HAM-D is intended to measure clinical changes in the symptoms of depressed individuals during treatment, and fans of the test argue that it is still well suited to that purpose.

Another drawback to the HAM-D is that each rating must take into account two different dimensions of symptom severity: intensity and frequency. Yet the original scale offered no guidelines on how much weight to give each dimension. To address this concern, a team of scientists from the International Society for CNS Drug Development has published the GRID-HAMD, a modified version of the scale that includes specific guidance on which probing questions to ask during the structured interview and how to interpret the answers. The goal of the GRID-HAMD is to simplify and standardize the administration and scoring of the scale in research and clinical practice.

*See also:* Diagnosis of Depression

***Further Information.*** International Society for CNS Drug Development, P.O. Box 910443, San Diego, CA 92191, (858) 646-2541, www.iscdd.org.

## *Bibliography*

Bagby, R. Michael, Andrew G. Ryder, Deborah R. Schuller, and Margarita B. Marshall. "The Hamilton Depression Rating Scale: Has the Gold Standard Become a Lead Weight?" *American Journal of Psychiatry* 161 (2004): 2163–2177.

Corruble, Emmanuelle, Patrick Hardy, Rasmus W. Licht, Per Bech, Ching-Lin Hsieh, Cheng-His Hsieh, et al. "Why the Hamilton Depression Rating Scale Endures." *American Journal of Psychiatry.* 162 (2005): 2394–2396.

Depression Rating Scale Standardization Team. *GRID-HAMD-17, GRID-HAMD-21: Structured Interview Guide.* San Diego, CA: International Society for CNS Drug Development, 2003.

Hamilton, Max. "A Rating Scale for Depression." *Journal of Neurology, Neurosurgery and Psychiatry* 23 (1960) 56–62.

Hamilton, Max. *This Week's Citation Classic.* August 17, 1981, http://www.garfield.library.upenn.edu/classics1981/A1981MA25900001.pdf.

Yonkers, Kimberly A., and Jacqueline A. Samson. "Mood Disorders Measures." In *Handbook of Psychiatric Measures,* 2nd ed., by A. John Rush Jr., Michael B. First, and Deborah Blacker, eds., 499–528. Washington, DC: American Psychiatric Publishing, 2008.

**HAMILTON, MAX (1912–1988).** Max Hamilton is a German-born British psychiatrist who developed the **Hamilton Depression Rating Scale** (HAM-D), the most widely used measure of depression in studies of **antidepressants**. The HAM-D consists of a scale on which a mental health professional rates the severity of a particular person's depression symptoms based on a thorough interview. Originally developed in the late 1950s, the scale was first published in 1960.

Hamilton helped pioneer modern clinical trials of psychiatric medications in other ways as well. He carried out some of the earliest double-blind studies, in which both the experimenter and the participants are unaware of who is getting the medication and who is getting a placebo—a dummy pill that looks like the real thing but does not contain an active ingredient.

***Career Highlights.*** Hamilton was born in Offenbach, Germany, but his family moved to England when he was three years old. Raised and educated in London, he eventually graduated from University College Hospital Medical School. After a stint as a physician in a deprived area of the city, Hamilton became a medical officer in the Royal Air Force during World War II. His wartime experiences—especially his observations of flight personnel returning from missions—awakened an intense interest in psychiatry and psychology.

Hamilton soon became intrigued by psychometrics, the science of mental measurement. In 1956, while a senior lecturer in psychiatry at the University of Leeds, he organized a study of a new anti-anxiety medication. Soon afterward, he began working on a scale for measuring the severity of psychiatric symptoms for research purposes. This work coincided with the introduction of the first antidepressant medications, which produced a need for a suitable way of evaluating them. Hamilton's rating scale filled that need admirably, and his 1960 journal article titled "A Rating Scale for Depression" became one of the top-cited papers in all of medical literature.

Hamilton rose to the position of professor of psychiatry at the University of Leeds, where he continued to research, publish, and lecture even after his official retirement in 1977. In 1988, at age 76, he died unexpectedly while on holiday. But his rating scale for depression lives on, influencing the way drug treatments for depression are evaluated to this day.

## Bibliography

Ewards, J. Guy. "Professor Max Hamilton, MD, FRCP, FRCPsych, DPM." *Human Psychopharmacology* 4 (1989): 77.

Hamilton, Max. "A Rating Scale for Depression." *Journal of Neurology, Neurosurgery and Psychiatry* 23 (1960): 56–62.

Hamilton, Max. *This Week's Citation Classic.* August 17, 1981, http://www.garfield.library.upenn .edu/classics1981/A1981MA25900001.pdf.

Sheehy, Noel, Antony J. Chapman, and Wendy Conroy, eds. "Hamilton, Max," in *Biographical Dictionary of Psychology.* New York: Routledge, 2002.

**HEART DISEASE.**   Heart disease is a general term for several more specific heart conditions. In the United States, the most common of these conditions is coronary heart disease (CHD), which can lead to a heart attack. Depression occurs about three times more often in people who have had a heart attack than in the population as a whole. The risk of depression after a heart attack is especially high in women, people who have been depressed before, and those who lack social support.

CHD occurs when the coronary arteries that supply blood to the heart muscle become hardened and narrowed by plaque—a buildup of fat, cholesterol, and other substances. Plaque itself reduces the flow of oxygen-carrying blood to the heart. It also makes it more likely that blood clots will form and partially or completely block the heart's blood supply.

Angina is chest pain that occurs when not enough oxygen-rich blood reaches an area of the heart muscle. When blood flow to the heart is severely restricted or completely blocked, heart muscle cells may become so starved for oxygen that they begin to die. The result is a heart attack. Without prompt treatment, a heart attack can lead to serious problems or even death.

Because there is such a close link between depression and heart disease, the American Heart Association has recommended that all heart patients be screened for depression. By asking a few quick questions, doctors can identify people who may require further assessment and treatment.

***Risks of Untreated Depression.***   For people who have CHD or who are recovering from heart attacks, untreated depression can be especially dangerous. People with depression are less likely than those who are not depressed to take their heart medication, quit smoking, **exercise**, or participate in a cardiac rehabilitation program.

These differences help explain why depression in the year after a heart attack is a risk factor for greater disability, delayed return to work, and poorer quality of life. Depression after a heart attack also at least doubles the risk of further cardiovascular events (such as another heart attack) and premature death. Most studies have found that the worse the depression is, the more severe any further cardiovascular events tend to be.

These findings have been well established by dozens of studies conducted in many thousands of patients in North America, Europe, and Asia. They underscore a critical point: Getting treatment for depression is important for anyone, but for those who also have heart disease, it is doubly beneficial.

***The Depression Connection.*** The relationship between CHD and depression cuts both ways. CHD increases the risk of becoming depressed, and depression increases the risk of developing CHD. In fact, initially healthy people with depression are 2.5 times more likely to later have a heart attack or die from heart disease than the general population. Scientists are still trying to sort out all the psychological and physiological factors that play a role in this complex relationship.

On a psychological level, being diagnosed with heart disease or having a heart attack can be stressful in itself, and **stress** may trigger or worsen depression in some vulnerable individuals. Beyond that, feeling isolated or having little emotional support are two sources of stress that are related to both CHD and depression. Being depressed, in turn, may contribute to unhealthy behaviors, such as smoking, eating a poor diet, or being physically inactive.

*Physiological Links.* On a physiological level, depression in people with CHD is associated with dysregulation of the autonomic **nervous system**, the portion of the nervous system that controls involuntary bodily functions such as circulation, breathing, and digestion. The autonomic nervous system is comprised of two opposing sets of nerves: sympathetic and parasympathetic. The sympathetic branch is activated during the body's stress response, and the parasympathetic branch is activated during the body's relaxation response.

People with CHD who are depressed tend to have increased activity in the sympathetic nervous system and decreased activity in the parasympathetic nervous system. One symptom of this type of pattern is decreased heart rate variability. Normally, heart rate varies in response to the demands of different situations, such as mental stress and physical exertion. In general, the more variability in heart rate, the better. Decreased heart rate variability is associated with both heart disease and depression.

Too much sympathetic activation keeps the body's stress system revved up and pumping out stress hormones, including **cortisol**. Excess cortisol, in turn, may contribute to increased clot formation and inflammation, and it is also associated with high blood pressure, high cholesterol, and poor blood glucose (sugar) control in people with diabetes. All these factors increase the risk of cardiovascular disease. An overactive stress response also is frequently found in people with depression.

In addition, depression is linked to low levels of **serotonin**, a chemical that helps regulate mood, sleep, appetite, and sexual drive. Serotonin **receptors** are found not only in the brain, but also on platelets, components of blood involved in clot formation. Lack of serotonin may make it easier for platelets to stick together, forming a clot that could block a coronary artery. Platelet stickiness may also be related to the same autonomic dysfunction that leads to decreased heart rate variability and increased cortisol.

Finally, depression is associated with elevated levels of substances in the blood that are markers of **inflammation**, the body's reaction to infection, irritation, or injury. Inflammation, in turn, plays an important role in atherosclerosis, the process by which plaque builds up inside the arteries.

***Treatment Considerations.***    Lifestyle changes—such as staying physically active, eating a healthful diet, losing excess weight, reducing stress, and not smoking—play a central role in the management of heart disease. People with CHD also may take various medications intended to reduce clotting, lower cholesterol or blood pressure, decrease the heart's workload, or relieve CHD symptoms. In some cases, an angioplasty (a procedure to open blocked or narrowed coronary arteries) or bypass surgery (an operation in which blood vessels taken from other parts of the body are used to bypass narrowed coronary arteries) may be needed.

When depression is an issue, the main treatment options are **antidepressants**, **psychotherapy**, or both. In the case of antidepressants, research has shown that sertraline and citalopram, two **selective serotonin reuptake inhibitors**, are safe and effective for treating depression in people with CHD. These medications are considered first-choice treatment options. In contrast, **tricyclic antidepressants** and **monoamine oxidase inhibitors**, two other types of antidepressants, can actually make heart problems worse. They are generally not recommended for people with heart disease.

Studies have shown that **cognitive-behavioral therapy** (CBT), which helps people recognize and change maladaptive patterns of thinking and behaving, also can reduce depression in heart disease patients. The Enhancing Recovery in Coronary Heart Disease Patients (ENRICHD) study included almost 2,500 people who had suffered a heart attack within the last month and who were at high risk for further heart problems due to depression or low social support. The researchers found that CBT decreased depression and improved social connectedness. However, it did not reduce the risk of having another heart attack or dying over the next two-and-a-half years.

*Double-Duty Lifestyle Changes.*    Some lifestyle changes that are good for the heart are equally good for the brain. Getting regular physical activity can help relieve depression at the same time as it improves heart health. **Relaxation techniques**, which help people keep stress under control, can be beneficial for both conditions as well. These two approaches lie at the core of cardiac rehabilitation programs, which help heart patients recover faster, feel better, and develop healthier habits for life.

Eating a diet rich in **omega-3 fatty acids**, the healthy type of fat found in fish, also may pay double dividends. It is well documented that omega-3s have benefits for heart health, such as reducing triglyceride (blood fat) levels and possibly lowering blood pressure slightly. In addition, a growing body of research suggests that omega-3s may help protect the brain against depression.

*See also:* Physical Illness; Stroke

***Further Information.***    American Heart Association, 7272 Greenville Avenue, Dallas, TX 75231, (800) 242-8721, www.americanheart.org.

National Heart, Lung and Blood Institute, P.O. Box 30105, Bethesda, MD 20824, (301) 592-8573, www.nhlbi.nih.gov.

## Bibliography

*About Heart Disease.* Centers for Disease Control and Prevention, September 10, 2008, http://www.cdc .gov/heartdisease/about.htm.

Andrews, Linda Wasmer. "Healing Hearts and Minds." *Heart-Healthy Living* (Fall 2009).

Barth, Jürgen, Martina Schumache, and Christoph Hermann-Lingen. "Depression as a Risk Factor for Mortality in Patients with Coronary Heart Disease: A Meta-analysis." *Psychsomatic Medicine* 66 (2004): 802–813.

Carney, Robert M., Kenneth E. Freedland, and Richard C. Veith. "Depression, the Autonomic Nervous System, and Coronary Heart Disease." *Psychosomatic Medicine* 67 (2005) S29-S33.

*Coronary Artery Disease.* National Heart, Lung and Blood Institute, June 2008, http://www.nhlbi.nih.gov/health/dci/Diseases/Cad/CAD_All.html.

*Depression After a Heart Attack.* American Academy of Family Physicians, November 2006, http://familydoctor.org/online/famdocen/home/common/heartdisease/recovery/702.html.

Kemp, David Eric, Shishuka Malhotra, Kathleen N. Franco, George Tesar, and David L. Bronson. "Heart Disease and Depression: Don't Ignore the Relationship." *Cleveland Clinic Journal of Medicine* 70 (2003): 745–761.

Kronish, Ian M., Nina Rieckmann, Ethan A. Halm, Daichi Shimbo, David Vorchheimer, Donald C. Haas, et al. "Persistent Depression Affects Adherence to Secondary Prevention Behaviors After Acute Coronary Syndromes." *Journal of General Internal Medicine* 21 (2006): 1178–1183.

Lespérance, François, and Nancy Frasure-Smith. "Depression and Heart Disease." *Cleveland Clinic Journal of Medicine* 74 (2007): S63-S66.

Lichtman, Judith H., J. Thomas Bigger Jr., James A. Blumenthal, Nancy Frasure-Smith, Peter G. Kaufmann, François Lespérance, et al. "Depression and Coronary Heart Disease: Recommendations for Screening, Referral, and Treatment—A Science Advisory From the American Heart Association Prevention Committee of the Council on Cardiovascular Nursing, Council on Clinical Cardiology, Council on Epidemiology and Prevention and Interdisciplinary Council on Quality of Care and Outcomes Research: Endorsed by the American Psychiatric Association." *Circulation* 118 (2008): 1768–1775.

*Mood Disorders and Other Illnesses.* Depression and Bipolar Support Alliance, September 1, 2006, http://www.dbsalliance.org/site/PageServer?pagename=about_mooddisorders.

*Top Ten Things to Know: Depression and Coronary Heart Disease (CHD).* American Heart Association, 2008, http://www.americanheart.org/downloadable/heart/1222379335251topTenDepression.pdf.

Van Melle, Joost P., Peter de Jonge, Titia A. Spukerman, Jan G.P. Tussen, Johan Ormel, Dirk J. van Veldhuisen, et al. "Prognostic Association of Depression Following Myocardial Infarction with Mortality and Cardiovascular Events: A Meta-analysis." *Psychosomatic Medicine* 66 (2004): 814–822.

Writing Committee for the ENRICHD Investigators. "Effects of Treating Depression and Low Perceived Social Support on Clinical Events After Myocardial Infarction: The Enhancing Recovery in Coronary Heart Disease Patients (ENRICHD) Randomized Trial." *JAMA* 289 (2003): 3106–3116.

**HERBAL REMEDIES.**    An herb is a plant or plant part that is used for its scent, flavor, or therapeutic properties. It can include a plant's flowers, leaves, bark, seeds, fruit, stems, and roots. Herbs are sold as fresh or dried products; liquid or solid extracts; teas; tablets; capsules; or powders. **St. John's wort** is the best-studied herb for managing mild to moderate depression. But a number of other herbs are sometimes recommended for depression, too, based largely on traditional practice rather than scientific evidence.

Many herbs have a long history of therapeutic use. Because herbs act like drugs on the body, it is easy to see how the right herb in the right amount could be beneficial. But it also follows that any herb powerful enough to help is also strong enough to do harm if misused. Some herbs may cause unwanted side effects, and others may interact harmfully with certain medications. For example, St. John's wort may affect the way the body processes many drugs, including **antidepressants**, birth control pills, and certain medications used to treat heart disease, cancer, and HIV infection.

To be on the safe side, people should talk to a health care provider before trying an herbal remedy. This is particularly important for those who (1) have a chronic health condition, (2) take any medication, (3) plan to have surgery, (4) are pregnant or breastfeeding, or (5) are considering giving a supplement to a child. Even if the provider is not familiar with a particular herb, he or she can access the latest scientific guidance on usage, risks, and interactions.

*See also:* Dietary Supplements

**Further Information.** American Herbalists Guild, 141 Nob Hill Road, Cheshire, CT 06410, (203) 272-6731, www.americanherbalistsguild.com.

*Bibliography*

*Botanical Dietary Supplements: Background Information.* National Institutes of Health Office of Dietary Supplements, April 11, 2006, http://ods.od.nih.gov/factsheets/BotanicalBackground.asp.
*Herbal Supplements: Consider Safety, Too.* National Center for Complementary and Alternative Medicine, December 2006, http://nccam.nih.gov/health/supplement-safety/herbal-supplements.htm.

**HIPPOCAMPUS.** The hippocampus is a seahorse-shaped structure in the brain that plays a role in memory, learning, and emotion. In people with **major depression**, the hippocampus often shrinks, and the more prolonged the depression, the greater the loss of volume tends to be. This helps explain the declines in memory and thinking ability that frequently go hand in hand with depression.

In part of the hippocampus called the dentate gyrus, new brain cells are created throughout adulthood. **Serotonin**, a brain chemical that helps regulate mood, also is involved in the creation of these new cells. Most **antidepressants** boost the availability of serotonin in the brain, and they also increase the production and survival of new brain cells in the hippocampus. The new cells, in turn, help account for some of the beneficial effects of antidepressants.

### The Lesson of Cushing's Syndrome

Cushing's syndrome is a hormonal disorder caused by prolonged exposure to high levels of cortisol. Like people with major depression, those with Cushing's tend to have shrinkage of the hippocampus.

Some people develop Cushing's from taking glucocorticoid medications, which are used to treat asthma, rheumatoid arthritis, lupus, and other inflammatory conditions. Others develop Cushing's because a tumor causes the body to overproduce cortisol. In either case, the syndrome can lead to a variety of symptoms, including upper body obesity, easily bruised skin, fragile bones, severe fatigue, weak muscles, high blood pressure, high blood glucose (sugar), excess hair growth on women, and decreased fertility in men. Depression is another common symptom of the disorder.

Treatment depends on the reason for the excess cortisol. If the cause is glucocorticoid medication, the dose may be decreased or another medication may be prescribed instead. If the cause is a tumor, options include surgery, radiation, chemotherapy, and cortisol-inhibiting medication. When the cortisol problem is fixed, the hippocampus often regains some or all of its normal volume.

This is encouraging news not only for people with Cushing's, but also for those with major depression. It suggests that hippocampal shrinkage in depression may likewise be partially or fully reversible with the right treatment.

***Effects of Chronic Stress.*** Why does the hippocampus shrink in people with prolonged depression? Scientists think long-lasting **stress** may be a key piece in the puzzle. Sustained stress can decrease neurogenesis (the creation of new brain cells), and it also can lead to neurotoxicity (damage to brain cells that are already there). Both of these effects may contribute to hippocampal shrinkage.

Much of the research in this area has focused on **cortisol**, a glucocorticoid hormone released by the adrenal glands in response to stress. About half of people with major depression overproduce cortisol. Excessive cortisol has a variety of harmful effects on the brain, centered in the hippocampus, an area rich in glucocorticoid **receptors**. In addition to decreasing neurogenesis and causing neurotoxicity, cortisol can cause brain cells to pull back the tiny, branchlike extensions through which they receive messages.

The good news is that treatment with antidepressants can help counter the harmful effects of excessive cortisol. Some antidepressants reduce cortisol directly, and others affect it indirectly by altering the activity of chemical messengers within the brain. As already noted, antidepressants may increase neurogenesis in the hippocampus. Certain antidepressants also stop the pulling back of receiving branches on brain cells there.

*See also:* Brain Anatomy; Brain-Derived Neurotrophic Factor; Hormones

## Bibliography

Campbell, Stephanie, and Glenda MacQueen. "The Role of the Hippocampus in the Pathophysiology of Major Depression." *Journal of Psychiatry and Neuroscience* 29 (2004): 417–426.

*Cushing's Fact Sheet.* Pituitary Network Association, January 2006, http://www.pituitary.org/news/Articles/CushingsFactSheet.php.

*Cushing's Syndrome.* National Endocrine and Metabolic Diseases Information Service, July 2008, http://www.endocrine.niddk.nih.gov/pubs/cushings/cushings.htm.

McEwen, Bruce S. *Stress, Depression and Brain Structure.* Depression and Bipolar Support Alliance, August 30, 2006, http://www.dbsalliance.org/site/PageServer?pagename=about_depression_mcewen.

Paizanis, Eleni, Michel Hamon, and Laurence Lanfumey. "Hippocampal Neurogenesis, Depressive Disorders, and Antidepressant Therapy." *Neural Plasticity* (2007): art. no. 73754.

Patil, Chirag G., Shivanand P. Lad, Laurence Katznelson, and Edward R. Laws Jr. "Brain Atrophy and Cognitive Deficits in Cushing's Disease." *Neurosurgical Focus* 23 (2007): E11.

Sahay, Amar, and Rene Hen. "Adult Hippocampal Neurogenesis in Depression." *Nature Neuroscience* 10 (2007): 1110–1115.

Sapolsky, Robert M. "Depression, Antidepressants, and the Shrinking Hippocampus." *Proceedings of the National Academy of Sciences of the USA* 98 (2001): 12320–12322.

**HISPANIC AMERICANS.** Hispanic (or Latino) Americans are the largest ethnic minority in the United States, comprising 15 percent of the total population. Because this group is growing so rapidly, however, it is expected to make up nearly one-quarter of the U.S. population by 2050. Two-thirds of Hispanic Americans trace their ancestry back to Mexico. The rest have roots in Cuba, Puerto Rico, Central America, South America, or another Spanish culture. This diverse community is bound together by the Spanish language, sometimes still spoken by the current generation, and by shared traditions and cultural values.

In general, rates of mental illness for Hispanic Americans are similar to those for non-Hispanic whites. Looking specifically at **major depression**, most studies have found that Hispanic Americans have similar or lower rates than non-Hispanic white individuals. But certain subgroups of Hispanic Americans—most notably, immigrants and youth—are at increased risk for serious emotional distress.

Although Hispanic Americans are vulnerable to the same mental health challenges as anyone else, they use mental health services less often than average. A large, national survey of U.S. adults who had experienced major depression within the last year found that just 52 percent of Hispanic Americans received treatment, compared to 73 percent of non-Hispanic whites. Among young people ages 12 through 17, the treatment rate was even lower—only 36 percent, compared to 41 percent for non-Hispanic white youth.

In part, this disparity may stem from cultural attitudes toward mental health disorders. Depression, for example, may be viewed as simply a passing case of nerves, tiredness, or physical illness. Rather than turning to a mental health professional for help, Hispanic Americans often reach out first to their family, friends, community, and church, or to a traditional healer.

***At-Risk Groups.*** Ironically, some of the lowest rates of mental health care are found in high-risk subgroups. Among Hispanic immigrants with mental disorders, for example, fewer than 5 percent receive treatment from a mental health specialist.

*Immigrants.* Immigrants face many challenges. They must adapt to a new culture with foreign customs and often an unfamiliar language, and they must make this difficult transition without the support of loved ones left behind. Many also are faced with discrimination, financial hardship, and poor living conditions in their adopted country. It is little wonder that immigrants sometimes experience considerable **stress**, which may trigger or worsen depression in vulnerable individuals.

In addition, many immigrants from Central America are refugees who fled political turmoil and violence in their homelands. Over 90 percent of these immigrants arrived in the United States between 1970 and 1990. However, the **traumatic events** that brought them to this country may have lingering repercussions to this day, putting them at high risk for **post-traumatic stress disorder** and depression.

*Youth.* Hispanic American youth are another subgroup with an increased risk for poor mental health outcomes. They have the highest rate of **suicide** attempts among all ethnic minorities in the United States. Plus, they are at greater risk for depressive symptoms, anxiety-related behaviors, delinquency, and drug use than non-Hispanic white youth.

Young Hispanic Americans may experience the same stress and discrimination as their parents, but without the secure grounding in traditional values. In addition, immigrant parents often invest high hopes for the American dream in their children. Although some youngsters are propelled to success, others buckle under the pressure.

***Barriers to Care.*** Lack of access to appropriate, high-quality care is a problem for many Hispanic Americans with depression. One hurdle is the language and culture gap between Hispanic patients and non-Hispanic treatment providers. Another hurdle is the disproportionately high number of Hispanic Americans in low-income, underserved communities.

*Language.* About 12 percent of Hispanic Americans speak Spanish at home. Lack of fluency in English is a major barrier for many of these individuals. Bilingual treatment providers and translators are in limited supply, making it difficult for Spanish speakers to get adequate assessment, treatment, and emergency care for pressing mental health problems.

*Providers.* Even Hispanic Americans who speak English fluently may have trouble finding culturally appropriate services. An individual's culture can influence such things as how depression is expressed, how symptoms are understood, and which treatments are most acceptable. Yet Hispanic Americans are underrepresented in the mental health field.

There are only 29 Hispanic mental health professionals per every 100,000 Hispanic Americans, compared to 173 non-Hispanic white professionals per 100,000.

*Socioeconomic Factors.* Low **socioeconomic status** is a well-established risk factor for depression. Although eight percent of non-Hispanic whites live at the poverty level, the poverty rate for Hispanic Americans is 21.5 percent. A low income, and the poor living conditions that go along with it, may contribute to depression directly by causing long-term stress. At the same time, people with limited social and financial resources are apt to have trouble accessing high-quality mental health care.

*Insurance.* Hispanic Americans have the nation's highest rate of uninsured individuals—37 percent, compared to 16 percent for the general population. Another 18 percent of Hispanic Americans rely on public health insurance. Only 43 percent have employer-based health coverage.

***Protective Factors.*** Helping balance out these risks are **protective factors** that decrease the likelihood of becoming depressed. For instance, the traditional Hispanic value of strong family ties may offer social support. This support, in turn, may promote resilience in the face of hardship or stress.

Interestingly, there is evidence that resilience may decrease as Hispanic individuals spend more time in the United States or become more fluent in English. Researchers have found lower rates of mental health disorders for Mexican-born immigrants and island-born Puerto Rican adults compared with those of Mexican or Puerto Rican descent who are born in the United States. The more acculturated these individuals become, the less protected they may be against mental health problems.

*See also:* Adolescents; Cultural Factors; Ethnicity; Susto

***Further Information.*** National Latino Behavioral Health Association, 1616 P Street N.W., Suite 109, Washington, DC 20036, (202) 797-6530, www.nlbha.org.

Office of Minority Health, U.S. Department of Health and Human Services, P.O. Box 37337, Washington, D.C. 20013, (800) 444-6472, www.omhrc.gov.

## Bibliography

*Hispanic/Latino Profile.* U.S. Department of Health and Human Services Office of Minority Health, July 31, 2009, http://www.omhrc.gov/templates/browse.aspx?lvl=3&lvlid=31.

*Hispanics/Latinos.* American Psychiatric Association, http://healthyminds.org/More-Info-For/HispanicsLatinos.aspx.

*Latinos/Hispanic Americans.* U.S. Department of Health and Human Services Office of the Surgeon General, http://mentalhealth.samhsa.gov/cre/fact3.asp.

Mendelson, Tamar, David H. Rehkopf, and Laura D. Kubzansky. "Depression Among Latinos in the United States: A Meta-analytic Review." *Journal of Consulting and Clinical Psychology* 76 (2008): 355–366.

*Mental Health and Hispanics.* U.S. Department of Health and Human Services Office of Minority Health, July 27, 2009, http://www.omhrc.gov/templates/content.aspx?lvl=3&lvlID=9&ID=6477.

Riolo, Stephanie A., Tuan Anh Nguyen, John F. Greden, and Cheryl A. King. "Prevalence of Depression by Race/Ethnicity: Findings From the National Health and Nutrition Examination Survey III." *American Journal of Public Health* 95 (2005): 998–1000.

*2008 National Healthcare Quality and Disparities Reports.* Agency for Healthcare Research and Quality, http://www.ahrq.gov/qual/qrdr08/index.html.

U.S. Department of Health and Human Services. *Culture, Race, and Ethnicity: A Supplement to Mental Health: A Report of the Surgeon General.* Rockville, MD: U.S. Department of Health and Human Services, 2001.

**HISTORICAL PERSPECTIVE.**   The systematic study of **mood disorders** dates back some 2,500 years to the time of the ancient Greeks, and written descriptions of depressive states go back even farther. Depression itself seems to be a universal human malady that may well be as old as *Homo sapiens.*

Some of the earliest references to depressive moods are found in the Old Testament. One story involves Hannah, mother of the prophet Samuel, who at first struggled to conceive. As the story relates: "Then said Elkanah her husband to her, Hannah, why weepest thou? and why eatest thou not? and why is thy heart grieved? am not I better to thee than ten sons?" (1 Samuel 1:8). Hannah responded to infertility with bouts of **crying** and lack of appetite—in short, she apparently became depressed.

The article below surveys historical perspectives on depression from antiquity through the nineteenth century. More recent historical developments, dating from 1900 to the present, are described in various articles throughout this encyclopedia.

*Ancient Greece.*   In times past, **mental illness** was often attributed to the actions of evil spirits or punishment by the gods. In ancient Greece, however, supernatural explanations gradually gave way to biological ones. Greek physician Hippocrates (ca. 460 BC–ca. 375 BC) is credited with the first clear-cut statement attributing **melancholia**—a condition that included a despondent mood—to dysfunction of the brain.

The Latinized term "melancholia" comes from two Greek words, *melas* and *khole*, meaning "black bile." It reflects Hippocrates' belief that the underlying brain dysfunction was caused by an excess of black bile—one of four basic body fluids, called humors, that determined a person's emotional and physical makeup. According to Hippocrates, those with a melancholic **temperament** were prone to despondency, sleeplessness, irritability, restlessness, and an aversion to food—a description that still echoes through modern definitions of depression.

In the second century AD, Greek physician Aretaeus of Cappadocia (ca.150–ca. 200) stated the first coherent theory connecting the mood extremes of melancholia and **mania**—a theory that anticipated current thinking about **bipolar disorder**. Aretaeus described those with a melancholic disposition as "dull or stern, dejected or unreasonably torpid, without any manifest cause. . . . [They] also become peevish, dispirited, sleepless, and start up from a disturbed sleep. Unreasonable fears also seize them." In patients whose illness grew more urgent, he noted that "hatred, avoidance of the haunts of men, vain lamentations are seen. They complain of life and desire to die."

Around the same time, the prominent Greek physician Galen (129–ca. 216) concluded that the functioning of nerves was mediated by something called "animal spirits." Galen believed that animal spirits were formed in the brain and passed through the nerves to the body's feeling and moving parts. This notion foreshadowed the current concept of **neurotransmitters**—chemicals by which nerve cells communicate.

*Islamic Medicine.*   The ancient Greek concept of melancholia persisted in both Europe and the Middle East through the Middle Ages. Islamic physicians of this period viewed melancholia and mania as manifestations of a single disorder. Notable among them was Persian philosopher and physician Avicenna (980–1037), whose Arabic medical encyclopedia, *The Canon of Medicine,* is among the seminal texts in the history of medicine.

Beginning in the late thirteenth century, love became an important concept in Arab medicine, and it was thought that pining over the object of unrequited love could at times turn into lovesickness. A person in the grips of lovesickness grew dejected, low in spirits, and melancholic—in modern parlance, a classic case of a **depressed mood** triggered by interpersonal loss. If the love object became available, lovesickness was instantly cured, and the person's mood immediately lifted. But if the love object remained unattainable, lovesickness could be lasting and dangerous—even fatal.

**Sixteenth and Seventeenth Centuries.**   During the sixteenth and seventeenth centuries, fresh perspectives on melancholy—the Anglicized term for melancholia—began to emerge in Europe. English physician Timothy Bright (1551–1615) had a dual interest in medicine and theology. He differentiated between natural melancholy and melancholy arising from "the heavy hand of God upon the afflicted conscience." His 1586 treatise on melancholy suggested therapeutic remedies for the former and spiritual consolation for the latter.

Bright's contemporary, French physician André du Laurens (1560–1609), focused attention on delusional aspects of a melancholic state. His memorable descriptions of melancholic madmen, such as one man who thought himself made of glass or others who were convinced they had swallowed a serpent or frog—were cited for two centuries to come.

Yet it was left not to a physician, but to a clergyman from Oxford University to write what is arguably the most important book ever penned about depression. *The Anatomy of Melancholy*, by **Robert Burton** (1577–1640), was an immediate popular success when first published in 1621. For the rest of his life, Burton continued to revise and expand his magnum opus, which went through five subsequent editions.

Burton's book is an eccentric mix of medicine, literature, wit, and whimsy. In it, he presented an expanded theory of humors, attributing the presumed excess of black bile to a number of possible

### The Bard on Melancholy

The works of English playwright and poet William Shakespeare (1564–1616) contain no fewer than 69 references to melancholy. In one example, taken from *The Comedy of Errors*, Shakespeare writes:

> Sweet recreation barr'd, what doth ensue
> But moody and dull melancholy,
> Kinsman to grim and comfortless despair,
> And at her heels a huge infectious troop
> Of pale distemperatures and foes to life?
> (V.I.78–82)

causes, including poor diet, overindulgence in alcohol, disturbed biological rhythms, and intense love or grief. In addition, he described what he called "causeless" melancholy.

The prevailing treatment of the day—little changed from the time of the ancient Greeks—consisted largely of exposing patients to amusing games, beautiful art, lovely gardens, and other pleasant experiences. Burton also espoused the therapeutic power of music. He noted that, of the many and sundry means to lift a heavy heart, there were "in my judgment none so present, none so powerful, none so apposite as a cup of strong drink, mirth, music, and merry company" (Pt. 2, Sec. 2, Mem. 6, Subs. 3). Interestingly, modern researchers have confirmed the depression-fighting power of pleasant activity scheduling (used in **behavioral therapy**) and **music therapy**.

**Eighteenth Century.**   The first detailed account of blood circulation by British physician William Harvey (1578–1657) had a profound impact on medicine. Around the dawn of the eighteenth century, various theories ascribed melancholic moods to the dynamics of blood circulation. Many of these theories focused on thickening of the blood, which was thought to cause sluggish circulation in the brain. That, in turn, was believed to affect the flow of animal spirits.

One example of this type of model was advanced by Scottish physician Archibald Pitcairne (1652–1713), who attributed melancholy to thick blood and sluggish circulation in the brain. German physician Friedrich Hoffmann (1660–1742) ascribed it to animal spirits that had turned sluggish and acidic. In 1751, English physician Richard Mead (1673–1754) added a new twist to these schemes, theorizing that the animal spirits underlying melancholy might be electrical in nature.

A major figure of the era, Scottish physician William Cullen (1710–1790), developed a theory that essentially attributed mental disorders to excessive irritation of the nerves. He believed the precipitating cause was acute brain activity. Yet he also emphasized psychological factors, stressing an unusual and hurried association of ideas, which led to "false judgement" and "disproportionate emotions." To a large extent, it was Cullen who put the "mental" back in mental disorders.

***Nineteenth Century.*** Toward the end of the eighteenth century, psychological theories of mental illness began to dominate the field. By this point, the definition of melancholy had been stretched far beyond its original meaning. French physician Philippe Pinel (1745–1826) described melancholy as a tendency toward not only marked inactivity and gloomy taciturnity, but also violent passion and outbursts of gaiety. Mania, in turn, was described as a tendency toward not only excessive joviality and immoderate laughter, but also crying jags and intense **sadness**. It seems that the two mood extremes had been conflated into a single, far-reaching condition.

French psychiatrist Jean-Étienne Esquirol (1772–1840), a pupil of Pinel, criticized the prevailing view of melancholy as too broad and too vague. Esquirol subdivided melancholia into narrower disorders, called monomanias, in which the mind focused on a single subject. Esquirol coined the term *lypémanie*, from the Greek for "sad-madness," to signify the monomania focused on a sad mood. Meanwhile, physician Benjamin Rush (1746–1813), a founding father of the newly formed United States, suggested an alternate term: *tristemania*. Although neither term for depression lasted, the narrower mood state they described comes much closer to current thinking about the disorder.

In 1856, French psychiatrist Louis Delasiauve (1804–1893) finally hit upon a name with more staying power: depression. It was one of the first medical uses of the term, although the noun had previously debuted in other contexts. For example, English author Samuel Johnson (1709–1784) had used depression as a synonym for "low spirits" a century before.

Starting in the late 1800s, German psychiatrist Emil Kraepelin (1856–1926) pioneered the modern classification of mental disorders. Kraepelin distinguished between two main categories of severe mental illness: manic-depressive psychosis and dementia praecox (schizophrenia). Kraepelin's concept of manic-depressive psychosis encompassed what is now considered not only bipolar disorder, but also **major depression**. He described the main signs of a depressive state as a low mood, inhibition of thought, and weakness of decision making.

Kraepelin ushered in the contemporary era of scientific psychiatry as well as the current view of depression. In the intervening years, knowledge about the disorder has grown exponentially. Yet it is still possible to trace the pedigree of many new discoveries back for centuries or even millennia. In the quest for the next big step forward, today's scientists might be well advised to look backward for inspiration.

*See also:* Melancholic Depression; Traditional Chinese Medicine

*Bibliography*

Burton, Robert. *The Anatomy of Melancholy.* New York: New York Review of Books, 2001.
Davison, Kenneth. "Historical Aspects of Mood Disorders." *Psychiatry* 5 (2006): 115–118.
Evans, G. Blakemore, ed. *The Riverside Shakespeare.* Boston: Houghton Mifflin, 1974.

"History 1450–1789," in *Encyclopedia of the Early Modern World.* Farmington Hills, MI: Gale Group, 2004.

Jackson, Stanley W. "Melancholia and Mechanical Explanation in Eighteenth-Century Medicine." *Journal of the History of Medicine and Allied Sciences* 38 (1983): 298–319.

*King James Version Bible.* BibleGateway.com, http://www.biblegateway.com/versions/index .php?action=getVersionInfo&vid=9&lang=2.

McDonald, Ian. "Impulses Good and Bad." *Brain* 128 (2005): 227–231.

Porter, Roy. *Madness: A Brief History.* New York: Oxford University Press, 2002.

Radden, Jennifer, ed. *The Nature of Melancholy: From Aristotle to Kristeva.* New York: Oxford University Press, 2000.

Shorter, Edward. *A History of Psychiatry: From the Era of the Asylum to the Age of Prozac.* New York: John Wiley and Sons, 1997.

Stone, Michael H. "Historical Aspects of Mood Disorders." In *The American Psychiatric Publishing Textbook of Mood Disorders,* by Dan J. Stein, David J. Kupfer and Alan F. Schatzberg, eds., 3–15. Washington, DC: American Psychiatric Publishing, 2006.

**HOLIDAY DEPRESSION.** The holidays are a time for fun, family, festivity—and for some people, depression. The added demands of holiday shopping, socializing, and cooking can be quite stressful, and **stress**, in turn, can set off depression in vulnerable individuals. At the same time, many people fall into bad self-care habits during the holidays. Overeating, lack of exercise, drinking too much, and sleeping too little can make matters worse.

Relationships are a common trigger. Family conflicts often flare up when far-flung relatives come together for the occasion. At the other end of the spectrum, the pain of a loved one's absence may be felt especially acutely, leading to deep **sadness** or **grief**.

Financial concerns are another frequent trigger. Overspending on gifts, travel, or entertainment can cause substantial stress. If the financial burden is too heavy, it may lead to feelings of hopelessness, helplessness, and guilt. Fortunately, by taking steps to limit spending and reduce stress, it may be possible to prevent or minimize holiday depression.

---

**Happy Holidays**

These tips can help reduce holiday stress and depression.

***Keep Expectations Realistic***

Don't try to match an unrealistic Hollywood image of holiday perfection. Expect that some problems or disappointments will inevitably occur. It may help to spread out the festivities over the whole season rather than pinning a year's worth of hopes on a single day, which is likely to lead to an emotional letdown.

***Prioritize and Prune Activities***

Give some hard thought to which activities are truly important and which are expendable or even burdensome. Eliminate less important activities if you find yourself stretched too thin. Allow plenty of time for exercise, sleep, and rest.

***Hold Spending in Check***

In a survey conducted by the American Psychological Association, people cited lack of money and the pressures of gift-giving as the top two sources of holiday stress. So make a budget, and stick to it. Pare down spending by giving homemade items or the gift of your time (for instance, by sharing a hobby you love with a child or by going cycling, sledding, or ice skating as a family).

***Seek Help When Needed***

Realize that depression may sometimes crop up or get worse over the holidays despite your best efforts. If you are feeling so sad, empty, or hopeless that it is hard to go about your daily life, talk to your doctor or mental health care provider.

---

*Bibliography*

*Holiday Depression and Stress.* Mental Health America, March 9, 2007, http://www.nmha.org/
go/information/get-info/depression/holiday-depression-and-stress.
*Holiday Stress Tips.* American Psychological Association, 2006, http://apahelpcenter.org/articles/
article.php?id=149.
*Holiday Stress: How to Stay Calm During the Mad Scramble of the Holidays.* American Psychological
Association, 2006, http://apahelpcenter.org/articles/article.php?id=8.
*Holiday Stress: What's Stressing You out This Holiday Season.* American Psychological Association, 2006,
http://www.apahelpcenter.org/articles/article.php?id=67.
*Stress, Depression and the Holidays: 12 Tips for Coping.* Mayo Clinic, October 19, 2007, http://www
.mayoclinic.com/print/stress/MH00030/METHOD=print.

**HORMONES.**   Hormones are chemical messengers secreted by endocrine glands or other organs. They travel around the body in the bloodstream and have effects on distant organs or tissues. These chemicals play a crucial role in controlling body functions, such as growth, reproduction, and metabolism. They also influence basic behaviors, such as emotion, sexuality, and **stress** responses.

Although hormones are carried around the whole body, they act on only certain target cells. These cells are equipped with **receptors**, specialized sites that bind to and react with a particular chemical. Once a hormone binds to its matching receptor, it modifies the activity of the cell, causing characteristic effects in the body. Many hormones have receptors in the brain, where they affect mental functions and disorders, including depression.

Minute amounts of hormones can have large effects. Because hormones are so potent, they must be carefully regulated by the body. The physiological changes triggered by hormones are healthy up to a point, but once that point is passed, a mechanism to reverse the changes may kick in.

***Production of Hormones.***   Hormones are produced by glands that make up the **endocrine system**, including the pineal gland, pituitary gland, thyroid, parathyroid, adrenal glands, pancreas, thymus, ovaries, and testes. Some other organs—such as the stomach, intestines, and heart—also produce hormones. But because this is not their primary function, they are not considered endocrine glands.

Chemically speaking, there are two main types of hormones: steroids and proteins. Steroids, produced by the sex organs and the outer part of the adrenal glands, react with receptors on a cell's surface. Proteins or protein derivatives, which account for all other hormones in the human body, typically react with receptors inside a cell. Because this process involves the synthesis of proteins, such hormones act more slowly than steroids do.

***Hormones in the Brain.***   Hormones affect the brain, altering the structure and function of cells there. Over a period of hours to days, this can bring about changes in the circuitry of the brain and its capacity for sending chemical messages. When all goes well, such changes are adaptive. But when there is a hitch, the changes may lead to maladaptive behaviors, including symptoms of depression.

The brain affects hormones as well. A small brain structure called the **hypothalamus** releases hormones that strongly influence the pituitary gland, located at the base of the brain. The pituitary, in turn, secretes hormones that influence almost every other gland in the body.

***Rise of Neuroendocrinology.***   In theory, the endocrine and nervous systems are two distinct communication networks. Hormones are the chemical messengers of the endocrine system, and **neurotransmitters** are the chemical messengers of the **nervous system**. In practice, though, some chemicals do double duty, serving as both hormones and neurotransmitters. An example is **norepinephrine**, which is involved in the body's stress response and helps regulate arousal, sleep, and blood pressure.

Beyond that, some cells of the nervous system make substances that act strictly as hormones. For example, cells in the hypothalamus secrete hormones that regulate the pituitary gland.

The more scientists learn, the more apparent it becomes that the nervous system and endocrine system are not as separate as once believed. There is considerable overlap and interaction. This recognition has given rise to a hybrid scientific field called neuroendocrinology, which studies relationships between the nervous and endocrine systems.

*The Depression Connection.* When it comes to moods, emotions, and behaviors, the effects of hormones and neurotransmitters are closely intertwined. Abnormalities in several hormones have been linked to depression.

### Hunger Hormones and Mood

Ghrelin and leptin are two hormones best known for their role in weight control, but recent research indicates they may be important in mood control, too. Ghrelin is produced mainly by the stomach, and leptin is produced by fat cells throughout the body. Both hormones work largely through the hypothalamus to regulate appetite and metabolism—and both also may be involved in depression.

In mice, at least, ghrelin seems to have an antidepressant effect. Researchers in one study looked for depression-like behavior in mice using standard lab tests. For instance, the mice were put in water, and those who gave up sooner on trying to swim their way out were considered "depressed." Then the researchers increased ghrelin levels in the depressed mice both naturally, by withholding food, and artificially, by giving them an injection. In both cases, the mice began swimming normally after their ghrelin levels were raised.

Leptin also seems to have antidepressant properties. In other studies, when mice were repeatedly stressed, they tended to isolate themselves and show less interest in sugar water—another way of approximating depression. But when researchers gave the depressed mice leptin, their behavior returned to normal. Low leptin also has been linked to human depression, and some researchers think drugs targeting leptin could one day be used for treating the disorder.

**Corticotropin-Releasing Hormone (CRH).** This hormone made by the hypothalamus stimulates the release of another hormone by the pituitary gland. CRH plays a key role in the body's stress response. Depression is associated with overproduction of CRH.

**Cortisol**. This hormone made by the outer part of the adrenal glands is released as part of the body's **stress** response, arousing various body systems and getting them ready to cope with a threat. People with depression often have an overactive stress response and abnormally high levels of cortisol in their blood.

**Estrogen**. This hormone is produced chiefly by the ovaries, but it is also made by the adrenal glands and other tissues. Estrogen plays a critical role in female puberty and menstruation, but it also has nonreproductive functions. Fluctuations in estrogen levels during the menstrual cycle or over the lifespan may disrupt brain chemicals that affect mood, increasing the risk of depression in susceptible women.

**Melatonin**. This hormone made by the pineal gland helps control sleep patterns. Changes in the daily timing of melatonin production may be a factor in **seasonal affective**

**disorder**, a form of depression in which symptoms start and stop around the same time each year, typically beginning in fall or winter and subsiding in spring.

*See also:* Appetite Disturbances; Hippocampus; Hypothyroidism

*Bibliography*

*Brain Facts: A Primer on the Brain and Nervous System.* 6th ed. Washington, DC: Society for Neuroscience, 2008.

*Characteristics of Hormones.* National Cancer Institute, http://training.seer.cancer.gov/module _anatomy/unit6_2_endo_hormones.html.

*Depression in Women: Understanding the Gender Gap.* Mayo Clinic, September 6, 2008, http://www.mayoclinic.com/health/depression/MH00035.

*Endocrine Glands and Their Hormones.* National Cancer Institute, http://training.seer.cancer.gov/ module_anatomy/unit6_3_endo_glnds.html.

*Endocrine System and Syndromes.* American Association for Clinical Chemistry, December 21, 2005, http://www.labtestsonline.org/understanding/conditions2/endocrine_table.html.

Lu, Xin-Yun. "The Leptin Hypothesis of Depression: A Potential Link Between Mood Disorders and Obesity?" *Current Opinion in Pharmacology* 7 (2007): 648–652.

Lutter, Michael, Ichiro Sakata, Sherri Osborne-Lawrence, Sherry A. Rovinsky, Jason G. Anderson, Saendy Jung et al. "The Orexigenc Hormone Ghrelin Defends Against Depressive Symptoms of Chronic Stress." *Nature Neuroscience* 11 (2008): 752–753.

Sukel, Kayt. *"Feeding" Hormones Affect More Than Hunger.* Dana Foundation, September 2, 2008, http://www.dana.org/news/brainwork/detail.aspx?id=13178.

*The Wired Brain: Advanced.* Canadian Institute of Neurosciences, Mental Health and Addiction, http://thebrain.mcgill.ca/flash/a/a_01/a_01_cr/a_01_cr_fon/a_01_cr_fon.html.

*The Wired Brain: Intermediate.* Canadian Institute of Neurosciences, Mental Health and Addiction, http://thebrain.mcgill.ca/flash/i/i_01/i_01_cr/i_01_cr_fon/i_01_cr_fon.html.

**HOSPITAL ANXIETY AND DEPRESSION SCALE.** The Hospital Anxiety and Depression Scale (HADS) is a self-report questionnaire designed to assess the severity of depression and anxiety in patients with general medical conditions. Introduced in 1983, the HADS was developed by British psychiatrists Anthony Zigmond and Philip Snaith. They were responding to a colleague's request for a simple test that could help distinguish **clinical depression** from the **sadness** and **grief** that often go along with having an illness. The HADS was a big step forward in that regard, and it has since been used in more than 700 scientific papers.

The HADS consists of 14 items, each of which presents four statements about a particular symptom of depression or anxiety arranged in order of severity. By design, the items do not cover the full range of symptoms. Instead, the test intentionally excludes symptoms, such as trouble sleeping and loss of appetite, that also are common in **physical illness**.

The questionnaire, which takes just a few minutes to complete, is quick and easy for patients to fill out in a waiting room. The questions are nonthreatening, avoiding any mention of severe symptoms that would clearly indicate a serious mental disorder. This makes the test ideally suited for use as a screening tool in medical clinics and hospitals.

***Pros and Cons of the HADS.*** The HADS is scored on two subscales: Depression and Anxiety. Research shows that the test does a good job of distinguishing between these two conditions. For both depression and **anxiety disorders**, the HADS performs well at identifying the problem and assessing symptom severity.

When scores on the HADS are compared to those on other common tests for depression and anxiety, most studies have found moderate to strong correlations. This is one way of establishing that the HADS does indeed measure what it purports to measure.

Research has shown that the HADS has good internal consistency, the degree to which all the items are measuring the same thing. The fact that the internal consistency holds up in various translations is an indication of the test's robustness. There is also a strong correlation between test scores when the same person retakes the HADS within a short time.

*See also:* Diagnosis of Depression; Screening Tests

## Bibliography

Bjelland, Ingvar, Alv A. Dahl, Tone Tangen Haug, and Dag Neckelmann. "The validity of the Hospital Anxiety and Depression Scale: An Updated Literature Review." *Journal of Psychosomatic Research* 52 (2002): 69–77.

Snaith, R.P., and A.S. Zigmond. "The Hospital Anxiety and Depression Scale." *British Medical Journal* 292 (1986): 344.

Yonkers, Kimberly A., and Jacqueline A. Samson. "Mood Disorders Measures." In *Handbook of Psychiatric Measures,* 2nd ed., by A. John Rush Jr., Michael B. First, and Deborah Blacker, eds., 499–528. Washington, DC: American Psychiatric Publishing, 2008.

Zigmond, A.S., and R.P. Snaith. "The Hospital Anxiety and Depression Scale." *Acta Psychiatrica Scandinavica* 67 (1983): 361–370.

**HOSPITALIZATION.**   Psychiatric hospitalization refers to inpatient treatment in a facility that provides intensive, specialized care and close, 24-hour monitoring. Because it is the most restrictive and expensive mode of treatment, it is reserved for the most severe or high-risk cases. The majority of people with depression never need hospitalization. But for those who are suicidal or having extreme difficulty getting along in daily life, it can be a very helpful—even lifesaving—option.

A hospital stay for depression typically lasts no longer than several days. It may be advised for those who pose to a threat to themselves or others, are behaving in a disoriented or destructive manner, require medication that must be closely monitored, or need round-the-clock care to become stabilized. Hospitalization also may be necessary if people have not eaten or slept for several days, or if they become so incapacitated by depression that they are unable to take care of basic needs, such as bathing and dressing. Finally, a stint in the hospital may be recommended if people have tried several outpatient treatments and still are not getting better.

The hospital provides an environment where people can get away from outside distractions and focus completely on starting to feel better. The goal is to keep people safe while bringing their most severe symptoms under control and helping them learn new ways of coping with their illness. While hospitalized, people also may undergo a battery of physical and mental tests to assess their condition, monitor their progress, and check blood levels of medication.

***Voluntary versus Involuntary.***   Voluntary hospitalization occurs when people willingly sign the forms consenting to inpatient treatment. Patients who sign in voluntarily also may request to leave. Unless patients are a threat to themselves or others, the hospital must honor this request within a set period of time—two to seven days, depending on state law.

Involuntary hospitalization is used only as a last resort when people become so ill that they are in danger of hurting themselves or others in the near future, but are unwilling to accept help. The law recognizes that involuntary commitment is a serious curtailment of liberty that is only appropriate in narrowly defined circumstances. Yet in a true emergency, it is also sometimes the most compassionate choice.

***Further Information.*** American Hospital Association, One North Franklin, Chicago, IL 60606, (312) 422-3000, www.aha.org.

National Association of Psychiatric Health Systems, 701 13th Street N.W., Suite 950, Washington, DC 20005, (202) 393-6700, www.naphs .org.

*U.S. News and World Report* Best Hospitals: Psychiatry, www.usnews.com/directories/hospitals.

### O'Connor v. Donaldson

In *O'Connor v. Donaldson*, the U.S. Supreme Court addressed the issue of involuntary commitment to a psychiatric hospital. The court's ruling in this case, issued in 1975, has been called the single most important decision in mental health law.

The case revolved around Kenneth Donaldson, who was confined for 15 years as a psychiatric patient in a Florida state hospital. During this period, Donaldson petitioned the court for release on several occasions. Both a halfway house and a personal friend offered to provide a home and supervision. Yet his petitions were repeatedly denied. Donaldson eventually brought action for damages against the hospital superintendent and other staff members, alleging that they had intentionally and maliciously deprived him of his constitutional right to liberty.

Donaldson won his case and had his victory reaffirmed by the Supreme Court. In its landmark decision, the Supreme Court stated:

> A finding of "mental illness" alone cannot justify a State's locking a person up against his will and keeping him indefinitely in simple custodial confinement. Assuming that that term can be given a reasonably precise content and that the "mentally ill" can be identified with reasonable accuracy, there is still no constitutional basis for confining such persons involuntarily if they are dangerous to no one and can live safely in freedom.

## Bibliography

Evans, Dwight L., and Linda Wasmer Andrews. *If Your Adolescent Has Depression or Bipolar Disorder: An Essential Resource for Parents.* New York: Oxford University Press, 2005.

*How Do I Find Inpatient or Residential Treatment?* Mental Health America, http://www.nmha .org/go/help/finding-help/find-treatment/in-patient-care/how-do-i-find-inpatient-or-residential-treatment.

*O'Connor v. Donaldson, 422 U.S. 563 (1975).* FindLaw, http://caselaw.lp.findlaw.com/scripts/ getcase.pl?court=US&vol=422&invol=563.

*O'Connor v. Donaldson, 422 U.S. 563 (1975).* Treatment Advocacy Center, http://www.psychlaws .org/LegalResources/CaseLaws/Case1.htm.

*Position Statement 22: Involuntary Mental Health Treatment.* Mental Health America, http://www .nmha.org/go/position-statements/p-36.

*Position Statement on Involuntary Commitment.* Bazelon Center for Mental Health Law, http://www.bazelon.org/issues/commitment/positionstatement.html.

*Psychiatric Hospitalization: A Guide for Families.* Depression and Bipolar Support Alliance, 2004, http://www.dbsalliance.org/pdfs/familyhospitalization.pdf.

*Understanding Hospitalization for Mental Health.* Depression and Bipolar Support Alliance, 2004, http://www.dbsalliance.org/pdfs/patienthospitalization.pdf.

**HUMAN IMMUNODEFICIENCY VIRUS.**   Human immunodeficiency virus (HIV) is a virus that lives and multiplies in white blood cells. These cells of the **immune system** normally protect the body from infection and disease. Over time, HIV weakens the immune system, leaving the body vulnerable to everything from pneumonia to cancer. The most advanced stage of HIV infection is acquired immunodeficiency syndrome (AIDS). Depression is a common problem in HIV and AIDS patients, affecting up to 37 percent of people with HIV infection.

The first sign of HIV infection may be a flu-like illness that starts within a month or two of exposure to the virus and usually goes away in a week to a month. More severe, long-lasting symptoms can take up to a decade or longer to develop. But even during the symptom-free period, the virus is multiplying and slowly disabling or destroying cells in the immune system. The most obvious result is a decline in the number of CD4 cells, the immune system's premier infection fighters.

As the immune system grows weaker, people eventually start getting sicker. Many develop swollen lymph nodes that stay enlarged for several months. Other symptoms that may occur during the months to years leading up to full-blown AIDS include lack of energy, weight loss, frequent fevers, persistent skin rashes or yeast infections, short-term memory loss, severe herpes outbreaks, and a painful nerve disease called shingles.

Once people reach the AIDS stage, the immune system is too weak to fend off infections and certain cancers. People may get life-threatening diseases, called opportunistic infections, which are caused by germs that usually do not make healthy people sick.

The latest treatments can postpone the development of AIDS, and people infected with HIV today generally have longer, healthier lives than their predecessors. But when HIV patients also have depression, it may be harder for them to stick to a complicated treatment regimen. Depression in HIV patients also has been linked to a more rapid decline in CD4 cell counts and a faster increase in HIV viral load—a measure of the amount of the virus in a blood sample.

Some might think depression would be the least of concerns for people infected with HIV. But depression adds to the burden of their disease, affecting their physical health and diminishing their quality of life. Getting proper treatment for depression when required is important—not only for mental well-being, but also for HIV management.

***The Depression Connection.***   The connection between HIV and depression is both psychological and physiological. On a psychological level, an HIV-positive diagnosis is apt to provoke strong emotional reactions, ranging from shock and denial to grief, hopelessness, fear, and anger. Most people eventually work through these feelings, but some who are predisposed to depression may sink into a dark mood that they are unable to shake on their own. As time passes, the **stress** of living with HIV and the prospect of developing AIDS may trigger new episodes of depression or worsen existing ones.

Certain milestones in the progression of HIV infection are especially likely to be stressful. These milestones include telling family and friends about the diagnosis, starting medication, recognizing new symptoms, being hospitalized for the first time, grieving the death of a loved one, getting a diagnosis of AIDS, and making end-of-life decisions. It is common and normal to experience some sadness, grief, discouragement, or demoralization at such times. For those who are prone to depression, however, the emotional response may be longer-lasting and more disabling.

On a physiological level, HIV can directly affect the health and functioning of brain cells, leading to symptoms such as confusion, forgetfulness and behavioral changes.

These symptoms may mimic or worsen those of depression. In addition, about 30 percent of people with HIV are also infected with hepatitis C. The standard treatment for chronic hepatitis C includes interferon-alpha, a medication that may cause depression as a side effect.

***Treatment Considerations.*** HIV infection is treated with a powerful group of medications called antiretroviral drugs. These medications can reduce the viral load, preserve CD4 cells, and dramatically slow immune system damage. Typically, two or more different types of antiretroviral drugs are combined, a treatment strategy known as highly active antiretroviral therapy (HAART). The use of HAART has greatly reduced the number of HIV/AIDS deaths.

Yet it takes more than medications to keep HIV in check. A positive outlook is needed to stick to complicated medication schedules, keep frequent doctor appointments, avoid high-risk behaviors, and live a healthy lifestyle. That is why, if depression occurs, getting prompt professional help is crucial. The mainstays of depression treatment are **antidepressants** and **psychotherapy**.

Antidepressants are generally safe for people with HIV. But because these medications may interact with antiretroviral medications, close monitoring for side effects is important. In addition, people with HIV may want to avoid taking **St. John's wort**, one of the most popular **herbal remedies** for depression. This herb can reduce blood levels of some antiretroviral medications, which might allow HIV to rebound, perhaps in a drug-resistant form.

Psychotherapy also can help relieve depression associated with HIV. In particular, **cognitive-behavioral therapy** (CBT), which aims to identify and change maladaptive thought and behavior patterns, may be beneficial. Research has shown that combining CBT with training in how to manage a complex medication plan may not only improve people's mood, but also enhance the effectiveness of HIV treatment.

*See also:* Mood Disorder Due to a General Medical Condition; Physical Illness

***Further Information.*** AIDSinfo, U.S. Department of Health and Human Services, P.O. Box 6303, Rockville, MD 20849, (800) 448-0440, aidsinfo.nih.gov.

amfAR, 120 Wall Street, 13th Floor, New York, NY 10005-3908, (212) 806-1600, www.amfar.org.

Centers for Disease Control and Prevention, 1600 Clifton Road, Atlanta, GA 30333, (800) 232-4636, www.cdc.gov/hiv.

National Association of People with AIDS, 8401 Colesville Road, Suite 505, Silver Spring, MD 20910, (866) 846-9366, www.napwa.org.

National Institute of Allergy and Infectious Diseases, 6610 Rockledge Drive, MSC 6612, Bethesda, MD 20892, (866) 284-4107, www.niaid.nih.gov.

Project Inform, 1375 Mission Street, San Francisco, CA 94103, (415) 558-8669, www.projectinform.org.

## Bibliography

Alciati, Alessandra, Luciana Gallo, Antonella D'Arminio Monforte, Francesca Brambilla, and Carmen Mellado. "Major Depression-Related Immunological Changes and Combination Antiretroviral Therapy in HIV-Seropositive Patients." *Human Psychopharmacology* 22 (2007): 33–40.

*Depression and HIV/AIDS.* Depression and Bipolar Support Alliance, August 25, 2006, http://www.dbsalliance.org/site/PageServer?pagename=about_depression_hiv_aids.

Leserman, Jane. "Role of Depression, Stress, and Trauma in HIV Disease Progression." *Psychosomatic Medicine* 70 (2008): 539–545.

*Let's Talk Facts About Psychiatric Dimensions of HIV and AIDS.* American Psychiatric Association, 2006, http://healthyminds.org/factsheets/LTF-HIVAIDS.pdf.

*NINDS Neurological Complications of AIDS Information Page.* National Institute of Neurological Disorders and Stroke, December 9, 2008, http://www.ninds.nih.gov/disorders/aids/aids.htm.

Safren, Steven A., Conall O'Cleirigh, Judy Y. Tan, Sudha R. Raminani, Laura C. Reilly, Michael W. Otto, et al. "A Randomized Controlled Trial of Cognitive Behavioral Therapy for Adherence and Depression (CBT-AD) in HIV-Infected Individuals." *Health Psychology* 28 (2009): 1–10.

*Understanding HIV/AIDS.* National Institute of Allergy and Infectious Diseases, http://www3.niaid.nih.gov/topics/HIVAIDS/Understanding.

*Update: Depression and Mania in Patients with HIV/AIDS.* New York State Department of Health AIDS Institute with Johns Hopkins University Division of Infectious Diseases, June 2008, http://www.hivguidelines.org/GuideLine.aspx?guideLineID=39.

**HYPOTHALAMIC-PITUITARY-ADRENAL AXIS.** The hypothalamic-pituitary-adrenal (HPA) axis is a body system comprised of the **hypothalamus**, pituitary gland, and adrenal glands along with the substances they secrete. The HPA axis is involved in the body's **stress** response. Overactivity in the HPA system, leading to an exaggerated stress response, is found in many people with depression.

The HPA response to stress occurs in a series of steps that follow one after the other like dominoes falling in a line: (1) When a person encounters a threat, it is perceived by the brain's cortex, the seat of conscious perceptions and thoughts, and **amygdala**, a structure involved in emotional learning and the fear response. (2) The threat message is then relayed to the hypothalamus—part of the brain that serves as a command center for the **nervous system** and **endocrine system**—which releases **corticotropin-releasing hormone** (CRH). (3) CRH travels to the pituitary gland, located at the base of the brain, where it triggers the release of adrenocorticotropic hormone (ACTH). (4) ACTH travels to the adrenal glands, located just above the kidneys, where it stimulates the release of another stress hormone called **cortisol**. (5) Cortisol arouses various body systems and gets them ready to cope with a threat. Later, it facilitates the body's return to a normal state.

***The Depression Connection.*** Several lines of evidence point to the importance of the HPA axis in depression. For example, many people with **major depression** produce excessive CRH and cortisol. Also, the pituitary gland and adrenal cortex—the outer part of the adrenal glands where cortisol is produced—are often enlarged in depressed individuals.

In contrast, the **hippocampus**—an area rich in **receptors** that bind with cortisol—often shrinks in people with long-lasting depression. The shrinkage may be due to prolonged exposure to excessive cortisol, which decreases the creation of new brain cells in the hippocampus and also damages existing cells there.

Successful treatment of depression with either an antidepressant or **electroconvulsive therapy** tends to reduce high levels of CRH in cerebrospinal fluid. But when CRH levels stay high even after symptoms improve, there is an increased risk of relapse. This suggests that above-normal CRH levels, which affect the rest of the HPA axis, may be a marker for vulnerability to depression.

*See also:* Dexamethasone Suppression Test

*Bibliography*

Belmaker, R.H., and Galila Agam. "Major Depressive Disorder." *New England Journal of Medicine* 358 (2008): 55–68.

*Brain Facts: A Primer on the Brain and Nervous System.* 6th ed. Washington, DC: Society for Neuroscience, 2008.

Evans, Dwight L., and Linda Wasmer Andrews. *If Your Adolescent Has Depression or Bipolar Disorder: An Essential Resource for Parents.* New York: Oxford University Press, 2005.

Gillespie, Charles F., and Charles B. Nemeroff. "Hypercortisolemia and Depression." *Psychosomatic Medicine* 67 (2005): S26-S28.

**HYPOTHALAMUS.**   The hypothalamus is a structure deep inside the brain that links the **nervous system** to the **endocrine system** via the pituitary gland. Although only about the size of a pearl, the hypothalamus has a wide array of important functions. Among other things, it monitors information from the autonomic **nervous system**, directs the activities of various body organs, controls the pituitary gland, and helps regulate sleep and appetite. In addition, the hypothalamus plays a role in regulating mood and emotion.

In interactions with the endocrine system, the hypothalamus partners with the pituitary gland and adrenal glands to make up a body network called the **hypothalamic-pituitary-adrenal axis**. This network plays a central role in the body's **stress** response. When the brain perceives a stressful situation, the hypothalamus sends **corticotropin-releasing hormone** (CRH) to the pituitary, which sets off a series of physiological changes. Under normal circumstances, this is a helpful response that gears up the body and brain when increased activity and alertness are called for. But in some people with depression, the system goes into overdrive, producing too much CRH and leading to an overactive stress response that is harmful in the long run.

In interactions with the nervous system, the hypothalamus joins the **amygdala**, **hippocampus**, and part of the thalamus to make up a brain network called the limbic system. As a whole, this system helps regulate the expression of emotion and emotional memory. The hypothalamus in particular plays a major role in organizing hormonal, physiological, and behavioral aspects of emotion.

*See also:* Brain Anatomy

*Bibliography*

*Anatomy of the Brain.* American Association of Neurological Surgeons, June 2006, http://www.neurosurgerytoday.org/what/patient_e/anatomy1.asp.

*Brain Basics: Know Your Brain.* National Institute of Neurological Disorders and Stroke, May 1, 2007, http://www.ninds.nih.gov/disorders/brain_basics/know_your_brain.htm.

*Brain Facts: A Primer on the Brain and Nervous System.* 6th ed. Washington, DC: Society for Neuroscience, 2008.

Drevets, Wayne C., Joseph L. Price, and Maura L. Furay. "Brain Structural and Functional Abnormalities in Mood Disorders: Implications for Neurocircuitry Models of Depression." *Brain Structure and Function* 213 (2008): 93–118.

**HYPOTHYROIDISM.**   Hypothyroidism is a condition in which the thyroid gland makes an insufficient amount of two thyroid **hormones** to meet the body's needs. Without enough of these hormones, basic bodily functions slow down. Among many other symptoms, people with hypothyroidism may develop depression, ranging from mild to severe. At times, depression is the first sign of an underactive thyroid.

The thyroid is a two-inch-long, butterfly-shaped gland located in the front of the neck, right below the larynx (voice box). Two main hormones are produced there: triiodothyronine

(T3) and thyroxine (T4). These hormones regulate metabolism, which is the body's use of energy, and affect nearly every organ in the body. They are involved in a host of functions, including brain development, breathing, body temperature, muscle strength, skin health, menstruation, body weight, and cholesterol levels.

The symptoms of hypothyroidism tend to develop gradually over several years. At first, they may be barely perceptible, but as the disease progresses, the problems become more pronounced. Besides depression, common symptoms include fatigue, sluggishness, sloweddown heart rate, hypersensitivity to cold, vague aches and pains, dry skin and hair, heavy or irregular menstrual periods, weight gain, and constipation.

Women are much more likely than men to develop hypothyroidism, and it is especially common in women older than 50. The condition may be caused by an autoimmune disorder, in which the body's **immune system** mistakes thyroid gland tissues for foreign invaders and attacks them. Other possible causes include surgical removal of all or part of the thyroid, radiation treatment of the thyroid, inflammation of the gland, and medications that interfere with the normal production of thyroid hormones.

**The Depression Connection.**   Along with a depressed mood, hypothyroidism can lead to other psychological symptoms, such as forgetfulness, lethargy, irritability, and a low sex drive. These symptoms can also occur independently in depression. In fact, there is so much overlap in symptoms between the two conditions that some doctors routinely test for thyroid disease before diagnosing depression.

Although depression may be a sign of thyroid dysfunction, it is unclear whether the reverse is also true. The majority of people with **major depression** do not have full-blown hypothyroidism, but about 20 percent to 30 percent have subtle signs of early thyroid disease. Although their output of thyroid hormones is still normal, they have anti-thyroid antibodies in their blood, which suggests that the immune system is starting to react abnormally to thyroid tissue. Doctors are still sorting out the significance of this finding, but many people with anti-thyroid antibodies later go on to develop hypothyroidism.

It is easy to understand why depression and hypothyroidism might go hand in hand. Thyroid hormones act directly on the brain. In some parts of the brain, high or low levels of these hormones can greatly increase or decrease the **receptors** for brain chemicals that may play a role in depression, including **serotonin**, **norepinephrine**, and **gammaamino-butyric acid**.

The chain of events leading up to the production of thyroid hormones is started by another substance, called thyrotropin-releasing hormone (TRH), which is made by part of the brain known as the **hypothalamus**. TRH also may play an important role. It affects how easy it is to excite activity in brain cells. It also affects the process by which certain brain chemicals, including norepinephrine and **dopamine**, transmit messages from one brain cell to another.

**Hypothalamic-Pituitary-Thyroid Axis.**   The hypothalamic-pituitary-thyroid (HPT) axis is a body network comprised of the hypothalamus, pituitary gland, and thyroid gland along with the substances they secrete. This network controls the release of thyroid hormones, which in turn have wide-ranging effects throughout the body.

At the top of the axis, the hypothalamus releases TRH, which travels to the pituitary gland at the base of the brain. TRH prompts the pituitary to release thyroid-stimulating hormone (TSH), which travels to the thyroid gland. There, TSH prompts the thyroid to release thyroid hormones.

Several HPT abnormalities have been reported in people with major depression. For instance, the pituitary's response to TRH may be blunted, and the normal nighttime surge in

TSH may be decreased. Depressed individuals who show such signs of HPT underactivity are less likely than those with normal HPT activity to respond well to **antidepressants**.

*Treatment Considerations.* The usual treatment for hypothyroidism involves taking a synthetic form of the thyroid hormone T4 every day. This restores adequate hormone levels, revving the body up to normal speed. Proper treatment typically improves both emotional and physical symptoms, including depression that is caused by the thyroid problem.

### TSH Test

When someone shows up at a doctor's office complaining of constant tiredness, lack of energy, mental fuzziness, and loss of interest in sex, the problem might be major depression—or it might be hypothyroidism. To rule out the latter possibility, the doctor may order a blood test that measures TSH, the pituitary hormone that triggers the release of thyroid hormones.

Normally, the pituitary gland boosts TSH output when the body needs more thyroid hormones, and the thyroid gland responds by ramping up production. Once thyroid hormones reach the required level, TSH output drops. But in people with hypothyroidism, the pituitary pumps out TSH continuously, trying in vain to get the thyroid to make enough hormones. Therefore, an above-normal reading on the TSH test generally means a person has hypothyroidism.

The standard treatments for depression are antidepressants and **psychotherapy**. When these treatments alone do not provide enough relief, adding the thyroid hormone T3 to an antidepressant sometimes boosts effectiveness, even in people without overt thyroid disease. In a major study called **Sequenced Treatment Alternatives to Relieve Depression**, a group of people who still had symptoms after trying two antidepressants were randomly assigned to add T3 to their treatment plan. About one quarter became symptom-free—a good result in a group of patients with hard-to-treat depression.

There is less evidence that T4 is helpful for depression in people who do not have full-blown hypothyroidism. That might simply be because T3 has been better studied in this context. But there is another possibility: Because T4 is converted to T3 in the body, some researchers have argued that people with depression may have a problem making this conversion normally.

*See also:* Mood Disorder Due to a General Medical Condition; Physical Illness

**Further Information.** American Thyroid Association, 6066 Leesburg Pike, Suite 550, Falls Church, VA 22041, (800) 849-7643, www.thyroid.org.

Hormone Foundation, 8401 Connecticut Avenue, Suite 900, Chevy Chase, MD 20815, (800) 467-6663, www.hormone.org.

National Endocrine and Metabolic Diseases Information Service, 6 Information Way, Bethesda, MD 20892–3569, (888) 828-0904, www.endocrine.niddk.nih.gov.

## Bibliography

*Ask the Doctors: What Is the Relationship Between Thyroid Dysfunction and Mood Disorders?* Depression and Bipolar Support Alliance, December 9, 2004, http://www.dbsalliance.org/site/PageServer?pagename=empower_QA_thyroidquestion.

*Hypothyroidism (Underactive Thyroid).* Mayo Clinic, June 12, 2008, http://www.mayoclinic.com/health/hypothyroidism/DS00353.

*Hypothyroidism.* American Thyroid Association, 2005, http://www.thyroid.org/patients/patient _brochures/hypothyroidism.html.

*Hypothyroidism.* Hormone Foundation, 2008, http://www.hormone.org/Thyroid/hypothyroidism.cfm.

*Hypothyroidism.* National Endocrine and Metabolic Diseases Information Service, May 2008, http://www.endocrine.niddk.nih.gov/pubs/Hypothyroidism.

Nierenberg, Andrew A., Maurizio Fava, Madhukar H. Trivedi, Stephen R. Wisniewski, Michael E. Thase, Patrick J. McGrath, et al. "A Comparison of Lithium and $T_3$ Augmentation Following Two Failed Medication Treatments for Depression: A STAR*D Report." *American Journal of Psychiatry* 163 (2006): 1519–1530.

Seidman, Stuart N. "Psychoneuroendocrinology of Mood Disorders." In *The American Psychiatric Publishing Textbook of Mood Disorders,* by Dan J. Stein, David J. Kupfer, and Alan F. Schatzberg, eds., 117–130. Washington, DC: American Psychiatric Publishing, 2006.

Thase, Michael E., J. Craig Nelson, George I. Papakostas, and Michael J. Gitlin. "Augmentation Strategies in the Treatment of Major Depressive Disorder." *CNS Spectrums* 12 (2007): 10–12.

*Thyroid Disease: Can It Affect a Person's Mood?* Mayo Clinic, December 13, 2008, http://www .mayoclinic.com/health/thyroid-disease/AN00986.

*TSH.* American Association for Clinical Chemistry, March 8, 2008, http://www.labtestsonline.org/ understanding/analytes/tsh/test.html.

**IMMUNE SYSTEM.**   The immune system is a complex network of organs, tissues, and cells that work together to defend the body against foreign invaders, such as bacteria, viruses, parasites, and fungi. Normally, the immune system does an admirable job of keeping such invaders out of the body or, failing that, seeking them out and destroying them. But a faulty immune response can give rise to a wide range of disorders—everything from rheumatoid arthritis and allergies to **cancer** and acquired immunodeficiency syndrome (AIDS). Although depression is not usually considered an immune disorder, there is good evidence that it may be affected by problems in immune function as well.

When faced with infection, irritation, or injury, the immune system responds with a surge of chemical signals that lead to **inflammation**. The classic signs of inflammation—redness, swelling, and heat—result from an influx of immune cells and their secretions coupled with increased blood flow to the affected area. During the initial period of recovery from an illness or injury, inflammation promotes healing. But if inflammation is inappropriate or prolonged, it can be harmful. A growing body of evidence indicates that depression may be associated with long-lasting inflammation.

*The System at a Glance.*   White blood cells are the workhorses of the immune system. They come in two main forms: phagocytes and lymphocytes. Phagocytes protect the body by chewing up invading organisms. Lymphocytes help the body remember previously encountered invaders and destroy them.

Scattered throughout the body are organs where white blood cells are produced or stored, called lymphoid organs. These organs include the thymus, bone marrow, lymph nodes, spleen, and various other clusters of lymphoid tissue.

White blood cells are carried in a yellowish fluid, called lymph. A body-wide network of channels, called lymphatic vessels, transports lymph to the immune organs and into the bloodstream. White blood cells also circulate around the body through blood vessels.

The cells of the immune system communicate with one another via chemical messengers known as cytokines. Types of cytokines include interleukins, interferons, and growth factors. Depression has been linked to increased production and blood levels of inflammation-promoting cytokines.

*A Whole-Body Disorder.*   A connection between immune dysfunction and depression is plausible because of the close ties between the immune system and **nervous system**. Some **neurotransmitters**, chemical messengers that carry signals from one nerve cell to another, can communicate with cells of the immune system. Networks of nerve fibers also

## Psychoneuroimmunology

A whole new branch of science has sprung up to study the interaction between psychological factors and the nervous and immune systems. In the 1970s, U.S. psychologist Robert Ader (1932– ) coined the term psychoneuroimmunology (PNI) to describe the burgeoning field. Although the term was a tongue-twister, the concept behind it caught on. The interdisciplinary research it inspired led to a fundamental shift in the way scientists think about mind-body health.

connect directly to lymphoid organs. The communication flows both ways, because some cytokines can send messages to the nervous system.

Scientists now believe that immune cells may function much like sense organs, detecting foreign invaders and relaying chemical signals to alert the brain. For its part, the brain may send chemical signals to the lymphoid organs that direct cellular traffic there. The **endocrine system** is another point of connection, communicating with both the nervous and immune systems through **hormones**.

Depression is still classified as a mental disorder, involving primarily the brain and behavior. But given the interplay of all these systems, depression may more accurately be described as a disease of the whole body.

*See also:* Human Immunodeficiency Virus; Inflammation

**Further Information.** American Academy of Allergy, Asthma & Immunology, 555 E. Wells Street, Suite 1100, Milwaukee, WI 53202, (414) 272-6071, www.aaaai.org.

American Autoimmune Related Diseases Association, 22100 Gratiot Avenue, East Detroit, MI 48021, (800) 598-4668, www.aarda.org.

Immune Deficiency Foundation, 40 W. Chesapeake Avenue, Suite 308, Towson, MD 21204, (800) 296-4433, www.primaryimmune.org.

National Cancer Institute, 6116 Executive Boulevard, Room 3036A, Bethesda, MD 20892, (800) 422-6237, www.cancer.gov.

National Institute of Allergy and Infectious Diseases, 6610 Rockledge Drive, MSC 6612, Bethesda, MD 20892, (866) 284-4107, www.niaid.nih.gov.

Psychoneuroimmunology Research Society, www.pnirs.org.

## Bibliography

Azar, Beth. "Father of PNI Reflects on the Field's Growth." *APA Monitor* 30 (1999).

*Immune System.* Nemours Foundation, November 2007, http://kidshealth.org/parent/general/body
_basics/immune.html.

*Understanding Cancer: The Immune System.* National Cancer Institute, September 1, 2006,
http://www.cancer.gov/cancertopics/understandingcancer/immunesystem/allpages.

*Understanding the Immune System: How It Works.* National Institute of Allergy and Infectious
Diseases, September 2007, http://www3.niaid.nih.gov/topics/immuneSystem/PDF/theImmune
System.pdf.

**INDIVIDUALS WITH DISABILITIES EDUCATION ACT.** The Individuals with Disabilities Education Act (IDEA) of 2004 is the federal special education law in the United States. It is the latest revision of a law first enacted by Congress in 1975 to ensure that youngsters with disabilities have access to a free appropriate public education, just as other children do. The most recent update of IDEA governs how states and public agencies provide early intervention, special education, and related services to more than 6.5 million eligible **infants**, **children**, and **adolescents**.

IDEA outlines 13 categories of disability under which children may qualify for special services. One category is "emotional disturbance," which includes a general pervasive mood of unhappiness or depression that exists over a long period of time and to a marked degree that adversely affects a child's educational performance. Not all children with depression are affected severely enough to meet this standard, but some do.

A potential pitfall to being labeled emotionally disturbed is the **stigma** attached to that term. In some settings, the term may be seen as synonymous with troublemaker. In others, children with this label may be routed into programs based on behavior modification, which use a system of rewards and punishments to change behavior. Children with depression are not always capable of responding as intended to the consequences, which only serves to increase their frustration and sense of low self-esteem.

To avoid these pitfalls, children with depression are sometimes placed into another category, called "other health impairment." This category includes **attention-deficit hyperactivity disorder** as well as other medical conditions that affect children in an educational setting. One advantage to this label is that it encourages teachers and school staff to consider biological aspects of depression as well as mental and emotional ones.

***Individualized Education Programs.*** Qualifying for services under IDEA requires going through a rather lengthy, involved evaluation and planning process. Therefore, it only makes sense for children with relatively long-lasting, extensive needs. Those found to be eligible for special services receive an individualized education program (IEP)—a written educational plan that details how a child's particular needs will be met.

The IEP is developed, reviewed, and revised according to guidelines spelled out in the law. The type of services covered by an IEP can range from minor modifications within the classroom to placement in a special education class or therapeutic school. To pay for these individualized services, the federal government provides extra funding for children served under IDEA.

A central tenet underlying the IEP process is that education should be provided in the least restrictive environment. As much as possible, then, children with disabilities should be educated alongside their peers who are not disabled. Special classes, separate schools, and other approaches that remove children from the general educational environment should only be used when necessitated by the nature or severity of the disability.

*See also:* School Issues

***Further Information.*** IDEA Partnership, 1800 Diagonal Road, Suite 320, Alexandria, VA 22314, (877) 433-2463, www.ideapartnership.org.

National Dissemination Center for Children with Disabilities, P.O. Box 1492. Washington, DC 20013, (800) 695-0285, www.nichcy.org.

**Another Law to Know About**

Section 504 of the Rehabilitation Act of 1973 is a federal civil rights law that prohibits discrimination based on a disability. This law has a broader definition of disability than IDEA. To be eligible for special school services, a student must simply have a mental or physical impairment that substantially limits one or more major life activities. The 504 process is faster and more flexible than the IDEA one, making it an attractive option for many students with depression.

U.S. Department of Education, 400 Maryland Avenue S.W., Washington, DC. 20202, (800) 872-5327, idea.ed.gov.

*Bibliography*

*Building the Legacy: IDEA 2004.* U.S. Department of Education, http://idea.ed.gov.

Evans, Dwight L., and Linda Wasmer Andrews. *If Your Adolescent Has Depression or Bipolar Disorder: An Essential Resource for Parents.* New York: Oxford University Press, 2005.

*Free Appropriate Public Education for Students with Disabilities: Requirements Under Section 504 of the Rehabilitation Act of 1973.* U.S. Department of Education Office for Civil Rights, September 2007, http://www.ed.gov/about/offices/list/ocr/docs/edlite-FAPE504.html.

Gilcher, Donna, Ruth Field, and Martha Hellander. *The IDEA Classification Debate: ED or OHI?* Child and Adolescent Bipolar Foundation, 2004, http://www.bpkids.org/site/DocServer/field _idea_clasification.pdf?docID=169.

*IDEA Parent Guide.* National Center for Learning Disabilities, April 2006, http://www.ncld.org/ images/stories/downloads/parent_center/idea2004parentguide.pdf.

*IDEA: The Individuals with Disabilities Education Act.* National Dissemination Center for Children with Disabilities, http://www.nichcy.org/Laws/IDEA/Pages/Default.aspx.

*Key Terms to Know in Special Education.* National Dissemination Center for Children with Disabilities, http://www.nichcy.org/SchoolsAndAdministrators/Pages/KeyTerms.aspx.

*Public Law 108-446.* U.S. Congress, December 3, 2004, http://idea.ed.gov/download/statute.html.

*Section 504.* National Dissemination Center for Children with Disabilities, http://www.nichcy.org/ Laws/ADA/Pages/Section504.aspx.

**INFANTS.**   Infants may react to stressful situations with withdrawal, apathy, fussiness, tantrums, unusual responses to strangers, or changes in their eating and sleeping habits. This type of behavior is normal and even healthy in most cases. But when the behavior leads to serious problems, occurs in a wide range of situations, and lasts four months or longer, many mental health experts believe it might signal infant depression.

It is still unclear whether infant depression is an early stage of the same kind of depression seen in older individuals or a distinct condition. Diagnosis of infant depression also poses a challenge. Although asking parents a few quick questions might be enough to flag a possible problem, a full evaluation requires interviewing the parents at greater length and observing how the parents and baby interact, ideally on multiple occasions.

Once a problem has been identified, early intervention may help improve life for the whole family. Depending on the situation, potential solutions might include parenting skills classes, **family therapy**, or individual treatment for parents struggling with their own **mental illness** or **substance abuse**. In addition, social service programs may take some pressure off families affected by poverty, homelessness, or lack of access to health care.

***Failure to Thrive.***   Efforts to formally diagnose and treat infant depression stretch back over 60 years. In the 1940s, Hungarian psychiatrist and psychoanalyst René Spitz (1887–1974) coined the term "**anaclitic depression**" for an extreme reaction seen in some infants who were abruptly separated from their mothers during the second six months of life. His work represented one of the first attempts to describe depression in infancy.

Today, Spitz' term has fallen out of favor, but a related term in current medical use is "failure to thrive" (FTT). Infants with the nonorganic form of this condition are consistently underweight or do not gain weight as expected, but no physical disease that would explain their failure to grow has been identified. If FTT continues, it may lead to iron deficiency, behavior problems, and developmental delays.

In some cases, unexplained FTT may have a medical cause that simply has yet to be identified. But in other cases, the condition may have a psychosocial cause—such as child neglect or abuse, chaotic family relationships, or **parental depression**—that blunts an infant's appetite and interferes with normal feeding behavior. The infant may become withdrawn, undemanding, and disinterested in food, which leads to even less responsiveness from the parents, which just makes the FTT worse. A vicious cycle is established that may lead to serious malnutrition if left unchecked. Some experts equate this particular pattern of FTT with infant depression.

Treating severe FTT is frequently a team effort, which might involve a dietitian, psychologist, social worker, pediatrician, pediatric nurse, and other health care providers. The first priority is to help the baby gain weight with nutritious, high-calorie feedings on a regular schedule. Hospitalization is occasionally needed. At the same time, parents may be counseled about how to break the dysfunctional cycle and promote a healthier style of interaction that benefits the entire family.

*See also:* Attachment Theory; Bowlby, John

**Further Information.** Zero to Three, National Center for Infants, Toddlers and Families, 2000 M Street N.W., Suite 200, Washington, DC 20036, (202) 638-1144, www.zerotothree.org.

## Bibliography

*DC: 0–3R: Diagnostic Classification of Mental Health and Developmental Disorders of Infancy and Early Childhood.* Rev. ed. Washington, DC: Zero to Three, 2005.

"Failure to Thrive." *Merck Manual of Medical Information.* 2nd home ed. Merck, http://www.merck.com/mmhe/sec23/ch267/ch267j.html.

Garber, Judy, Catherine M. Gallerani, and Sarah A. Frankel. "Depression in Children." In *Handbook of Depression.* 2nd ed., by Ian H. Gotlib and Constance L. Hammen, eds., 405–443. New York: Guilford Press, 2009.

Krugman, Scott D., and Howard Dubowitz. "Failure to Thrive." *American Family Physician* 68 (2003): 879–884.

**INFLAMMATION.** Inflammation is the body's reaction to infection, irritation, or injury. When one of these problems occurs, the **immune system** swings into action, sending immune cells and their secretions to the affected area. When all goes as it should, this response helps protect the body from harm. But when something goes awry, the response may wind up damaging body tissues rather than protecting them. Inflammation plays a role in many diseases, including type 1 diabetes, rheumatoid arthritis, asthma, and **multiple sclerosis**. A growing body of evidence suggests that depression should be added to the list.

Numerous studies of depressed individuals have found elevated levels of substances in the blood that are inflammatory markers. For instance, depression has been linked to increased levels of C-reactive protein in the blood. This protein produced by the liver normally is present in only trace amounts, but levels go up during periods of active inflammation.

**Role of Cytokines.** Cells in the immune system communicate with one another through chemical messengers known as cytokines. Release of cytokines may lead to many of the same kinds of chemical changes in the brain that are brought on by **stress**. For instance, both stress and cytokines affect **serotonin**, **corticotropin-releasing hormone**, and **brain-derived neurotrophic factor**—three brain chemicals that have been implicated in depression.

Because stress can trigger or worsen depression, it seems likely that cytokines might do so as well. And in fact, depression has been linked to increased production and blood levels of inflammation-promoting cytokines, such as interleukin-6 and tumor necrosis factor-alpha.

***Depression as Sickness Behavior.*** In both humans and lab animals, high blood levels of inflammation-promoting cytokines are associated with something called "sickness behavior." This pattern of behavior is normally an adaptive response that helps the body rest and heal. It shows up as increased sleeping, decreased sex drive, reduced appetite, and withdrawal from the environment.

Although sickness behavior is helpful during the initial period of recovery from an illness or injury, it is no longer adaptive if it continues too long. Many long-lasting inflammatory diseases include some or all of these behavioral changes as unwelcome symptoms. Such changes also may occur as unwanted side effects of treatment with synthetic interferons, manmade versions of natural cytokines that are used to treat conditions such as **cancer** and multiple sclerosis.

There is a striking similarity between sickness behavior and **major depression**. Noting this fact, some scientists have theorized that depression might result from inappropriate sickness behavior that is perpetuated by chronic inflammation and abnormal cytokines.

***Looking to the Future.*** Current **antidepressants**, including the widely prescribed **selective serotonin reuptake inhibitors**, have been shown to reduce the body's immune response. It may be that one way they relieve depression is by indirectly affecting cytokines and decreasing inflammation. In the future, it is possible that new antidepressants might target inflammation directly.

Recently, scientists from the University of Miami identified variants in two inflammation-related genes that are associated with major depression and antidepressant response. One day, a blood test that looks for these genes might help identify people at risk for depression.

*See also:* Appetite Disturbances; Heart Disease

## Bibliography

Anisman, Hymie. "Cascading Effects of Stressors and Inflammatory Immune System Activation: Implications for Major Depressive Disorder." *Journal of Psychiatry and Neuroscience* 34 (2009): 4–20.

Charlton, B. G. "The Malaise Theory of Depression: Major Depressive Disorder Is Sickness Behavior and Antidepressants Are Analgesic." *Medical Hypotheses* 54 (2000): 126–130.

Dinan, Timothy G. "Inflammatory Markers in Depression." *Current Opinion in Psychiatry* 22 (2009): 32–36.

Gimeno, D., M. Kivimäki, E. J. Brunner, M. Elovainio, R. De Vogli, A. Steptoe et al. "Associations of C-Reactive Protein and Interleukin-6 with Cognitive Symptoms of Depression: 12-Year Follow-Up of the Whitehall II Study." *Psychological Medicine* (June 4, 2008): e-publication ahead of print.

*Inflammation: What You Need to Know.* Cleveland Clinic, http://my.clevelandclinic.org/symptoms/inflammation/hic_inflammation_what_you_need_to_know.aspx.

*Nonspecific Immunotherapies and Adjuvants.* American Cancer Society, March 18, 2008, http://www.cancer.org/docroot/ETO/content/ETO_1_4X_Nonspecific_Immunotherapies_and_Adjuvants.asp?sitearea=ETO.

Raison, Charles L., Lucile Capuron, and Andrew H. Miller. "Cytokines Sing the Blues: Inflammation and the Pathogenesis of Depression." *Trends in Immunology* 27 (2006): 24–31.

*Understanding the Immune System: How It Works.* National Institute of Allergy and Infectious Diseases, September 2007, http://www3.niaid.nih.gov/topics/immuneSystem/PDF/theImmuneSystem.pdf.

Viljoen, Margaretha, and Annie Panzer. "Non-termination of Sickness Behavior as Precipitating Factor for Mental Disorders." *Medical Hypotheses* 65 (2005): 316–329.

Wilson, Debra Rose, and Lita Warise. "Cytokines and Their Role in Depression." *Perspectives in Psychiatric Care* 44 (2008): 285–289.

Wong, Ma-Li, Chuanhui Dong, Jorge Maestre-Mesa, and Julio Licinio. "Polymorphisms in Inflammation-Related Genes Are Associated with Susceptibility to Major Depression and Antidepressant Response." *Molecular Psychiatry* 13 (2008): 800–812.

**INSURANCE PARITY.**    Parity refers to equity in insurance coverage between the benefits provided for medical and surgical services and those provided for mental health care. Historically, physical and mental illnesses have been covered quite differently by health insurance plans. However, the Paul Wellstone and Pete Domenici Mental Health Parity and Addiction Equity Act, signed into law in October 2008, should erase some of the inequities of the past.

This act is the culmination of nearly two decades of advocacy efforts by organizations such as the **National Alliance on Mental Illness** and **Mental Health America**. The Mental Health Parity Act of 1996 was a tentative first step toward ending discriminatory insurance practices. But that law fell short of guaranteeing true parity in several regards.

The 1996 law banned the use of disparate annual or lifetime dollar limits for medical/surgical coverage and mental health coverage. Yet many health insurance plans set arbitrary caps on how many outpatient treatment sessions or inpatient hospital days were covered for mental health care, regardless of medical need. They also frequently required higher copayments for mental health services, leading to greater out-of-pocket costs for patients. The 2008 law is intended to close many of those loopholes.

*Wellstone-Domenici Parity Act.*    The Wellstone-Domenici Parity Act, which goes into effect in 2010, applies to employer health plans offered by companies with 51 or more employees. Some states already had strong mental health parity and consumer protection laws in place, and the Wellstone-Domenici Parity Act preserves these laws. But it also extends mental health parity to about 82 million health plan members who were not previously protected by state laws.

The act does not define which conditions must be covered. However, it does require that whatever is covered be on par with medical benefits. It prohibits health plans that cover mental health and substance abuse conditions from imposing treatment limits or financial requirements that are stricter than those for medical and surgical conditions. If a health plan offers out-of-network benefits for medical and surgical care, it must also offer out-of-network benefits for mental health and substance abuse treatment.

*Further Information.*    Mental Health America, 2000 N. Beauregard Street, 6th Floor Alexandria, VA 22311, (800) 969-6642, takeaction.mentalhealthamerica.net/parity.

National Alliance on Mental Illness, 2107 Wilson Boulevard, Suite 300, Arlington, VA 22201, (800) 950-6264, www.nami.org/parity.

## Bibliography

*Fact Sheet: Paul Wellstone and Pete Domenici Mental Health Parity and Addiction Equity Act of 2008.* Mental Health America, October 3, 2008, http://www.mentalhealthamerica.net/go/action/policy-issues-a-z/parity.

*New Law Covers Mental and Physical Health Services Equally.* American Psychological Association, http://www.apahelpcenter.org/articles/article.php?id=167.

**INTERPERSONAL THERAPY.**    Interpersonal therapy (IPT) is a form of **psychotherapy** that focuses on addressing the interpersonal triggers for mental, emotional, and behavioral symptoms. Originally developed for treating depression, IPT continues to be one of the best-validated therapies for that condition.

The underlying premise is deceptively simple: Whatever genetic, biological, cognitive, or **personality factors** are involved in causing depression, the immediate trigger is often an interpersonal problem. A loved one dies, a marriage dissolves, a teenage child rebels, a boss gives the promotion to a coworker—these are the kinds of problems that can set off depressive symptoms or make them worse. In IPT, patients learn to recognize and correct interpersonal problems that are contributing to their depression.

There is good evidence that depression and dysfunctional relationships are closely intertwined. For instance, children who grow up in families characterized by lack of emotional support, poor parental bonding, and harsh discipline are at increased risk for developing depression as teenagers and adults. The depression, in turn, often leads to further relationship problems, such as family conflict, emotional dependency, or social withdrawal. The aim of IPT is to break this cycle and thus help lift the veil of depression.

***Historical Roots.*** IPT was first described by **Gerald L. Klerman** (1928–1992) and his colleagues in a 1984 book titled *Interpersonal Psychotherapy of Depression*. From the start, the creators of IPT envisioned it as a therapy that would focus on one or two core interpersonal problems related to depression and address them in a relatively short period of time. IPT has stayed true to that vision. It generally is completed in 12 to 18 weekly sessions.

The interpersonal focus of IPT can be traced, in part, to Harry Stack Sullivan (1892–1949), a U.S. psychiatrist who emphasized the importance of interpersonal factors in shaping personality and mental illness. Sullivan also regarded psychotherapy as an interpersonal process, and he stressed that therapists who were interviewing patients needed a structure for their questions to ensure that they elicited all the pertinent information. This type of structured interview still plays an important role in the diagnosis of depression and other mental and emotional disorders.

Sullivan's approach was an outgrowth of **psychodynamic therapy**, and IPT bears surface similarity to some newer versions of psychodynamic treatment that focus on interpersonal conflict and put a time limit on treatment. Overall, though, there seem to be more differences than similarities between IPT and psychodynamic therapy. Compared to psychodynamic therapy, IPT is oriented more toward action than insight.

IPT and Psychodynamic Therapy Compared

IPT evolved from some recent formulations of psychodynamic theory that emphasize interpersonal relationships. However, IPT and psychodynamic therapy differ in several critical respects.

|  | **Interpersonal Therapy** | **Psychodynamic Therapy** |
|---|---|---|
| Number of Sessions | Has a time limit—typically, 14 to 18 weekly sessions— that is established at the outset. | Traditionally, was open-ended. However, newer, time-limited variants have been introduced. |
| Treatment Goals | Solving one or two core interpersonal problems and relieving symptoms of depression. | Increasing insight into the psychological conflicts that underlie mental disorders. |
| Temporal Focus | Emphasizes events in the patient's current life. | Stresses experiences in the patient's childhood. |
| Therapist Role | Serves as a supportive, optimistic ally. The therapist actively offers suggestions for change. | Maintains a neutral stance. The patient projects feelings toward others onto the therapist. |

***The Process at a Glance.***    The two main goals of IPT are improving relationships and reducing symptoms. The focus is on solving problems and helping patients regain better functioning within a relatively brief time rather than on making fundamental changes in personality that might require longer-term treatment.

To help patients achieve their goals, therapists provide active direction and support. Although patients are encouraged to explore their own ideas, the therapist provides suggestions as needed. When patients make progress, the therapist offers congratulations. When patients get stuck, the therapist offers encouragement and suggests ways to get back on track.

*Initial Phase.*    IPT is divided into three phases. The initial phase, which encompasses the first couple of sessions, is used to assess the patient's symptoms and identify one or two problem areas that are closely tied to current symptoms. The four problem areas most often seen in people with depression are abnormal **grief** reactions (for example, delayed or unresolved grief), interpersonal disputes (for example, conflicts with a spouse, child, friend, or coworker), role transitions (for example, adjusting to a new job, going away to school, relocating to a new home, or getting divorced) and interpersonal deficits (for example, social isolation or poor social skills).

*Intermediate Phase.*    The intermediate phase is the stage in which most of the therapeutic work occurs. After a general exploration of problem issues, the therapy narrows in on specific goals and strategies for achieving them. Consider the example of a patient who is struggling with unresolved grief over the death of a loved one. Typical goals might be to facilitate the mourning process and help the person find other relationships and interests to fill the void.

Strategies might include encouraging the patient to talk about the loss and associated feelings as well as reassuring the patient that expressing these feelings will not lead to loss of control. Because abnormal grief reactions sometimes stem from an unwillingness to confront negative feelings about the deceased, the therapist might suggest revisiting the lost relationship in all its complexity by looking through old photo albums with family or friends. The release of strong, pent-up emotions is viewed as healthy, so the therapist also might suggest going through the deceased's belongings. Even though the resulting feelings may be quite painful, the patient learns that such feelings are neither as frightening nor as intolerable as he or she had feared.

Such psychological exploration is regarded as helpful, but it is only a starting point in IPT. The necessary next step is to change interpersonal behavior. In our example, the therapist might encourage the patient to consider ways of becoming involved with others again; for instance, by dating, taking a class, joining a club, or attending religious services. The whole therapeutic process turns on this critical step of behavior change.

*Termination Phase.*    The last stage of IPT is devoted to gradually weaning the patient away from therapy. To promote the patient's self-confidence that he or she is ready to handle problems independently, the therapist may point out successes and help the patient identify support resources in the community.

***Benefits for Depression.***    IPT's effectiveness at treating depression has been well documented in controlled studies. Most research has looked at **major depression**, the form of the disorder that involves being in a low mood nearly all the time and/or losing interest or enjoyment in almost everything. These feelings last for at least two weeks, are associated with several other symptoms, and lead to significant impairment in the ability to function in everyday life. IPT can help decrease the symptoms of major depression.

There is also some evidence that IPT is useful for treating **dysthymia**, a less intense but longer-lasting form of low mood. However, improvement has been somewhat smaller in people with dysthymia than in those with major depression.

The other type of psychotherapy that is backed up by similarly strong research evidence is **cognitive-behavioral therapy** (CBT), which helps people change habitual patterns of thought and behavior that are associated with their depression. In general, the effectiveness of IPT and CBT seems to be comparable. However, in the National Institute of Mental Health's Treatment of Depression Collaborative Research Program study, IPT appeared to be more effective than CBT in those with severe depression.

IPT exemplifies many recent trends in psychotherapy. It is grounded in solid research, focused on current problems, and streamlined for relatively fast results. By improving people's ability to interact with others, it also fosters the development of a social network outside of therapy. In this way, it decreases dependency on the therapist and promotes change that is supported by other people in the patient's everyday life.

*See also:* Relationship Issues; Treatment of Depression

**Further Information.** International Society for Interpersonal Psychotherapy, www.interpersonalpsychotherapy.org.

## Bibliography

American Psychiatric Association Work Group on Major Depressive Disorder. *Practice Guideline for the Treatment of Patients with Major Depressive Disorder.* 2nd ed. Washington, DC: American Psychiatric Publishing, 2000.

Klerman, Gerald L., Myrna M. Weissman, Bruce J. Rounsaville, and Eve S. Chevron. *Interpersonal Psychotherapy of Depression.* New York: Basic Books, 1984.

Levenson, Hanna, Stephen F. Butler, Theodore A. Powers, and Bernard D. Beitman. *Concise Guide to Brief Dynamic and Interpersonal Therapy.* 2nd ed. Washington, DC: American Psychiatric Publishing, 2002.

Markowitz, John C., Martin Svartberg, and Holly A. Swartz. "Is IPT Time-Limited Psychodynamic Psychotherapy?" *Journal of Psychotherapy Practice and Research* 7 (1998): 185–195.

Weissman, Myrna M., John C. Markowitz, and Gerald L. Klerman. *Comprehensive Guide to Interpersonal Psychotherapy.* New York: Basic Books, 2000.

*What Is IPT?* International Society for Interpersonal Psychotherapy, http://www.interpersonalpsycho therapy.org/whatis.htm.

**INVENTORY OF DEPRESSIVE SYMPTOMATOLOGY.** The Inventory of Depressive Symptomatology (IDS) is a questionnaire that measures the severity of depression symptoms. The IDS was first published in 1986 by U.S. psychiatrist A. John Rush (1942–) and his colleagues. It consists of 30 items and comes in two versions: one designed to be taken as a self-report test and another designed to be completed by a mental health clinician. A shorter 16-item form, called the Quick Inventory of Depressive Symptomatology (QIDS), also is available. The IDS and QIDS are unique among depression tests in that self-report and clinician-rated versions were developed concurrently.

Another feature of the IDS and QIDS is that both assess all the defining criteria for **major depression** as set forth in the *Diagnostic and Statistical Manual of Mental Disorders, Fourth Edition.* In addition, the IDS assesses some other symptoms, including ones that are characteristic of the **atypical depression** or **melancholic depression** subtypes.

The IDS takes about 15 to 20 minutes to complete, whether the self-report or clinician-rated version is used. The QIDS requires five to 10 minutes. For each item on either scale, a series of sentences are presented that describe a particular symptom of depression in increasing order of severity.

The most common use of the tests is to measure the severity of symptoms at the outset of treatment and then periodically thereafter to see how well treatment is working. The tests also can be used as screening tools to identify individuals who might be depressed and need a full diagnostic workup.

***Pros and Cons of the IDS.*** Scores on the IDS range from 0 to 84. This is a wider range than is found on many other tests of depression, allowing for finer gradations. As a result, the IDS may be better able to detect depression in people with less pronounced symptoms.

Research on the IDS and QIDS has found good internal consistency—the degree to which all the items on each test are measuring the same thing. Scores on the IDS and QIDS also are highly correlated with those on the better-known **Hamilton Depression Rating Scale** and **Beck Depression Inventory**.

Unlike these other tests, the IDS and QIDS have not been as widely used up until now. But the IDS and QIDS may become more prominent in the future, thanks to their use in the **Sequenced Treatment Alternatives to Relieve Depression** (STAR*D) study, the largest and longest trial ever conducted to evaluate depression treatment.

*See also:* Diagnosis of Depression; Screening Tests

## Bibliography

American Psychiatric Association. *Diagnostic and Statistical Manual of Mental Disorders.* 4th ed., text rev. Washington, DC: American Psychiatric Association, 2000.

*IDS/QIDS: Instruments in English and Multiple Translations.* University of Pittsburgh Epidemiology Data Center, 2008, http://www.ids-qids.org.

Rush, A. John, Madhukar H. Trivedi, Hicham M. Ibrahim, Thomas J. Carmody, Bruce Arnow, Daniel N. Klein, et al. "The 16-Item Quick Inventory of Depressive Symptomatology (QIDS) Clinician Rating (QIDS-C) and Self-Report (QIDS-SR): A Psychometric Evaluation in Patients with Chronic Major Depression." *Biological Psychiatry* 54 (2003): 573–583.

Rush, A. John, Madhukar H. Trivedi, Stephen R. Wisniewski, Andrew A. Nierenberg, Jonathan W. Stewart, Diane Warden, et al. "Acute and Longer-Term Outcomes in Depressed Outpatients Requiring One or Several Treatment Steps: A STAR*D Report." *American Journal of Psychiatry* 163 (2006): 1905–1917.

Rush, A. J., C. M. Gullion, M. R. Basco, R. B. Jarrett, and M. H. Trivedi. "The Inventory of Depressive Symptomatology (IDS): Psychometric Properties." *Psychological Medicine* 26 (1996): 477–486.

Rush, A. J., D. E. Giles, M. A. Schlesser, C. L Fulton, J. Weissenburger, and C. Burns. "The Inventory of Depressive Symptomatology (IDS): Preliminary Findings." *Psychiatry Research* 18 (1986): 65–87.

Trivedi, M. H., A. J. Rush, H. M. Ibrahim, T. J. Carmody, M. M. Biggs, T. Suppes, et al. "The Inventory of Depressive Symptomatology, Clinician Rating (IDS-C) and Self-Report (IDS-SR), and the Quick Inventory of Depressive Symptomatology, Clinician Rating (QIDS-C) and Self-Report (QIDS-SR) in Public Sector Patients with Mood Disorders: A Psychometric Evaluation." *Psychological Medicine* 34 (2004): 73–82.

Yonkers, Kimberly A., and Jacqueline A. Samson. "Mood Disorders Measures." In *Handbook of Psychiatric Measures,* 2nd ed., by A. John Rush Jr., Michael B. First, and Deborah Blacker, eds., 499–528. Washington, DC: American Psychiatric Publishing, 2008.

**IRRITABILITY.** Irritability refers to a state in which people are easily annoyed and provoked to anger. In **children** and **adolescents**, irritability can be a diagnostic symptom of either **major depression** or **dysthymia**, a milder but very long-lasting form of depression. For people of all ages, irritability can also be a characteristic of **mania**, an overly high mood that alternates with depression in **bipolar disorder**.

Irritability is not included in the diagnostic criteria for major depression in adults, and it is not assessed by most depression rating scales. Nevertheless, research indicates that it may be quite common in depressed adults—even those without bipolar tendencies. Of 1,456 people with major depression in one study, 40 percent reported feeling irritable more than half the time. Other studies have found similarly high prevalence rates.

Depressed adults who feel irritable are more likely than their nonirritable counterparts to be young, female, and unemployed. Irritability also tends to be associated with more severe and persistent depression. Although irritability is an often-neglected symptom, there may be a high price for ignoring it. Depressed individuals with irritability may be at increased risk for coexisting anxiety as well as suicidal thoughts and behavior.

## Bibliography

American Psychiatric Association. *Diagnostic and Statistical Manual of Mental Disorders*. 4th ed., text rev. Washington, DC: American Psychiatric Association, 2000.

Fava, M., I. Hwang, A. J. Rush, N. Sampson, E. E. Walters, and R. C. Kessler. "The Importance of Irritability as a Symptom of Major Depressive Disorder: Results From the National Comorbidity Survey Replication." *Molecular Psychiatry* (March 10, 2009): e-publication ahead of print.

Pasquini, M., A. Picardi, M. Biondi, P. Gaetano, and P. Morosini. "Relevance of Anger and Irritability in Outpatients with Major Depressive Disorder." *Psychopathology* 37 (2004): 155–160.

Perlis, R. H., M. Fava, M. H. Trivedi, J. Alpert, J. F. Luther, S. R. Wisniewski, et al. "Irritability Is Associated with Anxiety and Greater Severity, but Not Bipolar Spectrum Features, in Major Depressive Disorder." *Acta Psychiatrica Scandinavica* 119 (2009): 282–289.

Perlis, Roy H., Renerio Fraguas, Maurizio Fava, Madhukar H. Trivedi, James F. Luther, Stephen R. Wisniewski, et al. "Prevalence and Clinical Correlates of Irritability in Major Depressive Disorder: A Preliminary Report From the Sequenced Treatment Alternatives to Relieve Depression Study." *Journal of Clinical Psychiatry* 66 (2005): 159–166.

$\diamond$  K

**KETAMINE.**   Ketamine was developed in the 1970s as an anesthetic for both humans and animals. Because it produces psychedelic effects—distorted perceptions, thoughts, and feelings—ketamine is also one of the more popular "club drugs" abused by teens and young adults. Now provocative new research indicates that ketamine given at a lower dose may have another effect: acting as a potent antidepressant. Unlike traditional **antidepressants**, which require weeks to take hold, ketamine appears to relieve depression within a few hours, and the effects of a single intravenous infusion can last up to a week.

Ketamine itself is unlikely to ever be used as an antidepressant outside a research setting due to the risks involved. Possible psychological effects include hallucinations, dreamlike states, confusion, feelings of invulnerability, paranoia, and aggressive behavior. Possible physical effects include slurred speech, faster heart rate, increased blood pressure, lack of coordination, muscle stiffness, breathing problems, temporary paralysis, and stimulation of the cardiovascular system. At high doses, ketamine can cause seizures, coma, and even death. Users can also become dependent on the drug.

Yet the positive results from studies on ketamine might point the way to a new class of antidepressants that act much faster than current ones. In one study, when 17 people with hard-to-treat **major depression** were given a single infusion of ketamine, 71 percent were substantially better the next day, and 29 percent were symptom-free. About a third were still feeling better a week later.

*The Brain on Ketamine.*   How can a single treatment with ketamine have such a quick and long-lasting impact on depression? Scientists think the key may lie in the drug's effect on **glutamate** receptors. Glutamate is a natural chemical with an excitatory effect on brain cells. Excessive glutamate activity may interfere with healthy brain function, and it is thought that one way traditional antidepressants work is by helping brain cells keep their sensitivity to this chemical in check.

In the brain, glutamate acts on two types of **receptors**: N-methyl-d-aspartate (NMDA) and alpha-amino-3-hydroxy-5-methylisoxazole-4-propionic acid (AMPA). Ketamine is an NMDA antagonist—in other words, it blocks NMDA receptors. This, in turn, may activate AMPA receptors, and researchers think the latter action may account for ketamine's depression-fighting ability.

In lab studies on mice exhibiting depression-like behavior, their behavior quickly returned to normal after a shot of ketamine, and the antidepressant effects of that one shot were still apparent a couple of weeks later. Two other chemicals that, like ketamine, block

NMDA receptors had similar but shorter-lived effects. But when the mice were given a drug that blocks AMPA receptors, the antidepressant effect of ketamine disappeared.

Researchers are now looking for other, safer drugs that block NMDA receptors and/or modulate the sensitivity of AMPA ones. One reason traditional antidepressants take so long to work may be because they hit targets close to the beginning of a long chain of chemical reactions that ultimately control mood. It then takes weeks for the brain to work through the chain of events before people start to feel better. Scientists think drugs such as ketamine act much faster because they hit targets closer to the end of the chain. The hope is that future drugs will be able to zero in on such targets more precisely.

## Bibliography

Berman, Robert M., Angela Cappiello, Amit Anand, Dan A. Oren, George R. Heninger, Dennis S. Charney, et al. "Antidepressant Effects of Ketamine in Depressed Patients." *Biological Psychiatry* 47 (2000): 351–354.

Brown, Walter A. "Ketamine and NMDA Receptor Antagonists for Depression." *Psychiatric Times* (February 1, 2007).

*Club Drugs: Ketamine.* National Clearinghouse for Alcohol and Drug Information, September 1, 2000, http://ncadi.samhsa.gov/govpubs/prevalert/v3i28.aspx.

*Experimental Drug Against Depression Works in Hours, Not Weeks.* National Alliance for Research on Schizophrenia and Depression, August 9, 2006, http://www.narsad.org/?q=node/466/latest-research.

Kudoh, Akira, Yoko Takahira, Hiroshi Katagai, and Tomoko Takazawa. "Small-Dose Ketamine Improves the Postoperative State of Depressed Patients." *Anesthesia and Analgesia* 95 (2002): 114–118.

Maeng, Sungho, Carlos A. Zarate Jr., Jing Du, Robert J. Schloesser, Joseph McCammon, Guang Chen, et al. "Cellular Mechanisms Underlying the Antidepressant Effects of Ketamine: Role of α-Amino-3-Hydroxy-5-Methylisoxazole-4-Propionic Acid Receptors." *Biological Psychiatry* 63 (2008): 349–352.

*NIDA InfoFacts: Club Drugs (GHB, Ketamine, and Rohypnol).* National Institute on Drug Abuse, August 2008, http://www.drugabuse.gov/Infofacts/clubdrugs.html.

Yan, Jun. "Ketamine's Antidepressant Effect Offers Drug-Development Target." *Psychiatric News* (September 7, 2007).

Zarate, Carlos A. Jr., Jaskaran B. Singh, Paul J. Carlson, Nance E. Brutsche, Rezvan Ameli, David A. Luckenbaugh, et al. "A Randomized Trial of an *N*-Methyl-D-Aspartate Antagonist in Treatment-Resistant Major Depression." *Archives of General Psychiatry* 63 (2006): 856–864.

**KINDLING EFFECT.**    The kindling effect is a physiological process by which exposure to **stress** sensitizes brain cells in vulnerable individuals. The more sensitized the cells become, the less it takes to disrupt them the next time. Some researchers have suggested that this type of sensitization might occur in depression.

The first episode of depression often is brought on by a life event that is clearly very stressful. As time goes on, though, clinical experience suggests that it may take less and less stress to trigger the illness. Because milder stressors are encountered more often, episodes start to occur more frequently. Kindling is one possible explanation for this pattern.

Supporting that hypothesis, research has linked depression to changes in brain structure and function over time. For example, in people with **major depression**, part of the brain called the **hippocampus** often shrinks. The longer the depression lasts, the greater the loss of volume there tends to be.

The pattern seen in **recurrent depression** also is consistent with kindling. About 60 percent of people who have recovered from a first episode of major depression go on to have a **recurrence**—a repeat bout of the illness. The risk goes up with successive episodes, until after three bouts, the odds of a fourth rise to 90 percent. As the illness progresses, episodes typically get closer together and more severe.

***Alternative Viewpoints.*** The kindling model described above, called stress sensitization, sounds plausible. Definitive evidence for the effect is still lacking, however. Some researchers have suggested an alternate possibility: Rather than making the brain more sensitive to stress, kindling might actually have the opposite effect. In this model, called stress autonomy, early episodes of depression are triggered by external stress, but later episodes are brought on strictly by internal changes in brain chemistry and function.

Both stress sensitization and stress autonomy are rooted in physiological changes. Another view focuses on cognitive changes instead. In this model, when people are depressed, an elaborate network of depression-related thoughts and memories is activated. A bias in favor of processing negative information is established, and it gets harder to access material that could disconfirm negative thinking. According to this view, recurrences get closer together over time as it takes less and less to activate the depression-related network of cognitive material.

The physiological and cognitive models of kindling are not mutually exclusive. Changes in brain function may underlie changes in thinking, which in turn may lead to depression itself. Either or both models could help explain the inexorable worsening of depression that is often seen when it is not interrupted by treatment.

*See also:* Cognitive Factors; Rapid Cycling

*Bibliography*

Christensen, Bruce K., Colleen E. Carney, and Zindel V. Segal. "Cognitive Processing Models of Depression." In *The American Psychiatric Publishing Textbook of Mood Disorders,* by Dan J. Stein, David J. Kupfer, and Alan F. Schatzberg, eds., 131–144. Washington, DC: American Psychiatric Publishing, 2006.

Monroe, Scott M., and Kate L. Harkness. "Life Stress, the 'Kindling' Hypothesis, and the Recurrence of Depression: Considerations From a Life Stress Perspective." *Psychological Review* 112 (2005): 417–445.

Monroe, Scott M., George M. Slavich, and Katholiki Georgiades. "The Social Environment and Life Stress in Depression." In *Handbook of Depression.* 2nd ed., by Ian H. Gotlib and Constance L. Hammen, eds., 340–360. New York: Guilford Press, 2009.

**KLERMAN, GERALD L. (1928–1992).** Gerald L. Klerman was a U.S. psychiatrist who developed **interpersonal therapy** (IPT), a form of **psychotherapy** that focuses on addressing the interpersonal triggers for depression and other psychiatric disorders. IPT was first outlined by Klerman and his colleagues in a 1984 book titled *Interpersonal Psychotherapy for Depression.* Since that time, the effectiveness of IPT for treating depression has been demonstrated in numerous studies.

In other work on depression, Klerman studied the benefits of combining medication and psychotherapy. He also conducted a study that found depression to be on the rise and occurring at earlier ages. Other areas of interest included **anxiety disorders** and schizophrenia, a severe form of mental illness.

***Biographical Highlights.*** Klerman was born in New York City. He graduated from Cornell and the medical school of New York University, then completed his residency at Harvard. Klerman's professional career began as a researcher at the National Institute of Mental Health. From there, he moved to Yale, where he was a professor as well as director of the mental health center. Next came a stint at Harvard, where he taught at the medical school, directed a mental health center, and served as director of psychiatric research at Massachusetts General Hospital.

From 1977 through 1980, Klerman headed up the federal Alcohol, Drug Abuse, and Mental Health Administration. After leaving that post, he was a professor of psychiatry and vice chairman of research at Cornell Medical College and New York Hospital, as well as a practicing psychiatrist. Klerman died of kidney disease at age 63 in New York City.

## *Bibliography*

Keller, M. B. "In Memoriam: Gerald L. Klerman, MD, 1928–1992." *Journal of Clinical Psychopharmacology* 12 (1992): 379–381.

Klerman, Gerald L., Myrna M. Weissman, Bruce J. Rounsaville, and Eve S. Chevron. *Interpersonal Psychotherapy of Depression.* New York: Basic Books, 1984.

Lambert, Bruce. "Gerald L. Klerman, 63, an Expert on Depression and Schizophrenia." *New York Times* (April 6, 1992).

Weissman, Myrna M., John C. Markowitz, and Gerald L. Klerman. *Comprehensive Guide to Interpersonal Psychotherapy.* New York: Basic Books, 2000.

# L

**LEARNED HELPLESSNESS.**   Learned helplessness is a giving-up reaction that stems from exposure to unpleasant events that are beyond the individual's control. The theory of learned helplessness was developed by U.S. psychologist **Martin E. P. Seligman** (1942– ) in the 1960s and 1970s. Seligman found that when animals received electric shocks that were inescapable, the animals became unable to act in future situations, even when escape was possible. The animals had learned to be helpless. Seligman later extended this concept to humans. He reasoned that human motivation to take action also is undermined when people have little control over their surroundings.

Seligman noted that some people become depressed after being subjected to a traumatic or stressful situation, but others do not. The differentiating factor, according to this view, is the extent to which people believe they have control over their situation. Those who have some success at avoiding or easing the pain, or at getting support from others are more likely to keep trying to escape the bad situation. Those who are unable to avoid the pain, in contrast, learn to feel helpless, hopeless, and depressed.

*Explanatory Style.*   Some psychologists criticized the original theory of learned helplessness for being too simplistic. In response, the theory was reformulated to include explanatory style—the way people habitually explain negative events to themselves. Seligman described a pessimistic explanatory style in which people see negative events as long-lasting, wide-ranging, and due to their own flaws.

From this perspective, people with depression often stay in bad situations because they feel more helpless than they really are and see their plight as worse than it actually is. They believe the situation is hopeless, so any effort to improve their lot in life is futile. The antidote to such **pessimism** is more realistic thinking. The same viewpoint is found in **cognitive therapy**, which aims to help people identify and change irrationally negative thoughts.

*Early Childhood Roots.*   Further research by Seligman and others has shown that learned helplessness can interfere with normal development. The seeds of helplessness may be sown as early as infancy, if babies do not learn that they can affect their own environment. This may occur in babies who are institutionalized or suffering from parental neglect, if their cries, smiles, and coos fail to get a response from others.

Learned helplessness can lead to depression in **children**, just as it does in adults. The consequences may be particularly severe early in life, when gaining a sense of mastery over the environment helps lay the foundation for healthy emotional development in the future.

*Bibliography*

Abramson, L. Y., M. E. P. Seligman, and J. D. Teasdale. "Learned Helplessness in Humans: Critique and Reformulation." *Journal of Abnormal Psychology* 87 (1978): 32–48.

Acton, G. Scott. "Cognitive Social Theories." *Great Ideas in Personality,* October 2005, http://www.personalityresearch.org/cogsocial.html.

"Learned Helplessness." *Encyclopedia of Childhood and Adolescence,* 1998, http://findarticles.com/p/articles/mi_g2602/is_0003/ai_2602000349.

Peterson, Christopher, Steven F. Maier, and Martin E. P. Seligman. *Learned Helplessness: A Theory for the Age of Personal Control.* New York: Oxford University Press, 1993.

Schwartz, Arthur, and Ruth M. Schwartz. *Depression Theories and Treatments: Psychological, Biological, and Social Perspectives.* New York: Columbia University Press, 1993.

Seligman, Martin E. P. *Helplessness: On Depression, Development, and Death.* San Francisco: W. H. Freeman, 1975.

**LEARNING DISORDERS.** Learning disorders—also called learning disabilities—affect the brain's ability to process, store, and use information. Such disorders interfere with people's performance at school or their ability to function in everyday situations that call for academic-type skills, such as reading, writing, and doing math. **Children** with learning disorders are more likely to have symptoms of depression than their peers without learning problems.

Learning disorders can affect anyone of any age. As a practical matter, though, they are usually diagnosed in a school setting. Studies show that up to 10 percent of U.S. students under age 18 have some type of learning disorder. These students have normal or above-normal intelligence and no major sensory problems, such as blindness or deafness. Their learning difficulties are not strictly due to emotional problems, cultural differences, or social or economic disadvantages. Yet they have serious trouble keeping up in school. When they take standardized tests, they score well below what would be expected for their age, grade, and level of intelligence.

Researchers think learning disorders are caused by differences in how the brain handles information. Such differences can be thought of as normal variations in mental development. They only become disorders when they get in the way of school or daily life. Specific skills that may be affected include reading and writing (dyslexia), math (dyscalculia), handwriting (dysgraphia), and listening (auditory processing disorder).

Special educational services and classroom accommodations can help students correct or compensate for such problems. The basic approach is to build on academic strengths while addressing weaknesses. The exact strategies used are based on a student's individual needs, but they might include such things as small-group instruction, one-on-one tutoring, or assistive technology. They also might involve such simple changes as providing extra time or a quiet spot with minimal distractions for taking tests.

***Relationship to Depression.*** Having a learning disorder can lead to constant struggles at school or in everyday life, especially if the disorder is not properly diagnosed and addressed. The resulting **stress** may trigger or worsen depression in susceptible individuals. In addition, young people with learning disorders often experience low self-esteem, a symptom that also characterizes depression. When a young person has both problems at once, the two may fuel each other, intensifying feelings of worthlessness and despair.

Children and **adolescents** who are depressed often have trouble functioning at school, regardless of whether they have a learning disorder or not. Depression itself makes it harder to concentrate and remember things, and it also saps energy and motivation. The combination of depression and a learning disorder makes it doubly difficult to cope at school. When students have both conditions, it is important that they get treatment for depression along with any special teaching or classroom changes that might be needed to help them learn.

*See also:* Comorbidity; Individuals with Disabilities Education Act; School Issues

**Further Information.** International Dyslexia Association, 40 York Road, 4th Floor, Baltimore, MD 21204, (410) 296-0232, www.interdys.org.

Learning Disabilities Association of America, 4156 Library Road, Pittsburgh, PA 15234, (412) 341-1515, www.ldaamerica.us.

National Center for Learning Disabilities, 381 Park Avenue South, Suite 1401, New York, NY 10016, (888) 575-7373, www.ncld.org.

National Dissemination Center for Children with Disabilities, P.O. Box 1492, Washington, DC 20013, (800) 695-0285, www.nichcy.org.

Office of Special Education and Rehabilitative Services, U.S. Department of Education, 400 Maryland Avenue S.W., Washington, DC 20202, (202) 245-7459, www.ed .gov/about/ zoffices/list/osers/osep.

*Bibliography*

*Accommodations for Students with LD.* National Center for Learning Disabilities, http://www.ncld .org/content/view/306/377.

American Psychiatric Association. *Diagnostic and Statistical Manual of Mental Disorders.* 4th ed., text rev. Washington, DC: American Psychiatric Association, 2000.

*Childhood Depression.* Learning Disabilities Association of America, May 1999, http://www.ldaamerica .org/aboutld/parents/mental_health/depression.asp.

*LD at a Glance: A Quick Look.* National Center for Learning Disabilities, http://www.ncld.org/index .php?option=content&task=view&id=452.

*Learning Disabilities at a Glance.* National Center for Learning Disabilities, http://www.ncld.org/ index.php?option=content&task=view&id=448.

*Learning Disabilities.* National Institute of Child Health and Human Development, http://www.nichd.nih.gov/health/topics/learning_disabilities.cfm.

Maag, John W. *Research Results: Depression in Children with Learning Disabilities.* GreatSchools, March 2004, http://www.greatschools.net/cgi-bin/showarticle/2784.

Maag, John W., and Robert Reid. "Depression among Students with Learning Disabilities: Assessing the Risk." *Journal of Learning Disabilities* 39 (2006): 3–10.

*NINDS Learning Disabilities Information Page.* National Institute of Neurological Disorders and Stroke, March 12, 2009, http://www.ninds.nih.gov/disorders/learningdisabilities/learning disabilities.htm.

**LEWINSOHN, PETER M. (1930– ).** Peter M. Lewinsohn is a U.S. psychologist who developed an influential theory of depression that is based on learning principles. In Lewinsohn's view, depression results from a reduction in positive reinforcement— rewarding circumstances that increase the likelihood of a behavior occurring in the future. When people receive fewer rewards for their behavior, they begin doing less, which leads to even fewer rewards. The goal of treatment is to interrupt this downward cycle and provide more positive reinforcement for staying actively engaged in life.

To achieve this goal, Lewinsohn devised a therapeutic technique called pleasant activity scheduling. It has since become a mainstay of **behavioral therapy** for depression. Using this technique, clients learn to monitor their moods and daily activities, looking for connections between the two. Then the clients work with a therapist to develop a plan for increasing the number of pleasant, satisfying activities in which they participate. Social activities are especially encouraged.

***Early Career Highlights.*** Lewinsohn was born in Berlin, Germany, but he was educated in the United States. In 1951, he received his bachelor's degree from Allegheny College in Meadville, Pennsylvania. Four years later, he earned a Ph.D. from Johns Hopkins University in Baltimore. After a series of short-term positions, Lewinsohn joined the psychology faculty at the University of Oregon in 1965, where he eventually served as professor and director of clinical training. Today he remains an emeritus professor at the university.

Since 1985, Lewinsohn also has held a post as senior research scientist at the Oregon Research Institute, a nonprofit behavioral research center in Eugene, Oregon. That year, he began the Oregon Adolescent Depression Project, a longitudinal study funded by the National Institute of Mental Health. The goal of the still-ongoing study is to increase knowledge about **risk factors** and **protective factors** that make it more or less likely that an adolescent will become depressed. The study also aims to provide insight into how the course of adolescent depression affects later functioning.

***Pleasant Activity Scheduling.*** A loss of interest or enjoyment in almost all activities is one of the hallmarks of **major depression**. In the 1970s, Lewinsohn and his colleagues conducted research showing that depressed individuals not only find fewer activities pleasant, but also take part in pleasant activities less often than those without depression. As a result of lower participation, people with depression have less opportunity to receive positive reinforcement. According to Lewinsohn, the reduced reinforcement is a critical antecedent to the development of other depressive symptoms.

Pleasant activity scheduling is designed to reverse this situation by increasing positive reinforcement. In the 1970s and 1980s, Lewinsohn and his colleagues conducted several studies looking at the use of this technique for treating depression. The results were generally positive, and several treatment approaches of the day incorporated activity scheduling into their manuals. The most notable of these approaches was the version of **cognitive therapy** developed by U.S. psychiatrist **Aaron T. Beck** (1921– ). Lewinsohn and his fellow researchers also incorporated activity scheduling into their Adolescent Coping with Depression Course, a well-validated cognitive-behavioral treatment program for depressed **adolescents**.

Because pleasant activity scheduling is a relatively simple technique, other researchers have since applied it successfully to the treatment of groups for whom more complex approaches might not be feasible. Examples include people with dementia and psychiatric inpatients.

***Lewinsohn in Perspective.*** Lewinsohn is considered one of the founders of behavioral treatment for depression. He is the author of eight books and over 200 articles describing strategies for treating depression across the life span, from adolescence to late adulthood. Over the decades, he has received numerous honors and awards, including the 2002 American Psychological Foundation Gold Medal for Life Achievement in the Application of Psychology.

Although Lewinsohn made many contributions to the field, his crowning achievement was the development of pleasant activity scheduling. The technique seems to be valuable for both depressed individuals who are feeling lethargic with too little to do and those who are feeling overwhelmed by too much to do. In addition, by making abstract plans more concrete, activity scheduling is helpful for people who seem mired in procrastination. Finally, activity scheduling can help counter suicidal thoughts that are based on the belief that all the fun has gone out of life. In short, the technique is well suited to helping many people who are struggling with depression find joy in their lives again.

## Bibliography

Cuijpers, Pim, Annemieke van Straten, and Lisanne Warmerdam. "Behavioral Activation Treatments of Depression: A Meta-analysis." *Clinical Psychology Review* 27 (2007): 318–326.

Lewinsohn, Peter M., and Christopher S. Amenson. "Some Relations Between Pleasant and Unpleasant Mood-Related Events and Depression." *Journal of Abnormal Psychology* 87 (1978): 644–654.

Lewinsohn, Peter M., and Julian Libet. "Pleasant Events, Activity Schedules, and Depressions." *Journal of Abnormal Psychology* 79 (1972): 291–295.

Lewinsohn, Peter M., Ricardo F. Muñoz, Mary Ann Youngren, and Antonette M. Zeiss. *Control Your Depression.* Rev. ed. New York: Fireside, 1992.

MacPhillamy, Douglas J., and Peter M. Lewinsohn. "The Pleasant Events Schedule: Studies on Reliability, Validity, and Scale Intercorrelation." *Journal of Consulting and Clinical Psychology* 50 (1982): 363–380.

Persons, Jacqueline B., Joan Davidson, and Michael A. Tompkins. *Essential Components of Cognitive-Behavior Therapy for Depression.* Washington, DC: American Psychological Association, 2001.

*Peter M. Lewinsohn, Ph.D.* Oregon Research Institute, http://www.ori.org/Research/scientists/lewinsohnP.html.

**LIFE REVIEW THERAPY.**   Life review therapy is a treatment approach for **older adults** that involves reflecting upon the past and evaluating their lives in a structured way. Research has shown that at least some forms of life review can reduce symptoms of depression. But because there is no single standardized protocol for the treatment, it is not possible to draw blanket conclusions about how effective life review is and which elements are most beneficial.

Studies have shown that depressed individuals tend to have less specific memories of the past than those who are not depressed. Instead, people with depression are more likely to recall general summaries of repeated events, such as taking tests in school or receiving scoldings by a parent. This tendency, known as overgeneral memory, is associated with more difficulty solving interpersonal problems, greater hopelessness, and a poorer prognosis. Life review therapy may help people learn to access more specific memories, which is one way it might be helpful for depression.

Another way life review might be beneficial is by helping people resolve old conflicts. By recalling and reevaluating what happened years ago, people may be able to come to terms with a difficult past. In some cases, they might be motivated to atone for personal misdeeds or reconcile with family members. In other cases, they might simply be able to forgive themselves or other people for past mistakes and let go of negative feelings.

***Historical Roots of Life Review Therapy.***   Life review therapy is inspired, in part, by the life stage theory of German-born U.S. psychologist Erik Erikson (1902–1994). In the last of Erikson's eight stages of development, older adults reflect on the lives they have lived. According to Erikson, if this stage is navigated successfully, people develop integrity—a sense of satisfaction with their lives and the ability to approach death calmly. The alternative is despair—a feeling of bitterness about lost opportunities and wasted time along with a dread of impending death.

The life review process itself was first described in 1961 by U.S. gerontologist and psychiatrist Robert N. Butler (1927– ). At the time, Butler was studying the characteristics of healthy older adults. He found that this group of vibrant older people tended to be engaged in the process of looking back over the past and coming to terms with everything that had happened. He concluded that they were striving to make sense of the lives they had led.

Since that time, Butler and others have developed life review into a therapeutic technique for older adults who are struggling with psychological problems such as depression. Some forms of life review therapy are structured as a cognitive exercise designed to enhance the recall of memories. Others more closely resemble **psychodynamic therapy**, which involves reflecting upon early experiences to understand ongoing problems.

***How Life Review Therapy Works.*** The goals and techniques of life review therapy vary depending on which method is used, but a common thread is the structured way in which memories are elicited. This differentiates life review therapy from informal reminiscing, which also can be beneficial. As might be expected, some studies have shown that structured life review leads to greater improvements than unstructured reminiscence. Others have found no difference, though, so more study is needed to find out what advantage, if any, is gained by formalizing the process.

In one form of life review therapy for depression, the goal is to encourage more specific memories. Clients focus on a different life period at each session. For each life period, they answer a list of preset questions that are designed to spark specific memories, both positive and negative.

In another form of life review therapy, the goal is to uncover and resolve old conflicts that are contributing to current problems. Clients are guided through a discussion that focuses primarily on difficult life experiences and the anger, guilt, or other strong emotions still associated with them.

***Benefits for Depression.*** Because of differences in methodology, it is hard to generalize about the benefits of life review therapy. However, several studies using various types of life review to treat late-life depression have found positive effects. These effects may be comparable to those seen with **antidepressants** or **cognitive-behavioral therapy**, a well-established treatment that focuses on changing self-defeating thoughts and behaviors. Some studies have suggested that life review therapy may be especially valuable for older adults with severe depression.

A major advantage of life review therapy is that it is specifically geared to the developmental needs of late life. The technique resonates with many older adults, which might increase their willingness to stick with treatment. More research is still needed, however, to clarify how best to deploy life review as a weapon against depression.

*See also:* Treatment of Depression

## Bibliography

Bohlmeijer, Ernst, Filip Smit, and Pim Cuijpers. "Effects of Reminiscence and Life Review on Late-Life Depression: A Meta-analysis." *International Journal of Geriatric Psychiatry* 18 (2003): 1088–1094.

Butler, Robert N. *Living with Grief: Loss in Later Life.* Hospice Foundation of America, 2002, http://www.hospicefoundation.org/teleconference/2002/butler.asp.

Lewis, Myrna I., and R. N. Butler. "Life Review Therapy: Putting Memories to Work in Individual and Group Psychotherapy." *Geriatrics* 29 (1974): 165–173.

McDougall, Graham J., Carole E. Blixen, and Lee-Jen Suen. "The Process and Outcome of Live Review Psychotherapy with Depressed Homebound Older Adults." *Nursing Research* 46 (1997): 277–283.

Serrano, Juan Pedro, Jose Miguel Latorre, Margaret Gatz, and Juan Montanes. "Life Review Therapy Using Autobiographical Retrieval Practice for Older Adults with Depressive Symptomatology." *Psychology and Aging* 19 (2004): 272–277.

Watkins, Ed, and John D. Teasdale. "Rumination and Overgeneral Memory in Depression: Effects of Self-Focus and Analytic Thinking." *Journal of Abnormal Psychology* 110 (2001): 353–357.

**LIGHT THERAPY.** Light therapy—also known as phototherapy—is a treatment that involves daily exposure to a very bright light from an artificial source. It is a well-established treatment for **seasonal affective disorder** (SAD), a form of **major depression** in which symptoms start and stop around the same time each year, typically beginning in fall or winter and subsiding in spring. It also has been tested as a possible treatment for other forms of depression, but with mixed results.

Light therapy is thought to work mainly by affecting **circadian rhythms**, the body's internal system for regulating physiological and behavioral cycles that repeat daily, such as the sleep-wake cycle. Circadian rhythms are normally synchronized to the external cycle of sunlight and darkness, and disruptions in this process may play a role in many types of depression. Light therapy can move the timing of daily body cycles forward or backward so that they sync up better with the 24-hour day. It also may magnify day-night differences in physiology.

Beyond that, light therapy boosts energy and stimulates production of **serotonin**, a brain chemical that influences mood and helps regulate sleep, appetite, and sexual drive. It is still unclear whether these effects are independent of light's impact on circadian rhythms.

*The Process at a Glance.* In light therapy, people sit in front of a light box—a small, portable device containing fluorescent bulbs or tubes. The light emitted is much brighter than ordinary indoor lighting—typically 10,000 lux, versus less than 400 lux in an average living room with the lights on in the evening. By comparison, a bright, sunny day may reach 100,000 lux. A special screen covering the light box helps block out potentially harmful ultraviolet rays—the type of rays in sunlight that can cause skin cancer and cataracts.

For light therapy to work, light must enter the eyes and strike the retinas, the light-sensitive tissue on the inner back surface. The light creates a signal that travels along the optic nerve to the brain, where it sets key changes in motion. Simply exposing the skin to light is not enough. But looking directly at the light box is not necessary or recommended, either. Instead, people simply sit near the box with their eyes open. They are free to go about activities such as reading, writing, eating, or making phone calls.

Daily treatment sessions usually last 30 minutes or longer, although as little as 15 minutes may be sufficient for some people. The sessions are generally most effective if scheduled in the morning soon after waking up. Doing light therapy at night should be avoided, because it can interfere with sleep.

Light therapy boxes are sold without a prescription. But before trying one, it is smart to talk to a health care provider and follow the provider's directions for proper use. Done improperly, light therapy may not be helpful for depression and might even be harmful.

*Risks and Precautions.* Side effects of light therapy are uncommon, but they occasionally occur. Possible side effects include headaches, eyestrain, jitteriness, irritability, and mild nausea. Such

### The Great Outdoors

Some people with SAD report feeling better after simply spending more time outside. Even on a cloudy day, the intensity of light outdoors can far exceed that from a light box. But for many SAD sufferers, the greatest improvement is seen when they are exposed to bright light in the early morning, while it is still dark outdoors during the winter. Even if they are outside regularly, bright light from an artificial source may still be helpful.

problems often go away on their own within a few days. If they persist, the health care provider may advise cutting back on treatment time, sitting farther from the light box, or taking breaks during long sessions.

Light therapy is generally not recommended for people with degenerative diseases of the retina, such as age-related macular degeneration and retinitis pigmentosa. Also, people who have skin that is extra-sensitive to light or who are taking medications that react with sunlight should only use light therapy under a doctor's guidance.

In addition, extra care should be taken by those with a history or high risk of **bipolar disorder**, a condition in which people cycle back and forth between a very low mood (depression) and an overly high mood (**mania**). Infrequently, light therapy triggers a sudden switch from depression to mania.

***Benefits for Depression.*** For many people with SAD, light therapy leads to marked improvement in their symptoms within about a week. But the symptoms may return just as quickly if the therapy is stopped too soon, so it is important to keep up the treatment until spring. A typical regimen involves starting light therapy at the first hint of trouble in early fall and continuing it until late April.

Studies indicate that light therapy is about as effective as treatment with **selective serotonin reuptake inhibitors**, a widely prescribed class of **antidepressants**. In one study by Canadian researchers, 96 people with SAD were randomly assigned to one of two groups: light therapy plus a placebo pill, or **fluoxetine** plus a placebo light treatment (dim light). Light therapy and fluoxetine had comparable effectiveness, although light therapy led to faster improvement.

Other researchers around the world also have demonstrated the effectiveness of light therapy in people with clear, longstanding histories of SAD. As a result, light therapy is now the first-choice treatment for many people with the disorder. In those with severe symptoms, light therapy is sometimes combined with antidepressants or **psychotherapy**.

*Other Types of Depression.* The benefits of light therapy for other forms of depression are not as well studied, and results so far have been less clear-cut. Nevertheless, research to date suggests that year-round light therapy might be helpful for treating **chronic depression**, unpredictably recurring **major depression**, and depression associated with **bipolar disorder**. An analysis of the best-controlled studies of nonseasonal depression concluded that light therapy may reduce symptoms by an amount comparable to what is seen with most antidepressants.

Light therapy also has been tested for **premenstrual dysphoric disorder** (PMDD), a mood disorder that begins in the week before the onset of a woman's menstrual period and subsides within a few days after her period starts. Some studies have found a benefit, but more research is needed.

The mechanism by which light therapy might act on forms of depression other than SAD is still being investigated. Some scientists believe that circadian disruptions may play a role in these conditions as well. Take PMDD, for instance. Studies have found that changes in female sex **hormones** during the menstrual cycle are linked to several physiological functions with a circadian pattern, and the effect on these body functions is different in women with PMDD than in women without the disorder.

People with depression also may withdraw from the world, spending more time indoors and closing the blinds. This tendency to shut out natural sunlight might affect them, mentally and physically, in ways that are still not understood. There is much to be learned, but it seems likely that the future may bring expanded uses of light therapy.

*See also:* Dawn Simulation; Treatment of Depression

**Further Information.**    Center for Environmental Therapeutics, www.cet.org. Society for Light Treatment and Biological Rhythms, www.sltbr.org.

## Bibliography

American Psychiatric Association Work Group on Major Depressive Disorder. *Practice Guideline for the Treatment of Patients with Major Depressive Disorder.* 2nd ed. Washington, DC: American Psychiatric Publishing, 2000.

*Frequently Asked Questions at CET.* Center for Environmental Therapeutics, 2007, http://www.cet.org/q-and-a.htm.

Golden, Robert N., Bradley N. Gaynes, R. David Ekstrom, Robert M. Hamer, Frederick M. Jacobsen, Trisha Suppes, et al. "The Efficacy of Light Therapy in the Treatment of Mood Disorders: A Review and Meta-analysis of the Evidence." *American Journal of Psychiatry* 162 (2005): 656–662.

Lam, Raymond W., and Anthony J. Levitt, eds. *Canadian Consensus Guidelines for the Treatment of Seasonal Affective Disorder.* Clinical & Academic Publishing, 1999.

Lam, Raymond W., Anthony J. Levitt, Robert D. Levitan, Murray W. Enns, Rachel Morehouse, Erin E. Michalak, et al. "The Can-SAD Study: A Randomized Controlled Trial of the Effectiveness of Light Therapy and Fluoxetine in Patients with Winter Seasonal Affective Disorder." *American Journal of Psychiatry* 163 (2006): 805–812.

Lam, Raymond W., Diana Carter, Shaila Misri, Annie J. Kuan, Lakshmi N. Yatham, and Athanasios P. Zis. "A Controlled Study of Light Therapy in Women with Late Luteal Phase Dysphoric Disorder." *Psychiatry Research* 86 (1999): 185–192.

*Questions and Answers About Seasonal Affective Disorder and Light Therapy.* Society for Light Treatment and Biological Rhythms, May 2000, http://www.websciences.org/sltbr/sadfaq.htm.

Rosenthal, N. E., D. A. Sack, J. C. Gillin, A. J. Lewy, F. K. Goodwin, Y. Davenport, P. S. Mueller, et al. "Seasonal Affective Disorder: A Description of the Syndrome and Preliminary Findings with Light Therapy." *Archives of General Psychiatry* 41 (1984): 72–80.

*Seasonal Affective Disorder Treatment: Choosing a Light Therapy Box.* Mayo Clinic, January 5, 2008, http://www.mayoclinic.com/health/seasonal-affective-disorder-treatment/DN00013.

*Seasonal Affective Disorder: Treatment with Light Therapy.* Mayo Clinic, January 5, 2008, http://www.mayoclinic.com/health/seasonal-affective-disorder/MH00023.

Terman, Michael, and Jiuan Su Terman. "Light Therapy for Seasonal and Non-seasonal Depression: Efficacy, Protocol, Safety, and Side Effects." *CNS Spectrums* 10 (2005): 647–663.

Terman, Michael. "Evolving Applications of Light Therapy." *Sleep Medicine Reviews* 11 (2007): 497–507.

**LITHIUM.**    (Brand names: Eskalith, Lithobid.) Lithium was the first mood stabilizer medication introduced in the United States. Approved by the Food and Drug Administration in 1970, it has since proved to be one of the most effective weapons in the psychiatric arsenal. Lithium is used to treat **bipolar** disorder, a mood disorder in which people alternate between an overly high mood (mania) and an overly low one (depression). The medication can help get a current episode of mania under control, and it can also help prevent the next bout of mania or depression.

In addition, lithium may help some people with hard-to-treat **major depression**. Several studies indicate that adding lithium to antidepressant medication may enhance the benefits.

Lithium is a salt, chemically similar to sodium, potassium, calcium, and magnesium. The mechanism by which it acts on mood is still not well understood. Among other things, it may affect the transport of sodium across cell membranes, altering communication between brain cells. It may also boost **serotonin,** a brain chemical thought to play a key role in mood. In addition, it may affect **second messengers**—brain chemicals that relay messages from a cell's outer membrane to the inner biochemical machinery.

***A Brief History of Lithium.*** Lithium is a naturally occurring substance with a long history of therapeutic use. Eighteen hundred years ago, Greek physician Galen (129–ca. 216) had manic patients bathe in and drink from mineral springs, and it is believed that this water contained lithium. Today, many such springs still have a reputation for being healing waters that can ease mental and physical ailments.

Modern medical use of lithium dates back to the 1840s, when it debuted as a treatment for gout. Over the next century, lithium was touted as a cure for a wide range of maladies, including epilepsy, diabetes, insomnia, and cancer. In the 1940s, lithium was even used as a salt substitute for people with heart or kidney disease on a low-salt diet—unfortunately, with disastrous results. It turned out that, without salt to offset it, lithium could rise to toxic levels in the body. By the time this danger came to light, several people had fallen victim to lithium poisoning, and some had died.

*Cade's Discovery.* Against this backdrop, an observant Australian psychiatrist named John F. Cade (1912–1980) stumbled upon one of the greatest discoveries in the history of psychiatry. While working as medical superintendent at a veterans' hospital in a suburb of Melbourne, Cade developed a hunch that mania might be associated with excessive uric acid. To test his hypothesis, he experimented with guinea pigs, utilizing an unused hospital kitchen as a primitive laboratory. Cade wanted to inject the guinea pigs with uric acid, but to control potency, the uric acid needed to be put into a soluble form that could be diluted. Cade chose a lithium salt solution for this purpose.

Cade noticed that the guinea pigs became unusually lethargic after being injected with the solution, and he realized that lithium might be the reason. After testing lithium on himself with no ill effects, Cade used it to treat 10 human patients with "psychotic excitement." The calming effect of the lithium was dramatic, and Cade published his findings in 1949.

Cade's paper failed to attract much attention at first, in part because of the obscurity of the source and in part because of the salt substitute debacle. But it did not go unnoticed by Danish psychiatrist Mogens Schou (1918–2005), a meticulous researcher who had bipolar disorder in his own family tree. At the time, randomized controlled clinical trials—in which patients are randomly assigned to receive either an active treatment or an inactive placebo—were just beginning to be used in psychiatric drug research. Schou commenced a randomized controlled trial of lithium, and his positive results, published in 1954, attracted the interest of scientists around the world.

U.S. psychiatrists were relatively late to jump on the bandwagon. When the United States finally gave lithium the stamp of approval in 1970, it became the fiftieth nation to do so. Despite the subsequent introduction of newer **mood stabilizers**, lithium remains a widely used medication to this day.

***Use and Precautions.*** Lithium is available to take by mouth as a regular or extended-release tablet, a capsule, or a liquid. To keep a steady amount in the blood, lithium should be taken around the same each day. It is important not to skip doses and not to stop the medication without consulting a doctor.

It may take several weeks for the full effects of lithium to kick in. Eventually, though, it is effective for nearly three-quarters of people with bipolar disorder. One drawback is that the dose must be precisely calibrated. Lithium can build up in the body over time, and too much lithium may be dangerous. On the other hand, too little lithium may not be effective. Regular blood tests are needed to make sure the dosage is right.

The side effects of lithium may be worsened by dehydration and low levels of sodium in the body. People taking lithium should not make any dietary changes that reduce their salt intake. They may also need to drink extra fluids to avoid becoming dehydrated. Extra caution is needed during hot weather and in situations that cause heavy sweating, such as saunas and strenuous exercise.

***Risks and Side Effects.*** Lithium can lead to a number of side effects, some of which may become serious. Possible side effects include excessive thirst, frequent urination, upset stomach, weight gain, loss of coordination, blackouts, seizures, slurred speech, abnormal heartbeat, hallucinations, vision changes, trembling hands, itching, skin rash, and swelling. Lithium can also cause kidney or thyroid problems, so tests to check kidney and thyroid function should be done periodically.

Numerous medications may interact with lithium. People should tell their doctor about all the prescription medications, nonprescription medicines, **dietary supplements**, or herbal products they are taking.

Lithium is a powerful drug that must be handled with care. The risks and side effects are generally manageable, however, and many people have successfully stayed on low-dose lithium for decades.

*See also:* Augmentation Therapy

## Bibliography

*Antidepressants Plus Lithium.* BMJ Group, 2009, http://www.guardian.co.uk/lifeandstyle/besttreatments/depression-in-adults-treatments-antidepressants-plus-lithium.

Cade, J. F. "Lithium Salts in the Treatment of Psychotic Excitement." *Medical Journal of Australia* 2 (1949): 349–352.

Ironside, Wallace. "Cade, John Frederick Joseph (1912–1980)." *Australian Dictionary of Biography.* Vol 13. Melbourne: Melbourne University Press, 1993.

*Lithium.* National Library of Medicine, September 1, 2008, http://www.nlm.nih.gov/medlineplus/druginfo/meds/a681039.html.

*Lithium (Oral Route).* Mayo Clinic, July 1, 2009, http://www.mayoclinic.com/health/drug-informatino/DR600869.

*Medication Information Sheet.* Depression and Bipolar Support Alliance, May 4, 2006, http://www.dbsalliance.org/site/PageServer?pagename=about_treatment_medinfosheet.

*Mental Health Medications.* National Institute of Mental Health, July 28, 2009, http://www.nimh.nih.gov/health/publications/mental-health-medications/complete-index.shtml.

Papolos, Demitri, and Janice Papolos. *The Bipolar Child: The Definitive and Reassuring Guide to Childhood's Most Misunderstood Disorder.* Rev. ed. New York: Broadway Books, 2002.

Schou, M., N. Juel-Nielsen, E. Strömgren, and H. Voldby. "The Treatment of Manic Psychoses by the Administration of Lithium Salts." *Journal of Neurology, Neurosurgery, and Psychiatry* 17 (1954): 250–260.

*Serotonin and Other Molecules Involved in Depression.* Canadian Institute of Neurosciences, Mental Health and Addiction, http://thebrain.mcgill.ca/flash/i/i_08/i_08_m/i_08_m_dep/i_08_m_dep_lithium.html.

Shorter, Edward. "The History of Lithium Therapy." *Bipolar Disorders* 11 (2009): 4–9.

Wilens, Timothy E. *Straight Talk About Psychiatric Medications for Kids.* Rev. ed. New York: Guilford Press, 2004.